THREE SHATTERED SOULS

James Wilde

authorHOUSE®

AuthorHouse™
1663 Liberty Drive
Bloomington, IN 47403
www.authorhouse.com
Phone: 1-800-839-8640

The people and events have been changed to protect the innocent, and any similarities to actual persons, either living or dead, are merely coincidental

First published by AuthorHouse 8/24/2010

ISBN: 978-1-4490-3352-1 (e)
ISBN: 978-1-4490-3353-8 (sc)
ISBN: 978-1-4490-3354-5 (hc)

Printed in the United States of America

This book is printed on acid-free paper.

I dedicate this book to my supportive wife, lovely daughter and two wonderful sons

When mother and father stand opposed
And daggers are stained
Children's souls will shatter

CHAPTER 1

I sat in the hallway outside the courtroom, watching as a number of families and attorneys bickered back and forth. Everyone was up in arms about something to do with their case, causing the noise to be unbearable. People of all races and ethnicity were there fighting and screaming. It looked like the whole city was getting divorced. Some were actually trying to fist fight for their children and I'm not referring to the men. The mothers were the toughest and loudest, making it nerve-racking while sitting there. I did my best not to look at these crazies, but couldn't help myself. Mitch, Julie and I sat as quiet as mice in the old greenish hallway, sucking in whatever air was available. In those days smoking anywhere was permissible, so between the smoke and heat my heart was racing non-stop. The three of us stuck to the old beaten bench like discarded chewing gum under a school desk, sweating and waiting impatiently to find out who we were going to live with, our mother or father.

They were in the final stages of a long drawn out custody battle over us, emotionally draining me from being dragged to court so often. By the time I was eight years old, the courthouse reminded me of an evil beast. The front door its teeth and mouth while the actual courtroom its hungry belly. I pictured the belly being the pit of hell as my own churned from the horrors that evolved within there.

We soon heard the gavel bang, followed by a muffled voice announcing court was adjourned. As young children, we didn't realize how that poignant sound was the death of our old lives and the hatching of our new ones. That resounding noise was the decision we had to accept and live with forever, leaving our votes uncounted, not understanding the impact of the verdict. By being so very young, forever didn't mean much and trying to perceive it meant even less. Regardless of our understanding, our fates were sealed and ready or not we had to survive it.

The bizarre outcome was surprising since men normally didn't win custody from the birth mother and that was exactly what happened. My father was awarded custody of my brother Mitch, my sister Julie and me. I was the eldest sibling with probably the best understanding of what was happening to us. For two years my parents had been fighting over who would retain custody of our lives. Both of them fought like nasty rabid dogs, even involving us. By being involved, I mean seeing shrinks, speaking with social workers and of course, the infamous attorneys. None of them cared about the awful effects it had on us, especially my father who was the most embittered. Every visit was grill time, "What did your mother do? Did your mother have a friend over? Were you taken care of or were you left alone? Did you see any naked people walking around the house?" My father continuously accused my mother of being a whore, trying to convince us she was screwing everyone.

The court's decision was based on the grounds of infidelity and my mother being an unfit parent. Given that we lived in the same house, I never witnessed her with other men nor did my siblings. That's what was so comical about us being grilled by all the involved parties. Even if we had seen an infraction, we were in no position to know. Most of our day-to-day education derived from the television and in those days TV showed married couples sleeping in separate beds.

After the people started filing out of the courtroom, we were confused about our situation. Were we to go with our father or mother? We had been pulled in so many different directions in the past that we didn't know who was going to claim us this time. But our father quickly cleared that up, charging out like a bull and pushing all three of us through the crowd. My mother, grandmother and grandfather were trailing behind him. They didn't seem like they were attempting to catch up, but rather fading away in the thick commotion. They reminded me of sheep being led to a spring slaughter, following the rest of the people out of the courtroom.

My father kept shoving and telling us to move faster with an agitated tone in his voice. It was the familiar voice which conveyed punishment if we didn't start moving at a faster pace and we certainly wanted no part of that. Eventually we made it to his car, the old white LTD sedan. He opened the door behind the driver's seat, quickly pushing us in with his shaky hands. Then slamming the door shut, he literally leaped into the driver's seat in one smooth motion as if previously planned out. Our heads were spinning as we were trying to comprehend the immediate rush. No goodbyes. No kisses or hugs. No one saying, "We will see you next weekend." It resembled a movie in fast motion. He quickly sparked up a cigarette while hastily squealing out of the parking lot. All of us looked back through the rear window, finding it difficult to conceive what was happening. I saw my mother hunched over crying, as my grandmother was trying to comfort her. My grandfather looked like a man defeated, shaking his head with his frail arms crossed against his chest. He appeared to be fighting off the tears which my mother and grandmother were spilling all over the sidewalk, by the expression painted on his gaunt face. At that moment, I remember feeling cold and empty inside. Through the process, I truly felt our answers to the court somehow impacted this outcome. I harbored a deep guilt complex which tore at my insides for years to come. This was the turning point of our lives and I thought we had sabotaged our mother.

The windows were rolled up as the air conditioning was on full blast, fighting the recycled smoke. My father was a habitual chain smoker and was on his second cigarette when he started to explain our future plans.

"Ok kids, court is over and we never have to go back there again," he said, sounding relieved. "That was it kids. The judge agreed, you all are not allowed to ever see or call your mother or grandparents ever again. Your mother did a bunch of bad things to you kids and the judge doesn't want her to hurt you anymore. She and your grandparents could mess up your heads and make you crazy like your mother. The judge felt by not ever talking or seeing them again would keep you kids from going crazy."

We all sat in the back of the car in shock without responding. It was as if someone sucked the life out of us. "Go crazy," I thought. "What did she do to go crazy? I never thought of my mom as crazy." Throughout this terrible mess, my father threatened to send us to a psychiatrist whenever we acted up. He told us we would be locked up if the doctor thought we were nuts and it naturally worked. We were deathly afraid of his threats and the word "crazy" was generously thrown around by my father. My darkest fear at that time was being dumped in a loony bin.

My father rambled on with his impassionate explanation, becoming more emotional about the new situation. "I want you kids to know that I married Hamar. You remember her? She was the lady we visited a while back and had two kids. You remember, Shlomo and Samara? They lived in that apartment and we all went out for ice cream." Mitch and Julie sat there in the smoke-filled car emotionless, but I remembered them. Who could forget? The lady's English was so horrid that I couldn't understand a single word she spoke. I had no idea what country she was from, but I sure knew she wasn't from here. When we met Hamar, she was cold and aloof towards us, presenting a face that had difficulty forming a complete smile. She didn't seem to have an interest of who we were at all, even though my father looked excited to introduce us. It was as if she were too good to make our acquaintance, basically looking us up and down like she was rating a dive at the Olympics.

"Yes." I finally answered, after thinking about that day.

"Good." My father replied. "How about you two? Mitch or Julie, do you remember meeting Hamar and her children?"

They simply nodded their heads in agreement, passively answering, "Yes." Considering Mitch was five and Julie was three, they most likely had no idea who they met yesterday but for his happiness, they agreed.

"Alright, good. Well kids, here it is," he began, making it out to be a simple task for us. "From now on Hamar will be your new mother and Shlomo and Samara your new brother and sister. In my house the word stepmother or step-anything will not be permitted. From now on she is your real mother," he distinctively announced. "You are not to call her Hamar. Is that understood?" We all nodded our heads. He asked again, as if he wanted a verbal confirmation on the deal, "Is that understood?"

All of us chimed back in unison, "Yes."

"Good," he bellowed back. "Because if any of you call her Hamar or refer to her as your stepmother you will get a beating. That goes for calling Shlomo or Samara your stepbrother or stepsister. Is that understood?"

Not knowing what else to say to that offer we all answered, "Yes."

We knew his temper and I, for one, tasted a sample of his threats before. It wasn't something any of us wanted to be a part of. When he became enraged, it was a bloodcurdling freak show. Our father stood approximately six foot two and from our point of view, he looked like a giant. On occasions when he lost his temper, his scream alone was enough to rattle my nerves. It was so ferocious that I imagined the roof lifting completely off the house and slamming down with a crashing explosion. In the years to come, I wondered how no one ever heard what was going on in our house. I always hoped someone would step in, saving us from the beatings since he never knew when to stop. Thank God he smoked because once he started gasping for air the beatings were usually concluded. During his enraged fits, my father's entire demeanor and physical appearance drastically changed. His eyes and eyelids would turn red as he seemed to forget we were just children by the language he used. Being the eldest, I had far more experience with his transformation, profoundly feeling the grunt of his punishment more than my brother and sister. They were too young for that kind of beating, considering his cruel style of delivery. I recall being physically thrown across the room like a paper airplane, then repeatedly punched in the stomach with full force. He finished up by slapping my face with the fury of a boxer hitting a speed bag. It seemed like a beating he would give another man in a street fight rather than his own son. At the end of a pounding like that, my brain was so jolted I honestly could not remember what day it was.

I recall one instance when he caught me fishing with a few of my neighborhood friends. We lived adjacent to a country club called Comanche Creek, where the play area was very enticing due to the manicured lawn and alluring ponds. One of the neighborhood kids had an extra bamboo rod, offering it to me if I went along. After my father had forbidden me to go, I shrugged him off figuring he would never find out. He was concerned about me crossing streets, but the only dangerous part of the trek was the road to the pond. It was an old dirt road with little traffic, but since I was only five my father didn't want me crossing any roads, quiet or busy. My friends and I fished and played for hours. In fact, it was so long I lost track of time. I was planning to be home before dinner, seeing how we started out so late in the afternoon. But just as I was throwing my fishing line into the pond, I happened to catch a glimpse of a car pulling up and stopping on the side of the road. It was a familiar looking car and at first, it didn't hit me that it could be him. I thought it very peculiar to see his automobile on this old dirt road, considering we didn't belong to the club. Then noticing through the passenger window who was driving, I immediately knew I was dead.

When seeing the horrific expression on my father's face, I instantly dropped the bamboo rod and stiffened up. I was praying he wouldn't pick me out from the group of boys, but knew I was out of luck when hearing, "Jim, get the hell in this car. Right now, GOD DAMN IT!" I nearly had an accident in my pants at that very unfortunate moment. My face quickly went flush from fear as I ran, not walked, but ran to the passenger side of his car. I knew when opening the car door what was in store for me, but it would be far worse if I just sauntered over.

Once I jumped into the passenger seat after slamming the door shut, I felt a giant sweaty hand grab my entire head, smashing my face into the filmy window. It stung something awful, as my face stuck to the glass with the immense pressure from his hand. I actually felt my ear pop from the tremendous collision with the window. Then the yelling started, with my friends fearfully looking on, as my face appeared to adhere to the glass.

"God damn it! Didn't I tell you not to go fishing with your friends? What the fuck were you doing out here?"

I was trembling so badly that my windpipe was uncontrollably closing, making it difficult to get the words out. "I, I don't know," I squeaked.

"You don't know," he hollered back. "Wait until I get your ass back home. When I tell you something, you better listen. Do you understand me? Don't you ever pull this shit again." Then out of nowhere "*SMACK*" right across the face. It stung like a solid wood board had been crushed against my skull. I felt the blood rise to the occasion, filling my cheek up and knew this was just a taste of what was to come.

We walked through the front door with his right hand squeezing the life out of my scrawny neck. My mother was sitting in the living room entertaining some friends from New York, when she immediately looked over saying, "Good, you found him. Where was he?"

My father sternly replied, "Fishing over at Comanche Creek Country Club. I pulled up and found him there with his buddies fishing. Do you believe this shit? After I told him no and he goes anyway. I'll be right back."

I was embarrassed to be seen by their friends, feeling a welt developing on the side of my face from where he had smacked me earlier. Tears were running down my cheeks with the feeling of humiliation reddening my face. I knew the worst was only a few seconds away. Picking me up by the seat of my pants, my father banged his way up the stairs, dangling me in midair. He kicked open my bedroom door and "*WHAM*" threw me across the room. I hit the wall like a stray bird smashing into a glass window. He powerfully grabbed the front of my shirt and wildly started pinning me to the ceiling, then slamming me down on the bed. Every time he pinned me to the ceiling, he yelled, "You better damn well listen to me next time! Do you understand me?"

The whole time I felt like I was losing the ability to breathe. I was crying while panting at the same time from the pain, praying for someone to come in and stop the beating. Finally, the pinning and slamming stopped as he started whacking away at my face, screaming, "Did you hear me? You better not pull this shit again! When I tell you something, you listen!"

The sweat from my father's forehead was dripping everywhere and his breathing was more like a raspy sound. It was getting to the point that he was losing his strength to scream. At last my mother flung open the door, panicking for my life and hollered, "Get off of him! You're going to kill him! Let him go!"

He turned to my mother while huffing and puffing, screaming for her to get out. His hands were bright pink from slapping me and he was shaking like he had just been outside in the dead of winter. Suddenly, she began pulling on him until he released the front of my shirt. My father stood looking at me lying on the bed with my mother standing behind him. She had a firm grip on the back of his shirt as her knuckles turned pure white from struggling to hold him back. I laid on the bed profusely sobbing and panting. I must have looked like I was ravaged by a wild bear or some other kind of ferocious beast. He pointed his index finger at me and said, "This shit better not happen again. You're damn lucky your mother walked in when she did."

He was losing the ability to scream since he was out of breath. "If I ever catch you fishing over there again," then he took a deep breath, "your ass is dead. Do you hear me?" His hands and entire body were wildly trembling. I guess the thrashing took a toll on him too.

Attempting to get the words out to answer him felt extremely improbable for me. I was panting, sobbing and shaking so rapidly it was hard enough to even breathe, let alone exhale a single word. Finding the strength, I cried out, "Yes. I hear you."

"*BAM*" the door slammed shut, sending the both of them walking out of my bedroom. Before my mother left, she gave me a pitiful look. A look disclosing guilt for not coming to my rescue sooner. I sat helplessly panting on my bed with tears trickling down my cheeks, thinking of ways to get even.

It was getting late and we all felt the hunger banging in our bellies, but my father wouldn't stop, saying we would have to wait until we got home to eat. The ride to Rolling, Virginia was far. It was only two hours but to little children it might as well have been twelve. We were familiar with the ride since we were living with him six months out of the year and the other six with my mother in Red Hill, Delaware.

During the grueling drive, all I could think about was calling a stranger mom. Who was this woman I was supposed to show so much respect to as to call her mother. I didn't even know her, except that she had some kind of strange accent and married my father. It didn't come easy to me as I am sure it didn't come easy to my brother and sister either. My dad portrayed a possessed man, acting like he was more interested in pleasing this woman and her children than us. We were the ones who went through this nasty experience, apparently losing our mother and grandparents forever. I couldn't believe we could never see nor speak to them again. He absolutely showed no sense of empathy towards us, painting an image as if we should simply forget about them, like they never existed. How in God's name could we accept such a horrific scenario to accommodate his selfish outlook on our future?

CHAPTER 2

My mother and father married very young, she being twenty and my dad twenty-one. Before traditionally married, my parents threatened to elope because my mother's parents were adamant about them not getting married. They were a well-to-do Jewish family, insisting their daughter marry a professional or at least wait until she was older. Unfortunately, my father did not come from such a prosperous family, falling short of fitting the bill. Living in a more modest part of town, he worked odd retail jobs to earn a living. After several arguments, my grandparents gave their consent, deciding that rather than lose a daughter they would prefer to gain a son-in-law. So shortly after they received the green light, my parents were married.

My mother was a tall slender woman with long blond hair and an extremely pretty face. I always remember her stylishly dressed and looking very attractive. She was a highly likable person, with a knack for making a bounty of friends. When we spent time together, I perceived her as fun-loving, finding reasons to laugh rather than be sad. She viewed life lightheartedly and I think that's what I loved most about her. Through the years she kept her youthful childlike personality. Even in her later days when fatally ill, she still projected that youthful quality. My mother never seemed to grow up, which may have played a major factor to her ultimate demise.

Paula, my mom's older sister, was a pretty lady, who looked very much like the actress Natalie Wood. Aunt Paula was thin, almost frail but very well put-together. She was like a friend to me when I was growing up. Not having any children of her own, she spoiled me to death with attention. I remember going many places with her and her husband, Charles. Most times it was to the circus or carnivals that came to town.

My father grew up in Cedar which was a tough area in those days, especially if you were Jewish. He lived in a little comfortable two bedroom home with his older brother, Stewart. It was one of those neighborhoods where each house looked like they were manufactured from the same mold. My father was a sharp looking fellow, slightly resembling John Travolta in the movie "Grease". A significant difference were his bucked teeth, eventually growing a mustache to disguise them. Like Travolta, he had the dark hair slicked to the side and was tall with a slim build. He was more serious than my mom, not having that lighthearted side to him the way she did. He told me he had a reputation as a hell-raiser, finding himself in plenty of spats with other young men in his day.

After my parents married, my father went to work for my mom's father, who owned a well established electrical supply house in the heart of Delaware. My grandfather hired him on to learn the electrical supply business, considering he had no sons of his own. He had plans to make my father the manager of his new store in Walden, Delaware. My father never worked in the electrical industry before, but my grandfather wanted to help him out since he was married to his daughter.

Shortly after being married my grandparents were very generous, making sure their daughter and new son-in-law had a home to start a family. Mitch came into the picture soon after the purchase, but it wasn't long before we had to move again. The Walden store was completed and my father wanted to live closer to work.

CHAPTER 3

Walden held many great memories for me, mostly for receiving my best birthday present there. We moved into a very nice ranch home with an oversized fenced in backyard. On my fourth birthday, my parents drove the family to a farm that bred ponies. They surprised me when arriving, offering to buy a pony for my birthday present. We all walked inside the dim barn, where a distinct smell of horse poop was emanating, as I started my search. The pungent odor didn't bother me much, but my mother was close to giving birth to my sister, Julie and wanted to wait outside. Slowly pacing back and forth, I peered in all the stalls until finding the perfect pony. My perfect pony was a Mr. Ed look-a-like. "Mr. Ed" was a popular television show in the late sixties and I watched it religiously. When my folks asked what I was going to call him, I enthusiastically replied, "Mr. Ed, of course!" with no hesitation.

Once the owner heard my choice, he asked if I would like to ride him out of the barn. I was a bit hesitant, having never rode a horse before and there were a few steps to contend with as well. Feeling perplexed, I looked up at my father for his approval and he smiled, cautioning me to be careful. Mr. Ed was steady as I climbed up on his back with little trouble. I remember my dad bragging to everyone how brave I was to ride the horse up the stairs the way I did. He made me feel like a natural born cowboy.

Walden was an exceptionally rural town, so having a pony in our backyard was not unusual. Most of the homes sat on large parcels of land, surrounded by plenty of working farms. Mitch and I loved

Mr. Ed, taking care of him everyday as promised. My parents never bought a saddle, so we just rode him bareback whenever we could manage to get on him. One day my father came out, filling the feeding trough with oats and hay while I was on Mr. Ed's back. As soon as the pony saw the food, he darted off like a race horse at the Kentucky Derby. I was able to withstand his powerful galloping for a few seconds, but quickly got tossed off into a tree. It knocked the wind out me, vividly painting an array of stars. My father and brother laughed at my expense, although my mother didn't find it as humorous. After my jockey accident, she insisted we simply walk the pony to insure our safety. Of course when she wasn't around, we still rode him.

Shortly after having Mr. Ed, Aunt Carly and Uncle Stewart came over for a visit with their kids, Jeff and Dan. They were about the same age as Mitch and me and couldn't wait to jump on my pony's back. It felt like we were running a carnival the way everyone was acting, especially Uncle Stewart. They lived in Seneca, Delaware, so it was an unusual treat to visit kids who had their own pony in their backyard. Everyone had an opportunity to ride Mr. Ed, even Uncle Stewart, who looked awkward on my pony's back. He overwhelmed Mr. Ed, having to raise his feet so they wouldn't drag on the long grass as he was riding. He looked like an oversized kid while Mr. Ed struggled to carry him around the yard.

The next day while we were eating breakfast, my father was working around in the back and startled us when he screamed something to my mother. Mitch and I were ready to do our morning chores, but our mom kept us from wandering into the backyard. Apparently, my father followed a trail of dark red tainted grass, until he stumbled upon a bloody carcass resting on our lawn. As it turned out, Mr. Ed was really Mrs. Ed. The veterinarian said the pony was pregnant and my Uncle's weight induced the miscarriage. My mother was so upset that we had to send Mr. Ed back to the farm. Mitch and I were destroyed over her decision, crying the entire trip. I only had him, or her, for a short period of time and wasn't prepared to give him back. My mother gave one of those fairy tale stories, explaining how it was better for the pony to be back with his friends so he would never be hurt again. I bought into it, as she promised to get me something else for my birthday.

In September of 1969 my mother gave birth to her third child. After two boys, she finally had a girl and named her Julie. She looked completely different from Mitch and me, being born with red hair and blue eyes. We had light brown hair and dark brown puppy dog eyes and neither of us resembled our Papa Willie. Everyone found Julie on the funny-looking side, commenting how much she took after Papa Willie with her bright red hair. She was the only sibling I remember being born, and my mother's appearance reflected a difficult delivery. She was too shaky and weak to take care of Julie, so Papa Willie and Mama Ida hired a nurse to help out. I guess I was too young to remember how she looked after delivering Mitch.

My grandpa Henry, who was my father's father, died a year after Julie was born. His passing was the first time I experienced death at my tender age. I remember how frail and pale he had become. He was dying from brain cancer and in order to operate on him, they had to shave his head. After an unsuccessful attempt to operate, he was left somewhat scary looking to a small child. Prior to his illness, I recall perceiving him as healthy and strong, but when the doctors were finished he didn't appear to be the same guy.

In my five short years spent with my grandfather, it was always special. I remember just before his passing my cousin, Jeff and I were standing at the foot of his bed. He looked like God had deflated most of what was left of his body. The room was smothered in death and even as a child, I could sense it. Death doesn't discriminate against age and until this day his appearance is still vivid in my mind. He held out his arms, looking for a hug from my cousin and me. At first, we both retreated apprehensively with fear. Then something inside of me recognized him as I went over, giving him a big heartfelt hug. I knew deep inside it was probably the last time I would see him again. My father was exceptionally pleased, which was confirmed by the gentle wink he gave me.

A few months after my grandpa's death, my father came home late from work one night with a surprise for the family. He walked through the front door and there by his side was the biggest dog

I had ever seen. It was an enormous German Shepard, probably weighing in the vicinity of a hundred pounds. My father stood there, introducing his new found friend. "Hey everyone, here is our new dog, King." We all were frozen. Nobody wanted to be the first to lose a finger meeting King. Then he said, "Come on, he won't bite, look." Trying to convince us, he gave the dog a pat on the head, saying, "Shake, King." And immediately the dog lifted his paw, shaking my dad's hand.

"Hey dad, can I shake King's hand too," I shouted, feeling confident he wouldn't bite my hand off.

"Sure, come on. Don't be afraid. He won't bite."

My mother looked surprisingly happy about King, catching me off guard. I thought like most mothers, she would be opposed to the dog since she already had three kids to mess up the house. Instead, the dog seemed to appeal to her and she was fine with my father's decision. I walked over to King, quickly offering my hand for him to sniff while Mitch stayed back, watching from afar still frozen. My mother sounding overly concerned, warned, "Be careful, Jim. You must be gentle with the dog." She laughed a little from nerves when speaking to me.

I didn't fear the dog and wasn't too concerned by her warning either. I was more interested in trying to make friends, reaching out saying, "Here King, shake my hand." Without hesitation, he put out his giant puffy paw and sure enough shook my hand. I was ecstatic, hardly believing my eyes. I repeated the command a second time and again, King shook my hand.

My father glanced over at Mitch and looking amused, said, "Come on, Mitch. Don't you want to shake King's hand?" Getting his nerve up, he bravely walked over shaking King's paw too.

"Where in the world did you get this dog? You could've at least told me you were bringing him home," my mother said with an inquisitive expression on her face.

"It was the craziest thing. He just showed up in the warehouse and a few of the guys were playing with him. Before we knew it, the dog was doing tricks and stayed the whole day. Nobody came in to claim him, so I decided to bring him home. We think he's a lost police dog or something. I've never seen such a well-trained dog in my life." By the time my father finished his explanation, we all were shaking King's puffy paw, including my mom. He was immediately adopted into the family that night. We may have lost Mr. Ed but King was for keeps.

The following day, King proved to be indestructible. We were driving into town when my father opened the rear window of the station wagon to give King some air. While driving down the road, he must have spotted another dog or cat because he jumped out as the car was traveling fairly fast. Mitch and I instantly started screaming for our father to stop the car. He most likely saw King jump too, because he quickly spun the car around and chased him down. When my father caught up with him, he hastily hopped out of the car, yelling, "King, get back here. Come on boy, get into the car." King's ears perked up, obeying my father's order by leaping back into the car. We all took a good look at him and to our amazement, he wasn't injured at all. He was like a super dog, lying on the backseat panting, waiting to have his belly rubbed.

After the excitement of King jumping out from the car, my father told us how a policeman came by the store to claim him. Evidently, he lost his dog around the same time we found King and had been looking for him ever since. My father acted as if he wasn't convinced that King was the dog the cop lost and made a deal with him. He challenged the policeman to call the dog and if he came, then he could have him back. But, if he didn't, then we would get to keep him. My father dropped King's leash, instructing him to stay while walking away. He stood on one side of King, leaving the officer standing where he was.

Looking at the dog, the cop sternly commanded, "Fred! Come!" The dog merely sat there calmly looking at him. Then again he sternly shouted, "Fred, did you hear me? Come!" At that instant, the fur on King's back stood straight up as he arched his back in an attack stance. Something triggered him off because he lost his mind, barking like a wild crazed beast. He acted like he was going to tear the cop into a million pieces.

Then my father stepped up, gently calling for the dog to come.

King, as kind as he could be, graciously pranced over. The policeman, looking offended, shot my dad a long pensive stare. Then he shifted his attention, sending an appalling long look at King. Sensing the meaning behind the officer's stare, King began barking in a violent fit. My father struggled to hold him back, pleading to the cop, "Listen mister, you better leave before this dog bites your head off. I don't know if I can hold him back." The policeman practically ran out of the store and that was the last time anyone came back for King.

CHAPTER 4

Against my wishes, I was sent to a nursery school which also happened to be a working farm. On the first day, my father walked me around to see the chickens, ducks, pigs, cows and any other animal a working farm would have. When it was time for him to cut me loose, I remember crying and attaching myself to his leg like a starving tick. I was having a fit, refusing to let go of my father's pant leg. I hadn't been away from home alone before, except to sleep at my grandparent's house. The teacher was not fazed by my behavior, assisting my father in releasing me from his legs. Then smiling, he took off for his car as if he were running from a starving pack of wolves. At first, I was extremely intimidated and shy until I saw a familiar face. It turned out my father had an employee, big John, who sent his son, little Johnny, to the same school. Little Johnny attended my last birthday party and we played together a few other times when our parents got together. I felt much better about my situation after seeing him.

After the teachers gave us a little speech, we each introduced ourselves and were set free to go play. Johnny and I were playing with some blocks or whatever we could get our hands on when we heard an alarming loud scream. A little girl had accused a boy of stealing her stuffed animal, while one of the teachers was angrily getting to the bottom of it. She was extremely intimidating, seeing that she was large and not very pleasant to look at. She violently got directly in the little boy's face, shouting, "Did you or didn't you take her stuffed animal?" The lady was so loud that the hair on my back stood erect.

The little boy, shaking in fear, looked back at the teacher and innocently responded, "I don't know."

The teacher became infuriated and I vividly recall her yanking that little boy up and down by the locks of his hair. As he was crying and squealing, she was yelling, "Don't you ever steal again! Don't you ever steal again!" I must say, if she was trying to make an example out of that kid, it worked because nothing ever disappeared again. After some searching, the teacher found the little girl's stuffed animal tucked away under the boy's jacket in the closet. I couldn't believe she was permitted to hit someone else's child, so from that point on, I was very cognizant not to get on her bad side.

Sometime after that little boy had his hair relentlessly pulled out, I managed to get myself in trouble. Each day after lunchtime, the teachers sent us off to take a nap. That was their personal time in the day to eat lunch and watch their soap operas. They were very serious about their personal time and I found that out the hard way. There was a separate room where they had these uncomfortable cots set up for us to sleep on. They resembled army cots and all of them were green with thin itchy material. They had such a strong old musky scent to them that it made it difficult to fall asleep.

I was lying on mine, aimlessly staring up at the ceiling, when Johnny got up and smacked me on the head. After the attack, I justly marched off to go tattle on him to the overweight teacher. I remember the music playing in the background as my drawers were drawn down to my ankles and she repeatedly paddled my bottom raw with a wooden spoon. The melody belonged to the soap opera "*As The World Turns*". I never got up again after that.

My mother picked me up each day after nursery school in her big blue station wagon. Mitch and Julie were usually in the backseat, but on this particular day, Julie was missing from the car. I was so excited to go home that I never questioned where she was and nothing was mentioned. My mom had become obscenely obsessed with animals since we adopted King. She even brought home a companion for him, a big white German Shepard we named Queen. My father hit the ceiling the night he came home, finding another the dog. My mother argued how a king needed his queen, but he didn't laugh and that night he laid down the law, telling her no more animals in the house.

After jumping in the car, she announced we were going to the pet shop. I was thrilled, having my heart set on a baby turtle that she promised to purchase for me. When arriving at the pet shop, the saleslady immediately recognized us, greeting my mother using her first name. We were regular customers by now, having bought Queen and loads of dog food from her store. On that particular day, the saleslady had one request for my mom, which was to keep us away from the spider monkey. She cautioned her that he had just arrived and was a little rambunctious. My mother turned to us, rigidly warning to keep away from the monkey. Mitch and I agreed to keep our distance and started browsing around the exotic pet shop.

The place was great fun since it was so diversified. They sold an array of fish, puppies, kittens, reptiles and of course, the turtle I was itching to have. At one point, I wandered off alone and while turning the corner around an aisle, it happened. Something grabbed a handful of my hair, not allowing me to shake free from its grip. Initially, I thought it was a kid or an angry adult, but then remembered the saleslady's warning. The next thing I knew whatever had me was now slamming my head aggressively against a cage. It finally occurred to me that the monkey had grabbed my hair. I didn't want to scream for help, knowing they would think I disobeyed my mother's wishes. So, the monkey and I played a brief game of tug-of-war with my hair. After a few minutes of having my head brutally slammed against his cage and trying to wiggle out of his monkey hold, he let go. My head was throbbing from where he grabbed my hair as the side of my head was pulsating from hitting the cage so many times.

Once breaking free, I swiftly leaped back and frightened, stared at the monkey in the cage. It felt spooky at the time to be attacked by a wild monkey. He appeared to be smiling at me, tauntingly waving a handful of my hair in his small hands. I fearfully reached back to feel my head, thinking for certain there was a big bald spot where he grabbed me. My legs were shaking so badly from the struggle that I was wavering back and forth. I was hoping there was no evidence of a struggle with the monkey, knowing that if my mother saw a big bald spot on my head, she would surely want an explanation. As I walked away practically in tears, I gave that monkey the nastiest look I could conjure up.

I heard my mother calling for me, as I slowly made my way back to the front of the store. She found the little baby turtle I wanted and as promised, purchased it for me. She did have one request. A request I would hear many more times to come. "Jim, I will buy this turtle on one condition."

"Sure!" I replied, jumping up and down, quickly forgetting about the nasty monkey attack.

She looked at me very seriously and said, "You cannot tell your father. He will be very angry. Do you understand?"

That was an easy request and having no problem with that one, I answered, "You bet."

The saleslady was ringing up the turtle and the little plastic island with the palm tree when my mother screamed. "Oh my God, the baby!" My brother and I quickly looked up as her face lost all its color. She was frantically looking at her watch and stammering, told the lady we had to go. The saleslady hastily rang up the sale and we rushed out from the store.

"What happened mom? Did you forget the baby," I asked.

"No," she replied, with a panicky expression. "The housekeeper told me she had to leave in an hour and I lost track of time. Just, ah, keep it down and don't mention it to your father."

When arriving home, we could hear Julie crying from her bedroom. My mother repeatedly called out, "Hazel. Hazel, are you here?" Hazel was nowhere to be found. My mother then thought out loud, "Hmm, she must have left already."

We heard Mitch shriek from down the hallway and my mother and I instantly ran as fast as our legs would carry us. The crying was getting louder and louder by every step we took. Mitch was in a frozen state, staring at Julie from the doorway. When we arrived, the odor emanating from Julie's room was so horrific that it was enough to make me dry heave. She was naked in her crib, completely covered in her own poop. Her feces was everywhere. It was on the walls, in her hair, in her mouth, on her hands and even under her little fingernails. She was a complete mess with the smell knocking me unconscious. We all covered our noses as we stood in despair. Julie finally stopped crying and my mother broke down in tears.

After Julie was bathed and her room completely washed down, my mother called Hazel. She abruptly gave that housekeeper an earful. Later, when my parents were going through their divorce, this story repeatedly came up. It was one of those tales that never died but became more embellished over the years. My father's contention was that she irresponsibly forgot Julie at home, blaming the housekeeper who had nothing to do with it. That was one of many stories he used as a tool to prove she was an unfit mother. He even had us kids telling the story to the social workers, attorneys and judge. All we knew was Julie was covered in poop, but in private he would threaten us to tell his version of the story or *"SLAP"*, *"BOOM"*, *"BANG"*.

CHAPTER 5

During the time we lived in the Walden house, my father's big project was building out the basement. He paneled the walls and built a beautiful large bar made out of wood. The finished part of the basement also had a place for his new pool table. He loved shooting pool, especially with his buddies from work, who came to play quite often. They would shoot, drink and smoke for hours. Many times I would stand around watching, while my dad and his buddies would kid around with me. I knew many of them since frequently tagging along with my father to work. My favorite of his employees was Lyle. He was a big rugged African-American guy, who looked like he could play football on the offensive line for the Washington Redskins. I probably liked him best because of his vociferous funny demeanor. He seemed to enjoy my company, while I felt like a pain in the butt to the other guys. Lyle also cut an album and once in a while the radio station would play a song from it. He gave us a copy but unfortunately like everything else, it disappeared.

One evening after dinner, Mitch and I went out to play on the deck. It was a story high and the basement was directly beneath it with a walkout patio. The deck also had seating with a railing going around the entire perimeter. On this particular evening, Mitch was contemplating leaping off to see if he could fly like Spiderman. He asked my opinion on the idea and since Spiderman used a spider web rather than fly like Superman, I was interested whether or not he would succeed. He kept insisting he could do it, so being curious, I did not strongly advice him against attempting this feat. I was a huge

Superman fan, toying with idea once or twice about giving flying a try myself. Then before another thought entered my mind, off went Mitch. He stepped up on the railing and with no hesitation, calmly closed his eyes and jumped. It was almost like a dive with a *splat* at the end. Someone must have seen him plunge because I heard yelling followed by a sliding door slamming open.

My father and his work buddies were shooting pool at the time. Apparently in the middle of a shot, my dad caught a glimpse of Mitch falling out of midair and hitting the patio. I watched from the deck as my father rolled Mitch over, exposing a bloody gash in his chin. Blood was flowing everywhere and at that moment, my mother ran out on the deck screaming.

"What in the world is going on? What was all that banging?"

I didn't move from where I was standing and neither did my mom. She looked down astonished, figuring out what had happened on her own. Then my dad looked up, screaming, "Quick! Get me something to stop the bleeding! Get some towels fast! I need something!"

My brother was rolling back and forth in terrible agony, conjuring up tears like a wicked storm. My father was telling him to hold on, that towels were on the way. He looked up, giving me a nasty look as if I tossed Mitch off the deck. I just looked back in dismay and started my way down the stairs. I was a bit apprehensive seeing that I didn't want to catch the blame for Mitch trying to fly. I kept praying when my parents asked Mitch why he jumped, he wouldn't bring me into the equation. After seeing him so banged up, I realized I should have attempted to talk him out of trying to fly.

My mother rushed out of the basement with a bundle of towels and horrified started dabbing up the blood from his cracked chin. My father picked Mitch up, the way a groom would carry his bride over the threshold, rushing him into the house. My mother and I followed at almost the same pace. Mitch was lying on the couch when we caught up and his bleeding did not stop, nor did the terrible pain he was experiencing. My mother was panicked, shrieking to my father, "Get Mitch to the damn car now. We're going to the hospital!"

"We don't know how bad it is," my father shouted back. "Let me take a look. The towel seems to be slowing down the bleeding," he answered, inspecting the mess.

"Are you kidding me? Let's go now. You're no doctor and his bleeding hasn't stopped. He needs stitches. Let's go," my mother demanded. She was frantic and even I was worried from all the excitement. Blood was cascading from Mitch's slashed chin like a never-ending fountain of blood.

Finally, without another word my father lifted Mitch, spastically speeding to the car. My mother and I followed as she wildly waved the keys in the air, shouting, "Just go to the car, I have the keys."

While on the road, Mitch laid across my mother's lap as she firmly pressed the already soaked towel against his slashed chin. It was the color of deep burgundy, losing it's ability to absorb anymore blood. My mother's hands shook while helping Mitch and were covered in wet blood blots. During this fiasco, my father began asking Mitch why he jumped. He seemed like he was trying to find out who was behind this insidious stunt. I sat stiffly in the backseat biting my bottom lip, hoping he wouldn't implement me. Luckily, Mitch was in too much pain to comprehend the question and cried out in agony, making no sense at all. Looking frustrated, my father finally gave up on his inquiries which left me exhaling in relief.

CHAPTER 6

Going to the drive-in was a big deal to my family. There wasn't much to do in Walden, but the movies made for a great night out. My father would lay down the backseat in the family station wagon, making one long flatbed. Then my mom would bring out a blanket, spreading it out in the back for us to lie on. It was like one big king size bed and Mitch and I would also bring our pillows for extra comfort. The movies never started without the cartoons, which was the main event for Mitch and me. Our parents sat in their usual spot, snuggling up in the front seat. My father put his arm around our mother and she would scoot over to him real close. Most times we could hear her giggling or laughing. We guessed he was tickling or squeezing her in some funny way. Once the cartoons started, Mitch and I would mess around in the back. I would poke him in the eye or he would give me a pinch, dumb things kids do. Shortly after goofing around and watching the cartoons, we would fall asleep. We never seemed to make it through all the cartoons but it was still a blast to watch them in our car.

Eventually, the drive-in took a backseat to boating. My father decided weekends filled with boating would be much more exhilarating, so he purchased an eighteen foot motorboat. Mitch and I immediately fell in love with it. The boat looked like a beautiful convertible sports car without any wheels. It had back to back bucket seats with a padded bench in the rear. The windshield had a latch that opened which we used to get to the very front of the boat. The bow was our favorite place to sit since you could feel every bump and splash there. My father, thinking it would be cute, bought us the appropriate hats to go with the boat. Since being the eldest, I was awarded the skipper's hat and Mitch the first mate's cap. *"Gilligan's Island"* was a popular television show back then so we pretended I was the skipper and he was Gilligan.

Most weekends we went boating as a family, but my mother didn't always join us. She complained it was dangerous for Julie since we all wore life preservers with the exception of her. Julie was too small to fit in the ones we owned, so my mom used that to her advantage for getting out of boating. A large reason for her not wanting to come was because she couldn't stay away from the beauty shop. She spent every Saturday there getting her hair and nails done. There was no way she wanted all that work to go to waste and she sure didn't want to sacrifice the juicy gossip either. The beauty shop was her local news center as she could talk and listen for hours. Unfortunately, I had been dragged through that torturous routine many times before, mostly since she had no one to watch me when I was younger. Now it was Julie's turn, but in time she too would come to be a beauty shop junky like most girls. So it was decided, our new hobby was boating and hers the beauty shop. It made for a happy family. My father never put much of a fight up, mainly because they argued back and forth about the correct speed the boat should travel. My father, Mitch and I wanted full throttle while she wanted slow sightseeing speed, the kind that puts you to sleep. We all agreed that the beauty shop was best for her and Julie.

It was great to take the boat out on the Chesapeake Bay and speed through the water. The motion of the boat skipping over the waves with the wind jetting through my hair felt invigorating. Mitch and I enjoyed sitting way up in the front, watching the crabs swimming swiftly through the water. When our boat was just about to drive over them, they would quickly dive to the safe depths of the bay. We felt if we dragged a net along the water we could easily catch plenty of crabs. The days were long and filled with so much fun. We would anchor, jumping into the water to cool off or just fish for hours. Our father let us drive the boat once in a while for fun. When it was safe, he would stand behind us, letting Mitch and I take turns. He appeared to be a well seasoned captain, teaching us how to cross over the waves so the boat would feel smooth when cutting through them. The feeling of getting away from home and boating felt like going on vacation every weekend. All of us had so much fun spending time together.

On the weekends my mom came along, things were slightly different. We didn't speed around as fast and she would never stand for us fishing for any length of time. She was more enamored with going up and down the finger rivers, eating at the different restaurants. The Chesapeake had hundreds of winding finger rivers feeding into the bay where you could find the marinas and restaurants situated. The restaurants were these little rustic taverns that had the best seafood, especially if you liked crabs. The décor in these places were all the same. They were filled with anything to do with fishing and boating. I remember seeing trophy fish hanging on the walls, probably the ones caught by the local fishermen. It was strange because the fish always looked shocked, as if they couldn't believe they fell for the old bait trick. Fishnets usually accompanied the trophy fish, lavishly hanging from the ceilings and walls. Little model sailboats and fishing rods also adorned the musky smelling bars and dusty shelves. The fish tanks were the most interesting to see, garishly decorated while stocked with the most unusual fish. Fish unlike the typical ones you see in the store. They were so colorful with their odd faces and unique body shapes. It was like watching colorful candy in splendor motion.

Any time we stopped to eat at one of those seafood taverns the order was always the same, steamed hard shell crabs. That was the delicacy harvested from the Chesapeake Bay and no matter your age anyone from Delaware could pick a crab clean. Obviously Julie couldn't eat crabs being so young, but Mitch and I could. We were only four and five but were taught at a young age. Parents barely had enough patience to clean their own crabs without worrying about cleaning for their children. That's why kids were taught to perform this pesky task at such a young age.

The tables all looked the same, completely covered with newspapers, and the only utensils were crackers and mallets. The crackers were metal utensils that looked like the ones used for opening walnuts, but only bigger. The mallets were everyone's favorite since you could bang the hell out of the crab to gather meat. It wasn't the neatest way to eat and when used, juice usually sprayed everywhere. It would end up in your hair, eyes, clothes, anywhere if you happen to be in the vicinity of a crab feast. No one ever minded, seeing how it was understood that eating crabs was messy business and you were doomed to smell like one after feasting. When finished, your hands and clothes invariably smelled for the entire day.

The servers traditionally started the crab feast off with hush puppies and beer, no matter what restaurant you ate at. Beer was the side order for adults, accompanying the crabs instead of corn or coleslaw. The more they drank the happier they became, even tolerating our horseplaying at the table. Normally, there would be screaming and slapping but not on these occasions. Once the crabs were cooked and the server dumped a mountain of steamed ones on the table, the fun would begin. Eating crabs was serious business considering there wasn't much meat and what you did pick was usually quite small. So you had to work fast to get satisfied. I don't know whether or not it's a Delaware tradition, but during the feast when someone happened to be lucky enough to pull out a good lump of crabmeat, they had to show it off to the entire table. It grabbed everyone's attention and altogether we would say, "Wow." No matter how many crabs were devoured, we never felt full. The only reason we ever stopped eating was from being tired from all the picking and cleaning.

The Chesapeake Bay was a beautiful and serene place to be with the waters calm and easy for small crafts to cruise. But as beautiful and serene the bay was, that's how quickly she could change on you too. When a storm would blow in full force, it was quick with little warning. The Chesapeake was known for transforming into a violent maelstrom, swallowing sea vessels leaving little chance for escape.

It was early Sunday morning and my brother, Mitch, was already up getting dressed. I was still soundly asleep when I heard my father call to us with a horse sounding whispering voice. "Come on kids, hurry up. We're going to be late." He was standing at our bedroom door, waving for us to hurry with a cigarette hanging from his bottom lip. I quickly jumped up, throwing on my clothes. Without brushing our teeth or washing our faces, Mitch and I were sitting in the backseat of the station wagon in record time.

"Ok dad, let's roll 'em out," I said, sliding across the vinyl backseat. He already had the car running, quickly putting it in gear as we squealed off.

"I hope you kids went to the bathroom before we left. We have an hour drive and I don't want to stop every ten minutes."

"We did," we both sang back in unison. He hated to pit stop for us to go to the bathroom. It drove him crazy, especially when our mother was with us because he couldn't give her the same crap he gave us. She made him stop at least once every trip.

Every time we drove to the marina, it felt like he was trying to break a new record. We watched the back of his head swivel back and forth from the windshield to the speedometer to the clock, then back to the windshield again. He resembled a spectator watching a tennis match. When we made it to the marina, he constantly voiced how long it took to get there. Eventually, Mitch and I started getting interested and every five to ten minutes we would ask, "How much longer?" It probably drove him nuts but he was so engaged in making good time, he really didn't make much of a fuss about it.

We were speeding down the road to pick up my parent's friend, Melvin and his son, Norman. They met at Red Hill Hospital where I was born. My father met Melvin pacing in the waiting room, while my mother was giving birth to me. Melvin's wife, Rose, was also in the process of giving birth to their first child, Norman. They all bonded after our births, remaining friends for a few years. Living close to my parents, they got together quite often. Melvin was a dentist who truly looked the part. He was balding, featuring a swoop hairdo which was matted down with either Groom and Clean or Brylcreem. Those were the two popular hair gels back then. Melvin was also short and chubby, sporting black square rimmed eyeglasses. He looked like your ordinary Jewish doctor and his son, Norman, looked like a miniature version of him, minus the glasses. Norman's hair was even genetically receding exactly like his father's, unmistakably pinning them as father and son.

The boat was waiting in the water, hugging the side of the dock when we arrived. My father had called ahead, making sure our boat was fueled and ready for us to save time. It was one of those nice perks, if you could afford to store your boat in a marina. As we were loading our cooler full of beers, sodas and sandwiches, a dockworker was warning my father of a possible storm moving in. He smiled, thanking the man, but nonchalantly shrugged off the helpful warning. Piling into the boat, we pushed off from the dock teeter tottering slowly out to the bay. The sun was completely exposed, making the water appear as clear as glass. It was a glorious day for boating, so how could anyone take the dockworker's caution seriously?

As soon as we made it out of the no wake zone, my father gunned the boat in full throttle. We sped through the water, feeling the salty spray of the bay reflect off our bare skin. It felt so good under the vibrant sun as I listened to the cheerful music playing on my dad's little black radio. After some cruising, we began looking for a good place to fish and swim. Melvin and my dad pointed and argued over the best spots to stop. Eventually they agreed, anchoring in a nice quiet area which was a safe distance away from any oncoming boats. Once securely anchored, we all got ready to jump in with our bright orange life preservers. Each of us stood on the edge of the boat, waiting to see who was going to be the first to test out the water. There was always one character in the bunch that pushes someone in and that day it was my father. He gave me a good shove, sending me hitting the water face first. Of course water shot directly up my nostrils, giving me an immediate headache pushing against my skull. I splashed water back at him, whining, "Hey, you made me swallow water."

He simply laughed while lighting a cigarette, poking fun at me not to be such a baby. Once I gave the nod that the water was great, Mitch and Norman jumped in to join me. My dad and Melvin cracked opened their beers, sitting back watching us splashing around in the water.

When finished swimming and getting water logged, we decided to get back in the boat. My dad and Melvin helped lift us in since we didn't have a ladder. Shivering wrapped in our towels and feeling hungry, we started scrambling around in the cooler for something to eat. Then while eating our sandwiches my dad looked at Melvin startled, asking him to look up at the clouds. "Hey Melvin, I think a storm is moving in. Look how dark and fast those clouds are closing in on us."

"Wow, I think you're right," Melvin conceded with his head craned back, looking up at the sky. "Do you think it'll rain or just pass over us?"

"I think we should bring up the anchor just in case and start heading back," my father nervously answered.

Being so young, I didn't think much of it, complaining that we should wait to see what happens. Mitch and Norman chimed in but my father ignored us, having no interest in what we thought. He instructed Melvin to go to the front of the boat to start bringing in the anchor. As Melvin was tugging on the rope attempting to loosen the anchor from the sand, a huge gust of wind brushed across the water, wobbling our little boat. Then another gust of wind skimmed across the water, pushing us again. Finally, a sequence of strong winds picked up, scaring my father in to screaming at Melvin to hurry with the anchor. While Melvin struggled, my father furiously puffed on his cigarette, cursing as he was trying to start the boat. The engine only cried a little squeak with each turn of the key. His knuckles were turning white with every turn, as if his strength alone would ignite the engine. We knew better than to say anything when he was frustrated, so we silently stood and watched. Infuriated, my father looked up yelling, "I want you kids to sit down and be quiet!" Each of us took a seat, starting to take the situation more to heart, seeing how my father looked so panicked.

"Sheldon, the anchor is up. Can't you get the boat to start?"

"Hell no, the damn thing won't turnover. It might be flooded or the battery's dead."

As they spoke back and forth, the rain started. It fell from the sky, pelting us with cold little rain drops. We all kept wrapped in our towels, impatiently waiting for the engine to miraculously start. Gradually, my father got so frustrated that he threw the keychain in the glove compartment, yelling for Melvin to grab an oar. The boat was being pushed further and further out into the heart of the bay as the land seemed to be drifting out of reach. Melvin and my dad each took a side of the boat, beginning to paddle as the waves were becoming larger by the minute. They may not have been as big as we thought but considering how small the boat was in comparison to our size, they appeared ten stories high. We were all frightened, quietly watching as the wave's dumped buckets of water into our boat. As vigorous and fast as they were paddling, the boat wouldn't straighten out. We didn't seem to be going anywhere. "Are you sure you're paddling straight," my father called out to Melvin.

"Yeah, I can't get the boat to move against the waves. They're just too big and strong."

"Well, paddle harder damn it. We're losing sight of the shoreline."

"I'm doing the best I can," whimpered Melvin.

The waves were beating against our boat while the water was steadily creeping upon us. Unfortunately, there wasn't another boat around for us to flag down for help. Then as luck would have it, the wind changed course slowly starting to blow in our favor. My dad and Melvin were now making progress and my dad shouted, "Ok Melvin, we're in luck. The wind is blowing in the right direction. Paddle as quickly as you can."

With a sense of urgency, Melvin eagerly put his back into it as the rapid currents and waves assisted by pushing us towards the shoreline. We had no idea where we were going to land but all we wanted to do was get out of the bay. The water in the boat was inching higher, so I cried out to my father that the boat looked like it was going to sink. He didn't seem to flutter from my warning but kept on paddling while panting heavily. It was one of those rare times when he didn't have a cigarette in his mouth. While being pelted by cold raindrops, I whispered to Mitch that it looked like we were moving towards an island. To take our minds off the scary situation, we were kidding around suggesting we were headed for *"Gilligan's Island."*

When we were approximately a few hundred yards away from shore, the boat really took in a large amount of water, increasing the struggle for my dad and Melvin. As we approached, the enormous waves helped push us closer to the nearing beach. Sensing that we were close enough, my father safely jumped out from the boat. He carried a rope in his hand, using it to tug us in as Melvin continued paddling. The boat suddenly came to a jerking stop, which felt like a whipping sensation. Then Melvin jumped out, quickly helping us to join them on the sandy island. My father fumbled around until he found a big rock, placing it on the rope to secure the boat from drifting away. In retrospect, that wasn't the brightest idea since the boat disappeared when he came back the next day. Exhausted and panting, my father lifted his hands over his brow to see through the raging downfall, motioning for us to follow him. We eventually came to a house where a nice couple took us in and drove us back to the marina.

CHAPTER 7

Walden soon became a nice memory in our past when my parents decided to relocate back to Seneca. We moved on a quiet street in a modest middleclass neighborhood where it was refreshing to have other kids to play with again. The house was perfect for our size family, accommodating each of us with our own spacious bedroom. My father built a fine recreation room for us to play in, leaving him the basement for his pool table. It was off limits to us, but every so often he would take me down, showing me how to shoot pool. I wasn't quite tall enough to effectively play, but the magic of spending time with my dad was the important thing to me.

The backyard wasn't as large as Walden's but it was adequate for us and the dogs. Completely fenced in, it was fully stocked with all sorts of fun equipment to keep us busy. We had a swing set, sandbox and a little merry-go-round that my mother's parents bought for us. We even had an above ground swimming pool which was great in the scorching Delaware summers. Our house felt warm and full of love. It appeared that our parents purchased the house of their dreams and their happiness illuminated with love.

My mother enjoyed entertaining, throwing many parties that I remembered. One that sticks in my mind was a barbeque in the summer when a big storm rolled in, knocking out our electricity. My parents had Uncle Stewart and Aunt Carly over with their kids, Jeff and Dan. They also invited Aunt Paula and Uncle Charles but they didn't care to come. They never seemed to show up for anything except when one of us kids had a birthday party. I found out later that

they despised my father. Apparently, he drank too heavily when they were around, making wise cracks at their expense.

During the evening, all of us kids were playing on the merry-go-round, starting a silly game called smack King in the mouth. We were spinning around in a circle while King inquisitively sat watching us repeatedly go past him. Somehow it turned into a game by which we each started sticking out our hands, smacking him in the mouth as we went by. Jeff adamantly kept warning us to stop hitting King. In fact, he was the only one not hitting the dog, but as luck would have it, that made no difference to King. He ultimately had enough of our nonsense, using his sharp teeth to nab Jeff by his ass. Annoyed and angry, he lifted him from the ride holding Jeff in his mouth like a toy doll. We all stopped the ride in unison, staring in disbelief as King began shaking his head from side to side. It appeared as though he was going to rip off one of Jeff's ass cheeks. All the adults were inside eating, so no one was outside to save poor Jeff from King's perilous jaws. He must have quickly realized that, yelling for me to go get my father. Still in shock, I heard his cries but couldn't move as my feet felt like they were permanently super glued to the yard. Tears were cascading down his face while King continued working on his buttocks like a rubber toy. Finally, something woke me and alarmed, I started running to the backdoor. I stuck my head in yelling, "Dad, come quick. King is eating Cousin Jeff."

My father quickly bounced up from where he was seated, dashing through the sliding glass doors. When he came out, his eyes bulged from the surprise of seeing Jeff engulfed in King's mouth.

"King, drop it. Drop it, King," my father urgently commanded. He knew to listen to my father, immediately opening his enormous mouth, dropping Jeff flat on his face.

Uncle Stewart and Aunt Carly were directly behind my father when Jeff hit the ground with a loud *"THUD"*. My Uncle swiftly snatched Jeff up, jogging inside as my Aunt trailed behind screaming, "Oh my God. Oh my God. Hold on honey, mommy's here."

We curiously followed to see how Jeff was making out. When we walked in a few minutes later, he was sprawled across his mother's lap bare ass, as she was dabbing him with alcohol soaked cotton balls.

He was awfully sore with me, repeatedly asking, "Why didn't you get your father when I told you to? Why? Why? You knew your dog was biting me," he cried, still grimacing.

I felt badly about it but didn't have a logical reply, so I clammed up. My father, looking irritated, grabbed me by my shoulders asking what happened. I proceeded to tell him about our made up game with King, then turning to Jeff, he questioned why he was slapping the dog in the face. Of course Jeff denied doing it, asking me to attest to his story. I explained to my dad how Jeff was the only one not hitting King, having no idea why the dog chose him to bite. Running out of questions, my father gave up, simply sending us out to play as he sipped on his vodka. While traipsing out, he shot me an odd stare, almost looking like he was holding back from laughing.

After the party, we had a couple of other scary mishaps with King. The final blow was an attack that happened to a friend of mine. One morning my pal, Alan, came over to meet me behind my house, chastising my dogs while waiting for me. We had a six foot fence to keep them in, which worked for Queen, but not for King on that particular day. In his boredom, Alan repeatedly shot the heads off of daisies, popping the dogs in their faces. He kept at it until King lost his temper, leaping over the fence like a hunted deer. By the time I arrived King was all over Alan, tearing his clothes completely off his body. He was wailing terribly, trying his best to break free from the dog's attack. Grabbing King in desperation, I ordered him to stop. Then once freed, Alan jumped up, bolting home wearing only his undergarments.

He was never bitten by King but was badly scratched up and it didn't take long for the phone to ring. Naturally it was Alan's mother, calling to give my mom a nasty earful of threats. My mother insistently apologized but it didn't help her cause. I could hear his mother through the phone, rampaging about the attack. After what seemed to be an hour of raking my mother over the coals, she hung the phone up. Then looking at me with a blazing glare, she said, "I think King has to go. We need to find him another home. He almost killed your friend and I don't want another phone call like that again."

I couldn't believe my ears, so teary eyed I screamed back, "But mom, he was teasing King with flowers. He would've never gone after Alan if he wasn't being teased."

"I know honey, but this is the second time King has bitten somebody and we can't take the chance. Could you live with yourself if something horrible happened to your friend, Alan?"

"No." I answered. "But I'm not giving my dog away. He's my dog." I sat on floor petting King, while he looked at us as if he understood every word. He always seemed to have the ability to communicate with me through his humanly inquisitive expressions.

Frustrated, my mother yelled back, "Well, your friend's mother said he couldn't play with you again until the dog was gone. She also threatened to call the police and have him shot. You wouldn't want that? Would you," she shouted, with her eyes aggressively bulging from their sockets.

"No. I guess not," I answered. Mitch came walking in hearing all the commotion, asking what was happening but neither of us answered him.

While out of energy and patience from all the arguing, my mother said, "Listen Jim, when your father gets home we'll talk with him and figure out what to do."

A few days later the entire family was in the station wagon, carting King off to some farm in the middle of nowhere. During the drive, our parents were attempting to convince us that it was best for King. They were suggesting that since these people lived on a farm, there would be plenty of room for him to run around. Our parents relentlessly went on to say how King would be much happier there, living a longer life. Mitch and I sat in pensive silence, knowing there was nothing we could say to convince them to keep King.

The trip took forever as our hearts felt heavy with grief, knowing our dog was being dumped off at some stranger's farm. When we arrived, our parents spoke back and forth exchanging pleasantries with King's new family. They offered for us to visit him anytime we wanted, but of course that never happened. I took notice how there weren't any children for King to play with but they did have a daughter who was in her teens. It saddened me to digest that King was to become her new best friend.

As soon as King jumped out of the car, he made the place his own. He ran around in circles, loving the green spacious grounds. As we were getting ready to leave he took a little pee on a tree, then came over panting. I felt like sobbing when we shook his giant puffy paw for the last time. Then looking out the back of the station wagon, Mitch and I cried as we watched King sprinting around the yard. He acted happy, not noticing that we had left, so in the end I guess we did the right thing. I thought it better to miss him than have the police shoot him. Heading home, I could hear my mom sniffling in grief from the front of the car. I knew she didn't want to show us that she was upset, but deep down inside I knew she loved King as much as we did.

When school started, I was entering kindergarten as Mitch was attending his first year of nursery school. Kindergarten was far more superior to nursery school for me. The teachers were kinder, speaking in a civilized tone rather than yelling at us. They also insisted on keeping us busy with different creative activities. I was thrilled that naps were out of the question considering I had a difficult time falling asleep on an old musky cot. But the neatest thing about school was taking the bus. It was a new adventure, seeing how my folks permitted me to walk to the bus stop all by myself.

Our next door neighbors happened to be my mom's cousins who had a daughter my age named Lisa. I remember her as a cute little blond, walking to the bus stop with me every morning. During one of our strolls, she explained how her front tooth was loose, feeling like it was going to come out any day. I offered my help if she wanted it out earlier to get money from the tooth fairy, describing how I took out my own tooth out with thread and a little tug. "It was painless," I told her. "And the next morning I found money under my pillow."

She was wearing a rabbit fur bonnet that morning which had laces to tie around her chin to keep the wind from blowing it away. I suggested using the laces from the bonnet as thread to tie around her tooth for pulling it out. She was apprehensive about the idea but after some convincing, she agreed to accept my help. After all, what kid wouldn't want the tooth fairy arriving early with money, leaving it under their pillow? While standing patiently waiting for the bus, I started tying one of the laces around her loose tooth. She started to chicken out as the lace was slowly being wrapped. "Come on," I coaxed. "It's no big deal. One pull and it's all over."

"No," she argued. "It's going to hurt. I've changed my mind," she whined, trying to back away.

"I can't believe it," I said, sounding frustrated. "It'll only take a second." Then quickly snapping her head back, the tooth popped out. It bounced on the pavement, lying there in a little pool of blood.

"Look what you've done," she cried. "I told you to stop and now my mouth is bleeding. I can't go to school like this." She turned around crying, running home with the speed of a rabbit.

"Stop," I yelled from the bus stop. "Don't go home. You're going to miss the bus."

Then while standing there, the idea of being in trouble with my parents came to mind. "I'm sorry, please come back." She didn't listen to me, continuing to run back home yelling for her mommy. I knew I would be in for it, once my parents got the call from Lisa's mother. She was definitely one of those overprotective moms.

When school was over, I hurriedly raced home, curious to see whether or not Lisa's mom called my mother. To my surprise not a word was mentioned when I returned home. It was the same routine rolling in motion, finding Mitch and Julie watching cartoons on the television set. I kissed my mother hello while she was bringing in the cheese whiz and crackers for a snack before our lunch. But it didn't take long for the telephone to ring. My mom was eating her cracker when I promptly jumped up to grab it. Sure enough, it was Lisa's mom asking for my mother acting if she didn't know it was me on the line. I quickly hung up the telephone without saying another word, returning to the family room. Within seconds the phone rang again, sending me dashing to be the first to answer it again. "Hello," I said as if it were the first time she called.

"Jim, I know it's you. Put your mother on the phone this instant," she angrily insisted.

"Ah, she's busy," I replied, hanging up for the second time. I was hoping she would give up but as soon as I sat back down, the phone rang again.

My mother finally said, "Jim, who keeps calling?"

"I don't know," I innocently replied.

When the telephone rang for the fourth time, my mother beat me to it. She was on it for quite some time without a word escaping her mouth. While intently listening to her cousin, she stared at me with piercing eyes. I became nervous, thinking of the punishment I would get for the tooth pulling and hanging the phone up on her cousin. Not long after the phone call, she walked casually back into the room. I pretended to be immersed in the television show when she returned, hoping she wouldn't want to disturb me. To my surprise, she sat back down on the couch, picked up another cracker, squeezed some cheese whiz and never mentioned a word to me about it. She acted as though it never happened, which just didn't seem like my mother at all.

CHAPTER 8

Sometime after that day, we all piled into the family car to take my mom to John Hopkins Hospital in Baltimore. On the way, we stopped at a Jack in the Box for lunch. The table was fairly quiet with obvious tension in the air. It was like one of those times when your parents were arguing with neither of them speaking, creating a mute cloud hovering over everyone. Breaking the silence, I asked my parents why we were going to Baltimore. My father explained that our mother wasn't feeling well, so she needed to see a doctor to find out what was wrong with her. I looked at my mother and said, "You don't look sick mom. Do you feel ok?"

She looked as if her mind drifted off to a far away place and softly answered, "I'm fine, honey. The doctor just wants to have a look at me. That's all." As a child you feel like everyone lives forever, especially your parents, so I didn't give it another thought. Being naïve, I assumed she was going to have another baby or maybe suffered from a bad cold. That's as far as my intellect went on the subject of going to the hospital. The prognosis was not good, indicating she was in the beginning stages of MS. The specialist at John Hopkins told my parents that our mother's symptoms were triggered from the birth of Julie. His only suggestion was not to have any more children, feeling the disease would then be controllable. My mother would only need to come periodically for checkups to make sure the MS was not progressing. Not much was known about the disease in those days and if you had it, there was no effective treatment to combat MS. When leaving the hospital that day, none of us were made aware of our mother's condition. I found out about it years later when she was suffering terribly from the disease.

Things were different around the house after our visit to John Hopkins. My mother wasn't around much when we came home from school, but there was the housekeeper Mama Ida had hired. She spent the day cleaning our house while we were at school, then took care of us until my mom came home. My mother began spending more time with friends who I didn't recognize from any parties or events that I attended. Quite often they were over when we came back from school, one in particular being Marlo. She was a stubby looking red head with a funny personality, dressing as if she were going out on date. Anytime I saw her at my house, she was snacking on something which usually was my father's Wise potato chips. It caused countless fights between my parents since it interfered with my father's regular routine. When coming home from work, he liked his bag of potato chips with a glass of vodka on the rocks. If he couldn't find any, all hell would break loose with him calling for my mother, "Mindy, where are my potato chips?"

Invariably she would call back, "I don't know. Aren't they in the pantry?"

"No, damn it. Was your fat ugly friend Marlo here again? You know I can't stand that bitch. Every time she comes over she eats all my potato chips."

My mother always denied Marlo was over, instructing us to do the same. She even bribed everyone with candy to keep quiet, knowing my father loathed her, assuming the two of them were sleeping around. Marlo was a married woman but my father thought she was unhappily married, out cheating on her husband. He had a vile opinion of Marlo, thinking she was a bad influence on his wife.

"No, she wasn't here today. Maybe you ate them all last night. You should've told me so I could've bought another bag today," my mom hollered back, sounding miffed.

"I know damn well I didn't eat them all. Who the hell could eat a whole bag of potato chips in one sitting? Only your pig friend Marlo, that's who."

Then the fighting would commence with my mother defending her friend, arguing how she didn't appreciate my father calling her a pig. It usually escalated into a big chaotic mess, enticing us to turn the television up louder to block them out. Julie would wind up crying from the loud screaming, cutting their argument short since my mother needed to put her to bed. That was my father's cue to make a break for it, grabbing his drink then retreating down to the basement to shoot pool. This was the beginning of our day to day life while living at our dream house.

Coming home from school one day, I noticed my mother's car in the driveway. Our house was located on the corner of the street, making it easy to see who was home when they didn't park in the garage. I was excited to see her, given that most days she was out doing errands. As I walked through the front door, a big collie graciously greeted me. My mom came up behind the dog with a large childlike smile. "What do you think of the dog, Jim? I named her Princess. Do you like the name?"

I was excited, exclaiming, "Yeah, I love it. But I thought you would call her Lassie since she looks like Lassie from the TV show."

"I know, but I wanted something original," she said, looking down at the dog. "After you're done meeting Princess, go to your room. I have another surprise for you upstairs," she coaxed with a melody in her voice.

Overwhelmed with blinding curiosity, I immediately ran up the stairs, finding an aquarium with a little furry hamster in it. It was cute, even having it's own wheel to play on. I instantly stuck my hand in the aquarium, hastily snatching out the hamster. He looked frightened as he squirmed around in my hand, so I used both hands to keep from dropping him on the floor. Holding him up while taking a long gander, I decided to call him Teddy Bear. He looked just like one, so I thought it was a fitting name. After dropping Teddy Bear back into the aquarium, I ran downstairs to hug my mom for the present. She proudly smiled, asking me to take Princess outside to meet Queen.

Mitch's bus pulled up shortly after I was in the back with the two dogs. I sat watching and giggling as they familiarized themselves by sniffing each other's behinds. It didn't take long for Mitch to come dashing to the backyard, screaming. "Wow, we have another dog? Mom said the dog's name is Princess. That's great. Can I pet her or does she bite?"

"No," I answered. "Go ahead and pet her. She's such a nice dog. Not as great as King but she's nice." Mitch slowly came over, stroking Princess as she sat at his side with her tongue hanging out. "See, I told you she wouldn't bite," I said, sounding as if I trained the dog myself.

We were having a great time with Queen and Princess when Mitch said, "I heard mom got you a hamster. She said I'm getting one too, when I'm old enough to take care of it."

"Good for you," I sardonically said. "Do you want to come see my hamster?"

After Mitch agreed, we jogged into the house finding our mother busy preparing dinner. In mid-stride, I stopped as something odd grabbed my attention. She had a pan full of what looked like snail shells so startled, I asked, "Are you cooking snails for dinner?"

She cackled, saying, "Yep, but they're called escargot."

My mom never cooked anything crazy like snails before. The most creative she ever got was making tacos. Then she asked if I wanted to try one while opening a can of raw snails. I thought, "Why not," putting one in my mouth and chewing. Mitch winced as if he was going to get sick. When chewing the slimy snail, it tasted like chewy thick dirt, so I spit it out in my hand. It was absolutely disgusting.

"You didn't like the escargot," she said, laughing hysterically.

My expression alone should have answered her question, but I stuck out my tongue, shouting, "Gross. It tastes like slimy dirt. Is it a snail or escargot? Tell me the truth."

"It's a snail, silly. But I have to cook it first before you eat it. Your father loves them baked in tons of garlic and butter. He asked me to the make them for him. But don't worry, I'm also making spaghetti and meatballs."

With a touch of irritability in my voice, I looked up at my mother and said, "Gee mom, I wish you would've cooked the darn snail before you gave it to me to eat. I feel like I'm going to throw up now."

Staring at me with a big smirk on her face, she sent us off to go play. Mitch and I went upstairs to mess around with my new hamster, until we heard the front door open and our father walk in. Quickly putting the hamster back into his aquarium, we ran down to greet him. Each of us wanted to be the first to tell him about the new dog and hamster, so we pushed and shoved one another, scampering down the stairs. My father, hearing our noisy race, stood in the foyer waiting for us to emerge. We darted to him as he knelt on one knee, hugging us at the same time. In unison, Mitch and I proceeded to tell our father about Princess and Teddy Bear. As we rambled on about our new pets, he was getting that nasty look in his eyes. His eyelids were turning red and I could see he wasn't happy about the news. His attention quickly shifted towards our mother as he stood up, pushing us away. We both stopped talking, knowing it was a signal for us to shut up.

"Mindy, you got a dog today," my dad surprisingly asked, in a slowly agitated voice.

My mother, undisturbed by his question, calmly took the snails out of the oven, plopping them down on the counter. Then looking my father directly in the eyes said, "Yes, we had to give King away which was devastating to me and the kids. We all were sick about it and Queen needed a playmate. She seemed upset since King was gone and plus, we already had two dogs before. What's the big deal?"

"What's the big deal," my father said with a sarcastic tone in his voice. "I told you, no more *dogs*." White pasty film started to form in the corners of his mouth as he distinctively said dogs. "Didn't we agree there wouldn't be anymore *dogs*? Mindy, didn't we?" Waiting for an answer from my mom, he started preparing his vodka cocktail.

"You know something, Sheldon, I clean the house all day, take care of the kids, the baby and make you your favorite dish and you're going to give me crap about another dog. Screw it! This is my house too. In fact, my father bought it for us so if I want another dog, damn it, I'll get another dog."

My father took a big swig of his drink, looking at her through his reddish peeved eyes and said, "Ok, fine. This better be the last dog. I'm sick and tired of you spending time shopping at pet shops and bringing home strange animals. Listen closely, I do not want anymore dogs."

"We'll see," is all she replied. "Now everyone sit down. Dinner is ready."

For the first time my mom had a victorious look on her face. She was such an easy going person that she allowed people to push her around. I felt good for her as if she had just won her first battle with my father. He said nothing, but you could see he was burning inside. It seemed as though my mom found his hot button, money.

After things quieted down for a few days, my mother received a phone call from my school. The principal called to inform her that I had been sniffing glue in class, requesting she come pick me up. While in class working on an art project for Halloween, I decided to taste the paste since it smelled so good. One of my concerned classmates approached my teacher, explaining how I was sniffing glue rather than sampling paste. That's how it all started. There wasn't even any glue out for us to use, but I was sent down to the principal's office anyway.

It's funny how quickly rumors travel because when I went to gather my things, somehow it leaked out that I was sniffing glue. As I walked down the hallway to meet my doom, the older students proudly patted me on the back, saying, "Good job, kid." Some actually asked how it felt, others smiling like I was hero. I felt like a celebrity the way everyone knew who I was from this mistaken incident. Whatever it was, I sure wasn't going to argue about it. It felt good to be in the limelight, being that I was only a Kindergartener.

We lived two minutes away from the elementary school, so when I arrived at the principal's office my mother was already there. I could hear her muffled voice through the closed door while waiting for her to take me home. It struck me odd how they were sending me home when I didn't feel sick. I didn't understand sniffing glue was a crime and that was the issue. Not whether or not I was sick from the paste. It seemed like the whole thing was being blown out of proportion, so needless to say I wasn't afraid of getting in trouble. Finally, the door abruptly swung open with my mother storming out. She grabbed my hand with an intense grip, dragging me out from the office, all the way to the car. She didn't say a single word during this long trek and for the first time, I felt like I was going to be in trouble.

The car ride was deathly quiet like traveling in a slow moving hearse. I could tell my mother was beyond agitated, finally breaking the silence. "When we get home, I want you to go straight to your room and think about what you did." I didn't answer her, doing exactly as she instructed when we arrived home.

It didn't take long for Mitch to return from school, hearing my mother greeting him while clattering around in the kitchen for our snacks. Julie was still napping so my mother tipped toed to my bedroom, asking me quietly to come downstairs. When I came down, Mitch was consumed by the TV, eating M&M's out of a large ripped bag. As I walked by with my mother, he asked her to change the channel to cartoons, but all she found was "Mr. Ed". We sat on the couch facing each other, leaving Mitch glued to the TV set. My mother started the conversation by saying, "Do you know what you did today at school that got you in trouble?"

"Sure," I innocently said. "I ate some paste because it smelled so good."

"No, your principal told me that you were smelling glue. Now, is that what happened, Jim," she asked, looking for the truth.

"No mom. We were making Halloween masks and we used paste and I ate some," I said, simply raising my arms.

She appeared very confused, shaking her head in frustration. "Do you mean to tell me you ate the glue," she asked in disbelief.

"No. I ate the *paste*," I protested, getting a little upset.

Then she started talking to herself, "I can't believe this. He ate the paste and they're telling me he's sniffing glue. Unbelievable! I didn't think a five year old knew how to sniff glue."

While turning her attention to me, my mom grumbled, "Don't worry, honey. I couldn't imagine you would sniff glue but your principal assured me that you did. He said some children told the teacher they saw you do it. I argued with him but he was pretty convincing. I am ..." She couldn't finish her sentence, seeing how Mitch had caught her attention. Intrigued, I turned to look as well, noticing him stomping his right foot on the carpeted floor while shoving a finger up his right nostril in frustration. He continued doing this act, repeatedly walking in a circle. I honestly had no idea what he was doing. My mother, looking puzzled, called out to him. "Mitch, what are you doing? If you need a tissue, go to the bathroom."

He looked frustrated, strenuously working his index finger up his nose. He began crying and shrieked, "There's an M&M stuck. I think it's stuck up my nose."

My mom quickly jumped up and to her amazement, he did have an M&M stuck up his nose. Panicking, she yelled, "Why the hell did you put an M&M up your nose, Mitch?" She quickly called our doctor, describing in detail what Mitch did. In the middle of the conversation, I heard her ask the doctor to hold on a moment, saying she would check. Setting the phone in her lap, she gazed down on the table at the two bags of M&M's. We had two kinds, plain and peanut, so perplexed she asked Mitch which kind of M&M he put up his nose. He stood there thinking for a moment, then told her it was a plain one.

She hung up the phone, exhaling in relief. Then looking at Mitch, she calmly said, "You'll be alright the doctor said. The M&M will eventually melt out of your nose. You're real lucky though. He told me if it was the peanut one, we needed to get you to his office so he could get it out with a pair of needle-nose pliers." She snickered a little after her comment and I knew she was pulling his leg.

After resolving Mitch's problem, my mom reapplied her serious expression, resuming our conversation. She said we shouldn't mention anything to my father, since she would call the principal tomorrow to get this silly mess worked out. I listened as my mother explained the damage glue could do to my brain. She also threatened to kill me if ever finding out I was using drugs in the future. I'm sure it never occurred to her that she would have to explain drug abuse to a five year old, but considering the situation the subject was already at hand.

CHAPTER 9

I considered myself fortunate to be living in Seneca, given we were so close to both sets of grandparents. My father's folks lived in Cedar, which wasn't too far from The University of Delaware. In fact, that's where my parents met. My grandparents lived in a small modest two bedroom home where they raised my dad and Uncle Stewart. Mitch and I didn't stay over their house very often, so when we did, it was a special treat. My grandma was a chubby little Jewish woman with the biggest heart, always wearing an apron as if she were on kitchen duty twenty-four hours a day. It just seemed to be her daily attire. Due to her constant cooking, the greatest aromas cascaded from her kitchen. It was a miracle my grandpa stayed so skinny considering all the good food she prepared.

I recall my grandfather being a gentle fun-loving man, wearing thick brim glasses and slicking his thick wavy dark hair straight back. He was another fan of Brylcream. He looked old to us but was only in his fifties. My grandma, until the day she died, never revealed her true birth date but was around the same age.

When we stayed over their house, our grandparents pulled out the same box of old toys which my dad and uncle played with when they were kids. It was full of old blocks, metal cars and my favorite, the batman outfit. It was strange that they would have all those toys, hearing my dad talk, they never had anything to play with as children. My grandparents would sit, watching us play after dinner. Sometimes bringing out cards, so we could play war. My grandmother usually gave us dessert right before bed. My favorite being her famous pinwheel cookies which she stored in an antique tin that stayed around for years to come. We sat around the table eating as my grandmother watched with an elated expression on her face. It appeared to make her happy whenever we ate her food. After dessert it was straight to bed, there were no late nights for them and certainly not for us. That was the only rule in their house that my grandpa was strict about it.

On one of our sleepovers, I scared the hell out of Mitch. After we had dinner and dessert, my grandparents were tucking us in while a big storm was brewing outside. It was one of those thunderstorms that had all the ingredients to scare the heck out of a little kid. Initially it started with the heavy winds, followed by the kind of thunder and lighting which made the house feel as though it would collapse. My grandparents had a huge weeping willow tree that stood directly outside our window. It almost looked like a person trying to break in when the winds pushed and shoved at it. The tree made an eerie scratching sound against the window, which I used to compose a horrifying story about a monster trying to break in to kill both of us. I talked and talked about this monster until my brother finally jumped out of bed scared out of his wits. My grandma must have heard him get up because she came out of her bedroom to see who was walking around. She found Mitch sitting on the sofa in her family room just staring into the fireplace. I must have done a hell of a job since he refused to go back to bed, forcing my grandmother to stay up the entire night with him.

The next morning she gave me an earful about scaring my little brother. She said he was in pure shock, refusing to speak or go to bed the whole night. He simply sat on the couch staring in the fireplace. Telling me I could have damaged him for life, my grandma made me apologize to Mitch. She insisted that I explain that there were no such things as monsters. He was still out of it that morning, probably from being up all night more than anything else. He sat at the breakfast table not doing much but staring off into space. Until this day, Mitch and I still laugh about that evening.

Shortly after that night, my grandfather was diagnosed with brain cancer, dying a few months later. My father was terribly broken up over his death, moping around the house for days. It was the first time I experienced a loss of a family member, understanding my grandfather was gone forever. His passing was an awful event to comprehend at my age. The strangest thing about his death was the custom after he was buried. All the mourners returned to his house after the burial to eat and drink for hours. It appeared as though everyone was having a good time and I couldn't understand this custom. I was under the impression that people should be sobbing and lamenting over his death, not drinking wine and feasting on cold cuts.

****

I felt like I had a special bond with my mother's parents, most likely because I was their first grandchild and stayed over quite often. When embraced in their arms, I sensed a strong feeling of being loved and important to them. There was no notion of having to win their love since it came unconditionally. Thinking back, they were the last ones to honestly give me that kind of love and security. That internal bliss is what stayed with me all these years.

Mama Ida was a very attractive woman, a blond with deep blue eyes and a gentle oval shaped face. I remember seeing a picture of her when she was much younger and everyone who saw it, commented how much she resembled Marilyn Monroe. Papa Willie was on the other end of the spectrum, being of average height and oddly lanky. As a kid, I thought he was a bit funny looking with reddish brown hair parted to the side and a mouth stuffed with large teeth. They almost looked like false teeth considering how big and white they were when he gave one of his zealous smiles. My grandparents were one of these couples you wondered how they got together, but loved one another very much, staying married until death did part them.

My grandparents lived in a nice three bedroom ranch in Bass, Delaware, where I loved spending time with them. When staying over, I especially liked the fact that we went out to dinner most times since Mama Ida didn't cook very often. There were a couple of places we frequented, which were either Hamburger Hamlet or Hot

Shoppe's. Both of them being your typical kid-friendly hamburger restaurants. I enjoyed going alone with them, blabbing non-stop through dinner with people who actually cared about what I had to say. After eating, we usually went for dessert at Gifford's for ice cream. They were the king's of gourmet ice cream in those days, making the most amazing sundaes and shakes. When it is close to bedtime, my grandfather finished the evening by sitting me on his knee, reading one of my favorite books to me. My folks had little time for things like that, having their hands full with three children, so I appreciated my time with Papa Willie and Mama Ida.

Depending on what night I slept there, the next day I either went shopping with my grandmother or to work with my grandfather. Like my mother, Mama Ida fancied shopping, dragging me through Garfinkle's more times than I'd like to remember. Garfinkle's was a large expensive department store, before it closed, comparable to a Saks Fifth Avenue. After running through the women's clothing section and playing hide and go seek with the sales ladies, it was my turn to get suited up. She favored taking me to the Peppermint Tree, which was an upscale children's boutique. Shopping with her, made me feel like a life size doll being dressed for her amusement. It was not a day that a little boy would dream about, so I preferred going to my grandfather's electrical supply store instead.

My relationship with Papa Willie only lasted seven years, but I vividly recall what a sweet old guy he was. He was exceptionally proud to introduce me around to all his employees, constantly joking around with them. His big gag was how they were looking at their future boss, while laughing they all threw out sly remarks at his expense. After exposing me to his crew and secretaries, I shadowed him around the store or sat at an empty desk drawing pictures on scrap paper. The one activity I jumped to do with him, anytime the opportunity presented itself, was ride in the old rickety elevator. It wasn't the typical safe elevator I was used to, equipped with a manual fence that he had to pull down before moving. As it operated, I could see each floor when going up or down. It seemed very complex to me, like he needed to hire an elevator operator to run it. The ride took an eternity as it went from one floor to the next, feeling like a ride at an amusement park with the loud banging and jolting.

My grandfather had a brother named, Louie, who was sort of strange, spending most of his time in the warehouse alone. He appeared to be taking inventory or just looking for something anytime we ran into him. Louie didn't talk much or ask many questions. Usually, my grandfather would say, "Hey Louie, look who I brought to work with me." He would glance over simply mumbling something, then nonchalantly going on with whatever he was doing. A few years later my father told me that my grandfather screwed him out of millions. One of those things you don't share with your child, especially when it wasn't true.

The highlight of the day was going to lunch. Papa Willie closed the shop early on Saturdays and liked taking me to eat afterwards. We went to the same little diner across the street where everyone who worked and ate there knew him by name. It was one of those quaint rustic diners where everyone knew each other. When entering, it had the old eat-in style bar and adorned with those old wooden booths, which were so uncomfortable on your butt that you couldn't wait to finish your meal. He loved to show me off to the waitress' who invariably joked and laughed at my expense. The kind of cutesy things waitresses like to do with the hopes of getting a hefty tip. It was all in good fun, but I felt embarrassed. I shied away when the waitress reached to grab for my cheeks, saying how cute I was. After lunch, he would make it up to me by taking me to a toy store.

The holidays were the best at Mama Ida's and Papa Willie's house. We were Jewish but celebrated both Hanukah and Christmas since Uncle Charles was Christian and lived with my grandparents. Every year Aunt Paula and Uncle Charles setup an immense decorated Christmas tree. Aunt Paula was exceptionally artistic, really knowing how to dress up a tree. She also displayed these delicious candy canes, which were seven feet long, laying them by the fireplace beneath our Christmas stockings. Mitch and I favored her gingerbread house the most, sneaking little pieces whenever she wasn't around. Aunt Paula never caught us but commented how the house was slowly shrinking as the candy was disappearing. It was an eye boggling event for us.

At my house we only celebrated Hanukah but my parents did allow us to hang stockings over the fireplace. By mentioning stockings, I mean my father's long black dress socks. My mom made sure we used the clean ones, explaining how my father's feet stunk to the high heavens. His smelly socks were one of her pet peeves that they occasionally argued about. After coming home from work, my father would take his dirty socks off, flinging anywhere in the room. It drove her nuts, especially annoying her when finding them in the bed. Some nights my dad would fall asleep with his socks still on, simply shoving them under the blanket. One evening my mother became so livid that she hid his filthy worn socks under his pillow to get even. She told me the story a few years later, finding it hysterical seeing that he never noticed them.

Even though Hanukah wasn't as festive as Christmas, we still had great fun with it. On the mornings of Hanukah, we would all dash downstairs for breakfast while my father played the Fiddler on the Roof album on our record player. Mitch and I loved that album, dancing around the living room like drunken monkeys. Then our parents would let us open our gifts after lighting the menorah. After we finished celebrating at our house, it was off to our grandparent's for more Hanukah and Christmas gifts. We usually stayed the entire day, having dinner as one big happy family. It was that time of the year when everything was peaceful and there were no family quarrels.

Soon after the holidays, school started up again. My mother wasn't home much when we returned, leaving the housekeeper in charge of us, but it wasn't the same. I was saddened, utilizing the television set as a substitute for my mother's absence. Routinely, Mitch and I stayed glued to the TV, eating junk food until dinnertime. I eventually grew tired of it, confronting my mom about not being home enough. She acted shocked that I was so upset, justifying it by telling me how she joined a bowling league with her girlfriend, Marlo. She didn't want me to mention Marlo to my dad, but he was well aware she was bowling. It was then I noticed how free-spirited she was becoming, disregarding what was going on around the house. She did ask how school was with us, in addition to other small talk, but somehow appeared pre-occupied with her own affairs.

Coming home one day after school, I found my mother at home, but this time with another dog, a full grown docile Irish setter. I knew my father was going to lose his cool when seeing a new dog in our house. She just didn't care, as if it were a game to her. A few days later she dragged home another dog, which was a cute toy poodle puppy. My mom said she purchased the dog for me, suggesting I could name him anything I wanted. Overwhelmed with the idea of having my own dog, I decided on naming him Snowball since he was white and fluffy just like a snowball.

Seeing how indulged my mother was in her new bowling league, there was no one around to properly care for the dogs, so dog crap was piling up everywhere in the house. It sat around so long that it dried up, embedding itself in the carpet making it difficult to remove. The housekeeper grew tired of it, adamantly refusing to clean up the poop any longer. Feeling no responsibility for picking it up either, my father let it sit there stuck in the carpet drying out for days. By this time, it was difficult to breathe in the air without gagging. The house emanated a combined odor of dog crap and wet dog. I remember walking up the stairs or going to the bathroom in the middle of the night, was like walking through a mine field. I did everything in my power to avoid stepping in the poop. My father finally lost his mind, bickering about it nightly but my mother never caved in. A few nights I woke up from a sound sleep hearing them quarreling back and forth. I even heard slapping and hitting echoing from their bedroom but never dared to go see what was happening.

My world was spinning out of control with me feeling too small to hold it together. The housekeeper became the only consistent figure in our lives when it came to dinner and going to bed, since our parents had their own agenda's. One night still feeling hungry, I took a jar of apple sauce to bed. The next morning I awoke, feeling a strange itchy sensation throughout my legs. Lifting up my blanket, I was startled to find my legs completely smothered with little black ants. I don't mean a few, but hundreds of them scavenging on me. Panicking, I swatted the ants off, feeling them biting and stinging at the same time. I jumped out of bed, quickly darting into my mother's room to find her still asleep. Repeatedly, I shook her until she woke up. I must have had a horrifying expression on my face because she quickly sat up to attention, asking, "What's the matter honey? Are you ok?"

"No," I replied, standing in my t-shirt and underwear. "Look at my leg," I said, lifting it on her bed and balancing on one foot.

Jumping back, she yelled, "Get your foot off my bed and jump in your bathtub." I rushed towards my bathroom, quickly jumping in without turning on the water. Her reaction made my situation feel far worse than I perceived it to be. My mother ran behind me, shaking both hands at her sides as if she had ants crawling on her. I sat down as she turned the water on with her shaky hands, instructing me to get my clothes off. The ants slowly released themselves from my legs, drifting down the drain with the currents.

"How the hell did you get all these ants on you, Jim? Were you outside playing this early in the morning?"

"No," I shouted, noticing how funny her hair looked in the morning. "I was sleeping and found them crawling all over me when I woke up." The water still had not reached a warm temperature as goose bumps were covering my body. "Are they almost all gone? I'm freezing," I whined while she was furiously wiping my legs with a washrag.

"Just about done, how did they get in your bed anyway," she asked, looking intently at my legs. "Did you have food in your bed or one of the dogs?"

"I ate applesauce with a spoon, but I didn't leave it in my bed. I sat it on my nightstand. Do you think that did it," I curiously asked, wondering where they came from as well.

"I'm sure it didn't help," she answered, turning off the water and grabbing a towel to dry me off. "Let's go take a look in your room."

When we went into my room, I pointed to the applesauce on the table. "Not that, your bed. Lift the covers up."

Quickly throwing back the covers, there were plenty of little black ants crawling around. My mother ripped everything off my bed, making a mad dash for the back door. She rapidly shook all the bedding with a fussy look on her face. After a few shakes, out flew a spoon along with the top to the applesauce jar. "Ah ha," she exclaimed, walking back in. "Here's your spoon and top for the applesauce, Jim. Don't ever eat in bed again. Do you get it?" I nodded my head in agreement as she hastily dumped everything into the wash machine. She gave me a look of disgust, then ventured back upstairs shaking her head.

My mother was the one who usually gave us baths, but with no one around anymore, I started doing it myself. It sounds strange for a kid in kindergarten to bath himself, but after that ant episode, I liked staying soil free. No matter how many baths I took, there was a strange sensation of ants crawling up and down my legs. I don't recall what Mitch or Julie did for bathing. One can only assume that my mother cleaned them up in the mornings considering my father was out the door by the time we woke up.

Clothes were becoming seemingly scarce, not finding anything in my drawers to wear in the mornings. I started improvising by dressing in the same clothes that were worn the day before, providing they didn't stink. Having to wear something to school, I was too young to care what others thought. As it turned out, our loyal housekeeper finally quit after having enough of the dog crap and all the overtime she never requested. The house was perpetually deteriorating without anyone around to help fix the situation.

My mother broke down after the housekeeper left, inviting Mama Ida over for a visit. I'm sure she was embarrassed by the condition of the house but was desperate for another cleaning lady. Without someone to be home with us to cook and clean, she couldn't run her errands or bowl. My mother had her hands full with three needy children and she was only in her early twenties doing it all by herself. When my grandmother arrived, she was appalled by the condition of our home. My mom must have been very convincing because my grandmother eventually gave in, offering her housekeeper, Lisa, to help out.

Lisa was an awesome lady whom I loved spending time with. She had been working for my grandmother since my mother and Aunt Paula were little girls. I considered her my friend, excited to spend time with her whenever I was over my grandmother's house. While cleaning, I would shadow her every move, talking her ear off. Lisa was a very pretty African-American lady with the most alluring smile. She reminded me of one of those pretty women on the album covers that my mother collected. We had our little games we played when I helped her clean and the vacuum ride was my favorite. At lunchtime, I begged her to make my favorite sandwich, her famous BLT. She was a great cook, preparing many meals for my grandparents before leaving to go home. Upon hearing Lisa was coming to work for us, I couldn't have imagined a better person.

It was comforting coming home from school and finding Lisa there. She was gradually getting the house back in shape. The dog crap I once tip toe around had disappeared and I started to find clothes again to wear to school. When Lisa wasn't over cleaning, my mom was home waiting for us. She frequently had friends over or would be on the phone when we arrived. On the days my mother's bowling league overlapped, with taking care of us, she brought us along. It was something different to do rather than sitting in front of the television eating junk food. Her friends were nice to be around, acting friendly with amusing comments flowing from their tongues. My mom gave us money to go play games or get candy while she bowled. Her league played with unusually small bowling balls and pins. They called the game duckpins which made playing easier for children, providing how small the balls were. Whether we arrived early or had time after her team played, my mother would allow us to bowl a few games. It was great fun, so anytime she went bowling we begged her to bring us.

Things were going well around the house, we were even eating together like a regular family. My father decided to try boating again, purchasing another boat to replace the one that drifted away. We spent more weekends together on the bay, but it didn't take long for my mother to revert back to her old routine. Her presence slowly diminished as we saw much less of her on a daily basis. My father was coming home later and most nights we went to bed without seeing either of them. Lisa was staying over longer to make sure we were taken care of, but was growing tired as the hours were getting to be too long for her. I overheard her complaining to Mama Ida about the long hours, expressing how her significant other was getting upset with her. During the days Lisa was off, the dogs languidly found their way back in the house with no one around to let them out. Once again the dogs started crapping all over the place, which was the finishing touch for Lisa. She sure as hell wasn't going to clean up any dog crap for my mother.

Mama Ida dropped by periodically after Lisa's phone calls, terribly disappointed how my mother was allowing the house to become so untidy. She was also frustrated never finding her at home or getting a hold of her on the telephone. I would have to assume my father was getting an earful at work since he worked for Papa Willie. Luckily for Mitch, Mama Ida happened to be over on a day when he got stung by a yellow jacket.

Mitch followed a few of my friends and me into the woods to go play one afternoon. The woods backed up to the road leading to a nearby country club where we played all sorts of different games for hours. It happened to be warm that day as the bees were out pollinating and buzzing around in great numbers. Out of a dead silence, Mitch let out a screeching high pitched cry that made me jump. Stunned, we all stopped whatever it was we were doing, quickly turning to look at him. He had his hand held over his face, stomping up and down like he was putting out a small forest fire. I went over to see what happened and at first, thought a bee had stung him beneath his right eye. The mark on his face was slightly red, but he shook it off continuing to play. A few minutes later he asked me to take another look. The side of his face, where he was stung, was now swelling at an enormous rate. At the time, I didn't know he was allergic to yellow jackets, but after seeing his condition, I suggested he should go home. Mitch refused, wanting to stay and play. Eventually, the side of his face swelled so immensely that we all pressured him to go home. His eye was completely swollen shut and his face looked like a football was growing out of the side of his head. He finally succumbed to our advice, charging home not being able to see out of his one eye.

Later in the day, I came home looking to see how Mitch was doing, finding my parents battling in the kitchen. Mama Ida happened to be over when Mitch came home, then seeing his radical facial transformation, frantically hurried him to the hospital. The doctors determined that Mitch was stung by a yellow jacket and not by a bee, which we original thought. They told my grandmother if she hadn't been there to drive him to the hospital, Mitch would have surely died being so highly allergic to yellow jackets. My father continued hollering at my mother, repeating the story he heard about Mitch. Shaking with anger, he violently screamed how Mitch almost died because of her absence. My mother kept contending that while she was shopping her mother was supposed to be watching us. They were so involved in their screaming match that neither of them saw me walk in. While they argued, I went up to check on Mitch.

He was a total wreck when I found him sleeping in his bed. He must have been loaded on painkillers because he never heard me when I walked in. I noticed how Mitch's face looked even worse than it did when he left to go home. If I didn't know better, I would have never recognized him. His face was so badly swollen that the other eye was just about shut too. It looked like a pomegranate, brightly colored red and stretching well beyond normal capacity. I shook my head, feeling blessed it wasn't me who was stung by the yellow jacket. Leaving his bedroom, I couldn't believe he didn't wake up from the hollering and fighting going on from downstairs.

Things were getting tense around the house but it didn't deter my mother from doing her own activities. No matter the consequences she still continued disappearing from the house, coming back at all hours of the night. It never made much sense, until years later Lisa enlightened me on my mother's behavior during a phone call. She explained how my father drastically changed when they moved to Walden, showing her little affection. He regularly went out after work, drinking with his buddies and coming home late. My mother was very young, finding herself longing for attention and companionship. That was the reason for wanting children, coupled with the desire to bring home all the dogs. It was all motivated out of loneliness from the lack of love and warmth in her life.

While all this missing in action was going on, Julie was walking around in stinky filled eroded diapers, food was scarce and the house reeked of dog and dog crap. I can't remember who was around helping, being so consumed with the television set when I was home. Mitch and I would sit for hours in front of our new found babysitter, watching anything that was on the tube not to be engrossed with the goings on in our house.

Sometime after Mitch was stung by the yellow jacket, my dad came home finding my mother's car in the neighbor's yard. Mitch managed to get into the automobile and drop the transmission in neutral. Our house was built on a slight hill, so the car rolled down the driveway backwards with Mitch in it, ending up on our neighbor's lawn. He simply got out unscathed, returning to the house as if nothing happened. When my father came home, he was utterly shocked to find the car sitting in the middle of the neighbor's yard. He blew through the garage door screaming my mom's name but of course, she was nowhere to be found. Sensing his anger, Mitch never admitted his wrongdoing, so my father was confused how the car was moved.

When he went back to retrieve the car, our neighbor came out describing the incident. He proceeded to tell my father how he heard a big bang and when seeing what happened, was surprised to see Mitch getting out of the car. They tried calling a few times, but no one answered the phone so they gave up since Mitch didn't appear injured. Our mother gave us strict orders never to answer the phone when she wasn't home. She scared us into believing that it could be kidnappers, so we never answered while she was out. After my father brought the car back, he scolded Mitch for messing around with it, but it was a joke compared to his usual temper. He actually blamed my mother for not being home to supervise us. I figured he was saving his A game for her.

The next day, after school, presented an unusual scenario, finding my father home early loading our car. Walking over to say hello, I noticed that he had packed most of our clothing which struck me odd. I was excited at first, thinking we were taking a family trip but instead, he informed me that we were going to Uncle Stewart's to stay for a few days. He looked clumsy as he hastily ordered me to grab any toys I would like to bring from my room. I looked at him puzzled, asking, "Where's mom? Isn't she coming too?"

Without looking at me, he sternly said, "Go get your things. We need to leave now."

"I don't want to leave without mom," I said in a whiney tone.

Something seemed very strange about what he was doing, giving me a bad feeling in my gut. He was extremely edgy, looking around as if he were about to steal something from a department store. I never saw my father home in the afternoon, so his packing like we were going away for a long time, didn't sit well with me. It didn't look like a short holiday at Uncle Stewart's either, so I inquired again, "Where's my mom?"

"Listen," he said, while holding my shoulders. "We have to go. Your mother hasn't been around to take of you kids and we're going away for a little while."

I stood there stiff, not knowing what to say. At first, I thought it could be fun to spend some time at Uncle Stewart's and Aunt Carly's house, but slowly the idea became scary to go somewhere without my mother. As all these thoughts were viciously cycling through my mind, Mitch and Julie had already managed to get into the car. With everything moving in fast motion, I didn't want to be left behind, so quickly I ran up to my bedroom to grab a few toys. Jumping into the car, I had a sick feeling in my stomach about leaving my mother behind. I knew she would be hurt when coming home that evening, finding us gone. Feeling bad, I knew I didn't have a choice unless going head to head with my father in our driveway. He already had that pissed off expression on his face, so I didn't want to offer myself as his personal punching bag.

CHAPTER 10

When we arrived at Uncle Stewart's and Aunt Carly's house, they were definitely expecting us. As soon as my father pulled up the driveway, they popped out their side door. My cousins, Jeff and Dan, staggered out behind them like little ducklings looking confused. Everyone exchanged hellos, helping us in the house with all our belongings. Aunt Carly asked if we were hungry but none of us wanted anything. My appetite was lost the moment we left our home. My dad sat down with Uncle Stewart, instructing us to go play somewhere else so he could speak with our uncle. We gladly scurried up the stairs, leaving Julie with Aunt Carly.

While playing around, Jeff began asking questions about my mother, like where was she, did I see her before we left and was she upset? He was two years older, probably grasping what was going on better than me. Numb from all the excitement, I considered this a little vacation until my folks made up. Jeff acted as though it was serious business and I respected whatever he said. Little by little he was making me nervous, knowing more about my parent's situation than I did. After all of his questions, I succumbed to the fact that he really knew more than me. Everything was happening so fast, I just wanted my parents to make up and put their lives back together again. After I divulged a variety of stories of what went on in our house, Aunt Carly called us down for dinner.

When we came rushing down, I noticed my father and uncle having cocktails in the family room. Uncle Stewart looked up at me from where he was sitting and asked, "Are you ok, son?" He referred to me as son when it was serious business. Even to this day, he still does that.

I skeptically nodded my head, answering, "Yes, Uncle Stewart." My father didn't look up. He sadly sat with his head held low, holding on to his drink like a baby cradling a bottle. It looked as if he were in deep thought with tremendous issues to mull over. I honestly felt sick to my stomach and lonesome without my mom. I sure didn't want to share that with my uncle in case it would upset my father.

After dinner, Aunt Carly brought us all upstairs for a bath. She must have been extremely tired having three extra children to prepare for bed, a chore she didn't tackle every day. Once all of us finished, Jeff and Dan went to their rooms getting ready for bed as Aunt Carly went to put Julie to sleep. As soon as she came back for Mitch and me, a loud banging echoed throughout the house, sounding like someone was kicking in the front door. All three of us stopped what we were doing and stood at attention as though someone ordered us to lineup. We nervously became quiet, with no one moving to hear what was going on downstairs. I heard my uncle shout, "Hold on. I'm coming." Then my father and uncle whispered something, hearing their footsteps inching across the foyer floor.

The door echoed throughout the house again, with jolting kicks as my mother yelled, "Open the fucking door. I want my kids back."

My aunt held us tightly when the door opened. "What the fuck are you doing with my kids, Sheldon? I want them back this minute."

Standing on the doorstep, my mother was hyperventilating with a distinct odor of booze laced on her tongue. Her fists were clinched at her side, looking like someone had their way with her with a butcher knife. She was wearing a white dress which was garishly stained with fresh blood, literally outlining her vaginal area as it strayed down her legs.

I heard my father scream back, "Lower your God damn voice. Everyone can hear your big fat mouth."

"Fuck you. I want my kids now. You have no business taking my kids from me. If you want to leave, fuck you, but I want my kids back."

There were some shuffling noises, sounds of pushing and shoving going on. Then I heard my uncle say, "Sheldon, cool it. Stop, do you hear me?"

My father was trying to reach over my uncle to grab my mother. While this was going on, two big African-American guys were making their way up the front lawn. They apparently drove my mother, given it wasn't her car they were standing by.

Believing the two guys to be a threat, my father spitefully yelled, "What? Did you fuck these two and bring them along to get your kids? You better tell them to get the fuck out of here. You're not getting the kids. Do you hear me?"

My uncle was still holding on to my father who was attempting to get at my mother. "Let me go, Stewart. Let me go, I'm not kidding."

My mother stood strong, refusing to back down. Slurring her words, she started screaming, "Do you think I'm scared of you? Your brother has hit me before. Do you know that, Stewart?" My uncle couldn't do much but nod, holding my father back from attacking her. "You better just give me back my kids or these guys will kick your ass."

After sensing the intense hostility, my mother's two companions stopped in their tracks. They most likely didn't imagine there was going to be this much drama and started back peddling to their car. My mother, still waiting for the cavalry, decided to take a look behind her noticing the two fellas retreating. Looking defeated and knowing there was no way she was getting into the house, my mother ranted one last threat to my father. "If my kids are not back by tomorrow, I swear, Sheldon, the police will arrest you. I'll make sure they put your ass in jail." With that last threat, she disappeared into the car driving off into the dark night.

When the front door was slammed shut, I heard their footsteps wander back into the family room as my aunt asked if we were ok. Mitch and I nodded our heads, motioning that we were alright. At that she briskly put us to bed, rushing down the stairs to see how everything was. Laying in the dark, I stared up at the ceiling feeling sick. I felt bad that my father and uncle didn't let my mom in, forcing her to leave so late in the evening. This feeling of guilt overwhelmed me that maybe I should have gone down to help her. After all, it was two of them against her. I rolled around in deep anguish until I finally fell asleep.

The next day I anticipated the police or my mother coming by, but neither showed. We ended up at the doctor's office instead. Julie, Mitch and I came down with a vicious flu, succumbing to extremely high fevers. I had a history of high fevers, most times an alcohol rub or an ice cold bath would bring it down, but nothing was working this time. Aunt Carly became very concerned, dragging all three of us to the doctor's office. Julie was about three years old when this happened and I saw a side of her I never witnessed before. The doctor examined all three of us, concluding that we needed to be inoculated in order for our high temperatures to be reduced. Mitch and I were the first ones in and out. Then Aunt Carly left us in the waiting room as she went in with Julie.

It was summertime, but oddly enough the waiting room was jammed packed with sick kids. Besides a few crying babies, the waiting room was quite calm. Most of the kids were anxiously sitting along side their parents, awaiting their fate with the doctor. Then a horrific shrilling resounded from the examination room with the intensity to vibrate a ten story office building. The entire waiting room flinched in terror, reacting like fans doing the wave at a sporting event, with the exception of raising their arms. It sent a tingling sensation up my spine and I had no reason to be nervous, having been given my shot already. I could only imagine what it was doing to the other kids who had yet to get their turn with the doctor. Within a few more seconds, another loud high pitched scream came from the examination room. It sounded like a nasty struggle was going on in there as I heard the doctor bellow for help. He was demanding for more nurses to assist him while the ruckus sounded as though someone was getting a limb cut off. Suddenly, I heard a familiar voice, Aunt Carly yelling, "Julie, you have to calm down. The doctor can't give you a shot if you're screaming and carrying on like this."

After my aunt's attempt to help, the doctor chimed in rigidly saying, "Please young lady, you must relax. It will hurt worse if you're jumping around like this." Eventually, the doctor administered the shot and out strolled Aunt Carly holding Julie's hand. Every mouth in the waiting room was agape. No one could believe that this little girl could have put up such a terrible fight. In the end, Aunt Carly told my father it took one doctor, three nurses and herself to restrain Julie.

It didn't take long for my father to find an apartment for us. I was surprised, assuming our leaving was only temporary. I figured we would stay at Uncle Stewart's and Aunt Carly's house for a few days, then it was back home with my mom. There was no talking to my father when the subject of my mother was brought up. He was always pre-occupied with something, which was either an important phone call or a private conference with my uncle. We hadn't seen our mother in quite some time and I was getting nervous that we may never see her again. I regularly overheard my father cursing my mother on the telephone and in the presence of other people, so I didn't feel comfortable asking him about her. When her name was mentioned, he transformed into a raging hothead. The only person I felt comfortable confiding in was my Aunt Carly. She was a sweet woman, reminding me of one of those Hollywood moms that you saw on the television shows. I often thought how fortunate Jeff and Dan were to have such a wonderful caring mother. I expressed how upset I was about the whole situation to my aunt, constantly asking her when I was going to see my mother. She never gave me a straight answer, but tried comforting me as much as she could.

Before going to the apartment, my father took us back to the house. He made it clear that we were only going back to pick up a few things, appearing relatively nervous as we drove up. When we returned, I was excited hoping my mom would be there waiting. I was praying if they saw each other maybe they would reconcile their differences and we wouldn't have to go to the apartment.

Our house appeared abandoned when we pulled up. The lights were all out, giving the place a lifeless impression, as though the soul had been sucked out of the interior. The facade was as sad as I felt inside, remembering the strange chill lingering as we walked through the front door. The house looked and smelled utterly dreadful, appearing like no one had lived there in weeks. I wasn't surprised my mom wasn't there seeing as the condition of the house was unlivable.

A great deal of dog poop was dried up still embedded in the shag carpet. Heaps of soiled dishes and glasses were piled high in the sink and the family room was littered with empty bags and plates. It was an eerie feeling, imagining at anytime I would bump into a dead body. I didn't go upstairs but my father did, rushing around like a madman grabbing miscellaneous items. I didn't actively pay attention to what he was grabbing, as I was still in shock over the condition of our home.

Then we entered the garage, which was another scary sight to witness. It looked like someone released a few wild tigers in there after we found our boat shredded to tatters and the windshield completely smashed out. My father was hysterically swearing and cursing up a storm given that the boat was unsalvageable. It was his baby and for sure, one of the things he was coming back to claim. Mitch and I stood in the unimaginable mess as he kept screaming, "Do you believe this shit? Can you believe what this crazy bitch did?"

After my father was done lamenting over his boat, we all jumped into the car heading back to the apartment. On the way over, I still felt apprehensive about leaving our house. I had this crazy notion that my mom would show up at any time, ending this chaotic nightmare. It never happened though, confronting me with the fact that this was reality. Something I needed to embrace, whether I wanted to or not.

The apartment complex was located in Cedar, not far from the University of Delaware. It was a nice garden apartment on the first floor with three bedrooms. I liked the idea that it was on the first floor since I brought my bike which Mama Ida and Papa Willie bought for me. It was nice keeping it on our patio rather than bringing it up and down the stairs each time. Mitch and I shared a bedroom while Julie and my father had their own rooms.

My father had hired a lady to do the cleaning and watch over us while he was at work. She was very nice, making sure we were fed and had clean clothes to wear. At least we were getting by, but she didn't compare to having a mother. During our time there, Mitch, Julie and I spent most days watching a lot of television. When I wasn't pre-occupied with TV, I rode my bike around the parking lot. After living there for a short time, my bicycle was mysteriously stolen. I was shattered seeing how it was the only thing I took with me that had any kind of sentimental value. It was irreplaceable in my mind. When my father came home that night, I explained how the bike was missing when I went out to ride it. He repeatedly blamed and scolded me for leaving it out on the patio unattended. When finished reprimanding me, I begged him for another bike. He reluctantly made a promise that he would do his best.

Each night my father came home from work, I ran to greet him hoping to find a new bike. Night after night I was disappointed until he got tired of me bugging him, finally coming home with a bicycle. I remember him rolling it into the family room and being totally blown away by what I saw. The bike looked like something he picked out from the garbage since the style was from the days when he was kid. It was deplorable, so rusted that it didn't even have a color anymore. It looked like Pee Wee Herman's bike from his movie, except completely rusted out. I shamefully looked at it, saying, "Dad, I thought you were going to get me a bike like the one I had. This is old and rusted." Before taking my eyes from the bike to look at him, he hauled off smacking me across the face. I immediately flew across the room from the impact, slamming into the living room wall.

Then grabbing the front of my shirt, he held me against the wall screaming directly in my face, "You fucking spoiled brat. Who the hell do you think you are? That's all you get. You shouldn't have left your God damn bike on the patio in the first place. I didn't even have a bike when I was your age."

In tears, I was dangling in midair and didn't say a word. He finally put me down, hollering to get out of his sight, that I made him sick. Julie began crying as I wallowed back to my bedroom, feeling my face throbbing. Resting on my bed, I wondered, "Where could my mother be?" I couldn't understand why she wasn't looking for us and why we were just with our father. I was feeling homesick for Mama Ida and Papa Willie as it seemed my family had been completely stripped from our lives. It felt like we would never see them again, given that my father had such venomous hatred towards my mother. I thought of us as his prisoners. Mitch was unhappy too, constantly asking me when we were going to see our mother again. Being only six and Mitch four, we had no way of contacting anyone on our own. It was a hopeless feeling.

The lady who was taking care of us decided to quit. She was tired of changing Julie's diapers, not understanding why she wasn't potty-trained yet. My father determined that his mother would be a perfect candidate to take her place. She had been living by herself since my grandfather died, with no one around to keep her company. We all loved grandma very much and thought it was a sensational idea. For one thing, she was a terrific cook making anything she touched taste awesome. She also had tremendous patience and we knew she genuinely loved us. It was going to be a warmer environment with her looking after us, rather than a stranger merely looking for a paycheck.

It had been weeks since we left our home and laid eyes on our mother. During this period, my father was still working for my grandfather. Papa Willie was trying to make things work out between the two of them, but neither of my parents were willing to give in. My father likes to tell his fable of how my grandfather begged him to go back with my mother, insisting how he refused, even after my grandfather offered him a million dollars. No strings attached, having only to return home with us. My father said that once he refused the offer, my grandfather had no choice but to fire him. He explained that my grandfather felt bad firing him, but Mama Ida wanted him gone.

My father held the million dollar offer over our heads forever. But years later, I had an interesting conversation with Lisa about it. She was there the night Papa Willie came home, disgusted by my father's outlandish request. She didn't know the dollar amount, but my grandfather sat at the dinner table, describing to Mama Ida how my father requested money in exchange for returning home with us. She told me Papa Willie was sick to his stomach, refusing to pay him a dime.

A few days later, my father announced that he needed to go out of town for a couple of days. He never said why, no matter how hard I tried to weasel it out of him. Everything was beginning to be a secret with him, but when he left there was a nice calmness which settled in the apartment. All of us were feeling and acting relaxed, going about our days the way children do. We laughed, made noise and played around. There wasn't that anxious feeling of having to walk on pins and needles. After dinner that evening, my grandmother bathed us, then put Mitch and Julie to bed. She allowed me to stay up longer since I was the oldest. It was great bonding time, having the opportunity to be alone with her freely speaking my mind. My grandmother listened to all my concerns and gripes, but was very hesitant to comment on anything. Most of her answers ended with, "But you need to understand" or "But it's for your own good."

After my grandma put me to bed, there was a sudden knock at our front door. I quickly leaped up and quietly peeked through my door which was slightly ajar. No one ever came to our apartment, so I couldn't help snooping. Not even a Jehovah's Witness, who were knocking on everyone's door in those days. My grandmother was slow getting up as I heard another knock, but this time it was unmistakably louder. I watched as my grandmother approached the door, asking in her old lady soft voice, "Who is it?"

The apartment didn't come with a peephole, so she had to speak through the door. I suppose she couldn't hear what was being said on the other side, repeating herself again, "Who is it?" Still not understanding the person, she slowly opened the door while in a more aggravated voice said, *"Who is...?"* Before she could finish her sentence, someone attempted to shove open the door as it came to a screeching halt, slamming against her forearm.

Surprisingly, I heard my mother's voice as she yelled, "Open the door you fat old bitch. I want my kids back."

My grandmother's arms and legs were shaking while struggling to keep the door from opening. I didn't know what to do and alarmed, stood frozen behind my bedroom door. Then my grandmother, laboring to get the words out, angrily shouted, "Get your foot out of the door this instant, young lady."

"You better let me in. Those are my kids. Your fucking son has no right to keep them from me." My mother was huffing and puffing, hearing her voice as she hollered.

Slowly making my way out of the bedroom to get a better look, my grandmother somehow spotted me. "Get back, Jim," she softly said, trying not to alert my mother that I was there.

For a lady in her sixties, she was doing a hell of a job holding her ground. As the struggle continued, I heard another familiar voice chime in, "Yeah! Open this door bitch. They aren't your kids. Give them back. E..R..A.. lady. ERA. EQUAL RIGHTS!" It was my mom's best friend, Marlo, and at the time, I had no idea what that phrase meant but it stuck in my head for years.

I was still standing there, not knowing if I should charge the door and let my mother in or help my poor old grandmother, who was fighting for her life. After what seemed like an eternity, my grandmother used her large frame powering the door shut in their faces. I was amazed by her tenacity and strength. She was probably all of five feet tall and I won't guess her weight, but it was quite a bit. With her hands trembling, she quickly turned the bolt lock, shouting, "I'm calling the police, Mindy. You and your friend better leave. Do you hear me?"

I heard my mom kick the door and scream back, "Go ahead bitch and I'll tell them you kidnapped my kids."

After a few minutes, the commotion drizzled down to a silence but then there was an alarming crash, as if they threw bottles against our door. I heard a door slam shut in the hallway, knowing they were definitely gone then. My grandmother was wreck, practically having to catch her from falling down on the floor. Her hair was disheveled, her hands were trembling uncontrollably and she was sweating profusely. I gently walked her over to the lazy boy, where she sat straining to catch her breath.

"Are you ok," I asked, finding myself trembling as well.

"I'm fine dear. Let me just catch my breath." I stood waiting for her body and breathing to wind down to a normal rate. She looked like a person going through convulsions, but soon started looking and acting like her old self. Trying her best, my grandmother flashed me a sincere smile, but I could tell she was still startled by all the chaos. After gathering herself, she thanked me for my concern and sent me back to bed. We never spoke about what happened that night again.

That was my grandmother for you, never speaking poorly about anyone. She kept her thoughts to herself, especially, when it was inappropriate for a young child to hear.

The next morning my father called to find out how we were getting along without him. When the phone rang, we all rushed to follow our grandma into the kitchen. That was how bored and nosey we were. Then while pulling on her apron and asking who was on the phone, she quietly whispered that it was our father. They spoke for a few minutes when he detected something was wrong in her voice, inquiring if she was ok. He also asked if we were behaving ourselves, grilling her through a barrage of questions. My grandmother answered every one of them by curtly saying yes or no. Finally, you could hear him through the phone say, "What's wrong mother?" Then turning, my grandmother asked for us to leave the kitchen. She spent a long time speaking with him, while we went back to watching television.

Prior to my father calling, I told Mitch what had happened the night before with our mother. I could see how excited he was getting while telling the story. Hope was colorfully illustrated all over his face. It seemed as if he wanted me to tell him that we were going back home, but I couldn't lie. I explained that our mother appears to be trying, but couldn't say for sure. By Mitch's demeanor, I could see that he was as homesick as me. Julie was too young to know any different, looking content just to eat and poop. She was the most upbeat from all of us, since not being cognizant of what was going on.

The day our father returned from his trip, he had a smile on his face that none of us had seen in months. His two front teeth protruded outwards as he looked like a child who got the present they always wanted on Christmas morning. He joyfully informed us that we were moving to Rolling, Virginia. I looked over at my grandmother, watching for her consent but she simply stood in the background with her arms folded on her chest. He explained how he found a new job there and the need to move fast so he could start working.

"Rolling, Virginia," I said, sounding surprised. "Where's that?"

"It's in Virginia about two hours away," he answered still very excited.

"Two hours away. How are we ever going to see our mother again?" That was the wrong question to ask. His Christmas smile disappeared as quickly as it had appeared.

"Listen to me and listen good. I don't want to hear about your mother again. Do you understand me? None of you. She left you hungry and dirty," he screamed, holding my shoulders in his strong grips with his face directly in mine.

I was as stiff as a board, wondering what was coming next. "That bitch whore doesn't give a shit about you kids," he furiously squawked, as saliva sprayed in my face. "She was out screwing and drinking while I was working, so don't ask me about your God damn mother. If I hear another word or question of when you're going to see your mother, there'll be big trouble. Do you understand me, Jim? And that goes for all of you."

My grandmother swooped to my rescue, putting her hands on my shoulders as she swiftly pulled me back. "Ok, Sheldon. We all understand. Right kids?" We all nodded our heads in agreement with my father eyeballing us, looking like a beast ready to lunge on its prey. "Fine then. I think we have a lot of work ahead of us."

This was how it all started. There was no mentioning our mother in his presence at all. If I used profanity, I most likely had a better chance of not getting a beating than bringing up my mother. It was to the extent we couldn't ask when we could see her or our grandparents. He hated all of them, particularly Mama Ida. The words he used to describe his hatred towards her were astonishingly terrible to express in front of three little children. It didn't make a difference to him what he said in front of us, using no discretion when it came to our mother or grandparents. I was terribly hurt by his remarks and couldn't imagine what it was doing to Mitch and Julie.

CHAPTER 11

Driving to Rolling was grueling for us as two hours felt like a trip down to Florida. We did that trip the year before, with Miami being where I received my first formal swimming lesson. I was alone in the pool when my dad shocked me by throwing me up in the air and belly-flopping in the water with a hard thud. The pool water filtered through my nose while my brain felt like it exploded inside from the pressure. In a frightened state of dying, my father laughed instructing me to swim or drown. At first, I thought he was kidding and would reach out and save me. But when he didn't attempt to help, I panicked managing to swim back to safety. He loudly laughed, saying, "See, I told you, you could do it." Then extending out his hand, as if I should slap him five, I refused, jumping out of the pool in disgust. He waved me off, shouting, "Baby." I did become a strong swimmer, but that kind of lesson isn't something I would do with my own children.

My father loved smoking and anytime you saw him, there was a cigarette dangling from his mouth. His fingers were permanently stained yellow while his clothes smelled like they were scraped off the bottom of an ashtray. Unfortunately for us, he smoked the entire trip to Rolling with the windows rolled up. The people who saw us must have been mystified, seeing a cloud of smoke being driven down the highway in a car doing 70 MPH. My grandmother was recruited to move with us and thank God she was in the car, constantly requesting him to roll down his window. After each request, he complained how cold it was outside. She didn't accept his answer, insisting there were children in the car until he reluctantly gave in. There were no bathroom pit stops either. That was against his rules and if you didn't go before we left, you had to hold it in. The same set of rules which applied when we used to drive out to the marina.

When we arrived, I was surprised to see we were going to live in a townhouse community since only living in single family homes in the past. It was a nice area and I liked the idea of living directly across from the pool. Our home was a three bedroom unit with a spacious basement to play in. It was a nice change from the stuffy apartment we were at. Mitch and I shared a bedroom together as well as Julie and grandma. My father was obviously left with the master bedroom. The back of the townhouse was a great area for us to horse around in. There were plenty of woods to roam and a small ravine, where the water source came from an unusually large cement drainage pipe. Whenever a heavy rainfall would come, the small ravine would turn into a raging river. It looked like the Mississippi was running through our backyard. Mitch and I had found an old metal cement container which we used as a boat when the water was high enough. Eventually, someone else came up with the same idea, disappearing with our boat one day.

Living in Rolling agreed with my father. He started acting like a happier person, but we felt a sense of loss and remorse given we hadn't seen our mother or grandparents for months. I was slowly catching on to my father's elusive plan. He was on the run with us, doing everything in his power to elude my mother and grandparents. None of us attended school and I never remembered attending the first grade. We stayed home with our grandma each day, watching television or playing out in the backyard.

My father was hired by a large lighting distributor, selling and servicing to electrical supply stores within a certain area. Needless to say, he wasn't home much. His job demanded he stay out overnight most of the week, traveling from client to client. We saw very little of him except on weekends but the time we spent together started to be more enjoyable. He was taking the family out to do entertaining things, like on Saturday's, dropping Mitch and me off at the movies to see double features. He would buy our tickets, giving us a few bucks for popcorn and candy too. We practically spent the whole day watching movies as it helped take our minds' off our mother for a short while. Other times, he brought us to see random events that came to Rolling, like Disney on Parade, the Rolling Rockets hockey games, rodeos or whatever else came into town.

Surprisingly, it didn't take long for my grandfather to find out where we were stashed. The company my father worked for also sold lighting to my grandfather's electrical supply house. During a sales call, the rep servicing his account happened to mention that my father took a job with Hawke Lighting, working in the Virginia area. It didn't take long for Papa Willie to act on the new information. My father soon received a telephone call from his attorney, instructing him to let us go see our mother for Christmas. He was enraged, astonished they had found him. His intention was never allowing our mother or grandparents to see us, adamant to hurt them by keeping us away. In reality, he was hurting his own children, something he selfishly never understood. Until this day, it was all about him and his feelings with nothing meaning more to him than his own issues. His attorney must have convinced him to allow us to go because he would not have agreed to the visit on his own.

When receiving the news, all three of us were flabbergasted, but kept the excitement down not to upset our father. One word or expression of happiness to see our mother and grandparents would certainly bring painful repercussions. Being the eldest, I knew it better than my siblings. Mitch and I couldn't wait, counting down the days as we were looking forward to seeing everyone again. We began contriving different schemes not to come back home, hoping our mother could help. But delving deeper, we found ourselves too scared to try. If the plan didn't work, it would have been a living hell when we returned to him.

Julie was excited for the visit too, sadly growing up without even knowing our mother. It had been months since we last had any kind of communication with them and with time growing closer, I managed to get another high fever. This time it was tonsillitis, forcing my father to take me for a doctor's visit. I fought him along the way, not wanting a needle stuck in my behind. He tried giving me a guilty shtick, sarcastically saying, "Well, you want to go see your wonderful mother so badly. Don't you? So you better get it or you'll have to stay here with me." Instantly becoming brave, I decided to take the needle wherever the doctor wanted to stick it.

I don't remember how we were transported to our grandparents' house but regardless, all of us were ecstatic to see everyone again. My mother was now living with them and looked great. She couldn't have been happier to see us, with tears flowing from her eyes as we all hugged and kissed. Our grandparents followed her lead, embracing us and explaining how much they missed everyone. Aunt Paula and Uncle Charles were there too, giving a warm welcome with the same sentiments. The tree was decorated as beautifully as ever, adding to the warmth and love we felt filling the house. We didn't even care about the presents or stockings hanging over the fireplace, being so engaged in just catching up. Each of us were stepping on the other's words in order to be noticed. Our mother begged us to speak one at a time, intuitively asking a number of questions, but never a sour note about our father. I have to say through everything we endured, she didn't speak or act as vengeful or spiteful as he did. It was all about us and our well-being. She repeatedly apologized about not visiting, explaining how our father never let her know where we were. She even mentioned the story of how she attempted seeing us at Uncle Stewart's and at the apartment in Cedar. I told her I knew about the both times and was saddened that I couldn't see her. As our conversations rambled on, the night went by like a blur and before I knew it, we were being put to bed.

My mother crept back into my room, quietly smuggling me out so we could speak in private. Sitting alone in the living room, she explained how it was best for us to speak one on one. Her demeanor and facial expressions were a picture of cheerless gloom, apologizing for not being around as much as she should have. My mom explained how her marriage to my father was a sad issue and couldn't stay married to him. Tears filled her somber eyes, as her bottom lip quivered when she spoke. I found the conversation sincere and candid, but saddened by her sobbing. She felt like God was punishing her for some unknown crime, repeatedly asking him why he was taking away her children.

After settling down, my mother embraced me, professing how much I meant to her. She adamantly explained how Papa Willie was working hard to fix things with a great attorney, convincing me that he would bring us back together as a family again. I felt a soothing relief circulate through my body and divulged how unhappy we were without her. The moment seemed appropriate, so I questioned my mom about the nasty accusations my father was making about her. She quickly became enraged assuring me they were all lies. Her interest immediately peaked, wanting to know every nasty slanderous detail that he told us about her. I crooned all the horrible names he was calling her, as well as all the nasty things he said she had done. During my descriptive explanation, she appeared to being taking all this down in her head, like a student taking notes in class. When I was done, she hugged and rushed me off to bed. As we walked back to my bedroom, with her arm around me, she broke a faint smile, saying, "Fall asleep quickly or Santa won't drop off any of your gifts."

The next morning it was refreshing to wake up in my grandparents' house, seeing my whole family. My grandmother had a big breakfast prepared, but all of us were so impatient that we ran down to the basement to open our gifts. The adults followed us, as Aunt Paula sat next to the Christmas tree passing out the presents. None of us could read the labels, so Mama Ida suggested putting Aunt Paula in charge. We each received wonderful gifts and clothing to take back to Rolling. My grandmother mentioned a few times how she wasn't crazy about the clothes we were wearing. She especially wasn't fond of Julie wearing tomboy clothing, making sure we had plenty of proper things to bring back. The day flew by as did the time we spent with them and before long it was time for us to go back. I repeatedly asked my mother why we couldn't stay with her, since I wasn't keen on returning back to Rolling. She asked for us to be patient that Papa Willie was working on it.

It was rough returning home to Rolling. My father was extremely embittered about our trip to Delaware, giving us the cold shoulder treatment. By his actions, you would have thought we broke bread with Hitler instead of a short visit to our grandparents' home. He had a unique way of trying to make us feel guilty for seeing our mother and grandparents. We were pressed to feel like we were consorting with the enemy. I made sure to hide my happiness from the trip, not speaking over a whisper about it. He eventually came around, but not to genuinely find out if we had a good time or not. It was more to pry and grill us over all the things that went on. He was snooping around to get dirt on our mother and it was so obvious to me. The questions were all coupled with whom she was with and was she home or out. In reality, there was nothing negative to report and he appeared frustrated by my uneventful answers. All I had were pleasant memories, which I could tell didn't sit well with him by his dismal demeanor.

Soon after we were back, there was a big commotion concerning Julie. I didn't know who noticed it first, whether it was my father or grandmother, but apparently Julie had a new habit. When going to bed at night, she would slide her hand down her underwear, inserting a finger in her vagina while asleep. This blew my father's mind, bringing his hot temper to an extreme boiling point. He concocted a brilliant story, blaming my mother for this unorthodox behavior. He described her laying naked on the bed with Julie, while teaching her how to masturbate. Mitch and I had no idea what that meant when he asked if we witnessed our mother doing those kinds of acts. Neither of us admitted seeing any of that going on, not knowing what Julie was doing was bad. He insisted we must have seen her teach Julie how to do this, repeatedly attempting to pressure us into some kind of confession.

We continued sticking with our original answer, but he simply wouldn't accept that. "I want to know right now, God damn it. Which of you saw your God damn whore mother show Julie how to do this shit?" Neither of us answered, rattling like the tin man from the "Wizard of Oz". "Ok, if you don't want to say, then get the hell out of my sight. Get up to your rooms and think about it," he shouted with frustration in his voice.

My grandma never corrected him in front of us, but I knew she didn't subscribe to his ridiculous stories. He was trying to persuade us to lie, but Mitch and I refused to admit seeing our mother doing this appalling act. This incident was the catalyst which instigated a number of other insane accusations against my mother. These infamous stories were forced down our throats to enrich his case and share with his hired attorneys and child psychiatrists. They were so far fetched but he persistently tried brainwashing us to believe them. I thought he was using this horrific strategy in an attempt to warp our love and affection for our mother. He desperately wanted us to take his side, despising her as much as he did.

It didn't take long before we were on our way back to Delaware, but this time it was to meet with a child psychiatrist. After getting in and settled at Uncle Stewart's house, my father dragged Mitch and me to the doctor's office. During the entire drive, he was coaching us on what to say. He rigidly demanded we tell the psychiatrist how we witnessed our mother laying naked with Julie on the bed, teaching her how to masturbate. The pressure was overwhelming, as he physically threatened us if we didn't tell his version of the story. My hands were sweating and I couldn't stop gnawing on my fingernails. Mitch was just as edgy, sitting in the car while staring out into space. He was a reclusive kid, finding it hard to get a good read on him sometimes. I was physically ill, sitting in the backseat thinking about being pressured into lying about my mom. The guilt was terrible, stirring in my soul for not wanting to lie about my mother in order to save my own hide. Mitch and I were scared to death to be beaten, but I promised myself under no circumstances was I going to lie. I was hopeful my father would think we told his version of the story, praying the psychiatrist wouldn't tell him the truth.

My father proceeded to tell us how he hired a private detective to follow our mother and what she was doing was real bad stuff. He elaborated, explaining how the detective followed Mitch and my mother to a bowling alley where her league played. When pulling up, a man jumped in and they started kissing with Mitch sitting in the backseat. He paused for a moment, looking back to ask Mitch if he remembered that happening. Slowly shaking his head, Mitch mumbled that he didn't remember. My father became frustrated roaring, "God damn it, Mitch. The detective said you were in the backseat while they were screwing right in the front of you. He said it happened right in the front seat. How the hell could you not remember?"

Mitch languidly shrugged his shoulders in doubt, looking complacent with his answer. My father was looking forward again, glaring at the road as he drove. I could see his eyes getting redder and smaller in the rearview mirror. The car became very quiet as my father appeared to be strategizing in the front seat.

"The detective also told me that your wonderful mother was stripping in Shepard Park. She's taking her God damn clothes off for strangers. Did you know that," my father hollered, while lighting a cigarette. "The others who do it get paid. Your mother is doing it for free." He was simplifying the terminology so we could understand what he was saying.

He kept checking in his rearview mirror to see if we were actually following along. When convinced of having our attention, he irately continued. "He said she's getting drunk and standing up on tables taking her clothes off. That's your mother. Huh, a real good mother. She's also sleeping with black men. She's a God damn whore. A nymphomaniac like all the psychiatrists told me."

The term nymphomaniac rang through our ears for years, considering how my father always referred to my mother as one. It sounded like a disease to us, but he made it perfectly clear what a nympho was when we were very young.

Nothing he said was going to provoke us to change our minds and tell lies about our mother that day. He wanted us to take the bait, believing his erratic tales but we never believed she could do such disgraceful things. The accusations were shocking when he rattled them off, however I knew it was fabricated nonsense to destroy my mother's character. He repeatedly spewed out these bizarre and outlandish stories about her which continued through our adulthood. As time passed, Mitch and I pretended to believe him since that was our only defense against a beating. We played this fictitious game throughout the years, but in reality never believing his outrageous stories about her.

When pulling into the psychiatrist's driveway, my father put the car in park and turned around to face us. "Alright, we're here. Don't forget what I told you. This is very important and I'm trying to keep both of you and Julie from turning crazy from your mother. She's already nuts. Do you two want to be crazy too?"

He utilized that infamous line all through the custody battle, constantly trying to convince us that being crazy was contagious. I hate to admit it, but he did a fine job of persuading us.

The doctor's office was unforgettable since the waiting area was filled with toys. He had a neat train set which we played with while my father went in to speak with the doctor first. The wait felt like a long time before he returned, and once he was done, Mitch and I went in separately for our evaluations. When it was my turn to meet the doctor, I was taken away by the array of pipes adorning his office. I couldn't take my eyes off of them. They were densely scattered over his desk and shelves, coming in so many different shapes, colors and sizes. I specifically remembered one of the pipes which must have been about five feet long. It was interestingly huge and before we spoke about me, I curiously asked about his pipe collection. After a quick synopsis, the doctor switched the conversation around, asking me a number of questions. He wanted to know if I was happy living with my father and grandmother, what I thought about living in Rolling, Virginia and the rest were all about my mother. He was looking for me to deliver the dirt, which I could clearly see through his smoky charades. His questions were phrased like: was your mother home at nights, did you feel like your mother loved you, were there many dogs in your home, did you notice dog poop in the house and he went on and on. My head was spinning by the time he finished with his inquiry.

Even as young and naïve as I was, I knew my father fed him all those questions. Being completely straight with the doctor, I professed all the escapades with the dogs did happen, but also told him neither of them were around the house much. I needed him to understand it wasn't only my mom who wasn't around to watch after us. I went on to tell him how I enjoyed living with my father and grandma but did miss interacting with my mother and grandparents. Before going any further, I had my concerns about my well-being, asking the psychiatrist if he was going to tell my father what I told him. He assured me the conversation would stay between the two of us, promising my father would never know the answers I gave to his questions.

Sensing I was more comfortable now, the doctor continued with the more delicate questions. When he came around to asking me about the validity of the Julie story, I told him I never saw Julie with her hands down her pants. I also said I never witnessed my mother teaching Julie how to put her finger in her own vagina either. He asked if I was certain and I assured him I never saw it happen. I still felt nervous about being brutally honest, but counted on his honesty. I didn't fully understand the consequences if I had lied, but found out soon enough.

When asked the question, who would I rather live with, my mother or father, I spoke the truth. I explained to the doctor how much I loved my grandma and father, but wanted to live with my mother. The time spent away from her and my grandparents depressed me a great deal, making me feel homesick. Throughout the evaluation, the psychiatrist was writing everything down and after each answer I paused, waiting for another question. It carried on for a long time, feeling good to have someone listening to me. One question he never asked, which surprised me, was on the subject of physical abuse. Everything was aimed at my mother, allowing nothing detrimental to be mentioned about my father. It was a one sided interview, but at the time I thought this doctor would be able to help us get what we wanted. Unfortunately, I was dead wrong on that assumption. The one thing I avoided, which in retrospect was smart, was divulging how my father was beating and pressuring us to lie about our mother.

After Mitch and I were finished with our evaluations, my father went in to meet with the doctor for an overview. We sat out in the waiting room, mentally exhausted from the myriad of questions we had thrown at us. I nervously bit my nails, going over the answers to the doctor in my head. Then Mitch and I compared notes on what we discussed with the doctor. He shared with me that he told the psychiatrist he wanted to live with our mother and I told him I gave the same answer. Mitch also assured me when the doctor asked about

Julie he said he never saw anything happen either. The doctor went as far as asking if Mitch had seen our mother having sex or kissing a strange man in the front seat of the car. We both held our ground, knowing what we wanted and that was to go back home to live with our mother. The only obstacle in our way was this doctor, who was the wrong guy to confide in.

Finished with the overview, my father stormed out of the office acting forcefully belligerent. He grabbed Mitch and me by the back of our shirts, shoving us aggressively out of the doctor's office and into his car. By his behavior, I could see the doctor didn't understand the meaning of confidentiality.

Once all three of us were in the car, my father squealed out of the driveway, leaving skid marks on the street. It didn't take long for him to light a cigarette and for the inside of the car to grow into a cloud of smoke. I sat waiting for a tidal wave of nasty words and threats. The car loudly roared down the street, sounding as though the engine was in the passenger seat. The transmission jolted back and forth while he hammered the accelerator to the floor with his size 13 shoe. My hands were sweating with my fingers digging deeply into the vinyl backseat. We were on our way back to Uncle Stewart's and Aunt Carly's house and the anticipation of his yelling was killing me. My father vigorously rolled down his window, flicking out a lit cigarette then quickly lighting another while speeding recklessly down the road. He began the conversation with an acute monotone voice asking, "Why did you kids lie? I thought we had an agreement." As he spoke, his voice slowly increased in volume, dragging on the second cigarette. "The psychiatrist tells me that both of you want to live with your mother? Your wonderful fucking whore mother, is that fucking right? You want to live with that pig whore?"

We sat rigidly still, as if he wouldn't notice us in the backseat if we didn't make a move. "Did you hear me? God damn it! Did you or didn't you tell the doctor that you wanted to live with your mother?" I could see him eyeing us through the rearview mirror.

Since being the eldest, I figured it was up to me to begin, so I answered, "I *said*..." And before I could finish my sentence, my father reached over with his right arm and started spraying us with slaps.

He was like a human windshield wiper, going back and forth, not missing a beat. Mitch and I were screaming in terror as I ducked with my hands held over my head. Mitch followed my lead, covering up with our father viciously coming at us. The car started swerving all over the road as he repeatedly slapped us. The only reason I knew was because Mitch and I were rolling from one side of the car to the other. We were banging back and forth, from one backdoor to the next. He must have realized how unsafe it was to beat and drive at the same time, so he suddenly pulled over. I felt the car hit gravel as he slammed down on the brakes and the car came to a tremendous jerking stop.

He slammed the gearshift into park with a loud thud, swiftly swinging around. "You fucking spoiled brats," he screamed, while the hitting and slapping accompanied his anger. "You're going to tell the psychiatrist, behind my back, that you want to live with your fucking mother. Behind my back, after I took you away from that bitch whore. I got news for both of you. She wants nothing to do with you. All she cares about is going out and dancing naked in strip joints and getting fucked by black men. Is that what you want? To stay with your nymphomaniac mother while she's out all night getting screwed? Well is it?"

He was slapping and hitting us with great accuracy, now that the car was in park. "Ok. Ok," I cried. Hoping he would end his barrage of slaps and punches, but it continued without stopping. He started running out of breath with his breathing turning into a gruff coughing fit. Mitch and I still had our hands and arms protecting our faces and heads. I could hear Mitch crying next to me. Then the attack came to a halt, most likely due to my father's lack of oxygen.

Through a wheezing tense voice, he said, "I'll tell you this. This shit better not happen again. Do you understand me?" Then he paused, as if the crying was annoying him and shouted, "Stop your God damn crying or I'll give you something to really cry about. Do you both hear me? I barely touched you."

He stopped for a moment, then in a threatening tone said, "If I find out that you tell another psychiatrist or lawyer that you want to live with your mother, there's going to be big trouble. Sit up, both of you and stop your fucking crying."

We couldn't stop even if we wanted to. Our bodies were involuntarily controlling our emotions seeing how we were scared to death. He finally turned around coughing, slamming the car in gear. As we drove back onto the road, he lit another cigarette without a word spoken for the duration of our drive.

When we arrived at Uncle Stewart's house, my father yanked the keys out of the ignition and turned around. Disdain darted from his eyes as he callously said, "Alright, get out. I better not hear from either of you for the rest of the day. I mean nothing. You both disgust me. Now get the hell out of my sight."

Mitch and I did what we were told, sauntering in the house to escape our father's fury. Neither of us made mention of what we said or discussed at the psychiatrist's office. Jeff and Dan asked if we were ok, probably because we looked like we were trampled over by an entire NFL football team. We lied, saying everything was fine. That was one thing Mitch and I never did, talk about beatings or verbal abuse dished out by our father. He didn't threaten to do anything if we talked, in fact he never told us not to tell anyone. He simply just didn't give a damn. I never thought to share my horror stories with another person since I was ashamed of being beaten. I assume Mitch felt the same way. It was one of those plights that stayed within the family, tucked away like a nasty secret. There was no one to reach out to for help, so it was an ongoing dilemma that we conditioned ourselves to live with each and every day. We figured we were bad and that was what happened to bad kids.

CHAPTER 12

Memorial Day weekend finally arrived, an event I had been waiting for ever since we moved in to our townhouse. Living across from the pool, I watched the entire week as they cleaned getting it ready for the weekend. First thing that morning, I anxiously met my grandmother downstairs for one of her big breakfasts, which was the usual, two hardboiled eggs, toast with cream cheese and a bowl of cereal. Once everyone came down and ate, we immediately rushed over to the pool. My father rough-housed with Mitch and me, throwing us up in the air and having us dive off his shoulders. Grandma kept Julie busy in the baby pool, while we played with our father, managing to keep from getting sunburned. The water was freezing from just being opened, but it didn't faze us, feeling invigorating to be outside doing something. The pool was packed with so many children from the neighborhood, who I never knew existed. Mitch and I met a few of the neighborhood kids, finding out they had a bunch of forts and tree houses built deep in the woods. They invited us to stop by sometime, so being curious we accepted their offer. Everyone was friendly and it was good to see so many new faces. That weekend kicked off our summer, pre-occupying Mitch and me from moping around the house, missing our mother and grandparents.

During the summer months, Mitch and I occasionally went to Grand's department store when we weren't at the pool. The summers were hot and muggy, feeling very similar to living in Delaware. The humidity was exceedingly bad too, causing my breathing to become actual work. Anytime I inhaled the air, it felt like my lungs were filling with thick moisture. Grand's was a nice escape from the heat, even if we didn't have any money to spend. We merely enjoyed walking around and looking at all the toys, but the main attraction was the motorcycle display. Mitch and I forever dreamed of having one. I hate to admit it but I was an avid shoplifter. Scouring the candy isles, waiting for the coast to be clear so I could stuff my pockets and run out from the store. I was getting so good that I actually considered stealing a motorcycle. Having my eye on a beautiful black bike, I would try concocting ways to get it out of the store without anyone noticing.

One afternoon at Grand's, I had my sites on something much smaller than a motorcycle but bigger than a candy bar. Mitch and I wanted to try smoking cigarettes like our father, so being a master thief I volunteered to steal the carton. It was a risky proposition and scary since they were stocked by the manager's booth. The booth was positioned towards the front of the store, not far from the exit door. The plan was for Mitch to be the lookout guy and when saying it was clear, I would steal the cigarettes. As we moved into position, my heart was pounding faster than percussionist banging on a snare drum. I was never caught before and didn't want this to be the first, especially since I was trying to pocket a carton of cigarettes. I was standing impatiently trying not to look obvious, waiting for Mitch's signal. Once he waved letting me know all was clear, I hastily grabbed the first carton of cigarettes. I quickly shoved them under my t-shirt as my heart raced. Then frantically looking around to make sure no one saw me, I dashed out of the store. Once outside, we ran down the plaza's sidewalk, slapping each other five in victory.

Our next predicament was where to smoke them without my father catching us. I wouldn't want to imagine how much trouble we'd be in if he were to see us. Even though he was a chain smoker, he always threatened to kick our ass if ever finding us smoking. With a warning like that, Mitch and I needed a place he would never spot us. After walking back home for some time, we decided on visiting the guys we met at the pool. They mentioned how their forts and tree houses were tucked deep in the woods. We figured our father would never bump into us out there. The first thing I wanted to do was drop off the carton at home and walk through the woods with just one pack instead. The carton looked awkward under my t-shirt, feeling very uncomfortable. When arriving home, I quickly ran upstairs stashing the carton of cigarettes under my pillow. Struggling to be inconspicuous, I managed to squeeze one pack into my shorts without it being visible. My grandmother heard me, calling out, "Hello." I shouted back to let her know it was me, explaining we would be back in time for dinner.

Mitch and I found the dirt path leading to the forts and followed it through the thick woods. Afraid of getting poison ivy, I made sure to watch every step I took along the way. When we finally made it there, it was shocking to see what those kids did. They literally made a little city which was something I had never seen before. I expected a few tree houses, but instead there were several neatly built forts. They looked good enough to actually live in fulltime. The doors were installed with hinges rather than just being leaned against the doorway and the windows had real glass. The community was still under construction as the kids were snatching lumber, plywood and other accessories to build their forts from the builder. Some of them were still in the progress of working as we walked around, peeking in a few of them. One of the kids offered to give us a little tour, explaining the different functions of each structure. They used one for a school house, another for a church, another for a meeting hall and the list went on. Then I remembered the pack of cigarettes in my pocket, so thanking him for showing us around, Mitch and I went off to smoke.

We didn't inhale the cigarettes once they were lit. Nervously, we sucked the tar tasting smoke into our mouths, coughing as we blew it out. It tasted foul but neither of us got sick or disgusted. While puffing away, we sat and talked, thinking how cool it was to smoke. I kept looking around feeling paranoid, making sure my father didn't creep up on us. He never did show so Mitch and I smoked a few more before returning home for dinner. Thinking back, it was strange how my grandmother never smelled the cigarette smoke on us. We had to stink from sitting in the heat of summer while smoking like feigns, but she never seemed to smell it. We continued to do this for a few days until my father found the carton of cigarettes under my pillow.

Coming home one afternoon with Mitch, I went upstairs to wash up for dinner. As I made it to the top of the stairs, my father was standing in front of his bedroom door holding a carton of my cigarettes. A black curtain immediately unraveled right in front of my eyes, while I stood there so dazed that all I could see was darkness. Becoming focused, I knew something had to be quickly done, otherwise I saw my last sunrise that morning. While standing and thinking of some bullshit story, my father grabbed a fistful of my shirt. With the front of my shirt clasped in his white tensed fingers, he pushed me against the hallway wall. His red eyes shrunk to slits as he said, "Whose fucking cigarettes are these?"

I hung there like a piece of meat in his grasp, fumbling around for some kind of answer. "I'm only going to say this one more time. Whose fucking cigarettes are these?"

Right before he was about to haul off and pound me, it came to me. "Wait," I shouted with clinched eyes and both hands in position to block oncoming slaps. "Alright, I got them for you. Ok?"

"What do you mean? You got them for me," he questioned, looking dumbfounded.

"For Father's Day. I got them f-f-for you for Father's Day from Grand's. It's your present." Somehow I pulled that out, remembering Father's Day was in a few weeks.

My father's grip loosened a bit, as his other hand stopped its forward motion for a moment. He had an inquisitive expression drawn across his face now, saying, "For Father's Day? You bought this for me for Father's Day?" I thought he took the bait until he said, "Where did you get the money?" Now I knew there was a new issue to deal with and I was fresh out of stories. His tight grip on my shirt returned, with an evil stare that shot right back at me once again.

Realizing defeat, I went with the truth deciding it was time to confess. "I took them. I didn't have any money and wanted to get you a gift so I just took the carton." With a quick jolt, he dragged me down the stairs by the front of my shirt, holding the carton of cigarettes in his other hand. Frightened and not knowing what was coming next, I cried out, "Where are we going?"

Standing at the front door, my father said, "Well, you have a choice. Either we can go to the police and you'll go to jail or we can go back to the store and you'll tell the manager that you stole the cigarettes." I faltered in fear of going to jail, so of course, opted to go back to Grand's to confess my crime. I knew it would be embarrassing, but better than sitting in a jail cell.

Still tightly holding the front of my shirt, he dragged me out to his car. After hearing all the turmoil, my grandmother came running to the door and in a panic called out, "Sheldon, where are you going with Jim?"

While getting in the driver's seat without looking at her, he called back, "Please mother, I'll be right back. Ok? Get back into the house." I could see the concerned look on her face, standing there watching the car back up, then quickly jetting off.

When we arrived at Grand's, my father abruptly hopped out of the car and slammed the door with a nasty appearance on his face. Carrying the carton of cigarettes in one hand, he waved for me with the other to get out of the car and follow him. I slowly trailed behind, wincing at the thought of having to admit stealing the carton of cigarettes. It was really sinking in what an idiot I was to have shoplifted. It never occurred to me how dumb it was to steal until I had to admit it out loud. Once I was close enough to my father, he forcefully grabbed my arm yanking me through the automatic doors. Then angrily he dragged me to the manager's booth, calling him down. While shoving the carton of cigarettes in my hands, he told me to explain what I had done. After confessing my crime to the store manager and apologizing, he thanked my father for his honesty. Proceeding to tell him, how he wished more parents would take the same kind of initiative with their own kids. After a few words between the two of them, they shook hands as my father and I left.

The car ride was silent until we returned home. As my father put the car in park, I turned to him, humbly saying, "Sorry Dad. I promise I won't steal again. Thanks for not putting me in jail."

"This better be the last time, Jim. That was embarrassing for me." After that experience, we never spoke of it again. My days of shoplifting came to a screaming halt.

For the remainder of the summer, I managed to stay out of trouble by keeping busy with my family. My father became more involved, bringing us on a variety of fun trips like, Jamestown, Williamsburg and even taking a week off to vacation at Virginia Beach. That was a blast for all of us, considering we had never been to the beach before. We traveled to Florida but stayed at the pool the entire time so this was a fresh experience. By now, we started to think of grandma as a second mother, seeing how she did such a wonderful job filling in for the role. She came with us everywhere we went, appearing to love the time we spent together. Her happy glowing face was there every morning we awoke and every night going to bed. As far as I was concerned, my grandmother was a gift. She didn't take the place of my mother but sure made up for her absence.

Summer came to a quick close as school was starting up. My father enrolled me for the second grade, not remembering attending the first grade, it proved to be a disastrous mistake. I was nervous for my first day of school and being the new kid made it even worse. Feeling like a loner, I stood at the bus stop keeping to myself. The other children playful spoke to one another with a familiarity in their demeanor. At least when attending kindergarten, I knew a few of the neighborhood kids, with my next door neighbor being my cousin removed once or twice. The one thing I discovered quickly while living in Rolling, Virginia was, you didn't want people to know you were Jewish. It was a horrendous place to live in the early seventies if you were Jewish, something I found out first hand. They were under the impression that Jewish people had horns and a tail, a characteristic I had never heard of before. It was hard conceiving how small children could hate and detest someone or something they knew nothing about.

After school I was coming home on the school bus when a few kids starting calling me a dirty Jew. They stood directly in my face, harassing me about being Jewish until we got to our stop. Along the way, they also mentioned kicking my ass which frightened the hell out of me. I didn't know another soul on the bus, so it was going to be me alone, fighting everyone who agreed that I needed a good ass kicking. As soon as the bus came to a stop, I hopped off while about ten or fifteen kids formed a circle around me. I felt like a trapped animal with the possibility of escaping being impossible. The bus stop was located in front of a library, where I was seriously thinking of hauling ass but didn't. Pride got the best of me and then the games commenced. All together the kids were calling me dirty Jew, piece of shit Jew, where are your horns Jew and it went on until one kid stepped into the circle with me. He viciously ran towards me, throwing a powerful punch but missed. We both wound up rolling around in the grass, punching and kicking in a wild state. When finding myself on top of him, the other children kicked and pulled me off. They were spitting and screaming more obscenities at me. Each time I got on top of the other kid, the rest of the children resumed kicking my back and yanking me off. Finally, someone from the library came out breaking up the fight. The strange thing was, the bus driver was still there after the fight was broken up. He was actually enjoying the whole thing as I watched him close the bus door and pull away. I couldn't believe a grownup could be so cruel but that was the mentality there.

After a fight like that, I thought the kids would respect me for standing up for myself but instead, it only got worse. Each day on the bus they decided who would be the next opponent to fight me in front of the library. They were enjoying this, but I had no intention of backing down. I didn't want to be known as a chicken, feeling for the first time like I was fighting for something. When I fought these kids, it was with bitterness for all the beatings my father gave me without being able to defend myself. It was non-stop fighting everyday after school with no one putting an end to it. I was getting exhausted fighting, wanting only to go home in peace for once. It was a demoralizing feeling that my father moved me into a hellhole like this. I never told him what was going on nor did I tell my teacher. Never advertising being Jewish, I found it strange how these kids knew which really bothered me most. It wasn't a conversation I would have ever had with any of them. My life was now pure torture.

After weeks of this torment, I came home from school one day finding my father's car parked in front of our townhouse. I thought it very unusual since he was never home at that hour. Casually totting in, I gave my grandmother her usual kiss hello, then found my father sitting on the couch smoking a cigarette. I was excited to see him, hoping he had tickets for a special event or maybe he was taking us out for dinner. Those thoughts fell rapidly by the wayside when I saw the expression on his face. He had a sullen and callous demeanor about him when I came over to kiss him hello. I was getting an uneasy vibe that something was very wrong and started chewing on my fingernails. He sat there with one leg crossed over the other while giving me a long look over. I broke the silence, asking, "Why are you home so early today, dad?"

"Jim, let me ask you a question. Someone tells me that kids are calling you a dirty Jew and you're running away like a chicken. Is this true? Because if it's true, I'll beat you up. Do you hear me?"

I couldn't believe what I was hearing, so proudly standing with my chin held high I said, "Who told you that?"

"It doesn't make a difference who told me that. I asked you a question." His voice was getting louder, as I could see he was grabbing my grandmother's attention. She stopped what she was doing, looking through the kitchen partition to see what was going on.

"I've been fighting everyday after school because these kids won't leave me alone. All they do is call me a dirty Jew, shit Jew and all kinds of stuff. They come to fight me and kick me in the back." Tears started flowing from my eyes out of frustration. I couldn't believe I had to convince my own father that I wasn't a chicken.

"Really, because someone told me that you're running home and not doing shit."

"That's a lie," I screamed in anger. I wasn't backing down from this argument, being very passionate on the subject since wearing the bruises to prove it. Then it struck me and I said, "Look. You can even see the bruises on my back and butt."

He didn't care to look. His mind was already made up as he shouted, "I'll tell you this. If I ever find out that you ran away from a fight, I'll beat you up when you come home. Do you understand me?

You'll have more to worry about when you come home to me than those little punks from your school."

Standing with clinched fists, I glared at him in bitter disappointment. I couldn't believe how he was coming down on me like this, after fighting these kids for weeks. Besides fighting these animals everyday after school, now I had to worry about my own father. It felt like my whole world was screwed up. I had nothing more to say and while leaving to go up to my bedroom, he shouted, "Remember what I told you, Jim."

I thought to myself, "Yeah, I'll remember and never forget."

My grades were suffering terribly while attending second grade. The other students could read and write fluently, but I was struggling, feeling the pressure of being way in over my head. No matter how much effort I put towards my school work, I couldn't possibly keep up. It didn't occur to me second grade was going to be so intense, expecting to be taught how to read and write rather than having to know it already. Before long, the teacher contacted my father, explaining how I was falling behind the other students. She made it clear if I continued on the same path, she would have no choice but to fail me. Her only suggestion was getting me extra help, so I would have a better chance of catching up with the rest of the class.

When my father came home from work that evening, he was furious with me after receiving the phone call from my teacher. In my defense, it escaped him that my only formal education was kindergarten. He was so concerned about my mother and grandparents finding us that he never sent me to the first grade. After eating dinner, my father had everyone leave to have a discussion with me. Leaning back in his chair, he held a cigarette between his two yellow stained fingers, kindly saying, "I got a call from your teacher today. Do you want to know what she said?"

I didn't see a need to answer, knowing exactly what she said and it wasn't good news for me. "I said, do you want to know what she said about you?" There was a slight pause as if he thought I was going to enlighten him. "I'll tell you what she said. You can't fucking read. You can't even write is what she told me. She said you can't even copy down on a piece of paper what she writes on the GOD DAMN blackboard! Are you fucking stupid?"

Looking down at the floor, I answered, "No. I'm not stupid. It's just too hard for me. I never learned how to read like these other kids." My finger was in mouth while I was gnawing on a fingernail.

"How did the other kids learn to read and write? Can you tell me that?"

"I don't know," I responded, sulking. "Maybe they went to first grade." I think that stumped him, as his tone changed appearing to be more sympathetic about my predicament. His attitude and demeanor showed some empathy when we continued our conversation.

"Well, your teacher told me that you need extra help and gave me a place to take you. I'll give them a call and set something up. You're going to need a lot of help, Jim. Otherwise she's going to fail you. That means you're going to have to work real hard, harder than the other kids to catch up."

A tingling sensation traveled up and down my spine as my knees wobbled from feeling weak. I understood that failing would precipitate more fighting and teasing, making my life even worse. Being Jewish would now be compounded by failing second grade and I would have to defend myself for two different issues. I prayed this extra help would work, promising my father to try extra hard.

My father took me for the additional help a few times a week after school; unfortunately I was too far behind by now to catch up. My teacher was pleased with my progress, but explained to my father that I needed to repeat second grade. She expressed concern, saying I needed a better foundation in order to survive the third grade. I was devastated by her decision since this was the first time I tasted failure and it was humiliating. Recognizing my life was going to be brutal when starting school next year, I fell into a deep depression. I carried this embarrassing failure on my back for years, a page in my volatile life which defines who I am.

Just when I felt like I was down on my luck, my father reluctantly told us the courts wanted him to split his custody time with our mother. We were so excited that we could barely hold in the explosive happiness which was bursting inside of us. The feeling was emotionally elating, but Mitch and I knew better than to display our excitement. We didn't want to be considered traitors and I didn't want another encounter like I had in the car after the visit with the psychiatrist. We were to spend the entire summer with our mother and the first half of the next school year. My father was so angry over the decision he could hardly get the words out of his mouth.

Still mourning the failure of second grade, I refused to allow my mother to find out. Failing haunted me, causing my imagination to run wild with the idea that a badge was sewn on my sleeve for everyone to know. It was an overwhelming embarrassment, one I did not want my grandparents finding out about either. The last thing I wanted was to be viewed as a loser in the eyes of the people I loved most in this world. This new adventure couldn't have come at a more appropriate time. The move was a great way to avoid the humiliation of walking past my former classmates without being ridiculed in the school hallway. The fighting and mental torture would cease as well, since God willing, they would forget all about me in good time. My strategy to avoid shame with my mother and grandparents was to lie. I elected to tell my mother I was in third grade when it came time for her to sign me up for school. Feeling confident that I studied hard enough to be able to swing it, which is exactly what I did.

CHAPTER 13

When we returned to our mother, Papa Willie had purchased a house in Red Hill, Delaware for us to live in. We were incredibly thrilled with the idea of living with her again. The neighborhood was much nicer than the one we came from and I had high hopes that the kids were as well. I didn't want to be picked on or fight anymore for being Jewish, praying I left all that behind in Rolling.

It was so exciting to see our new house and bedrooms. I remember it had a very unusual floor plan, like when walking in the front door, that was where the family room was and behind there was a wall concealing the basement area. Upstairs was where the kitchen, dining room, living room and our bedrooms were. I found it to be a comfortable ranch style home. The house had three bedrooms, so Mitch and I shared a room together, Julie had her own and my mother had the master bedroom. Everything in the house was brand new, symbolizing a new start in mind. Invigorated with my new life, I wanted my mom to succeed as a good mother, staying around to take care of us. I knew the clock was ticking and had no interest in returning to Rolling. I loved my father but was sick of his cruel beatings, in addition to that nasty neighborhood he called home. Seeing him on a temporary basis was safer for all of us in my eyes. He was looking for any excuse to badger my mother with nasty accusations, so I didn't want anything to go wrong. I wasn't interested in going back to the psychiatrist, with my father coercing me into making slanderous statements regarding my mother. I felt more mature and cognizant of the things going on around me by now, making a promise to myself, to see that my mom didn't screw up.

When we arrived, my mother looked sensational, resembling one of those fashion models on the cover of a magazine. Her hair was beautifully put together and wearing a very stylish outfit. Happiness burst from her shapely smile, glowing with a sincere aura which I hadn't seen in a long time. It looked like being away from my father and the fighting definitely agreed with her. She was grateful and overjoyed to have us back in her life again, a feeling like the days before we moved into the Seneca house. I was saddened by how much time had elapsed since we last saw her, but being back was like no time was lost at all. She proudly gave us a tour of the house, making our bedrooms the high ticket feature. She was especially proud of the way our rooms were decorated, bringing all our toys back from my grandparent's house and adding several more. By the looks of it, there was plenty to keep us busy and out of trouble. The bedroom belonging to Mitch and me was adorned with a seventies motif. What I recall most about it, were the 7 UP lamps that sat on our nightstands. They were constructed out of 7 UP cans with an unusual round light bulb on top, that when turned on illuminated a green flickering glow.

Julie's room was the typical girl's bedroom, entirely decorated in pink. It was perfect for a little girl as Julie was thrilled to have her own room. My mother walked her through it while Mitch and I went to play with all our new toys.

After the tour, Mama Ida arrived to welcome us. My grandfather must have still been at work because she came alone. She looked overwhelmed with happiness, warmly hugging and divulging how much she missed all of us. Then she asked what we thought of the house and by our reaction, she could clearly see that we all loved it. With a jovial smile, Mama Ida declared how she had another surprise for our summer stay. All three of us jumped up and down like little show dogs in a circus, asking what it was, but she wouldn't say until we came to her house. The rest of the afternoon was consumed with them watching us play with our toys. They were both striving to find out what they had missed on, but in between the noise and playing, it was difficult.

Having no correspondence with them for such a long period of time, there was plenty to catch up on. Mama Ida and my mom sat taking inventory, commenting on the same things most parents and grandparents remark about. They were pleasantly surprised by how much we had grown and the extent of our intelligence. My mother was devastated having missed an abundance of quality time with us, promising it would never happen again. Julie was the biggest surprise, seeing how she was capable of talking and potty trained. The last time they saw her she was only two years old, so much had changed between the ages of two and nearly four.

It was getting late and Mama Ida was busy gathering her things together when I noticed her motioning to me. I quickly went over to her as she pulled me away from the others. Handing me a piece of paper, she held my shoulders softly saying, "Jim, I need your help. This is very important." Her nose twitched from side to side with a sharp sniffle as she spoke. She had a habit of doing that with her nose. "My phone number is on this piece of paper. Your mother will be in big trouble if there are any men here or any parties. I need you to call me right away if you see any of this happening. You're the oldest, so I'm trusting you with this. Ok?"

I nodded my head in agreement, whispering, "Ok, but I don't want to tattle on my mom. I'm not a tattle tale, you know."

"You're not being a tattle tale, Jim. You're helping your mother, not hurting her. You kids could be sent back with your father if she's caught. Do you see what I mean?"

I understood when she put it that way. "No problem. If it happens, I'll call you right away. I promise."

"One last thing, Jim. No dogs. Your mother is not to bring any dogs home. If she should bring a dog home, you call me or Papa Willie. Ok?" I nodded my head again, promising I would. After our little discussion, we rejoined everyone as my grandmother said her goodbyes and left.

That night my mom made dinner, accepting our help since we all volunteered. She was in such high spirits, that it didn't even bother her how we were destroying the kitchen. It felt wonderful to be in her company again as she toyed around with us, acting full of life.

Her patience was grand, while the continuity between the four of us was so fluid, you wouldn't have guessed we spent a year and a half apart. After dinner, we all were bathed and as Mitch and I got ready for bed, my mom put Julie to sleep. When she returned to our bedroom, Mitch and I were pre-occupied tinkering around with our new toys. She playfully sat on the bed, patting her hand on the covers for us to join her. I guess she was interested in knowing how we were doing with the new home and all the changes. We assured her how much we loved it, and were glad to be here. Then she decided to get silly, asking, "More importantly, how much did you guys miss me? I hope as much as I missed you." We wholeheartedly agreed while she laughed out loud, giving us both a big hug.

As we sat around getting reacquainted, she explained how guilty she felt for not seeing us for so long. Becoming emotional, her bottom lip quivered non-stop as tears slid from her dark brown eyes. Then pausing for a moment to catch her breath, she said, "Your father just ran off with you guys. Your Papa Willie and me tried to fight him with our attorney but your father hid in Rolling. It was hard to get you guys back from there. I hope you're not mad at me."

I spoke up feeling sad, assuring her we didn't blame her at all. "No. We're not mad at you. I felt bad for you because he kept running away with us. Mitch and I talked about it all the time. I could see he was trying to hide from you, but we couldn't call. He would never let us call you or talk about you," I rambled while biting my nails.

"Don't you kids worry. You're here now and that'll never happen again. Papa Willie and Mama Ida promised the attorney will fix everything." I let out a big sigh, while inspecting my bloody thumb and felt a deep sense of relief.

"Jim, I noticed you're biting the skin around your fingernails. Why are you so nervous?" I shrugged my shoulders as if I didn't know why. "We need to get you to stop chewing your fingers. Tomorrow we'll try putting pepper on them. I used to bite mine too and that got me to stop. You'll hate the taste but it should work."

She youthfully sprung up from the bed and smiling said, "Ok kids, it's time to go to sleep."

She tightly tucked us in while kissing us goodnight, illuminating a special warm glow about her. There was a lot more I wanted to share with her, so as she was walking out the door, I called out, "Hey mom, I need to talk more."

She looked back, closing our door. "Don't worry, we can talk more tomorrow. Goodnight boys. Love you."

I laid in bed smiling, having this realization that at last we were where we were supposed to be. Feeling a strong sense of security and happiness, I thought to myself, "What a long journey it's been to get back to my mother." Before falling asleep, Mitch and I whispered to each other how grateful we were to be back. We both agreed that kids belong with their mother as we fell asleep.

The next day my mother was cheerfully energized. She was kidding and singing songs with us on the way to our grandparent's house to see Mama Ida's surprise. When we arrived, our eyes were glued in astonishment since the big surprise turned out to be an in-ground swimming pool. We couldn't believe it was ours. My grandparents were proudly smiling, then began laughing at our dazed reaction.

The pool was carved in the shape of a big snowman, coming equipped with all the bells and whistles. They installed a diving board, a winding slide and a variety of fun pool toys. Being so overjoyed and excited, we hugged and thanked everyone for the pool. Then we charged into the house to change into our swimsuits. Our mom had to leave to go to work, so my grandfather was left in charge of watching us. All day I begged him to get me a whistle, so I could be the acting lifeguard on duty. Eventually, he gave in, promising to take us to store later.

As the day progressed, Aunt Paula showed up excited to see us and delighted we were enjoying the pool. She was thankful we were there to use it because if not for us, it would sit empty. When she sat down, I jumped out and sat on the edge of the pool to visit with her. I really missed her company since we spent a lot of time together before my father ran off with us. She and Uncle Charles took me to all kinds of fun places like the circus, the state fair and the zoo. They never had children of their own, so I kind of felt like their adopted child. Aunt Paula and I had a special bond and talked alone for quite a while about different things. As the time quickly drifted by, Mama Ida ordered us out of the pool so we'd be ready for our mother when she showed up.

My mom was working at a beauty salon in Bass that happened to be down the street from where my grandparent's lived. It was convenient for her to drop us off when she had to work, which fortunately wasn't everyday. I found it very fitting for her to work at a beauty shop, remembering the majority of her Saturday's sitting and gossiping at the one in Walden. On the occasions I went to visit her, the place was a blast considering how all the ladies were so nice and pretty. They were genuinely friendly, hugging and kissing me whenever I came in. They played around, telling me how cute I was and if I were older they would date me. Invariably I blushed, becoming embarrassed but wasn't too young to enjoy a little flirting. The shop was full of energy, primarily from the upbeat music blaring from the speakers, which made me want to sing and dance. The one thing I could never forget about the beauty shop, was the array of overwhelming poignant scents. The salon reeked of hair spray, hair dye and a pinch of perfume. When I left there, my nostril hairs were permanently tainted for the entire day. Anything I ate or smelled, never dominated the odor from the beauty shop.

I was delighted to see how happy and fulfilled my mother was from working there. She was in her own element as everyone seemed to truly adore her. Memories of her being a hip lady and easy-going with a great sense of humor, is what sticks out in my mind. She utilized this side of herself at the beauty shop, which I thought was what people cherished most about her.

Music was one of my mom's passions, inspiring me to love it as well. She introduced me to all the big hits of the late sixties and early seventies. We frequently shopped at a record store not far from the beauty shop, where we purchased forty-fives to play at home. While we listened to the music on the record player, she would enthusiastically dance and sing with us. She inspired me to want to sing, which was always a dream of mine to write my own songs and become a singer. One day, she surprised us by coming home with a drum set for Mitch and a guitar for me. We pretended to have our own family band like the Partridge Family, making an abundance of noise as we pretended to play.

While digging around in my mother's albums, I came across this one, having a picture of a sharp looking guy on the cover. I didn't know who he was but liked the way he looked, so I decided to play the album. The music was moving and empowered by this dauntless voice, which provoked me to continuously play the album. Being so enamored by this guy's voice, I went to find my mother to see if she ever heard of Elvis Presley. She giggled since of course she had, and told me how much all the girls loved him. Anytime his songs were on the radio, my mom stopped whatever it was she was doing, to have me listen with her. If one of his movies happened to be playing on TV, she would call me to come and watch. Occasionally, whenever she had time or if it wasn't too late, we sat together watching his films. Our favorite was "Clambake". I was dazzled by his songs and the beautiful girls dancing in their swimsuits. The movies put me over the top though, motivating me to carry his albums around for weeks. He became my idol at the time, a component which gave me happiness.

As much as my father despised my mother, he started calling once a week to see how we were doing. It had been a while since we heard from him and I was more relaxed and comfortable than I had been in a long time. He spoke to each of us individually, asking if everything was alright. We always replied that everything was great and we were enjoying ourselves. We didn't want to go overboard sounding exceedingly happy. It wouldn't be worth paying the consequences the next time we saw him, so we all conveyed laconic replies. The conversations never ended without him fishing around for some gooey dirt on my mother. He was relentless, torturing me the most with this tiresome routine. The things he wanted to know, regarded my mother, was precisely what Mama Ida warned me to keep an eye on for her. I adamantly told him how she was taking great care of us, and putting us to bed every night. Usually, that was enough to end the conversation but if he wanted to dig deeper, I found clever excuses to hang up.

All that I told my father was the truth, whether he wanted to hear it or not. My mom was home every night with us, making sure dinner was on the table. After dinner was our playtime together, as she wholeheartedly played like she was one of us. We had a ball with her and laughed until our lungs hurt. My father never played with us like that, constantly pre-occupied with other things when he happened to be home. She played a variety of games, like chasing us around the house playing tag or hide and go seek. Sometimes we would just make up games as we went along. It was unusually fun because she really kept up with us and we could tell she was enjoying the games as much as we were. My mom's personality was a nice adjustment from the Seneca house. It was like spending time with another person. She really drew us in emotionally, making us feel like we were a part of her life, instead of a burden.

One evening, things got a little out of hand as I ended up going to the emergency room. My mother was chasing me around the house, after dinner, when I happened to trip over Mitch, hitting the frame of our bedroom door. After being stunned and seeing a myriad of stars, my earlobe was brutally sliced, bleeding non-stop. Eventually, the stars and pain stopped but my mother was petrified since the bleeding wouldn't subside. She insisted on dragging me to the hospital for a few stitches. I already had them twice in my chin and once in my pinky, so I was only too familiar with the horrible experience of getting stitched up. Adamant about not going again, I pleaded with my mom to try anything but the hospital. She agreed, attempting everything from bandages to gauzes but nothing would stop the bleeding. She finally gave up since the lobe was split in two, deciding to load the family in the car for a trip to the hospital. During the entire ride, she constantly apologized, begging me not to tell my father or Mama Ida what had happened. I pressed the paper towel firmly against my throbbing earlobe and said, "Why would I blame you anyway? It was Mitch's fault for tripping me."

An enlightened expression sprayed across her face, as she smiled looking back at Mitch. "Yeah Mitch, you shouldn't have tripped, Jim." She looked back at me as if to say, "Thanks for the alibi, kid. Why didn't I think of that?"

CHAPTER 14

During that summer, my mom started dating this character named, Roy, which tore me up inside. I understand now how a woman in her late twenties needs companionship, but back then, I thought he was interfering in our relationship with our mother. He was consuming too much of her time and I wasn't going to stand for it. My father had girlfriends, but it didn't bother me as much. I don't know why that was, other than it just wasn't as irritating. There was a time in Rolling, Virginia, when he was dating a woman who was divorced with two little girls. They happened to be around the same ages as Mitch and me. I think he was considering marrying her because the girls repeatedly expressed how neat it would be for us to become brothers and sisters, but nothing every came of it.

I gave this guy, Roy a run for his money, doing everything in my power to annoy the hell out of him. Hoping he would leave for good, I shot rubber bands or spitballs at him whenever he came over for a visit. Every so often, I would call him colorful names too, assuming he would get so frustrated that he would run away, but it never worked. Roy never retaliated either, but when my mother came back into the room, he would tell her what I did. I was surprised to see my mom with a guy who looked the way he did. He had long scraggly dead-looking hair, which looked like it was pressed down by the same heat press they used to put decals on t-shirts. His mustache was horrendous, looking as if he taped a dead rat under his nose. It was long and bushy, with constant debris nestled in it. He rarely said much but simply sat on the couch, waiting on my mother while she put us to bed. I didn't call my grandmother like she instructed, since I didn't have the heart to tattle on my mom. She had been doing a great job with us, so it didn't seem fair to get her in trouble with Mama Ida.

There was one inappropriate incident, but it was more my fault than my mother's. One morning, when going to the kitchen for breakfast, I noticed that my mom wasn't there. It wasn't unusual considering sometimes in the mornings, she would lay in her bed with the door open. When that was the case, I normally jumped into bed with her and we talked. But on this particular morning, the door was closed. That never happened before and not being in the habit of knocking, I just walked in. When pushing the door open, I observed something I never forgot, finding it more humorous than anything else. Unfortunately, the courts didn't find it as funny as me and it became a serious matter.

As the door slowly opened, I startled Roy who was comfortably laying on my mother's bed with a full erection. His look alone scared the hell out of me. His eyes popped out of his head, when I came into view, as he scrambled around for something like a pair of pants which weren't anywhere in reach. I literally caught this guy with his pants down, forcing my mother to jump into her closet. Completely naked, she swiftly threw on a robe, screaming, "Jim, get out of the room." But I stood there for a moment, drinking it all in. She was still in her walk-in closet when I heard her shriek again. "Jim! I mean now." I finally snapped out of it, walking out as the door loudly slammed behind me. It was so powerful that I felt a breeze, fingering through my hair.

Upset and embarrassed, my mother sent Roy home and came into the kitchen to find me eating cereal with Mitch. "Jim, I would like to talk to you for a minute, honey," she sweetly said. I was caught off guard, thinking for certain she was going to rip me to shreds. I followed her back to her bedroom as she closed the door behind us. "Listen Jim, I'm very sorry for what you saw, but you just can't walk into my room without knocking. Can you understand that?"

I nodded my head, answering, "But I didn't know Roy was

sleeping in there. If I did, I wouldn't of walked in. We normally sit in your bed and talk in the mornings."

"I know honey, but you have to knock in the future. I just want you to know that I'm sorry and I want you to forget about it. Ok? You're too young for stuff like that. I also need you to do me a favor, and not mention this to Mama Ida or Papa Willie. Oh, and whatever you do don't tell your nosey father, Sheldon, Beldon, Feldon."

My mother never made negative connotations about my father in front of us, but loved using rhymes to chastise his name. She wasn't vindictive like him either, clearly too content with her life to really care to be. I empathized with how badly she felt, having no intention of making it any worse than it already was for her. I promised not to mention a word to anyone, truly meaning it, but that was until my father blew into town.

Every so often, he drove into Delaware to visit with us. It never went well and I begged my mother not to make us go. When my father picked us up, it was a day spent seeing his attorney and/or his child psychiatrist. We didn't share much quality time together, as he constantly berated us with questions and threats about our mother. Before the interviews, he finely prepped all of us, even Julie. He started getting her involved since she was older, hanging his hat on the facts of her new habit. It was quickly getting trite, as my mind rapidly melted away. His lies and illusions were becoming hard to tell whether they were real or fantasy anymore. Maybe he was just wearing me down, but it was getting hard to live and breathe each lie. Being eight, I only had so much will power to fight off his arsenal and we were hard pressed to tell his fashioned fables about our mother. When saying hard pressed, I mean by physical violence.

Towards the end of the summer, my father picked us up to revisit the child psychiatrist again. The three of us sat stoically in the backseat of the car as he seemed somewhat pleased to see us. While we drove to the doctor's appointment, he looked like his mind was swirling somewhere else. No one freely spoke until he engaged us, asking what we had been doing all summer with our mother. Julie spoke first, describing the new pool and her large assortment of dolls. Mama Ida did buy Julie an extensive collection of dolls that ate, pooped, walked and did everything except breathe. I knew that wasn't the information my father was itching for as he turned the question over to Mitch. Not having much to say, he gave his usual laconic yes and no replies to my father's inquiries. Mitch didn't like long drawn out answers, looking to avoid a possible slap for composing the wrong response. Eventually the question came around to me, responding how we were having a great summer with our mother and grandparents. My answers were as short as Mitch's and I could see we weren't satisfying his appetite.

Then our father began his typical prepping before the doctor's appointment. "Hey kids, now when the doctor asks you questions make sure you answer him with what I told you to say. Do you all understand?" After his statement, he went through role call. "Julie, do you understand? You remember what we talked about, right?"

Julie innocently answered, "Yes daddy."

"Good girl. Mitch, you remember too, right?"

"Yes."

His voice wasn't as kind as it was to my siblings when my turn came. "Jim, you remember what we talked about, right? I don't want to look like an asshole again. Do we understand each other?"

I was apprehensive to reply, knowing I wasn't going to lie to the doctor. Biting the skin around my raw thumb, I pensively sat for a moment in silence. My heart was exceedingly pumping as my hands were dripping beads of sweat. Then my father bellowed, "Jim, did you hear me?"

"Yes," I echoed back.

"Yes, what? Yes, you're going to say what I told you to say or are you going to make me look like an asshole again." His temper was flaring up and I could feel the heat from the backseat.

"Yes. All I can say is yes." My mouth was parched, feeling like all the fluids in my body were being drained through my pours. There was no response from my father, with the car falling into a pit of silence. I could tell he was waiting for me to say more, so I said, "I'll see how I feel when I get there." Suddenly, I felt the car swerve off the road, while sharp sounds of stones popped under the tires.

In a fit of rage, he slammed on the brakes bringing the car to a skidding halt. Banging the car in park, he chucked out the cigarette he was smoking. Then with a lack of words, the hitting and slapping came over me like a sweltering storm. Mitch and Julie, fearing for their own lives, scooted away like I was a bundle of poison ivy. As I was blocking and trying to dodge his arsenal, the words finally flourished. "You're not going to fucking listen to me? Is that what you're fucking saying? This is it man. Today is the day that you will do what I fucking tell ya." His volume escalated to a raging roar and for every syllable there was a hit. "You are going to tell that fucking doctor what I said because if you don't, I will beat the fucking shit out of you. Do you understand me, God damn it?" While furiously hitting me, the rings on his fingers were slamming against my head. The pain was a terrible ringing sensation, echoing throughout my skull.

Crying and panicking for my life, I positioned my head between my knees with both arms trying to ward off his every hit. I knew I had to come up with something fast to get him off. He was practically standing in the front seat to get a better shot at me. "Ok. Ok. Stop! Stop! I'll tell you something if you promise to stop hitting me." After hearing an abundance of coughing and heavy breathing, I felt him retreat.

With a gruff coughing voice, he hollered, "What? What the fuck are you going to tell me?" Slowly peeking through my defense, I saw he was sitting down now. Mitch and Julie were scared to death, hysterically crying in fear. They were pinned so closely to the opposite car door, that if it were to open, they would have surely fallen flat on their asses. "You better tell me something, right fucking now God damn it. Otherwise it'll start again. What is it? Spit it out."

Sitting there uncontrollably shaking, I was attempting to form words through my quivering lips. I tried to speak but the muscles in my throat wouldn't allow me at first. After another violent threat from him, I flinched, pleading, "It's about my mother."

"What about your mother? Spit it out or I swear I'll kick your ass right now."

I didn't want to spill the beans on her, but I had no choice. No one was helping me and I didn't want go through another round of getting my ass relentlessly beaten. Reluctantly, I was able to squeeze out the story about seeing Roy sprawled out on my mother's bed naked. He sat quietly listening, loving every word as a devious smirk slowly emerged across his face. It was sweet music to my father's ears, hearing dirt on my mother. Especially, when there was a naked man with an erection involved. I could see him salivating while describing the story.

"Ok, this is what you're going to do and you better fucking do as I tell ya. You're going to tell the doctor the same story you just told me. Do you hear me? If I find out you changed the story, this beating is nothing compared to what you'll get." He turned around fixing his hair in the rearview mirror, then looking down at his palms, said, "God damn it, I busted a blood vessel. Shit. You made me break a God damn blood vessel. Ouch," he cried out in pain. "I must've done it on your head."

Mitch and Julie scooted back into their original seats, pitifully staring at me with their mouths agape. They were still quivering and panting as if they were the ones who had their asses pummeled. Neither of them squeaked a word to me, but I could read from their body language how they were hoping I was ok. They knew better than to ask, sensing it could lead to provoking my father into another fit of rage. Miserably, I sat in the backseat huffing and puffing, wishing I were dead. I did that as a kid, thinking if I were dead it would teach him a lesson. Imagining he would feel guilty for all the beatings he gave me. Then my father broke my concentration, bellowing for me to get myself together. He wanted me to fix my hair and wipe the tears away. The one thing he was very talented at, was not leaving visible bruises for anyone to see.

When we arrived at the doctor's office, it was the same old routine. My father went in first to have his session with the psychiatrist, then it was our turn. Sitting and waiting was the toughest part for me, consumed with the disturbing thought of having to tattle on my own mother. It was eating me up inside, but I knew it meant my life or at least an absorbent amount of pain. On the other hand, it was giving my father more ammo against my mother in court. I didn't want either to happen but I was caught in a no win situation. The stress was tormenting my insides with my fingernails absorbing the grunt of my frustration. My father sat in the waiting room with us chain smoking. He never mentioned another word to me, but I knew by his look what he was waiting for and I was going to deliver. He knew he had won, displaying a demeanor of confidence and victory with every drag on his cigarette.

It was my turn and I was curious what Julie had said when she cheerfully skipped out. I guess she voiced anything my father told her, definitely posing the worst damage to my mother's case. Her new habit of touching herself in bed was pretty damaging to my mom. Even though my mother never gave a demonstration, the testimony of a little girl could be awfully devastating. Especially, if presented the right way by a child psychiatrist in a court of law. I faltered in, reluctantly spilling the beans on my mother about the naked episode with Roy. The doctor didn't say much, scribbling intently on his notepad. Then he went through a series of questions. The same stale ones he hit me with the last time I was in his office. I wasn't too cooperative, seeing how I already gave him enough dirt on my mother to hold my end of the bargain with my father. What I wanted to tell him about, were the brutal beatings I received since our last meeting. I thought it would be interesting to see what his reaction would be to that. He never alluded to those types of questions and I wanted to let him know that his promise of confidentiality didn't mean squat. Using my better judgment, I decided to let it slide. After the doctor finished with the three of us, he called my father in for a synopsis of the appointment.

Since the entire harsh day was swallowed by the doctor's appointment, my father just drove us back to our mother's house. There was no thank you or you did a good job in the doctor's office. He came off as though owed the rotten confessions, triumphantly smoking his cigarettes while calmly driving in complete silence. As we were pulling into the neighborhood, he broke the silence promising the next time we would have more fun together. When he reached our house, we said our goodbyes and hastily jumped out of the car before he could walk us up. My mother was waiting on us when we came home, noticing we weren't happy as we each went our separate ways.

Later that night, after we ate and Julie went to sleep, Mitch and I sat on our bed talking with our mother. We described the different events which occurred before and during the doctor's appointment. Still upset, I told her how my father maliciously beat me in the car, forcing me to tell the psychiatrist about the thing I saw with Roy. Apologizing, I explained it wasn't something I wanted to do, but couldn't handle being slapped or hit anymore. She wasn't angry, giving me a gentle hug as I could see an expression of deep regret in her face.

"Don't worry. Papa Willie will fix everything," she said with a soft voice.

"You keep saying that, but I'm tired of getting beaten for not wanting to lie. How come we haven't seen your doctor?" I was thinking, we never met with a child psychiatrist from her side. It was strange that the only doctor we saw was my father's.

My mom looked at me confidently smiling, "Don't you worry, I said. Ok? Papa will fix it. Let's stop talking about Sheldon, Fleldon, Weldon and have some fun. I got you boys presents today. Jim, you're going to love yours." With that, she popped up disappearing for a moment, then returned with an armful of gifts.

She bought me a cassette tape recorder. So thankful, I immediately jumped up hugging and kissing her. The last time we were shopping for records, I saw one at the store and told her how much I wanted one. "Wow! I can't believe you got it for me. I love it," I shouted, ripping open the box.

She smiled and said, "Guess what? You can record yourself with it too. You can sing in it and play it back. Isn't that neat? I also got you this." She handed me a cassette of Don McLean's new album "American Pie". I was crazy about that song. My mother and I sang it together anytime it was on the radio. After quickly jamming the cassette into the tape recorder, we sat around singing as it played. Then my mom said, "Well, let's see if it records."

Excited, I pulled the microphone out of the box, plugging it in the tape recorder. "What should we say in it?"

"Anything you want. It's yours," my mother squawked.

While Mitch was looking at his gift, he let out a loud fart and we all broke out in laughter. Then he came up with a brilliant idea, while giggling. "Let's fart in it," he said. Hysterically laughing, I agreed, thinking it was a good idea but couldn't find the urge to fart.

My mother's mascara was running, as her tears flowed from laugher. "If you guys want to learn how to fart, I'll show you how."

Mitch and I looked at her as if she was crazy since after all, that was a boy's dream, to fart at will. Then our mother continued with her explanation. "First, jump up and down real fast." So, Mitch and I stood up, enthusiastically jumping up and down on our beds. It was fun but neither of us had to pass wind.

"Can you fart yet," she asked, laughing and crying at the same time. We both said no, continuing to jump around the room like two wild kangaroos. I couldn't understand how Julie wasn't waking up from the laughter and noise. My mom was chuckling even harder now, saying, "Ok, both of you get up on the bed and stand on all fours like a dog." Still cackling, we climbed onto the bed proceeding to get into a dog stance. Then barking like two canines, my mom told us to stop so we wouldn't wake up Julie. "Now put your butts in the air and that should make you have to fart." We were all giggling like muffled school girls when it happened. Mitch and I found the urge and farted. My mom started pointing while screaming, "See. It works. I told you it worked. Now go fast and record it." So that's what Mitch and I did the rest of the evening. I broke in my new tape recorder by taping the two of us passing gas.

After putting us to bed, my mother called Mama Ida up in a furious rage. I overheard her screaming on the telephone like I've never heard her yell before. She was describing what had happened to us when we were with our father, reiterating the stories Mitch and I told her. Her tone and demeanor had altered drastically while speaking to her mother. It sounded unlike the way she spoke to us, calling my father every name under the sun that could be spelled with four letters. She was nasty but I could tell it wasn't directed at my grandmother. She was just venting. It was strange because my mother did not react as angry in front of us when telling her the stories. I suppose she was waiting to speak to an adult to vent the way she was screaming.

With school on the verge of starting, my mom enrolled me in the third grade as requested. I felt edgy about lying but was confident I could keep up with the class. I went for the extra help in Rolling and practiced reading and writing each night during the school year. My mother was electrified by the idea of us going back to school, dragging everyone shopping for clothes and school supplies. I didn't realize shopping for school was going to be so much fun. We picked out all kinds of pens, pencils, erasers and other supplies, but the best part was shopping for shoes. Mama Ida and my mom persistently bought me saddle shoes in the past. It was getting embarrassing to be eight years old still wearing that style of shoe. I pleaded with my mother, explaining that it was time for a change. Finally agreeing me, she purchased a pair of cowboy boots I fell in love with. As we were waiting to pay, I could sense how fidgety she was by the way she repeatedly looked at her wristwatch. While the salesman was neatly putting the boots in a box, she handed him her credit card, instantly signing her name without even looking over the bill. Then quickly hurried us out of the store and began scurrying for the exit doors.

"What's the big hurry," I asked, as Mitch and I struggled to keep up with her through the mall.

"I have to stop and see someone real quick. They get off work soon," she said without turning around.

My mom was extremely difficult to lose in a crowd. While working at the beauty salon, she tried every hairdo and hair color known to women. Her latest hairdo was a coif in the front and long cascading hair in the back, thanks to an attachable wig. The color of her hair was the true reason why you couldn't lose her, given it was pure white. She started off blond, gradually changing until it turned white.

When reaching the car, we piled our things in the trunk as my mother sped off like we were in the Indy 500. She was flying down Georgia Road, then suddenly made a sharp turn into the Georgia Square shopping center. The place was under construction, so I thought it odd for her to be heading in that direction. While pulling up, a few construction workers were packing it in for the day. I couldn't understand what we were doing there, as my mom rolled down her window calling one of the workers over. Sitting in the front seat biting my nails, I watched as a workman came sauntering over. He leaned in the car with both hands on the roof supporting himself. "What's up honey," he said with a slight grin. He was profusely perspiring, taking notice how his hands and fingernails were also filthy dirty.

"Nothing much. Me and my girlfriends are having a party tonight. I was wondering if you and a few of your friends want to stop by for a drink?"

The guy bent his head down, then coming back up with an arrogant smile on his face, he laughed saying, "A party? Where?"

"My house. I only live a few minutes from here. Have you heard of Farmland before?"

"Sure."

My mother appeared to be getting impatient, saying, "Well, do you what to come?"

The guy reflected his coolest look, muttering, "Yeah, that sounds great. I'll bring a few of my buddies."

My mom scrambled around in her purse for something to write on. After scribbling her information on a flimsy scrap of paper, she handed him our address. "See ya around eight," she said, pulling off.

I couldn't believe what I was seeing. She was inviting complete strangers to party at our house, so looking at her in disbelief, I said, "Mom, do you even know that guy?"

"No, but I know a few of the other guys. Marlo dated one of them. She's coming tonight, so it'll be cool." She cruised out from the parking lot, displaying a sly smile, looking confident with her decision.

My mom let us help setup for the party as Mitch and I munched on some of the snacks she had out. I loved her parties, looking forward to having some fun. It had been quite some time since we had any company over. My mother made a deal with Mitch and me, permitting us to stay up for a portion of the party as long as we went to bed when asked. Not long after Julie went to sleep, everyone started arriving. There were approximately five guys who showed and about the same number of my mom's friends. Everybody was extra nice to me as the party carried on in a low key manner. My mom had music playing on the record player while her friends were drinking and dancing. She was busy talking to one of the fellows with me nagging them for part of the evening. I was showing off my new superhero dolls and blabbing about nothing in particular. When it was time, she sent us off to bed moving the party to the downstairs portion of the house.

It didn't occur to me, until lying in bed, that my grandmother wanted a phone call if there were any parties going on in our house. I didn't feel right telling on my mother, considering she was home and we were fed while safely in our beds. She wasn't keeping us up with loud noise or music and everyone was acting polite. I was fully aware that Mama Ida would be upset with me for not calling, but I didn't think she would ever find out.

The next morning we were eating breakfast when the front door opened. I heard a voice echo through the house, "Hello." My mom was still sleeping, so I instantly ran over to the stairs to see who walked in. When reaching the railing, I found my grandmother standing at the bottom. She routinely came by to checkup on us and my mom, making sure everything was copasetic.

She was attentively staring into the family room when I screamed back down. "Good morning, Mama Ida." Distracted by the mess, she didn't answer, looking around in shock with her neck outstretched like a crane.

As I approached, she was still looking at the number of empty beer bottles and cans, scattered either on the cocktail table or laying on the carpet. Some with cigarettes butts hanging out and others half full. With her penciled-on eyebrows raised, she squealed, "Jim, what happened here?" Before I could answer, she said, "It looks like your mother had a party. Didn't we have an agreement that you were supposed to call me if something like this happened?"

Her nose nervously twitched back and forth, waiting impatiently for an answer. "I didn't see any people. I must've been asleep when they came over."

My grandmother exhaled in frustration, shaking her head and calling out, "Mindy. Mindy. Are you upstairs?" Her voice was squeaky from old age as she tried projecting a powerful scream.

My mom came stumbling to the top of the staircase, wearing a robe. She looked like a wreck as she eased herself down the stairs, holding onto the railing. My grandmother stood there, shockingly taking it all in. Once my mother made it down, she folded her arms across her chest, casually saying, "Good morning, mother."

"Mindy, you are not to have parties. What went on here last night? There are potato chips on the floor and beer bottles everywhere. It smells like booze in here."

"I had a couple of girlfriends over. Is that a crime? I need some friends around sometimes too. I can't just put the kids to bed and not have any adult interaction in my life."

Mama Ida wasn't unnerved by my mother's remarks, shrieking, "I don't care what you want. If that ex-husband of yours should come by, you'd be in deep trouble. Do you want your kids? Your father is doing everything in his power to help you and this is not helping."

"I know mother, but it was only a few girlfriends. I was going to clean the place when I woke up," my mother combated back in a childish fashion.

Then flopping down on the couch she put an arm over her eyes, forcefully exhaling in frustration. I started to feel like an intruder and didn't think this was a conversation I should be hearing. While looking down at the carpet and biting my fingernails, Mama Ida yanked me by the arm. I grudgingly followed her up the stairs as she reamed me for not calling her, insisting that I must have heard the loud noises. Defensively lying, I promised her that I was sleeping and didn't hear a thing.

She was winded from all the excitement, asking, "Do you want to go back and live with your father or do you want to live here with us?"

Looking serious, her nose was twitching more than usual. I felt guilty for upsetting her, whining back, "Here. I want to stay here with you. I'm sorry. I promise to call next time."

"Please call me next time, Jim. Your mother told me about your father's temper and I'm nauseous thinking about him hitting you. Your mother will lose you kids if she keeps up this behavior, Jim. That disgusting father of yours is looking for anything. We understand each other, right?" She peered seriously in my eyes, waiting for reassurance. Not wanting to disappoint her again, I promptly told her not to worry.

I was feeling a sense of security, since school was in session for a few weeks without any harmful phone calls to the house. My paranoia was nagging at me, concerned my mom or teacher would somehow find out I flunked second grade. The overwhelming feeling was wrenching, as it haunted me everyday. The one thing I counted on was my father and mother despised each other so much, that there would never be a conversation blowing my cover. In addition to that my father recently called, telling us our court date was creeping up and we would be done going to court soon.

It was stressful and depressing to think about going back to court. I constantly had thoughts of being stretched in two different directions, like a tug-of-war competition. I always sucked myself into anticipating the worst scenario, which would be living with my father. He insinuated, with every call, how confident he was of winning custody over us. Sensing the clock ticking down, I felt completely helpless to the outcome. The most frustrating piece of the puzzle, was when they asked who we would rather live with. Upon saying our mother, the judge mysteriously sent us back with our father, sending the wrong message to us throughout the process.

With all the variables rolling around in my head, I couldn't concentrate in school and lost my ambition to go. I began faking being sick in order to stay home. My mother never fought me, so it began that I occasionally called off from school. Then it blossomed into two to three times a week. I played so much hooky that my teacher started calling my mother to find out why I wasn't showing up for class. Never knowing what my mom's responses were, the teacher was kind on the days I was in school. Being out so frequently, I became a guru on cartoons and until this day, I'm a walking historian on them.

My daily routine started by sitting around the house, eating Brach's candies while watching TV all morning. In the afternoons, my mom and I watched old movies and if lucky, an Elvis film popped on the tube. When my grandmother happened to stop by doing her checkups, my mother alerted me so I could jump in bed pretending to be sick. Other times when my mom was at work, I hid somewhere in the house waiting for Mama Ida to leave. Looking back, I am well aware she was guilty of allowing me to play hooky, but my mom sympathized with my issues. We conversed often about the problems. Many times she was more like a friend than a mother to me, seeing as she was the only one I could confide in.

CHAPTER 15

On one of our last weekends, before D-Day, my father came by to pick us up for the afternoon. He was unusually overjoyed when we squeezed into the car. I was very suspicious until he announced we were going to meet his new girlfriend and her children. This wasn't the first girlfriend we ever met, so I didn't understand the importance of this meeting. I was incredibly disappointed since he committed spending the day alone with us as a family. After our last dismal visit together, he promised we would do something fun. Introducing his girlfriend and her kids to us, didn't qualify as fun to me. It sure didn't make Mitch and Julie happy either. We already had a family that we were struggling to keep alive. We didn't know day to day where we could end up next, so who needed the pressure of another family. It seemed selfish to me but I reluctantly went along. I sure as hell didn't want to burst his bubble, taking a chance on another rumble in his car.

During the drive there, I felt like a trained circus dog as he instructed us on how to kiss her hello. He explained that we couldn't just give her one kiss on the cheek but had to give her a kiss on both. I had no intention of kissing her at all. She meant nothing to me and the only people I kissed were my family members.

My father was smoking his cigarette, still going through his explanation on kissing when I said, "Hey dad, why do we have to kiss her anyway? I don't want to kiss her. I don't even know her."

He gazed back at me with squinty eyes through his rearview mirror, sternly saying, "You'll kiss her because I asked you to. Don't make me look bad. Do you hear me, Jim? All of you, do hear what I'm telling you?"

"Yeah," I said in dismay. "I guess I don't know what the big deal is."

"The big deal is, she means a lot to me. I want her to see what good kids I have. Is that so bad?"

Now he sounded like he was asking rather than forcing, so giving in I said, "Sure, but I'm not kissing her kids."

My father laughed, agreeing as he lit another cigarette. "Did I tell you that she has a son around your age, Jim?" I shook my head, while he spoke through the rearview mirror. "Nice kid. I like him a lot. His name is Shlomo. By the way, my girlfriend's name is Hamar. She also has a baby girl, her name's Samara. I think she's too young to play with you yet, Julie, but she's cute. Anyways, I think you kids will have a good time."

My father parked the car in front of a large apartment building, announcing that we were here. We all jumped out, following him into the building. From the time we left the car until we reached their door, he repeatedly went over the instructions on how to kiss Hamar hello. I thought I was going to yank the hair out of my head. Then he added an additional ingredient to the mix. As we were walking down the hallway, he was stammering, "If her mother and father are there, make sure to call them mama and papa. Oh yeah, and make sure to kiss both of them the same way I told you to kiss Hamar, ok?"

Mitch and I looked at each other, shaking our heads in disbelief. Julie was still skipping along behind us, most likely not paying attention to a single word our father was saying. She mimicked everything we did anyway, so I guess my father felt assured by that. I could read he was really trying to impress his new girlfriend with all the preparation he went through with us. He never did this when we met his other girlfriend, so I assumed he must be in love. As we reached the door, I could smell a strong odor of something burning from inside, as my father boldly knocked. When the door opened, a blustery gust of smoke, with an array of aromas, exploded out almost blowing me over. My dad, gentlemanly-like, stepped up giving her a kiss on each cheek. After he was done with his noble deed, she stood stoically looking at us, with a look of expectation in her eyes. My father briskly stumbled back, pushing us towards her. I was the first to say hello, planting a kiss, like my father instructed, on each cheek. Then Mitch and Julie followed my lead, doing the same. She didn't actually kiss us back. It was more like she was offering her cheek to us. She appeared very cold and didn't act as happy to see us as my father was to see her children.

Hastily shoving us in the apartment, my father immediately went gaga over Shlomo. I never saw that side of him, as he exerted a lot of phony energy to impress someone. He put his hand out, lively shouting, "Hey Shlomo, give me five." After Shlomo slapped him five, my father gave him a playful hug and rubbed his knuckles into Shlomo's skull. I couldn't help noticing that the greeting Shlomo received was warmer than any hello we ever got. Then he turned to us with a quirky smile, calling out, "Hey kids, I want you to meet Shlomo. He's a real cool kid."

When meeting Shlomo for the first time, I thought he was strange looking. He had an unusually large head for a kid his age, in addition to a distinct oval pie-shaped face. I took notice how exceptionally thin his body frame was, surprised it could support such a large head. It looked like his mother gave him a very unfortunate bowl haircut, seemingly accentuating the size of his face. Each of us shook his hand while exchanging hellos. I kept my word to my father, making Shlomo the only person in the apartment that I didn't kiss. After the polite hellos, my father was leaning in a crib conversing in baby talk to someone. Shlomo was standing by his side, waving us over to meet his baby sister. She was standing in the crib as my father laughed, making baby noises and softly pinching her cheeks. He turned around smiling, saying, "This is Samara, kids. She's Shlomo sister. Isn't she cute?" None of us answered, as we stood watching a side of our father we never saw before.

Then two ancient people wobbled out of the kitchen smiling, where I noticed the poignant smell was emanating from. It smelled like they were burning peppers and beans in there, with the smoke violently following them in the living room. My father cheerful shouted, "Mama! Papa! Hello!" His arms were outstretched for a hug before the two of them were even in hugging range. He was obviously overdoing it, putting forth everything in his power to sell himself to these people. The lady he referred to as mama was a heavy set woman with a pleasant smile. The old man was slightly heavy, walking with a noticeable limp. They hugged when reaching one another, exchanging the two cheek kiss in the middle of the living room. Once they were done, my father instantly pointed in our direction, slowly saying, "Mama. Papa. These are my kids." Then he motioned for us to come over, flailing his hand in the air as if we needed to hurry. This whole experience was like we walked in on a family he had on the side. Watching my father's performance was getting weird. He reminded me of an actor, over playing a part in a B rated TV sitcom.

"Kids, this is Mama and Papa. Say hello," he slowly said so that they could understand his words.

Dumbstruck, the three of us stood there frozen, completely forgetting our father's instructions. He finally broke the ice when giving us the evil eye. With his encouragement we quickly thawed out, giving each of them a kiss on both cheeks. They appeared very pleased, saying hello in their best broken English. My father spoke up to brighten the mood, trying to hold a coherent conversation with the two of them. Listening to him speak was like hearing some parents reasoning with their baby. "Mama, you feel good? Papa, how leg?" Then they asked him how he felt, with him replying, "Me good."

Hamar was leaning against the wall, drinking everything in as though she was mentally taking notes. It was clearly evident she wasn't pleased we were there, acting withdrawn and aloof. Julie was fully energized, skipping around the room while everyone talked. Eventually she made it over to the baby, trying to play with her. While attempting to tweak the baby's cheek in the same manner as my father, I could see Hamar wasn't too keen on that. She abruptly walked over and removed Julie's hand from Samara's cheek, demanding that she not do that anymore. Julie looked disappointed, as my father interjected, saying, "Julie, you have to be gentle with the baby, ok honey?" She shrugged him off, skipping away to do something else.

Hamar appeared to look much older than my father. She was blond like my mom but very different looking. She had a foreign hard look about her, with a heavy harsh accent to match. Her eyes were thickly outlined with black eyeliner, accentuating her exceedingly intense and unfriendly stare. Hamar looked as if she had a big chip on her shoulder, noticeably not enjoying our company.

Shlomo took Samara out of the crib, wanting to show us how she could do sit-ups. He gently laid her on the carpet, while holding her legs securely down and to our amazement she was able to do it. We all clapped for her as she proudly smiled. Then Hamar, in her harsh accent, said to my father, "Ok, let's get going, Sheldon." My father made sure we said our goodbyes to the two ancient people, he referred to as mama and papa. Then we all crammed into his car.

He decided on taking us to a park, where we played and had ice cream. Hamar and my father sat on a bench talking as we played. While we were messing around at the park, Shlomo proceeded to tell me how my father wanted to marry his mother. I was taken back and alarmed at the same time. This was certainly big news that we weren't privy to, so I asked, "How do you know?"

"Your dad told me. My mom did too. I don't know when they'll get married but I know he loves my mom. Your dad said he loves me and Samara too. He told me if you come live with him that we can be brothers. Do you think you'll live with your dad?"

I couldn't believe what Shlomo was telling me. My ears were hearing it but my brain couldn't make sense out of it. It was shocking to have a stranger sharing my possible future with me. It didn't seem real since it came from him instead of my father. I felt foolish that he knew more about the plans for my life than I did. The news was unpalatable that my father had plans to start another family when he was still married to my mother.

After several thoughts ricocheted through my mind, I responded, "I don't know what's going to happen. We could live with my mom or my father. We just don't know. I didn't know my dad even knew you guys. He never told us about you all before." I was careful not to tell him that I didn't want any part of his mother in my life. "How long have you guys known my dad?"

It didn't take long for Shlomo to answer that question. "I don't know. Not long... I guess." It bothered me how my father kept these people a secret from us. I assumed he was doing it so my mom wouldn't find out. He figured if we knew, his secret would be shared with her. Receiving this information was mind boggling for me. I couldn't wait to be alone with my father to check out the validity of Shlomo's story. I was hoping he was talking nonsense.

After we dropped Hamar and her kids off, I finally had my chance. "Hey dad, can I ask you something?"

My father had a cigarette hanging out of his mouth, glaring at me through the rearview mirror. "Sure, what do you want to know?"

"Shlomo told me that you guys are going to get married. You and Hamar. Is that true?" I was praying it was a big misunderstanding, perhaps Shlomo got it wrong when hearing my father talking.

There was a long pause before my father responded. His eyes drifted upwards as if he were searching for an answer in the sky. Then appearing to contemplate something before speaking, he said, "I don't know, Jim. We like each other a lot, but we'll see." He looked back at Mitch and Julie, changing the subject real quick. "What did you guys' think of Hamar and her kids?"

Mitch was the first to reply. "Good. They were good."

"Good. They were good," Julie answered, following Mitch's lead.

Then my father eyeballed me through the rearview mirror, asking, "How about you, Jim? Did you get along with Shlomo? He's a nice kid, isn't he?" I could see he was smiling through the mirror like a kid who found a dollar bill on the sidewalk.

"Yeah, he's nice alright. He just told me a lot of stuff about you being his dad and all." I looked directly back into the mirror until our eyes met. I was waiting for a reaction.

"Well, kids can exaggerate things. You know how that goes. Like I said, we'll have to see. Nothing's set in stone." He slipped another cigarette between his lips and lit it.

When he dropped us off, I couldn't wait to see my mother and tell the big secret. I was so focused on running to the front door that I practically forgot to say goodbye to my father. He had to remind me to say goodbye. The words were drooling from my lips, as I was quickly making my way to tell my mom about this woman my father was planning on marrying. Mitch had the same idea, as we were pushing each other while jogging up the stairs. He loved reporting bad news, later I nicknamed him "The Bad News Reporter". My mom was watching TV when we found her sitting in the family room. Mitch and I began talking in unison, describing our day with Hamar and Shlomo. Becoming frustrated and annoyed with how the conversation was going, my mom said, "Ok, one at a time. What are you trying to say? Jim, you go first."

Mitch looked disappointed, as I spewed out, "My dad took us to meet this lady, Hamar, who he's going to marry. This kid with a real big head, her son Shlomo, told me everything." I was panting, spraying out the words faster than humanly possible. "Do you think it's true? My dad didn't admit it."

My mother cackled loudly, shaking her head from side to side. "Let Sheldon, Beldon, Fleldon marry whoever he wants. Who cares?"

"I care and Mitch cares and I'm sure, Julie cares. What if we have to live with him? I don't want that lady to be my mother. You should've seen her. She didn't like us. I could tell. She didn't even talk to us." I was very concerned when speaking, since I didn't want to live with someone who didn't want us.

My mom couldn't keep a straight face and giggling, said, "It won't happen. Papa Willie has everything under control. I promise you. I promise all of you." She looked at us for confirmation that we all understood.

Unfortunately, I was a worrywart. Always considering the worst because in reality the worst was a distinct possibility. When my mother was done with her promises, we sat around talking about our day with my father's new girlfriend and kids. I colorfully described how Hamar and her son, Shlomo, looked, cracking her up with my creative portrayals. I loved getting my mother going, because when she laughed, she cried at the same time. It was contagious and hilarious to watch. When bedtime came around, I laid anxiously biting my nails, thinking about my conversation with Shlomo. I couldn't imagine him as a new brother or even worse, Hamar as my new mother. Before falling asleep, Mitch and I spoke briefly on the possibility of living with Hamar and her children. We were in agreement that we wanted to stay with our mother.

Before our final court date was upon us, my mom came home with a St. Bernard. We were watching television in the family room, when she merrily walked in with this monstrous dog. "Look what I got. What do you guys think," she asked, while struggling to hold the dog by a leash.

Mitch and Julie instantly darted over, petting and hugging the dog. I went over too, but in complete shock, that she would have the moxie to bring home a dog. As I began to pet it, this anger built up inside me. "Mom, I'm calling mama. She told me to call her if you came home with a dog and I'm calling."

She half-smiled, handing the leash to Mitch. "What do you mean, you're calling? Don't you like the dog?"

Somberly standing in the family room, I held my ground. I knew calling Mama Ida was the right thing to do, so miffed, I shouted, "I'm calling. Mama Ida told you, no more dogs. You'll get in trouble with the court and we can't stay with you."

I started moving towards the telephone but my mom beat me to it, ripping the phone off its base. She angrily stared at me, while tightly squeezing the phone in her hand. Taking a good look at her for the first time, in a long while, I noticed how much weight she had lost. Her face was unusually gaunt and her nose was noticeably bulbous. It seemed to be the main attraction on her thin face. "I thought you wanted a dog, Jim," she yelled. Then peering at Mitch and Julie for support, she exclaimed, "How about you kids? Didn't you want a dog?"

Mitch and Julie nodded their heads, shouting, "Yes."

Then Julie shrieked, "Can I name him? Please!"

Grinning, my mother focused on Julie, saying, "Of course honey, you can name him anything you want."

"How could you bring a dog home? Mama told you, no dogs. I didn't tell when you had your party, but I promised her, I'd call if something else happened."

This was the first time I raised my voice to my mother, however I knew the consequences could be devastating if the courts found out. I also made a solemn promise to Mama Ida, which I did not want to break. She was right to instruct me to call if my mother was acting against her wishes. The outcome could be bleak if we had to live with our father and his new aloof wife. I unsuccessfully attempted to grab the phone out of my mom's hand, yelling, "Give me the phone. Mama told me to call."

After struggling with her for a few minutes, I simply gave up. Angry and out of breath, I threatened her. "When you're not looking, I'll call. You'll see."

On that note she hung up the phone, tauntingly saying, "Come on, Jim. Have some fun. Mitch and Julie are. Don't be such a party pooper." When done, she sat next to Mitch and Julie, playing with the dog as it drooled all over the carpet.

Later that day I kept my promise, calling Mama Ida as she came over faster than if I called 911. All hell broke loose once she barged into the house, with the two of them having it out in the middle of the family room. My mother resembled a little girl getting scolded by her mother, which was exactly what was happening. She was belligerently screaming how it wasn't fair that we couldn't keep the dog, but Mama Ida was unmoved. She was yelling and carrying on with all kinds of threats if my mother didn't get rid of the dog. After arguing back and forth, my grandmother was victorious. My mother was teary-eyed as she took the dog back to wherever it was she got it. She had no choice since mama said she wasn't leaving until my mom got rid of the dog. I didn't think she could be so tough at her age, but she proved me wrong, showing us who the boss was that day. I was a little sad for my mother, having caused her such grief. Sensing my sadness, my grandmother assured me that I did the right thing.

After that day, I became very rambunctious and a discourteous smartass towards my mother. I was using profanity like my father which my mother constantly reprimanding me for. She never hit me, but threw me in my bedroom many times for cussing. I had no reservations in the manner that I spoke to her anymore. It was getting so bad, I would rant and rage in front of strangers, family members and neighbors. One day, a lady from across the street heard me yelling at my mother. She suggested to her, that she break a branch off a tree and spank my ass until it bleeds. My mom threatened to do it, but never followed through. I was acting out from all the stress brought on by the custody battle, in addition to my mother's poor judgment. She wasn't following the rules my grandmother had set for her, realizing we would ultimately pay for it. Court was creeping up, as my father reminded me of it every time he called. He still continued harassing me over the phone for dirt on my mother or anything he could use to hurt her in court. It was getting intolerable as my nerves were getting the best of me. My nail biting progressed from all the stress, leaving the skin around my fingernails bleeding from the constant gnawing.

My impetuous behavior was easing its way under my mother's fingernails like bamboo shoots. She had grown weary of my foul mouth and erratic actions. Eventually, threatening to haul me off to the psychiatrist for an evaluation of my bad behavior. I was fearful of going, something my mom was well aware of since my father instilled that fear. She took full advantage of that weakness, knowing I was afraid of being locked up in a loony bin. That threat worked on me every time I was unruly and she kept it closely tucked away in her back pocket.

During one of our arguments, my mom terrorized me with a visit to the psychiatrist's office. Startled, I sprinted out of the house while grabbing her keys. She chased me outside, yelling for the keys back as I charged across the driveway to get into her car. I jumped inside just before she reached me, hastily banging all the door locks down. She furiously pulled on the door handle, screaming for me to get out of the car. I didn't listen, slipping the car key into the ignition and starting it after a few attempts. On special occasions, my mother sat me on her lap, allowing me to steer the car around the neighborhood as she worked the brake and accelerator pedals. With some practice under my belt, I was confident about going solo.

She was violently banging on the window when I put the car in reverse , backing out of the driveway. "Open the damn door, Jim. Stop the car, right now. You'll kill somebody." Tightly holding on to the door handle, she attempted to get in without any success. I could see her panicking when reaching the street and jamming the car into drive. Barely able to reach the pedals, the car powerfully jerked back and forth as I searched for the correct one.

While the car was slowly rolling down the street, my mom kept up with it, shrieking, "I mean it, Jim. Stop the FUCKING car." She was still hanging onto the door handle with her face expressing fear and wrath all rolled into one. Then she looked up, noticing there were some cars parked on the street. Fearful of an accident, she started crying, "Oh dear. Oh dear. Oh me. Oh my."

No matter how hard I tried, I could not reach the pedals, so the car essentially rolled down the street idling. I was concentrating on steering, with the speed not go over five miles per hour. By now my mother was worn out, so with little oxygen remaining in her lungs, she huffed, "Ok! I won't take you to the doctor. Just… stop… the… car."

Her face was a sweaty mess, causing her mascara to run around her eyes. She looked like an angry raccoon chasing me along side the car. While she was banging on the window for me to stop, I apprehensively shouted, "Are you telling the truth? Cause I don't want to go to the loony bin."

"Yes, I promise. No doctors," she spit out, gasping for air.

Taking her word, I partially stood up to reach the brake pedal, slamming the car in park. It came to a sudden halt with her frail fingers pounding on the window. "Open the damn door. I mean it. Open it, right now."

She was hunched over huffing and puffing, reminding me of a rabid raccoon with the white foam in the corners of her mouth. When I opened the door, she wearily rolled in and finding this superhuman strength, tossed me over the middle console. Breathing heavily she said, "This is it. You're punished. When we get back, go straight to your room. And no new toys for a long time. I'm sick of this crap!"

When we got home, I did exactly as told. Then heard my mother sobbing on the phone from the kitchen. "Mother, I've had it. I can't do this anymore. Jim is driving me crazy."

She was gradually becoming hysterical on the phone as the

conversation progressed. The hair on the back of my neck stood erect, sensing the damage I inflicted. I wasn't a mean-spirited kid, but could see by my mom's reaction that I really hurt her. While she was on the phone with Mama Ida, I faltered out of my room, lovingly hugging her.

"I'm sorry, mom. I promise that I'm sorry. Please stop crying. Please."

Sniffling, my mother wiped the tears from her saturated eyes, looking down at me. "Mother, let me call you back." After hanging up the telephone, she bent down to her knees with a shortness of breath, saying, "Listen honey, you scared the hell out of me. You can not behave like that anymore. I can't handle it and what you did was dangerous. You could've killed somebody or yourself."

"I'm sorry," I regrettably said. "I won't do it again."

"I know you are, but you have to promise me that you won't act like this anymore. I just can't handle you, Jim when you do things like this. I know you're nervous and confused about court, but we all are. You have to understand that papa, mama and I are doing everything we can. Ok?" She wiped my hair to the side with a trembling hand, smiling as if to assure me her words were sincere.

I took comfort in her words, promising to behave myself in the future. It was troubling, that it took her to breakdown for me to notice how badly I was acting at home. We naturally bonded once again, with everything reverting back to normal. At least as normal as normality could be, that is.

Halloween night was the last chapter in my life when I remember having fun with my mother. She was all revved up for it too, buying any costume we desired at Toy R Us that afternoon. Mitch and Julie were not excessively imaginative, choosing generic costumes. The ones that came in the cardboard box with the cellophane covers. I decided to be Batman, so my mom treated me to an awesome rubber mask with all the accessories that went with it. From the time we returned home, until Halloween evening, I wore that costume in great anticipation. Mitch and Julie, not wanting to be different, did the same. We played around the entire day, pretending to be the characters we dressed up like. Then my mom called us into the kitchen to help clean and carve the enormous pumpkin she purchased. My mother was funny, because anything she did had to be out of the ordinary, like the size of the pumpkin and kooky face we carved. When we were done, my mother lit the candle which burned for the rest of the afternoon and through the evening.

As soon as it was time to go out trick or treating, you couldn't hold my mother back. She was as excited as we were to get started. Not only did she supply us with bags but brought one for herself as well. Before we went out, she wanted us to learn the proper way to trick or treat, so she taught us the version she used to sing as a child. My mother was so engrossed that she laughed nonstop. "Listen guys, when they open the door you want to sing, 'Trick or treat smell my feet give me something good to eat.' Don't just say trick or treat, ok? Let me hear you guys sing it?"

All three of us burst into laughter and in unison we sang, "Trick or treat smell my feet give me something good to eat."

Uncontrollably laughing, my mother cried out, "You got it. Ok, let's go and don't forget the words. Keep singing so you remember."

That's exactly what we did. We sang that song the entire night whether we were at a door or not, we were singing. As we traipsed from door to door, it was apparent the neighbors presumed us nuts. I could see by their facial expressions how they couldn't believe we were singing that song in the company of our mother. We thought we were just being funny, but the people didn't appear to appreciate our antics. Some giggled, finding it amusing, while others didn't. Whenever a man answered the door, my mom would loudly sing along with us. After the candy was distributed in our bags, she would childishly say, "What about me? What do I get for trick or treat?"

The guys all had the same reaction, as they blushed and asked, "What do you want?" My mother usually asked for either a beer or a cigarette. It was funny because she walked back home with her own bag almost as full as ours, with all sorts of strange goodies. One guy who was smoking a cigar, offered her a pack of cherry cigarettes he didn't want. Mitch and I had our eyes set on that goody. We both wanted to try a cherry cigarette since Rolling.

When all the bags were stuffed with candy and our mother had her fill of acting like a goof, we headed home. She permitted us stay up extra late that night to check through our candy. She warned everyone not to eat anything that was opened, especially apples. After Julie went to bed, my mom started a fire in the fireplace, then lit up a cherry cigarette. While she opened a beer, I asked if Mitch and I could try one. She was shocked at first, cackling at my whimsical request. "You guys really want to try a cigarette? Come on, really?"

We perked up, surprised she would actually consider it. "Yeah, can we?"

Taking a lengthy second look at us, she appeared to be pondering the idea. "Ok, go for it. Just don't inhale, ok you two," she said with a devious laugh. We had no problem with that request, being ignorant on how to inhale anyway.

We each grabbed a cigarette, scurrying to the front of the fireplace. Getting up from where she was sitting, our mother squatted down on the floor joining us with a beer in her hand. "You guys aren't allowed to play with matches, so I'll have to light the smokes for you." Neither of us disputed her rule, shoving the cigarettes in our mouths while waiting on her to light them. "Don't forget. No inhaling guys, alright?"

When we began smoking, my mother broke out laughing at us. "You two look like the plastic monkeys they sell from the vending machines. You know the ones that smoke those fake cigarettes and blow out smoke?"

Catching on to her joke, Mitch and I started coughing as we laughed. "Come on mom, stop. You're making me cough," I said in between puffs.

The rest of the night my mother did her best, teaching us how to blow smoke rings. She giggled at Mitch and me, sitting in front of the fireplace, trying to mimic her technique. We kept trying but neither of us could get the hang of it. As it was getting late, she told us we had to get ready for bed. While saying goodnight, my mom asked, "Hey guys, make sure you don't tell Mama Ida or Papa Willie about this. This was a one-time thing. I don't want you kids picking up a bad habit. You don't want to start smoking like me or your bucktooth father. This is it. The end of it, right?" She gave us the most serious glare with us agreeing, as she kissed us goodnight.

CHAPTER 16

Court was afoot, blowing through our lives like a blustery winter storm and with it, went our souls and sanity. The mood at the courthouse was futile petulance and when everything was said and done, our father was awarded custody. No one was overly dramatic about the court's decision. There wasn't any dropping to the ground or rolling around crying in defeat. Everyone was too shocked that our father won the custody battle. I wasn't the slightest bit stunned, knowing there was a constant threat he could win. My mother and grandparents seemed the most shocked, as their postures and expressions went limp after the decision was rendered.

When the hush fell from the skies with all the vulturous sounds returning to the courtroom, my father abruptly dragged us out of the courthouse. He quickly rushed us by our mother, Mama Ida and Papa Willie, as they helplessly watched. We never had the opportunity to say goodbye nor did we know it would be the last time we would see them as children. They stood watching in defeat, while we were loaded in my father's car.

After the car began moving, my father told to us that he was awarded custody and we were going back to Rolling, Virginia. He aggressively shook a cigarette out of his pack, sliding one in between his lips. Then looking back at us through the rearview mirror, he calmly bellowed, "Are you kids alright?"

"No," I firmly said. "What's going on? Are we ever going to see our mom again?"

He coldly looked back at all three of us, shouting, "No! She's no good and the courts agreed. She's a bad mother and is sick too. Do you understand me? She's sick in the head." His voice was getting louder as he spoke.

"Who says?" I voiced, still having some backbone after living with my mom for a few months. I couldn't believe she lost us after all her promises.

"The courts say she's crazy, Jim. I took your mother to so many psychiatrists that you kids didn't even know about. They all said she was nuts and a nympho. The one doctor told me to grab you kids and get the hell out. He thought the whole bunch of them were nuts. Why do you think I left? I left to make sure you kids didn't end up living with her. I didn't want you all to grow up crazy like her. I begged your bitch grandmother for help. I told her that her daughter was fucked up in the head and I needed her help. She went crazy on me and told me that I was fucked up in the head. I knew after that, I had to get out."

"I know her. She's not crazy. You're just trying to tell us she is," I argued, trying to defend her.

My father's anger was peaking, with the volume of his voice increasing even louder. "Oh, really? That's why she had sex in front of Mitch in the car. Where do you think she was all the nights she wasn't home? She was out dancing in fucking strip clubs for free. Your mother was taking her clothes off and dancing naked. That's where she was, instead of being home with you kids. I hired a private detective to follow your mother. Do you know what he told me? Your wonderful mother had a boyfriend, who she hired to shoot me."

Mitch and I looked at each other in dismay. He was using his sarcastic tone as he spoke to us. "That's right. He was to be somewhere in the woods behind the cul-de-sac, waiting for me to come home from work. Then he was going to shoot me. I even had to get a gun from one of the warehouse guys who worked for your Papa Willie. Yeah, that's right. Love and protect your pig whore mother who is trying to have your father shot."

I couldn't believe what he was describing to us was true. My brother Mitch never saw this sex activity that he kept referring to and my father wasn't around at night either. I thought the detective thing sounded too far fetched. My mom never cared enough to even mention him in our presence. Now, we were supposed to believe that she would risk going to jail by hiring a boyfriend to shoot him. Nothing he said made any sense to me.

While lighting another cigarette, my father began explaining how he married Hamar and grandma was no longer living with us. Evidently, we were supposed to live harmoniously with Hamar and her two children, Shlomo and Samara. I was bewildered that my nightmare had actually come true. "When did this happen," I asked, lacking air to breathe after the news.

"Not long ago and it's a good thing. Hamar's a great woman. I love her and her kids. From now on, we'll be one big family." I was emotionally hurting inside with an inability to get a read on Mitch or Julie, since they were sitting like two stiffs. Neither of them said anything, probably because they were over tired from court all day. I was angry and whined, "Well, how come I can't see my mom and grandparents anymore?"

My father's patience was slowly eroding away from all my questions. "I already told you. Your mother is fucking nuts and your grandparents are too. I never want to hear you mention them again. Especially, your God damn mother. She's dead. Do you understand me? Dead! Hamar is your new mother and no one, under any circumstances, is to call her Hamar. Y'all will and I mean will, call her mom. Is that understood?" Before we could agree or disagree, he went on. "If I hear or find out that one of you didn't call her mom, there will be beatings. And I mean it. The word stepmother or stepbrother or step-anything will not be used in my house. For now on, this is your family and the others are dead to you."

I was too tired to argue anymore, so exhausted, I gave up. Grasping that I was flirting with a beating, I didn't want to continue.

It was late when we arrived at the townhouse. A few of the lights were on, but the place seemed lifeless. We were all so tired from the long day that we literally dragged ourselves into the house. Hamar was the first person we encountered when coming in, immediately warning us to be quiet. She looked unhappy as ever to see us. It was like a standoff between the three of us, seeing who was going to crack first and say hello. My father staggered in behind us, greeting her with a kiss while shooting us his famous evil look. We knew what that meant, so we followed his lead, kissing her on each cheek. Hamar repeated the same thing she did in Delaware, merely outstretching her face for everyone to anoint with kisses.

Hamar took control right away, curtly whispering in her best broken English, "You, go down to the basement and go to sleep." Then she motioned to Mitch and Julie, whispering, "You and you follow me. Be quiet."

While walking up the stairs, she impatiently waved her hand again, as if Mitch and Julie weren't moving fast enough for her. I stood watching, as they followed her up to their new bedroom. They ended up sharing a room together, giving the baby her own bedroom. My father and Hamar obviously occupied the master bedroom, which left the basement for me to share with Shlomo. I was curious to see what they did with the basement because before they moved in, we used it as a playroom. It had a bathroom, which saved us from running upstairs, but the floor was tiled and usually cold to walk on.

After getting down the stairs, I noticed the basement was furnished with two standard beds, divided by a large green hutch. My father snuck up behind me, as I was taking it all in. He smiled and whispered, "What do you think? It looks good, huh?"

Shlomo was sleeping, so I whispered back, "Sure. It looks nice."

Patting me on the back, he proudly said, "Ok, I'll see ya tomorrow." Turning around, I gave him a kiss goodnight. Then he disappeared, sauntering back up the stairs.

I had no luggage or toiletries, so after removing the clothes from my back, I fell into bed. While laying there and thinking about the various events that happened that day, I couldn't get my arms around the horrible fact that I would never see nor speak to my mom or grandparents again. Anger stirred in my stomach, with a sensation of acid percolating from the fury. I felt like a helpless trapped victim, who was tormented, having to call this stranger my mother. I thought long and hard over this devastating issue, telling myself, "I would try it for a little while, but if it didn't work, I wanted to go back to my mother." I figured that was how it worked. Even as scary as it sounded, I believed it was an option.

The next morning I was still tired from the day before. I could have slept the entire day, if it wasn't for the unruly screaming echoing from upstairs. Wiping my eyes, I looked over to see if my new roommate was still in bed, but he was gone. Hamar's voice was muffled but I could hear her screaming at someone about eating something. Gradually slithering out of bed, I felt groggy making my way upstairs. Hamar was badgering Mitch and Julie for eating all the cereal in the house. She had them plastered against the pantry, intimidating them with her nasty Arabic and Hebrew obscenities. "You stupid. You ate all our breakfast. What are we going to do for breakfast now? Stupid idiots." Mitch and Julie were dumbfounded. They nervously remained pinned against the pantry door, looking as if they had no idea what this woman was saying.

My father wandered down, looking disheveled, asking, "What's going on, Hamar?"

"Your kids ate all the cereal. Look at the floor. A mess everywhere. Like animals, those two. ANIMALS," she hollered.

Mitch and Julie timidly stood shaking with their mouths agape. None of us ever heard anyone scream like that over cereal before. Not fully awake, my father gazed at them, saying, "What happened kids?" Neither of them answered, acting as though their lips were glued together, so he asked again, "Mitch? What happened? Why is there cereal all over the floor?"

Mitch shrugged innocently, replying, "We were hungry, so me and Julie ate cereal." His hands were turned over as if to show he wasn't hiding anything in his palms.

Hamar interjected again, shouting, "You ate all the cereal. Look, it's on the floor. Stupid. Like animals. ANIMALS." Mitch and Julie were frightened and if they could have taken another step back, they surely would have.

My father was more serious now, roaring at them with an annoyed tone. "Ok Mitch and Julie, you two pick up the cereal from the floor and get up to your room. You know better than that." I didn't see much of anything on the floor, but they picked up whatever little bit there was, then gladly scurried up to their room.

Hamar was irritated, so my father rubbed her shoulders, tenderly saying, "See, everything's picked up now. Are you ok?"

He was babying her like Mitch and Julie permanently destroyed her kitchen by setting it on fire. The truth was, Hamar was more pissed off that they touched her kitchen without permission. We soon found out, that we were not allowed to eat or drink anything unless she gave her consent. Everything was Hamar's, a serious reality we had to learn. It didn't matter if my father worked and brought it home, everything was hers. If you were starving, you had to ask her for food, leaving it up to her discretion whether you ate or not. All Mitch and Julie did was eat some cereal, if that's all she had for breakfast, shame on her. It was loud noise to test my father. There was no way two little kids ate an entire box of cereal. I viewed it as my father's first test, giving him an opportunity to display his loyalty to her. Punishing his own children for bullshit, on her behalf, seemed loyal enough to me.

My father gently rubbed Hamar's shoulders as she angrily turned her face with a sourpuss expression on it. He reminded me of a little boy trying to make up for being naughty. The baby was oblivious to the fight, sitting in her highchair banging while Shlomo looked at his mother with deep empathy. I couldn't believe the big deal she was making over a box of cereal. My father didn't make matters much better, by allowing her to blow the situation out of proportion.

Hamar and her entire family were born in Morocco, later migrating to Israel. They spoke a combination of two languages, Arabic and Hebrew. It was a very foreign dialect to us with a heavy accent, making it even harder to comprehend. When communicating with us, she would blend English, Arabic and Hebrew all together, which made her extremely difficult to understand. Hamar hated when we repeatedly asked, "What" too many times. Shlomo was born in Israel, so he could clearly understand her, and the ranting Arabic and Hebrew obscenities. When they didn't want anyone to know what they were saying, Shlomo and Hamar communicated in their own language. They even did it in front of my father, irritating him terribly. He constantly shouted to them, "English. Speak English."

My father looked over at me, saying, "How did you sleep, Jim?"

Still frazzled by the commotion, I stammered, "Good. I guess."

Hearing that I was in the room, Shlomo quickly swiveled around on his barstool smiling at me. Hamar never looked up when I said, "Good morning." Shlomo returned the greeting, but Hamar never took her eyes off the bowls she was rinsing off in the sink. She was still frowning while my father had his hands gently on her shoulders.

"Are you hungry, Jim," my father questioned, with a little kick in his voice.

Focusing on him, I timidly answered, "Yeah, what do we have?"

Without raising her head from the sink, Hamar sarcastically squawked, "Nothing. Your brother and sister ate everything."

"Come on, Hamar. I can make some eggs. What about eggs, guys," he asked Shlomo and me with a nervous laugh.

Before I could reply, Hamar chimed in with an aggravated voice, demanding, "I'll do it. Get out of my kitchen." My father foolishly smiled, backing out in order to give her full run of the place.

The kitchen area was cutoff from the dining and living room by a partition with a counter. My father placed stools there, so we could eat instead of having to walk around the partition to get to the table.

My dad walked over, standing between Shlomo and me. "So guys, have you gotten a chance to get to know each other yet?"

We looked at one another, answering at the same time. "No."

"Well, you guys are going to be brothers now, so you need to get to know each other," he said, patting us firmly on our backs.

While my father was getting us acquainted, I heard a loud fart reverberate from the kitchen. Startled, I looked up seeing Shlomo giggling. Then suddenly a string of more farts followed, bellowing from the kitchen. I darted my attention there, as Hamar was working on breakfast without missing a beat. It was as if passing wind while cooking didn't constitute being offensive to her. My father pretended not to hear, but Shlomo and I chuckled knowing it was his mother.

As my father continued talking, I thought to myself how breakfast wasn't going to be appetizing with the smell of her gas circulating in the kitchen.

I never heard a grown woman fart before, so stunned, I took a closer look at Hamar. She still had that sour look stapled on her face, standing in the kitchen wearing a wrinkled nightgown. She didn't look like the same woman from the night before since her face looked different without all that caked-on makeup. Her hair wasn't as bouffant either, seeing how it was flattened and messed up from the bed. After noticing Hamar's striking appearance, her style of cooking was anything but neat. I watched as she sloppily cracked opened the eggs, getting fragments of shells into the mixing bowl. Then whatever spilled out from the egg, onto her fingers, she smeared off on the edge of the bowl. She let nothing go to waste. I prayed the eggs she was mixing were not going to be for me to eat.

When hearing laughter, I turned my attention back to my father, watching him give Shlomo another head rub with his rough knuckles. I was so focused on Hamar that I missed what they were laughing about. Then Hamar broke my concentration, gruffly shouting, "Come and get your breakfast."

As she abruptly dropped the dishes on the counter, we picked them up and went to the table to eat. I cautiously picked through my scrambled eggs for shells. When not finding any, I took a bite with my teeth immediately crunching down on shell fragments. I quickly spit it out, gulping down some milk to clean my palate. Feeling brave, I tried another bite of eggs and sure enough, bit into another eggshell. "I can't eat this," I said, walking my plate back to the counter.

My father peered at me oddly, saying, "What's wrong with it?"

Hamar was standing at attention in the kitchen while I turned, answering, "The eggs have shells in them. I can't eat this." I attempted saying it as nice as possible, but it didn't matter.

"Stupid. Like the eggs have shells in them. There's no shell. Stupid," Hamar spewed at me, trying to rectify the situation.

"Jim, the eggs are fine. Get your plate and sit down and finish. I want you to apologize to your mother."

Up to this point, I still hadn't referred to Hamar as, *mom*, simply not feeling the urge. I didn't feel comfortable calling her that on my first morning and above all, I had a mother. Partially giving in, I apologized but wasn't calling her mom or eating her eggs. "I'm sorry about the eggs, but I'm not hungry anymore," I pleasantly conveyed.

Hamar mumbled something I couldn't understand and my father, sensing she was upset, firmly said, "Either sit down and eat the eggs or get to your room. You have a choice. What's it going to be?" I could tell I was ruining his appetite, by the way he threw his fork down in frustration.

It didn't take long to figure out which option I was going with, as I faltered to the stairs. Before descending to my room, my father called out sounding irritated, "If you're going down, then you can stay there until lunch. Do you understand me?"

"Yes," I responded, making my way down to the basement. I tumbled into bed, feeling sick to my stomach from the food and confrontation. I rested there, hoping all her other meals weren't as bad as that breakfast.

Shlomo came down shortly after breakfast and we sat around getting to know each other. While exchanging our interesting war stories about how we came to be in Rolling, he seemed to be a nice enough kid. Apparently, Shlomo's father was slapping Hamar around, which provoked her to divorce him. He explained how terrible it was to watch his father leave, but couldn't stand to see his mother beaten any longer. Shlomo was obviously depressed talking about his parents, quickly changing the subject to football. He shared with me how he was a big Miami Dolphins fan, as a large smile broke across his lips. He also mentioned that the Dolphins were his father's favorite team too, since he won money every time he bet on them. I didn't know much about that team, being an avid Redskins fan, but he could name all the players and their jersey numbers. After getting acquainted, I felt like we connected. It was nice to have someone else around to assimilate with, besides Mitch and Julie. I also sensed that I could trust him after that day, which proved to be a serious mistake.

School was already in session, so I had missed almost the entire first half. My father registered me to repeat second grade, which was like somebody hitting me in the stomach with a sledgehammer. He was extremely adamant about me passing and let me know it. "I'm going to tell you, Jim. You better pass this time. There is no third try. I spent plenty of time and money, getting you extra help. If you don't know something, you better damn well ask the teacher. Don't come home asking me how to do your homework, because I'm not doing it. I'm not going to be embarrassed again. Do you want to be a moron and be in the same grade as your little brother, Mitch?"

He strongly hit home with that one, as I stuttered, "No. I'm really going to do good, I promise. You'll see." I meant it too. There was no way I was going to end up in the same grade as Mitch. For the first time in my life, I met my competitive side and was confident that there was no way I was going to fail. I didn't need threats of being beaten to be motivated. I knew I was doing this for me and my self-respect, eliminating the term "*failure*" entirely out of my vocabulary that day.

School was different when I returned. I anticipated being teased in the hallways for failing second grade but it never happened. It was strange, as if I grew another face with nobody recognizing me anymore. A tremendous relief circulated through my body, giving me the confidence to concentrate in school and progress with the other students. I even had a new teacher who really cared, giving me a little extra help in class. I assumed she must have known I was held back, to help the way she did.

Mornings in the townhouse were full of drama and chaos. I sensed Hamar's frustration, having to take care of five children instead of only two. She was miserable in the mornings, finding it best to keep my distance. Hamar enjoyed picking on everything and anyone who she came into contact with for some reason. One morning, Mitch came down with his hair looking like a ragged old mop. It was a bad case of bed head and Hamar was anything but gentle when speaking to him. "Mitch! Your hair looks like shit. Get back upstairs and brush it." Then she started mumbling under her breath, "Stupid. Coming down here, looking like shit. Idiot."

I wasn't accustomed to that kind of talk, at least not yet and neither was Mitch. Our mother and grandparents never spoke using nasty words like that to us. We didn't have carpeting on our stairs, so being enraged, Mitch turned around stomping up the stairs as loud as he could, each step of the way. She irritably yelled up, "Stop that kicking. Do you hear me?" But he didn't care, continuing down the same exact way. Hamar was livid when he didn't heed to her request, cruelly bawling Mitch out when he returned.

Mitch didn't say much, which in retrospect was a good thing. It meant fewer beatings, but he sure showed his temper when angry. Once when my father's mother was staying with us, I remember she sent him to his room for talking back and he furiously kicked a hole through his bedroom door. It was unbelievable how this little five year old kid had the strength to do that, which my grandmother talked about forever. I think my father was so shocked that he actually let him off the hook without punishing him.

Shlomo decided to antagonize Mitch that morning by imitating his hairstyle throughout breakfast. He was picking up a few strands of his own hair, pretending to give himself bed head. Mitch wasn't finding it funny, as I could see he was getting irritated. He didn't retaliate, but on our walk to the bus stop, he kicked every curb we approached. That was the way Mitch expressed aggression, by kicking things. He had kicked so many curbs and other hard objects that the fronts of his shoes were completely flattened. In fact, a portion of the sole had become exposed, acting as the toe area on his shoe. Mitch, like me, was taking this change of lifestyle very hard, since it was devastating not having a parent to confide in for comfort.

CHAPTER 17

One day after school, I was playing around in the family room when knocking over one of Hamar's candlesticks by accident. Feeling badly about it, I picked up the broken pieces to admit my crime to her. She was upstairs at the time, doing something when I casually called up to her. I still wasn't calling her mom yet, using any other vernacular to address her. "Excuse me," I called up, but she didn't hear me the first time. Then I tried again. "Excuse me. I broke your candlestick by accident. Can you hear me?"

Then she came to the foot of the stairs, as my voice reverberated off the stairwell walls and stared down at me. I could not see her face since it was hidden by the darkness in the hallway, but I held up the broken candlestick to show her anyway. "Sorry," I said in a humbled voice. "But by accident, I hit it and it fell on the floor. I…" Prior to finishing my sentence, a shoe struck me square in the stomach and I dropped the candlestick for a second time.

I froze at first, seeing how it knocked the wind out of me and fell to my knees. Surprised that she threw a shoe at me, I didn't know whether to heave it back or run for the hills. Then hearing footsteps rapidly pounding down the stairs, I glanced up seeing Hamar. She was enraged, hollering, "You stupid idiot. Where's my shoe?"

While looking for it, she screamed a number of foreign obscenities at me. When Hamar found her shoe, which was a hardwood wedge slip on, she started beating the hell out of me with it. She was like a deranged wild monkey, jumping up and down. Every time she came down, so did that shoe on my back and legs. I was lying on my stomach with my both hands and arms defending my head. The beating was terribly painful as she was striking me with her shoe, doing everything humanly possible not to get hit in my head. I couldn't move or get up to run away, feeling completely disoriented. Eventually, she grew tired of the shoe and jumped on my back, pulling out my hair through my defense. Then she started banging my head against the floor like a fierce animal trying to open a coconut. My brain felt like it was rattling around in my head with every slam to the floor. While this was going on, she repeatedly screamed, "You piece of shit. You stupid idiot. You broke my candle. IDIOT!" Then she switched languages, hollering in Arabic or Hebrew at me again. I couldn't interpret what she was yelling but it sounded nasty. Finally, she got off of me. I remained laying there covering up, waiting for another attack when she screamed, "Get out of here. Get! You stupid idiot."

I slowly stumbled to my feet, attempting to make my way down the basement stairs. My equilibrium was way off as my head pounded as though someone had thrown me down a flight of concrete steps. I was livid and in disbelief that she thought she had the right to beat me. Feeling violated and humiliated, I wanted to mouth off but wisely knew better than to scream at her. So I did what I thought was the only thing I could do. Managing to turn around with clinched fists, I gave her the dirtiest glare I could conjure up. It doesn't sound like much but I was surprised at the response I received from such a well done glare. It worked almost as good as if I hollered back. She stood there breathing heavily, with strands of my hair still in between her fingers, staring at me. Then slowly puffed out, "You're going to look at me like that. You piece of shit. Get out of my sight. You piece of shit. You should drop dead."

Then she began with that Arabic cursing crap of hers. Screaming and cursing even when I was downstairs in the basement. I could hear her through the basement ceiling, hollering for a good five to ten minutes more, while I sat on my bed trying to collect myself.

Shortly after I went down to the basement, Shlomo appeared. He had been upstairs during that vile commotion, checking to see if I was ok. Sitting on my bed fuming, I gave him an earful, but quietly, so Hamar wouldn't hear. "I'm done man. Your mother has no right to hit me. I'm going to tell my father that I want to go back to my real mother and live with her. I'm also going to tell him how your mom beat me with a shoe. She's not my mother to beat me and curse at me. I don't even know what the hell she's saying and her food sucks too."

Shlomo simply sat straight faced, allowing his ears to swallow all my deep rooted complaints. He never said a word, appearing to be listening as if he were genuinely concerned. During my discussion with him, I heard Hamar on the telephone harshly yelling to someone in her foreign language. I was confident it was about me. But not caring what she said, I told Shlomo when my dad came back I was leaving.

The unique thing about this turn of events was Hamar giving me the cold shoulder. I was the one who was beaten, having his hair pulled out and she was giving *me* the silent treatment. It didn't bother me in the slightest, but I couldn't wait for my father to get back into town. He was out on the road selling and on the way back, he was going to Delaware to pick up Hamar's parents. They were the ancient couple we had to call mama and papa at our first meeting. Hamar had shared an apartment with them in Delaware, which made her even closer with her parents. In fact, she was extremely close with all her sisters as well, but not particularly as close with her two brothers. It felt like every week a relative of hers was coming up for a weekend visit.

A few days later, my father returned home with mama and papa. I hadn't spoken with Hamar since the day of my beating, which was fine with me. I was certain my father had conversed with her, regarding our confrontation during his trip away. But I was going to give him my version, letting him know what she did to me. Hamar had the table fixed up extra nice that night. It was Friday, so that meant it was Shabbat and on that night we did a prayer over the wine and bread. Hamar's father was ultra religious, so she wanted to make sure everything looked special for him and her mother. When my father arrived, he came in the house behind Hamar's parents, hauling in their luggage. Hamar answered the door, being the first to greet everyone. They exchanged greetings in their language, kissing one another on each cheek. Her demeanor immediately changed once her parents were there. It was a complete personality overhaul as she turned into this person I had never met before. Shlomo instantly darted over, warmly hugging and kissing his grandparents. Then he spoke a few words to them in Hebrew or Arabic with some jovial laughter as they pushed down the hallway. Mitch, Julie and I had only met them once, but followed the same routine from our first meeting, saying hello with kisses, even though we were uncomfortable with it. The only thing on my mind was speaking with my father, since I was burning inside with anxiety. He was the last through the foyer hallway and when he glared at me, I instantly knew something was terribly wrong. He went from a cheery fun loving guy to a nasty looking maniac when our eyes met.

My father walked up to me, saying under his breath, "I'll be with you in a minute." He looked perturbed, but I just thought he got the story wrong from Hamar, something I would easily fix. After all I just broke a candlestick, which was nothing compared to the vicious beating his wife gave to me. Everyone was jabbering away as my father was running around with a cigarette dangling from his mouth, asking if anyone wanted a cocktail. He reverted back to that cheery fun loving guy, still looking like he was trying to win Hamar's parents over by all his ass-kissing. Hamar's father accepted a drink, so my father poured one for him and himself. Hamar's mother declined her drink, seeing how she was busy in the kitchen helping out. My father quickly slammed his cocktail down his throat, excusing himself. I was over by the TV with Mitch when he called me over.

Standing by the stairs in the foyer, my father grabbed my arm tightly when I approached, saying, "Let's fucking go, big mouth." He roughly yanked me up the stairs by my arm, swinging me into the bedroom while slamming the door shut. "What the fuck am I hearing? You told my wife's son that you're moving back with your fucking whore mother." Then *WHAP*! He slapped me across my face so hard that I hit the ground falling on my back, as he jumped on top of me. Both of his knees pinned down my arms as he yelled directly in my face, "You're going to tell my wife's son that shit." A slap to my face followed every word he screamed with precise rhythm. "Who the fuck do you think you are? I took you away from that fucking whore bitch and this is the thanks I get."

Then he picked me up like a rag doll, literally throwing me from one end of the bedroom to the next. I was brutally banging into the walls head first, feeling like a pinball stuck between two bumpers. As he continued throwing me in a fit of rage, he hollered, "This is the thanks I get. Do you hear me? You'll never talk that shit again." He began heavily coughing, getting raspy with every word he yelled.

I was shaking and crying as he was tossing me around and began pleading, "Ok. Ok. Stop. Please stop. I won't do it again."

That did nothing more than entice him to beat me even worse and while this went on, not one person came to my rescue. The combination of my body slamming into the walls and his screaming must have made a horrendous amount of noise. I was praying that someone would hear and pull this wild man off of me, but no one ever came. Then he grabbed me by the front of my shirt, with his breath reeking of vodka, shouting in my face, "If I ever fucking hear that you talked about my wife or going back to your mother again, I'll kill you. Do you fucking understand me? That fucking whore mother should die." I was painfully pinned against the wall by his hand that had my shirt and throat. His breathing drastically changed to huffing and puffing, as I sensed the beating was coming to an end.

"Yes, I understand." I managed to cry out, through what air I could exhale from my windpipe.

"I'm not fucking with you, Jim." He was looking me dead in the eyes while coughing. "You fucking pull this shit with me again and there won't be a next time, buddy boy. Now take your ass downstairs and you fucking apologize to your mother and your brother, Shlomo. And for your information, that is your mother whether you like it or not. You will call her mom and she has my permission to punish you anyway she wants." He still had a hold of my shirt and throat, when brutally throwing me towards the door, barking, "Now get your fucking ass downstairs."

My knees were knocking and I was quivering so badly that I couldn't calm myself down. The last thing I wanted to do was apologize to Hamar and her son, who dragged me into this situation in the first place. Everything I said was the truth, whether my father agreed or not, she had no business hitting me. I discovered the painful way that Shlomo was a damn snake, realizing now who I was dealing with the next time I wanted to speak out loud. Hobbling down the stairs like an amputee, I didn't know how I was going to face these people looking the way I did. It was humiliating having those strangers hear all that crying and screaming going on upstairs. Now my father had me marching in after all that chaos, so they could see me in this pathetic state. I noticed my face had a stinging sensation, imagining it looked as red as a baboon's ass. Limping into the dining room, I was hyperventilating while everyone was sitting around the table waiting on us. It was dreadfully quiet and I could smell the tension circulating in the air. Reluctantly, I went over to Hamar, who didn't even acknowledge me, squeezing a "*sorry*" out of my diaphragm. She simply looked straight ahead as if I didn't exist, not saying a word. "*Bitch*," is what I thought to myself. Then Shlomo was next, shaking my hand while smiling, as if he had no part in my horrible attack. "*Asshole*," is what came to mind after shaking his hand.

When finished apologizing, I hurriedly attempted to hobble back to my bedroom, but my father walked in after cleaning up, shouting, "Where are you going?"

Hunched over holding my stomach, I shyly said, "Down to my room. I don't feel so good."

"No. No. Sit down. It's Shabbat. You can go downstairs after dinner." I stumbled back to the table taking my seat, but didn't say a word throughout dinner. I was infuriated, thinking how the hell could I get away from this nightmare.

After that night, I began harshly resenting my mother and grandparents since I couldn't fathom how they allowed us to end up where we were. This was like purgatory with no door out and no one with any sense of compassion to help. In the midst of all my mother's promises, we still ended up here and I was frustrated that I couldn't speak with her or my grandparents. I was drenched with bitterness, feeling like they weren't trying hard enough. But deep down I knew, even if they tried to call, they would have never gotten through.

My father was busy doing his best to manipulate us into accepting his new found family. Unfortunately, my mom and grandparents were becoming a faint dream due to the threats and abuse we were taking from my father and his nasty wife. I still had hope, but it was progressively eroding away. In the meantime, I told myself that I would go along to get along, which became my motto. Living by that motto was what got me through all my crazy years living with these people. I put my game face on, masking myself like one of them, but deep in my heart always longing to get away. Playing their bullshit game was used solely to get by, so I could live in peace. I knew keeping my mouth shut and assimilating was the only way to achieve that.

After that brutal beating, I finally caved in, referring to Hamar as mom. I never used the term stepmother, stepbrother or step anything again and neither did Mitch or Julie. None of us wanted to experience another beating like the one I endured, so we called them anything they wanted to be called. Mitch and I spoke every so often about how much we missed our mother and grandparents, but never in front of anyone else. Especially, not in front of Shlomo. If I had to refer to my real mother, I used the term "the other mother", which caught on, giving Mitch and Julie a way to refer to her as well. We were forbidden to speak or even mention her or our grandparents, so that term for our mother was only for rare occasions. It's hard to describe the severity of using the phrase "my real mother", since we were supposed to believe that she never existed. That phrase was worse than walking up to my father and calling him a motherfucker to his face. I can't describe the seriousness of our reference towards our mother any better, other than saying it was a death sentence.

Since our father married Hamar, Mitch and I never went to anymore double features, or special events for that matter. All that fun stuff just melted in our memories, leaving our weekends to either playing around in the backyard or wandering the community. That was only when we didn't have to push Hamar's baby around in her stroller. She loved forcing us to take turns strolling Samara around the parking lot, allotting her time to do whatever it was she did. It was a big pet peeve of ours with none of us wanting to do it. I didn't know what Hamar and my father were doing, but it left little time for us to spend with him, since the strolling would last a majority of the afternoon. Hamar demanded all our father's attention, only sacrificing it if he was doing something with her children. I can't remember him playing ball or any type of activities with us. Hamar made it very apparent that she was making an effort to push us away. I knew she didn't want us living with them and in her perfect world, it would be just her and her two children. She declared on many occasions how she never wanted us, professing my father lied, telling her that he would never win custody. Hamar went as far as saying, if my father hadn't tricked her, she wouldn't have married him knowing we were part of the package. The only bonus about us being there was Shlomo had me as a play pal.

This was the sort of crap she confronted us with and my father condoned it, never correcting her. He was present many of the times she expressed her true feelings towards us, never making a comment on our behalf. Still, we were coerced into calling her mom, showing Hamar the outmost respect. It was enough frustration to make me want to pull the hair out of my head, failing to find the sense in it all. The hopeless situation was a one way street where we were getting bulldozed over by it.

Saturday night was the pinnacle of the week for Hamar and my father. They went out every Saturday night without ever missing a beat. They wouldn't dream of getting a babysitter either, with Hamar having so much confidence in Shlomo that she left him in charge. I was his assistant, but ultimately he was the boss. He was around nine years old at the time, being left in charge of a baby, Julie who was four and Mitch who was six. I loved that they left us alone so we could stay up late or at least until they came home. Before Hamar and my father went out, everyone was put to bed, relieving us from the burden of having to do it. This was about the time Mitch and I started drifting apart since my bedtime was the same as Shlomo's. I felt bad for him, thinking they should have made room for Mitch to bunk with us in the basement, instead of rooming him with Julie.

While our parents were out, Shlomo and I watched movies and snacked on whatever wasn't frozen. Hamar had this sneaky habit of freezing everything, so we couldn't eat it. The most fascinating thing was watching Shlomo pawing through the pantry and refrigerator, pulling out food and devouring it. I knew I was safe to eat the food as long as Shlomo opened it. He never knew what it was like not to be able to freely go to the pantry, getting something to eat. It blew my mind when watching him nonchalantly scrounge through their special stash too. Hamar hid food, which only my father and she were privy to eat. It consisted of goodies like roasted peanuts, M&Ms and Pepperidge Farm milano cookies. Whenever Shlomo dug into their stash, I stood waiting like a squirrel for him to toss me a nut. I knew there would never be any repercussions as long as he was the one passing out the goodies. When Hamar asked why I ate something, I simply responded that Shlomo gave it to me. He never caught the slightest bit of crap for eating anything, one of the perks that came with hanging out with him.

CHAPTER 18

Hamar made it clearly evident how much she despised Julie early on. It started when she was attempting to break Julie's masturbating habit. My father had given her full reign over the situation as she sadistically broke Julie out of the habit with repeated physical violence. Hamar was the one who woke us in the mornings and if she found Julie with her hands down her underwear, she would beat her relentlessly. The beatings went on day after day. Her tormented cries were heard so often that we were conditioned to think nothing of it. My father knowingly permitted Hamar to persistently batter his daughter, seeing nothing wrong with it. Mitch and I stayed away, minding our own business. They had us believing that Julie needed this abusive training in order to stop touching herself.

The violence was horrifying, hearing Hamar's infuriated screams as sounds of thunderous banging echoed from upstairs. Julie pleaded with her to stop, crying out for my father. "Addy, addy. Help!" She was so hysterical that she couldn't even put the D in front of daddy. The hairs on my back stood erect from her frightening screams, as I was sick that there was nothing I could do to help her. Afraid of being beaten as well, I emotionally vanished from the situation.

When Julie finally stopped touching herself, my father was proud of the fact that Hamar had cured her from this so-called affliction. He didn't care how she achieved breaking Julie's habit, opening the door for Hamar to mentally and physically torture Julie for years to come. I remember my father telling close friends and relatives how great and caring she was for helping Julie with her problem. I still get ill when thinking about the way Hamar beat the crap out of Julie to get her to stop touching herself.   With my father endorsing that kind of behavior, Hamar's abuse towards Julie became more frequent. She didn't like any of us from day one, but it was clear that she particularly detested Julie the most. I don't know if it was because she looked like my mother or Julie was the easiest to abuse since being too young to express herself.

Hamar was a stressed out ruthless person behind closed doors with anything setting her off. She screamed about the most insignificant things, going into these raging screaming fits, where she would keep repeating herself over and over again. Whatever aggravated her was normally taken out on Julie since Hamar pinned her as the family scapegoat. I remember coming home one day after doing errands with my father, finding Julie lying on the living room floor crying her eyes out. Her appearance portrayed a victim who just got sucked through a wind tunnel. Her hair was disheveled, as though a beautician teased it without putting it back in place, while her clothes were tattered like she was mauled by a ferocious carnivore. My father came in playing stupid. "What happened, Hamar?"

She was all worked up with a livid tension about her, screaming, "Your pig daughter tried to ride Samara like a horse."

My father didn't like Hamar using the term pig, so protesting he said, "Hamar, I told you I don't like you calling her a pig."

"Fuck you! I don't care what you like. Big shot. Like you're going to tell me what to say. Stupid. Your pig daughter was riding my daughter like a horse. What are you going to do about it? I'm sick and tired of taking care of your wild animal kids."

"I told you to stop using that word." Then looking at Julie, who was hysterical, my father asked, "Were you riding your little sister?"

Julie could barely speak from all her trembling, crying out, "No. I was just playing with the baby."

Instantly, my father discounted her response, sternly yelling, "I don't believe you. Get up to your room."

"I told you. I didn't want your animal kids and you came home with them anyways. You're a fucking liar." Having no respect for her husband, Hamar spoke without any reservations.

"Hey. Hey. Watch your mouth. I sent her up to her room. What else do you want? You already hit her."

Still livid, Hamar screeched out, "Fuck you! Idiot. I hit her? Of course I hit that pig. She's a pig to be riding my daughter. She could've broken my baby's back. You stupid." She picked up Samara, marching into the kitchen.

I was hopeful that maybe this would be goodbye for Hamar and her children. My father had a violent temper and I couldn't imagine he was going to allow her to speak to him in such a manner. I pictured him giving Hamar her walking papers, sending her and her two children packing back to Delaware. A little tune went off in my head as I sang to myself, "Ding dong the witch is gone. The wicked witch. The wicked witch. Ding dong the wicked witch is gone." Unfortunately, that's not what happened.

Hamar was on a wild rampage after their confrontation. Leaving me in disbelief that my father didn't physically pick this woman up, throwing her out on her ass. She became aggressively spiteful and rigid towards everyone in the house. My father was punished with the silent treatment, which I considered more like a blessing than a punishment. He continued to sweetly kiss her ass, while she treated him like complete garbage. But after a good amount of kissing up, she finally forgave him. Even when doing so, she was looking for any excuse to jump down our throats.

Mitch had made friends with a kid named Rudy, who lived next door to us. The kid's mother took notice one day, while looking out the window, that Mitch and Julie had climbed into a trash dumpster. She was appalled when seeing them feasting on other people's trash, provoking her to phone Hamar. These big dumpsters were located in the front of the town homes for everyone to see, which mortified Hamar with embarrassment. How could she explain two of her children eating other people's trash, other than the truth. It would have been difficult for her to admit, how we weren't allowed to touch or eat anything without her permission.

I watched her open the front door, screaming as Mitch and Julie were jumping in the scattered trash. "You two...! Get in the house." Mitch and Julie's heads instantly snapped to attention when spotting

Hamar standing at the door with her eyes fixed on them. I could read exactly what was going through their minds, grateful it wasn't me in their predicament. Abruptly, she waved them into the house with frustration scribbled upon her face. They somberly sauntered to the townhouse as I heard her voice from across the street when they entered their doom.

After all the action was done, I came home later finding Hamar hammering away at my father. She was cursing in English and Arabic. It appeared like she was working on him to either get rid of us or kill us. He never defended us against Hamar's bitching and squawking, but always taking her complaints to heart. Then to keep her complacent, he did his own punishing in addition to hers, to make himself look like the good supportive husband.

Mitch and Julie were in their bedroom weeping when my father went up for an explanation. In between their sobbing, Mitch did most of the squealing and complaining concerning how hungry they were. He told my father that Hamar never let them eat when they were hungry, describing how she hid all the food. My father intently listened to everything they had to say, but in no way confronted Hamar about it. She actually had to ask why they were eating out of the trash, given that he never offered an explanation after speaking with them. Then he told Hamar how they were hungry because she wouldn't give them any food. I could hear the tension in his voice as it choked his vocal chords.

"Give them food? You stupid, like I don't give them food. Idiot! Your children are animals. And that little bitch, Julie, is a pig too. Her and Mitch sneaking around stealing food all the time. They're like animals, always hungry. Hungry. Food food food that's all they can think about."

"Come on, already. What's with the pig? I told you I hate that word," my father barked back.

"Sheldon, don't put your nose in this. Do you understand me," she shrieked, as my father back peddled. "Keep your nose out of my business. I run this house, not you. One more thing from you and I'll throw this fork at your face." Her face wrinkled with frustration and hatred, as she held up a rinsed fork.

"Well, they said they were hungry. That's all, Hamar. I don't want this to be a big fight."

"Who's making it a big fight, stupid? Like I'm making it a big fight. Idiot. Just get out. Get lost already. You and your wild animal children."

She hit my father with an arsenal of nasty obscenities, while he walked away getting himself a cocktail. The ranting and raging would get ridiculously repetitive, as Hamar could carry on for hours like a lunatic. She knew damn well that she was keeping the food from them and so did my father. She had this faint expression of guilt when she was wrong, which was quite obvious at the time. If truly convinced that she was in the right, Hamar would have sent my father up for another round of beatings for Mitch and Julie.

We were so brainwashed that our judgment was tainted by Hamar's actions and cruel behavior towards Julie. Our mother seemed to have forgotten about us, so Mitch and I were becoming resentful. I felt myself hardening inside, hardly remembering my happiness when I was with my mother. It's hard to explain, but Hamar positioned Julie as a punching bag for our mother's shortfalls. She referred to Julie's actions and persona as being crazy and stupid like our mother's, so we started picking on her. Not right away, but eventually. My father and Hamar constantly pounded in our young minds that our mother was a whore and crazy. After a while, it began to stick because we were trying to find comfort in this new home since our hopes of being with our mother were slowly dwindling away.

School was going well and the one thing Hamar did to help was make sure we all read for an hour each night. I became a ferocious reader, primarily reading biographies on different football players. Whether it was to keep us out of her hair or not, I really enjoyed reading as it enriched my performance at school. My report cards exceedingly improved, with there being a hallowing light at the end of the tunnel. I was fairly confident of passing the second grade, redeeming myself so I wouldn't have to share a classroom with my younger brother. I felt a sense of accomplishment by my hard work. It was a therapeutic stepping stone in my life, providing me with a shred of self-confidence to get by this bullshit with Hamar and her children.

CHAPTER 19

Shabbat dinners were a big deal in our house and my father rarely missed them since Hamar considered herself an Orthodox Jew. Her parents were truly Orthodox, keeping kosher in their home as well as out of the home. They didn't drive on Shabbat or any other Jewish holidays, so I should simply say they followed very strict rules for being Jewish. Hamar was nothing like her parents, but still considered herself just as religious. For example, if you're kosher that means you don't eat shellfish, pork and mix milk with meat when consuming a meal. Those parameters stand in Jewish law whether you eat in your house or out. Meanwhile, this woman was out feasting on shrimp, lobster and barbequed ribs at a variety of restaurants. On many occasions, Hamar brought this food into our house, justifying it because she ate it off of paper plates. I didn't mind that she cheated, seeing how I grew up eating these kinds of foods and would have hated giving them up. What was interesting was the way Hamar ridiculed and judged other Jewish people for not following the religion as closely as she thought she did.

On Shabbat we sat down as a family to eat, after Hamar would begin the evening by lighting the Shabbat candles. My father commenced dinner by chanting a prayer over the wine, followed with a prayer for the bread. It was serious business in our house, with no one being permitted to speak during the prayers. Afterwards, we were allowed to talk which grew loud with four children and a crying baby. Hamar's cooking was still not my style, given she was Moroccan using an assortment of wacky spices which didn't agree

163

with my palate. Frequently, she made these Moroccan hamburgers, dousing them with a dreadful spice that made me gag. I practically vomited at the dinner table while attempting to eat her burgers. There were also moments when I uncontrollably dry heaved in the toilet from the foul taste. I begged for something else to eat, but we were forced to finish what was on our plate, whether liking it or not. Eventually, I had an idea of storing a few bites in my cheeks like a chipmunk, then running downstairs to spit it out in my toilet. With Mitch catching on, we scuttled to the bathroom so often, that Hamar prohibited us from going during dinnertime. Once that rule was implemented, I started stuffing my napkin to get rid of the evidence. There was no chance in hell I was going to swallow that Moroccan hamburger.

My father always had a vodka or two before dinner, influencing him to ask goofy questions once in a while. One evening he was feeling extra lovey towards Hamar, explaining why he loved her so much. She proudly sat next to him looking so pleased and flattered by his comments that she smiled, which was a true rarity. Then my father circled around the table, asking each of us to describe what kind of girl or guy we wanted to marry and why. He started with Shlomo who of course said he would like a woman just like his mother. Mitch was still upset about the beating for eating the trash, so he remained silent. Then the question was presented to me, as my father appearing cheerful from the booze, said, "Well Jim, how about you? What kind of girl would you like to marry?"

Hamar sat by his side, portraying a look of confidence on her face with her nose propped high in the air. Coming out of a deep moment of thought, I gave a slight smile, saying, "I'd like to marry a girl who is American for one. Also, she has to be pretty. Oh yeah, and she has to be a good cook." That was as honest as an answer I could have given, without it ever occurring to me that my response would invoke an all out fight.

Hamar's confident look shattered as if I threw a stone at her face, with her nose taking an immediate dive. Steam began emanating from her ears, hollering to my father, "Sheldon! Did you hear what your son said?"

My father was engaging Julie, just about to ask her the same question when he sluggishly said, "What? What did he say?"

"You stupid potato. Asshole! He said a girl that was American, so that means not Moroccan like me. Like Moroccan is a bad thing to be. You idiot." My father still looked stumped as Hamar was doing her best to open his eyes.

"Then he said a girl who is pretty. Like I'm not pretty." Then my father caught on while she pushed his shoulder, shrieking, "Do something shmuck. He insulted me, you idiot."

He quickly switched expressions, putting on a perturbed look. "You stupid shit," he shouted, smacking me across the face. "Get up and apologize to your mother and then get your fucking ass downstairs."

The powerful slap stunned me, with the stinging pain only increasing my hatred for Hamar. I honestly didn't think my answer was going to upset everyone. It wasn't meant to be a malicious comment, but it was funny how I unknowingly put together that witty insult. After apologizing and returning to the basement, I felt invigorated. The slap was well worth my innocent remark, finding it rewarding to my soul.

School finally came to an end, as I passed the second grade with flying colors. It also spurred some big news from my father and Hamar, announcing that we were moving back to Delaware. My father and Uncle Stewart decided to go into business together, with plans on opening a lighting store in Red Hill. I recall how well my father said he was doing with his current company, so I was surprised to hear we were leaving Rolling. But I was elated to get back to Delaware, seeing that Rolling didn't agree with me. During the course of our transition, we went back and forth to Delaware searching for a place to live and a viable location for the new store. We stayed over at relatives when visiting, remembering Hamar rarely getting along with Uncle Stewart.

I loved Uncle Stewart, but he could be a tough cookie at times. He was in the marines as a young man which made him a bit of a hard-ass, but overall he was a great father and uncle. Aunt Carly was a sweetheart as well as a good all around lady, making them a great pair. They were simple people living within their means and like most parents, took great pride in nurturing their children.

Hamar came off as the complete opposite. She lived vicariously through her sister, who married a wealthy attorney, portraying herself wealthy by association. When my father met her, she was a simple beautician without two cents to rub together. She lived with her parents driving a sixties VW Bug, but spoke as if she were a wealthy socialite. Fooling no one, Hamar lacked tact when speaking, spewing anything that came to mind without any discretion. She would tell someone, whom she just met, how awful they looked wearing glasses, then outwardly advising them not to wear them anymore. That was a brilliant comment made to my current mother-in-law.

Openly, Hamar hated fat people, boasting how they disgusted her. If a large person happened to be seated close to her in a restaurant, all hell would break loose. She ruthlessly made wicked comments loud enough for them to hear what she thought of their appearance. Continuously, she made comments like, "Look at that pig. How could they think they should eat that? I'm disgusted. Pig. Ooh, what a pig."

I wanted to disappear whenever she ran her mouth like that. It was terribly uncomfortable to be around, as she embarrassed everyone sitting with her. My father would usually tell her to be quiet from being humiliated, but she responded with cruel insults. "Just shut up, stupid, big nose, fool." He would back down, not to make a scene since there was no shutting her up. Hamar knew everything about everything, putting herself well above everyone else by her own estimations.

During one of the times we were in town, Uncle Stewart and Aunt Carly invited us over for a barbeque. My uncle and Hamar never actually got along, forever butting heads. Out of all my relatives, he was the only one who had the moxie to put her in her place, which was most gratifying to see. When we arrived, I was extremely excited to see Jeff and Dan, since living in Rolling didn't give us much of an opportunity to see one other. While Shlomo was around, Jeff began inquiring how things were going with my new family, but I couldn't be as candid as I would have. Through the years, Jeff and I were very close, with him being a strong support system for me. He knew just about everything that went on in my life, which encouraged his disappointed with Hamar's unacceptable behavior.

Aunt Carly and I spoke for a little when we were alone. She was interested in how I was adjusting to Hamar and her children. I didn't want to divulge too much, in fear of it getting back to either Hamar or my father. The only thing I did admit was liking her cooking far better than Hamar's, especially her hamburgers. Explaining how Hamar's burgers were so rancid that I couldn't stand eating them. It seemed like an innocent enough conversation but later proved to be disastrous one for me.

Soon after dinner, Hamar and Uncle Stewart got into a tiff. I didn't hear the conversation, but while playing around with my cousins in the family room, I heard Hamar screech, "Let's go, Sheldon. I've had enough."

My uncle taunted her, saying, "Come on Hamar, you're miss know-it-all. You know everything. Stay Hamar."

She stood up infuriated, glaring at my father shouting, "Let's go, Sheldon. I mean, now."

Slowly scooting his chair back, my father peered into the family room, barking, "Shlomo, Jim, everyone get up we're leaving."

"Oh, come on Hamar, you're right. Ok Hamar, you're right. You're always right." Uncle Stewart wasn't going to eat her bullshit like everyone else did, not letting up. Hamar ignored his sly mocking as my father was silent, short of coming to her rescue. I had a distinct feeling that he was in for a battle once we were in the car.

Hamar angrily stomped out before any of us, without saying goodbye to a single person. Looking frazzled, my father called out, "Ok kids, let's go. Your mother's in the car." While saying our good-byes, we were quickly shoved out by our father.

When my dad climbed into the car, it was as if he entered hell. Hamar furiously unloaded on him, skillfully using every curse word she knew in English, Arabic and Hebrew. "You potato. You let your brother make a fool of me. You piece of shit, asshole. You're finished for me. You'll see. Letting your big shot brother talk to me like I'm shit." I slumped into my seat, biting my fingernails while thankful it wasn't me on the receiving end.

"What are you talking crazy for? 'I'm finished.' What does that mean?"

Hamar's voice went from loud to a shrilling scream. "Just shout your mouth. Do you hear me? All of sudden you're going to answer me. Where was your fucking mouth when your brother was insulting me? Stupid idiot."

She was leaning in my father's direction, ranting to herself as he was driving. "Stupid idiot. Opening a big mouth to me. All of a sudden he can speak. Idiot!"

"Watch your fucking mouth already. Every word out of it is nasty. I'm God damn tired of your mouth." Hamar hastened his temper, but she didn't care, repeatedly provoking him with more insulting names.

"You're getting tired of my mouth. Fuck you and your brother. You just sat there like a big shmuck, letting your brother talk to me like that. What, do you think you're going to scare me? I've had it with your brother's big mouth. He knows everything. Right? Wait til we get home, you idiot. I'll show you."

"Oh, don't threaten me, Hamar. Ok?" My father calmly answered, still trying to be civilized.

I was surprised by her tenacity, being a woman who claimed her ex-husband beat her daily, as she continued attacking him. "Big shot. You just shut your mouth, asshole. Fuck you and shut your fucking mouth. Big shot."

My father completely lost it after her string of obscenities. Hamar set him off like an antagonized leopard, fiercely screaming and yelling which sent me hitting the ceiling of the car. "Watch your fucking mouth. Shut up! Shut up! Shut your fat filthy mouth already." While screaming, he was pounding the steering wheel so hard that the entire car was shaking. My heart began racing from anxiety and the baby started crying hysterically.

Through all his bawling, Hamar didn't even flinch, standing her ground with the confidence of an elephant. She stuck her face in his direction, sadistically hollering, "You watch your fucking fat filthy mouth. You're the one who taught me those words. Opening a big mouth on me. You should've opened your fat mouth to your brother, you idiot. Opening a big mouth on me. Idiot, you and your fucking son."

"What do you mean, my son? Who?"

Hamar swiftly turned around looking in my direction, as I turned white, feeling the blood slither to my feet. Then projecting her poisonous venom my way, hollered, "Huh, you told your Aunt Carly that my hamburger tastes like shit? Yes? Then you told her that my cooking makes you sick. You idiot asshole! You wait too. I'll show you shit. You piece of shit. You should drop dead."

My father instantly jumped to her defense, screaming, "What? You told Aunt Carly that your mother's food is shit?" As he was finishing the statement, he reached back, aimlessly slapping and punching me in the head. My father was so focused on hitting me that in his furious rage, accidentally hit Mitch causing him to cry out in pain.

"I just told her that I liked her hamburgers better," I cried out in my defense.

My father used this diversion to take the heat off himself, going ballistic on me with his screaming and hitting. "I've had it with your shit already. It never stops." With every syllable, he struck me as the car was swerving all over the road.

Hamar screeched, "Sheldon. Sheldon, the car is going off the road. You're going to kill us all. Stop!" My father's breathing became so heavy that I could hear it from the backseat. He finally stopped his brutal assault to avoid an accident. Then Hamar delved in, shouting, "You can eat shit. Do you hear me? I won't make you anything to eat again. Let your father make your food. I'm done with you. Piece of shit is going to tell people that my food tastes like shit. You're finished and I'm done with you. You should drop dead. Drop dead you piece of shit. Moron. Idiot."

Her threats meant nothing to me. If she never cooked for me again, I would've been ecstatic. I sat in the backseat shaking and festering over the whole incident. Obviously, Hamar embellished the story, but my father believed her version anyway, carrying out his vicious attack to impress her. I couldn't understand why Aunt Carly would have discussed our conversation with Hamar but in her defense, she didn't realize the consequences of telling her. Who would think a child would be beaten for not liking someone's cooking?

CHAPTER 20

No one was more overjoyed than Hamar about the move back to Delaware. She and her family were inseparable and she cursed the day we moved to Rolling. Hamar was constantly on the telephone with her three sisters and mother. I couldn't imagine what they had to speak about for all those hours, but it went on through the day into the early evening. Hamar never spoke English when conversing with her family either, which drove my father crazy. When home, he pleaded with her to get off the phone, but she never listened. Merely ignoring him, continuing on with her discussions as if he were invisible. It annoyed the hell out of my father but unless he wanted to go to war, he had to keep his mouth shut.

The summer after I completed the second grade, we relocated to Galley, Delaware. Looking back, I was surprised my father made the move. He once told me how he was earning $60,000 a year, which was a great sum of money back in the early seventies. But Hamar had been nagging him to move back to Delaware since the time they moved to Rolling. She desperately needed to be close to her family, so he finally gave in. When we moved, Uncle Stewart and my dad opened their lighting store. Their arrangement was for Uncle Stewart to be responsible for running the showroom and my father was in charge of bringing in the builder and contractor business. They were a good team, building a fine business together. The one nice thing they did was hiring my grandmother to be the bookkeeper. The job kept her busy and I never saw her happier as I did when visiting the store. It seemed to give her a sense of pride.

My father and Hamar rented a four bedroom townhouse for us to live in. It was practically new and felt refreshing to get out of Rolling to make a new start. The sleeping arrangements remained the same, which I could see frustrated Mitch to no end. He didn't appear happy about the situation, slowly drifting off into obscurity. Shlomo and I started bonding more, sharing many of the same interests while Mitch went off making his own friends. By this time, Hamar had done a good job pinning us against Julie to be the scapegoat, incessantly remarking how she was just like our mother. Over the course of time, Hamar repeatedly made comments how our mother was stupid, a whore and crazy, which started settling in our minds. For some reason my father condoned this type of behavior by never putting a stop to her appalling remarks. But instead, stressed how the courts wouldn't permit us to be around our mother because she was "so crazy and a nymphomaniac". He urged us to believe that her character flaws could be passed onto us, like a contagious disease, if we were in contact with her.

Many times while tearing down my mother's character, he told us she was so stupid and ignorant that she couldn't even spell her own name. With all these notions and comparisons instilled in our heads, we began treating Julie like she had leprosy. By doing so, it made it easy for Hamar to get away with all her mental and physical abuse. They succeeded in convincing us that Julie deserved whatever Hamar dished out, since she was stupid and crazy like our sick mother. She even had this colorful story how several times she saved Samara from Julie's attempts of strangling her to death. So here was Mitch, feeling like he was stuck sharing a room with a contagious mentally ill person.

The neighborhood was a pleasant change, filled with loads of children our age. Everyone was extremely friendly and it was interesting how easy it was for all of us to make friends. For all the time living in Rolling, I couldn't recall making a single friend. There was so much to keep us busy as well, which was great considering Hamar locked us out of the townhouse for the entire day. Her explanation was that we made her floors filthy dirty and she didn't want to keep cleaning up after us. Her infamous expression was telling us how she wasn't our maid. Anytime I would ask where something was or if she saw something I was looking for, her response was, "What do you think, I'm your maid? Stupid." Then she started ranting to herself. "Like I'm his maid. He comes and asks me like I'm the maid. Stupid idiot." All those insults for one measly question.

We were sent from the house after breakfast to go play and then return at noon. Upon our return, there was a mail chute built into the front door of our townhouse where we received our lunch. Hamar was so strict about us not entering the townhouse that we couldn't even come in to eat comfortably. She would actually pass the peanut butter and jelly sandwiches through the mail chute, which was our lunch everyday. There were no variety of sandwiches for us, so becoming tired of eating peanut butter and jelly, I began skipping the sandwiches across the parking lot like stones. I joked around with everyone, referring to her lunch as a peanut butter and shit sandwich.

The neighborhood had a large community pool where we spent most of our time. Hamar's sister and brother-in-law came by often with their two children to go swimming with us. Out of her three sisters, Rubel was the one whom we spent the most time with seeing as they enjoyed our company. Hamar claimed her rich sister, Muffy, was her favorite, but her husband didn't get along with Hamar, so their time together was fairly limited. Rubel was a tall dark-skinned woman, who was extremely funny with her off the cuff comments. She and her husband Gus were pleasant people to be around and I enjoyed the time we spent with them. Gus' claim to fame was his admiration for saying, "Wa wa wait a while. Would ya?" Initially, I didn't know whether it was a joke or he was serious, because I never heard anyone using that expression before. But anytime asked a question which he needed to ponder, he would exclaim, "Wa wa wait a while. Would ya?" I referred to him as "Uncle Wait A While", as it caught on, with our whole family referring to him as "Uncle Wait A While". He possessed a great sense of humor, never seeming to mind the nickname.

While Shlomo and I were out playing one afternoon, a few kids mentioned that a guy put together a little organized football league.

We were passionate about the game, tossing the ball around every day and running our own plays. But never playing on a team before, we eagerly went to go check it out. One of the kids, who played, had an older brother named, Bob. He put together two football teams who played each other throughout the summer. When we stopped by, he allowed us to tryout while putting together the team rosters. Bob decided to assign me as the quarterback, which was uplifting, since I always dreamed of playing that position. The only catch was we had to have our own uniforms. No one was allowed to play without at least wearing a helmet and shoulder pads. Shlomo and I didn't have either, so we planned on asking my father for the equipment that night. We waited for him to come home, but when he arrived his answer was no. He never believed in presents without there being a special occasion like a birthday. Then I remembered my cousins, Jeff and Dan, had some equipment, so they helped out by letting us borrow theirs. That was my first taste of playing football and I loved it. I spent more time playing football that summer than cooling off in the community pool.

We had a manmade pond in our neighborhood, which made fishing a popular activity. Shlomo and I became friendly with the kids next door who offered their bamboo fishing pole for us to use one afternoon. The pond was behind our development and they convinced us that everyone was catching fish there. It was not an enormous pond but nicely put together with picnic benches and a number of pretty trees surrounding the parameter. It was so peaceful like a little pocket of paradise, which I unfortunately avoided due to playing so much football. When arriving, we noticed that a couple of kids, who were already fishing, had caught a few bass. Nothing big but it gave us hope. Shlomo and I took turns using the fishing pole, although the waiting was getting boring, so I decided to improvise. Searching around, I found a discarded fishing line with a hook still attached in some nearby tall grass. We had no money for bait, so I dug up a few worms, threading one through the fishhook. Then wrapping the line around a thin stick, I sat up on a cement pipe which was draining into the pond. Within a few minutes of dropping my line in the water, a minnow quickly snatched the bait. I started screaming, "Shlomo, I caught my first fish, come look." While shouting for Shlomo, a bigger fish came from beneath the cement pipe, greedily swallowing the minnow I had caught. Jumping up and down, I hollered, "Shlomo, come quick. You're not going to believe this fish." Hastily reeling it in on my thin stick, I watched as it flipped and turned in the green grass. I was so thrilled. The fish looked as though it weighed approximately five pounds. Then a few kids dropped what they were doing to come see, agreeing it was the biggest fish they had ever seen pulled out of the pond.

Shlomo and I decided on bringing the fish home to surprise Hamar, knowing how much she enjoyed eating fish. When we arrived at our front door, it sounded as if somebody was committing a gruesome murder inside. We heard loud banging and pounding, and muffled noises of furniture sliding and slamming into walls. Then what really caught my attention were the hair raising yells and cries bursting out from the townhouse walls. I stood pensively outside the front door holding my trophy fish, wavering whether or not to go in. Finally, curiosity bullied my shaky hand into opening the front door. As Shlomo and I slowly stepped in, I never forgot what I witnessed when entering the house. Hamar had Julie's hair, in her clenches, as she was swinging her clockwise, perpendicular to the floor. It was an alarming sight, with poor Julie screaming at the top of her five year old lungs. I couldn't believe her hair didn't detach itself from her scalp. Julie's face was tainted bright-red from hollering out in pain, while Hamar had a look of determination, rotating Julie around the kitchen. She looked determined to rip the hair right out from Julie's sweaty red head. Our kitchen table was pushed against the wall with all the chairs scattered in various directions.

Hamar was so intent on physically destroying Julie, she didn't even focus on us when walking in. She was wildly yelling, "You fucking whore. Bitch. Just like your fucking pig mother." Then she dropped Julie flat on the floor, stomping on her back with her wedged wooded shoes. I was sweating watching this with my tongue going dry.

Julie was sobbing and crying out, "Addy addy addy." I had difficulty swallowing, watching Hamar wickedly beating Julie. I

175

could mentally feel every cruel stomp on my own back, seeing the pain she inflicted on her.

Finally finding the gumption, I asked, "What's happening? What did Julie do this time?"

Hamar was exceedingly self-absorbed, not even taking notice to my question. In fact, Julie didn't seem to hear me either, as she elusively tried wiggling off in an attempt to escape. Leaping on her back, Hamar grabbed her hair again, violently slamming her head into the linoleum floor. "I hate you. Hate you. You piece of shit, idiot whore." My head was spinning in fast motion as Julie was getting a wicked walloping. I wished there was something to do to help, but any attempt would surely trigger Hamar's anger towards me. Then Hamar was running out of steam as her breathing increased to heavy gasps, crowing, "Get up to your room, whore. Pig! You should drop dead. I hate you. Hate you!" After she rolled off from Julie's back, Julie hysterically darted up the stairs shrieking in terror.

It was a wonder no one called the police. The kitchen window faced the front of the townhouse, where we clearly heard all the chaos from outside. Stumbling up, Hamar came to her feet while wiping her brow. She looked like she just finished boxing a few rounds as her breathing was irregular when speaking. "That pig... was next door... with a boy. They were playing... a touching game... or kissing. Somebody... saw this whore." Then pausing, she noticed I was holding a bucket and angrily shouted, "What's that dripping on my floor?"

I lost my excitement over catching the fish, calmly replying, "Oh yeah, I caught a fish for you. I know how much you like fish, so I brought it home for you."

Looking fatigued, she staggered over peering into the bucket with a grumpy look. "Disgusting. Get it out of my house, fast. You're dirtying my floors. Stupid, like I need a fish." I looked at her stunned, thinking nothing I did could make this woman happy.

"Out fast. Why are you standing there, yala yala," she demanded, shoving me in the direction of the front door. Sauntering out, with my head hung low, I returned the dead fish back to the pond.

When my father returned home from work, he poured himself

a vodka on the rocks, listening while Hamar pounded him with a mouthful of threats and obscenities. She was outraged with Julie, demanding he straighten her up or she would kick her out of the house. "I'm sick and tired of being your maid and taking care of your fucked up kids. You don't have to be around. It's me. Your pig daughter, that you brought to me, is ruining my life. I hate her. Do you understand me? I hate her."

My father sat grinding his teeth in anger and harshly said, "Hey, I told you. I don't like that word *pig*. And don't say you hate her, ok?"

"You shut your mouth, stupid. I take care of her and I'll call her what I want." Hamar was furious, hating when my father attempted taking Julie's side. "Don't you defend her, you idiot. A pig whore is what she is. Do you hear me? Pig whore. I hate her."

"Hey, watch it." My father pleaded, pointing to the ceiling.

It was amazing how she had no respect for my father. Striking at him like a venomous snake, knowing how to push every one of his buttons. "You forgot already, how I had to take care of her in Rolling, when she was naked in the street with her finger up her papoo, huh? Your fucking whore wife had her in bed while she screwed different men in front of her. That's your pig daughter. A whore like your ex-wife."

My father shared so much crap with Hamar that it backfired on him, with her using it as a weapon during her raging fits. He told her that my mother had sex with strange men, while Julie was in the same bed watching. What disturbed me the most was Hamar describing the fabricated scenario as if our mother had Julie participating. They mentally tortured her with these vile stories. It was a crime how my father thought it acceptable for this woman to feed Julie such despicable lies at a tender age.

Turning white with anger, my father's hands trembled while Hamar forged on. The ice in his cocktail clinked against the sides of his glass, making a jingling noise. "I'll tell you Sheldon, you better take care of this or you'll be sorry. I'm sick and tired of this shit."

"Stop it. Will you? I'll talk with her but don't threaten me, ok? I don't need this shit now. I'm in the middle of opening the store and

I don't need it." The vodka was kicking in, enabling him to slightly defend himself, but he never got the last word.

Hamar wasn't backing off, violently hollering, "Big shot. You stop it and you shut your mouth. You better take care of that pig daughter of yours."

When hostile, Hamar constantly repeated herself, directing her angry words towards a person or other times to herself. "Big shot. Like you're going to open a big mouth on me. Open your big mouth with your whore daughter. Stupid. Like you're going to scare me."

As it turned out, it was too late for my father to have a one on one with Julie. Hamar sent her to bed, each evening, at an absurdly hour of 7:00. It was a good thing for Julie too, given that Hamar really got my father worked up to punish her. He surely would have used her as a punching bag in place of Hamar's face.

Hamar's bellyaching did not end with Julie that evening, rolling into another bitching session about my mother. Ever since we moved back to Delaware, someone had been calling the house and hanging up whenever Hamar answered. She was convinced it was my mom, hoping for one of us to pick up the telephone. It was a trite complaint, which my father had to listen to on a regular basis. He didn't argue, knowing when to pick his battles with Hamar and this one didn't warrant an all out confrontation. Because of the number of prank calls, none of us were permitted anywhere near the telephones. They wanted a tight grip around our throats, since my mother was hauling him back to court for custody over us. The only reason we were made aware of our return to court was because our father was prepping us.

Court was a complete blur to me. It was nearly a year prior to this, when I last saw my mom and grandparents and until this day, I don't remember if I saw them or not that afternoon. When leaving our townhouse to go to court, a frenzy brewed in my mind. As we walked out the front door, Hamar and Shlomo were patting us on our backs, saying, "Ok guys, don't forget to tell them that you want to live with us." I felt like I was walking through a tunnel, entering a football game, as my teammates were giving me encouragement. For the life of me, I couldn't figure it out. Hamar mentally and physically tormented us, relentlessly reminding everyone how she would have never married our father, knowing we were part of the package. I wondered about the million dollar offer my grandfather extended to him, maybe the story was the other way around. Perhaps they thought, if winning custody of us, we would fetch them a million dollar offer from Papa Willie. My father didn't mind that his children were getting their ass' kicked right under his nose. It always struck me odd how he fought so hard for his children, just to throw them in a snake pit with an abusive stepmother.

Interestingly enough, my current wife's mother had a conversation with Hamar during one of her visits to New Jersey. While I was engaged to Michelle, Hamar openly explained to my future mother-in-law how she came to acquiring us. As the conversation progressed, Hamar described that my father tricked her into taking on three of his children. My future mother-in-law was appalled when Hamar stated my father promised to come home with $1,000,000, not three children. She never knew the importance of Hamar's statement and didn't bring it to my attention until I happened to be writing my memoir. When enlightened of their conversation, I explained that she finally solved a lifelong question of mine. It neatly put together the last pieces of the puzzle, solidifying in my mind the reason for his resilient battle for us.

While at court that day, all I can recollect was being in the judge's chambers. My mind was crawling with all sorts of emotions, which were scaring me to death. I wanted to go with my heart, divulging to the judge how much I wanted to live with my mother. But I didn't want to risk anymore brutal beatings, seeing how consistent the courts were with their decisions. The odds of my father winning again were likely, considering I caved in, answering all the questions the way he intimidated me to. I don't remember how Mitch and Julie responded to the judge, but we were all asked the same questions as usual. Being so well versed, I knew the questions before they were even thrown at me. During the interrogation I felt like a robot, chewing my fingernails and spewing out the answers with little effort. I must have sounded like a programmed monkey, but the judge who conducted the interview never thought twice about my demeanor. After the interview, I had a sense of being whisked away by a magical giant broom. Then patted on the back and being told to enjoy hell. That's exactly what happened as I sat biting my fingernails in the backseat of my father's car, pondering whether or not I did the right thing.

That day in court was a defining moment in my life and from then on, I always wondered how my future might have turned out if my mother had actually won. I embraced a terrible guilt complex about the entire court proceedings, feeling weak for not going with my heart. I harbored so much remorse, with the notion of betraying my brother and sister. Being the eldest, the judge probably put more emphasis on what I had to say than Mitch and Julie. I wanted so badly to speak to my mother and grandparents, explaining the threatening situation my father had me under, but I knew that was out of the question. The courts left no provisions, from what my father told us, to ever have any contact with them again.

Life back at the townhouse was the same with Hamar after the court episode. She didn't loosen up on us and we didn't win any more attention or love for saying the right things to the judge. Her nasty temperament and bad treatment perpetuated just like it had before. The only thing that came out from all this was it concluded my mother's and grandparents' last attempts to win us back. We were entirely on our own, something we needed to be strong about and deal with to survive. I knew I had to get emotionally hard, forgetting about my mother and grandparent's existence in order to endure. Motherly love had to be obsolete from my vocabulary and emotions. It took conditioning to reach this mindset, but once adhering, it helped get me through the treacherous nightmare. I think my sanity stayed intact through the years only because of that mental conditioning. I wish I could say the same for Julie.

Fortunately school started, as I entered the third grade. I was thankful since it helped get my mind off our depressing home life, focusing more on my books and friends. It sounds unusual coming from a nine year old, but it was extremely therapeutic for me, giving a much needed sense of worth and accomplishment. My grades were flourishing, given a new daily routine I started when getting home from school. It was a very simple technique, which encompassed finishing my homework before running out to play. It proved to work like a charm. The only positive attention I ever received from my parents was when arriving home with good marks. They fancied my excellent grades, not because they were proud of me, but because Hamar was in constant competition with her sisters. It was one of those topics that came up in conversation, which equipped her with the ammo to look like she was doing a great job raising us. Whatever it was, I did it for my own satisfaction.

Sadly, life at the Galley townhouse didn't last long. On a Saturday afternoon, Hamar and my father left us alone, with Shlomo in charge of watching over Samara, who was napping upstairs. Since the baby was sleeping, we were only allowed to play quietly in the basement. While goofing around, the telephone repeatedly rang upstairs, but none of us dared to answer it, so it just kept on ringing. In the midst of messing around, a terrifying knock came at the basement door, which was a neighbor in complete panic. "I've been trying to call you guys. I saw from my window that you have smoke and flames coming from one of your bedrooms. Where are your parents?"

We casually looked at one another dazed, as Shlomo and I finally answered, "They're out."

She was rushing her speech, shouting, "Listen, you kids need to get out of here. Were one of you playing with matches?"

"No," I said. "We've been downstairs the whole time." I had a little dark past with matches, so I immediately grew defensive. One autumn afternoon, I was carelessly playing with a pack of matches behind Mama Ida and Papa Willie's house. Hiding behind a cord of wood, I set a leaf on fire which ignited another and another and before I knew it, the backyard shot up in flames. My father flew to the rescue, stomping out the fire. So after that scare, I didn't play with matches any longer.

Then Shlomo yelled out, "The baby! Samara is upstairs sleeping. I have to go get her." He sped off to grab Samara, while the rest of us followed the lady out of the house.

When Shlomo came out with Samara, the neighbor brought us over to her townhouse and we watched as the fire trucks loudly arrived. There wasn't much smoke, so out of curiosity I asked Shlomo, "What did it look like when you were upstairs?"

"Not bad. Just your bed was on fire," he casually said. I was surprised because by the lady's reaction, I imagined the entire second floor was burning in a raging fire.

After the firemen completed their job, it turned out the electrical outlet by my bed setoff a spark which started the fire. The fireman explained that when the townhouses were built they used aluminum wire, which corrodes and that's what caused the fire.

When we returned to see the damage, it was a spooky scene. The entire upstairs was either burned or blackened by the fire. We wound up losing all our clothing and furniture on the second floor. Hamar was an absolute wreck, screaming a smorgasbord of obscenities in English, Hebrew and Arabic at my father. I ventured off, trying to stay as far away as possible from her fury. The most devastating issue, which came up, was my father never insured our personal belongings. While renting the townhouse, he forgot to call the insurance company after Hamar reminded him several times. She pressed him so hard with insults; he didn't look like he could catch his breath. My father honestly didn't have a leg to stand on, so he couldn't do much but absorb her wrath. I think her cursing was choking him worse than the black soot permeating in the air.

After salvaging whatever we could, Shlomo and I were sent to stay with Hamar's brother and new wife, while the rest of the family stayed with other relatives. They were extremely nice, doing their best to comfort us. Shlomo and I were mourning over the loss of our Wacky Card collection. We had been saving them since living in Rolling, almost having every complete set. The cruelest thing was how we took such meticulous care of the cards, only to find that the neighborhood kids somehow got into our townhouse, stealing them. The reason for our deep-rooted pain was when going back, most every basement door was covered with our Wacky stickers. It was a big blow to us since we rarely even looked at the stickers, so to keep them in pristine condition. It would be like someone using thumbtacks to hang the Mona Lisa on their bedroom wall.

CHAPTER 21

My father and Hamar quickly picked out another house to rent. They found a four bedroom single family home in Red Hill, Delaware. It was a nice colonial, except for the bedroom I shared with Shlomo, it spooked me out. When we lived in Rolling, Hamar and my father went to see the "The Exorcist", which frightened the hell out me. My father's depiction of the movie was so horrifying that I slept with Shlomo for a week. He described how the little girl in the film became possessed when she went into the attic to play. My new room had two crawl spaces for storage, but I considered them the doorways to the attic. I wouldn't even go near them, scared of being possessed like the little girl in the movie. The bedroom also had an old style vaulted ceiling, casting the most unusual animated shadows I had ever seen. Needless to say, I was especially nervous when sleeping in that room.

Mitch and Julie were assigned to share the same bedroom again, irritating the hell out of Mitch. I realized he had to be grief-stricken over sharing a room with Julie for all this time, with the baby still having her own bedroom. Mitch must have been counting down the days when Samara was old enough to share a room with Julie. With Shlomo being the eldest, he would be the next in line for his own room, leaving Mitch and me as roommates.

We were enrolled in Woodley Gardens Elementary School, where I enjoyed learning, but still missed my former school and friends. Seeing how our clothes were burnt in the townhouse fire, my father and Hamar took us shopping at Sears to purchase new clothing for school. The only clothing any of us owned were the ones on our backs, so when done shopping, each of us had two outfits to wear. It felt embarrassing attending school looking that way, but fortunately no one gave me much grief about it. The only thing I actually did catch crap about was Hamar's lunches. Any time I brought a tuna fish sandwich to school, it spelled S T E N C H. Once in my classroom, my lunch smelled so rancid the teacher actually went back to where we stashed them, picking up an old, beaten up, wrinkled bag and asked who it belonged to. I sat quietly, biting my nails without daring to raise my hand. Hamar forced us to keep our brown paper lunch bags, as well as the plastic baggies that held the sandwiches. Eventually, the bag became so worn, I could have used it as a tissue to blow my nose. That's how soft and pliable it became from the excess use. I was so ashamed of having to save the bag that I hid in the bathroom, folding it up quickly, then jamming it in my back pocket before anyone could see.

My teacher held her nose, keeping the lunch bag at a safe distance from herself. I knew it was mine, but by the look on her face there was no way in hell I was going to take ownership of that lunch. She must have thought it was old by the condition of the bag, instructing us not to leave old lunches lying in the coat closet anymore.

Hamar's lunches were never prepared with love. After that incident in class, I would have preferred her peanut butter and jelly sandwiches. The lunches always consisted of the same thing, a sandwich, a small bag of Utz Potato Chips and a smashed cookie thrown at the bottom of an old greasy beaten up brown bag. I pictured her being upset while making our lunches and heaving the cookies as hard as she could to the bottom of the bag in hatred. The strange thing about her tuna sandwich was it never tasted like tuna to me. I think the fire put a strain on my father's wallet because the tuna I used to get was flaky and not so fishy smelling. This tuna was ground up and gritty, with an odor more poignant than normal tuna. Eventually, I found out what I was eating. A few years later, a buddy of mine was feeding his cat and I noticed how the color and consistency matched Hamar's tuna sandwiches. Mortified at first, I gave her the benefit of the doubt, attributing the mistake to her being from Morocco or

Israel and not being able to read very well. Then after noticing how cat food was sold in an entirely different isle that scenario didn't fly with me any longer.

Growing up, I had great memories of Halloween and trick or treating with my mother. She bought us great costumes, allowing us to run around collecting candy until we were too tired to continue. That year I was especially excited, since Hamar and my father decided on letting all four of us go trick or treating unsupervised. The only condition was Shlomo and I had to keep a close eye on Mitch and Julie, which we had no problem doing. It was the first time I was permitted to go without a parent and was counting down the days. Next to my birthday, Halloween was my favorite time of the year. The neighborhood we lived in was much larger than I was accustomed to, figuring we could make a killing trick or treating. That night Hamar gave each of us a large grocery paper bag, instructing us to visit a few homes close by and bring back the candy.

Perplexed, I gazed at her, asking, "Why do we have to do that? I thought we were allowed to go out and trick or treat as much as we wanted."

Hamar immediately grew angry, shouting back, "Just shut up and do what I said, stupid. Shlomo take them and do what I said." She looked at him as if they had some kind of understanding that I wasn't a part of.

He sharply nodded his head, responding, "Ok mom, we'll be right back."

As we walked off into the early night, confused I asked, "Hey Shlomo, what's going on? I thought we were going out to get a ton of candy. Why do we have get candy and bring it back to mom?" I was starting to get upset and Mitch and Julie looked confused as well.

"Oh, my mom didn't buy any candy to give out. She told me that she wants us to go get it and we can go afterwards."

I couldn't believe what I was hearing. Mitch and I looked at each other completely frazzled and frowned. "You mean, we have to give her our candy to give back out? That doesn't make any sense. I thought she was supposed to buy the candy to give out," I said, feeling as though this was so wrong to do.

Then Shlomo defended her as if this was the norm during Halloween. "Yeah, well this is what she does, so we have to do it." I didn't want to argue with him, in fear Shlomo would rat me out to his mother and I would get my butt beaten.

After visiting a few homes, we ran back chasing Shlomo to give Hamar our candy. I was reluctant to give it up, since it felt like she was cheating. When we returned, she instantly swung open the door, as if she were waiting on us. Acting extremely aggravated, Hamar squawked, "Come on already, give me the candy. I already had kids here knocking on the door." One by one, we stepped up as she stuck her greedy hands hastily in our bags, snatching out the candy. "Ok," she said, without a thank you. "Hurry up and get more. Yala yala, go fast." I stood in disbelief, as she gave me a wicked look, shrieking, "Go! What are you waiting for? A special invitation."

Hamar had a unique way of tainting a wonderful event and here we were collecting candy so she could give it away. Mitch, Julie and I tottered with our heads hung low, as we went from door to door, losing our enthusiasm to scream "Trick or Treat". None of us were inspired anymore, almost wanting to call it quits after returning with our second load of candy. There were so many children out that night, that they cleaned Hamar out of our first load. When we returned to the stoop, she was waiting on us again, screaming because she was running out of candy. "What took so long? I ran out again. After this, I'm turning off the lights so they don't wakeup Samara knocking on the door." Then greedily snatching the candy out of our bags, she told us we could go back out.

Shlomo asked, "Can we stay out instead of coming right back?"

"Yeah, go ahead but don't eat anything until you get back home," Hamar snapped back, pushing us on our way. I was excited now, knowing we had a lot of catching up to do. All four of us ran off into the streets, trick or treating until every porch light was finally extinguished.

On our way back home, we were so excited that we began comparing whose bag was the heaviest. Repeatedly, we passed the bags around until we couldn't hold back. Not one of us could resist eating a candy bar, since back then they were full size, making it even harder not to sneak a piece. When we got back, Hamar and my father were in the kitchen talking. He had a drink in his hand as they both looked like they were in the middle of an intense conversation. We walked in with our chests puffed out, as if just conquering a country. Then in unison, we smiled screaming, "Look! Look at all the candy we got." It was an all out contest, with each of us showing off how much candy we collected. Hamar shuffled over with a somber expression embroidered on her face, quickly claiming ownership of our hard work. Snatching the bags from us, she loudly poured them out on the kitchen counter as candy sprayed everywhere. Shlomo walked over joining her, with a big smile pasted on his pie face. Without speaking a word, Hamar pulled out two plastic bowls and started separating the candy. Shlomo helped her separate our candy into two categories, chocolate and hard candy.

"Isn't this great? Look at all the candy we have," he exclaimed, while the three of us looked on flabbergasted.

Before my father sucked us into this family, he and our mother permitted us to keep our own candy. They checked it for poison or razor blades, but it was ours to keep and eat.

Outraged by what she was doing, I asked, "How come we can't keep our own candy?" Then looking at my father for support, I stated, "My dad always let us keep our own candy."

Of course, my father didn't have my back, fixing his eyes on Hamar. She gave me a wicked glare, shouting, "Stupid. What am I, stealing your candy? Stupid, like I'm stealing his candy. Idiot!"

She shot my father an evil stare, provoking him to quickly stammer. "Look kids, now you have so much more by putting it together."

Cutting him off, Hamar said, "Here," as she threw each of us a candy bar. At that moment, I didn't realize it but that was the last candy bar Mitch, Julie and I would ever see again. She looked over at my father with a snarling expression, saying, "Here potato," tossing him a candy bar as well.

"That's it. Are you happy now? You'll get one candy a day and that's all. I don't care what your father says."

Hamar could see, by the expression on my face, I wasn't going along with her decision. She stood with Shlomo throwing the candy into separate bowls, screaming, "What did you think? I was going to let you take this candy upstairs so you can get cockroaches in my house. Stupid. Like I'm going to let you get cockroaches in my house. Cheap. That's what you are, cheap. Like I'm going to steal your stupid candy. Go. Go. Get out of my face and get ready for bed."

Walking away, I could still hear her babbling away. "Stupid. Like I'm going to steal his candy. Like I even eat candy. Cheap. Stupid idiot." She rambled on until her festering voice vanished, absorbed through the floors of the house. As it turned out, Hamar locked our candy away with her stash of goodies. Mitch, Julie and I were given the crap while she gave her son the chocolate candy bars.

We weren't living in our new house very long, before Hamar's parents came over for an extended sleepover. They were like traveling gypsies, making a habit of migrating back and forth between their children's homes. They stayed with us so often and for such long periods of time, I wondered if they still had their apartment. Hamar's folks didn't stay often at Rubel and Gus' home given there wasn't much room, primarily bouncing between our house and Muffy's. She had a large house with at least five bedrooms, which gave them their own room when staying over. At our home, Mitch and Julie had to vacate their beds, forced into sleeping on the floor in sleeping bags. Hamar constantly boasted how her parents liked staying at her house the best. It was like a contest between her and her sisters, although it never seemed to bother them. The only ones bothered and inconvenienced by all this were Mitch and Julie.

Neither of Hamar's parents spoke English and her mother never put forth the effort, considering how shy and quiet she was. Her father was the opposite, being far more the extravert, attempting to speak but in very broken English. I understood some of his phrases, mainly because he did an exceptional job playing charades when speaking. They came to America about the same time as Hamar, but never adjusting as well as she did. It was difficult referring to them as mama and papa, however, it didn't mean anything to me, seeing how I emotionally detached myself from my real grandparents anyway. These people never took their places, but like I mentioned earlier, I went along to get along. I sure didn't want to endure another beating like I had in Rolling.

Mama was a very sweet woman, with having little to say. She was heavy set and unmistakably looked Mediterranean, as Hamar and her entire family did. She was an older woman, but surprisingly spared the defining wrinkles to prove it. Mama mostly kept to herself, doing all the cooking and baking when staying over, definitely earning her keep. We used to joke around, calling her the kitchen police since she planted herself there during her waking hours. I always sensed she was taking notes whenever we entered the kitchen, informing Hamar of our activities. I don't think she ever did but it was an eerie feeling, having her just sitting there whenever I came in. Even when the lights were out, she was a permanent fixture and many times scaring the hell out of me. There were times when I came into the kitchen for a glass of water, then flipping on the light switch, *BOOM*, there she was.

Hamar's father was older than his wife and looked the part too. He only had hair on the sides of his head, walking with a terrible limp from falling on the steps of a bus, while attempting to get on. Usually, he wore the same clothes all week, consisting of polyester pants and a white short sleeve dress shirt. Being a religious Jew, he prayed when waking, before eating and practically all day. I thought praying was his fulltime job, leaving little time for anything else. When not praying, he made an effort explaining that he owned a successful bar in Israel or how he lost his hair. He insisted that he had a full head of hair, until it all fell out in a single day, due to a serious sunburn to his head. Shlomo and papa were close, since living together after Shlomo's father moved back to Israel. I could understand that, but never appreciated how he would look at me, declaring, "Shlomo my son. You nothing." He would pat himself on the chest while repeating the words, "Shlomo my son. You nothing." It didn't hurt me, but felt like he wasn't playing by the same set of rules I was. Here I'm trying to fit in, working on avoiding the whole step issue as he's telling me that I amount to nothing. Those were truly the times I missed my real mother and grandparents.

It was odd but papa truly took a liking to Julie. Out of all his grandchildren, he always had a kind way with her, managing to sneak Julie an assortment of candies. His pockets were a bottomless pit, regularly filled with goodies and Julie being the soul recipient. This made Hamar feel great, as if her father wasn't prejudice to our existence. She boasted about it like it was unusual for anyone to accept us in the family.

I had been around Hamar for about a year, never witnessing her smacking her own kids, except one time back in Rolling. Shlomo and I were jumping on our beds, pretending to be on a trampoline. After a few minutes, I heard Hamar creeping down the stairs. She was extra quiet so we wouldn't hear her, but I did. She wore approximately five different gold bracelets, which clinked anytime she moved around the house. It was like a cow wearing a bell and I used those bracelets as an alarm to warn myself when she was on the hunt. This day there was no clinking, as I froze when spotting her. Shlomo was still joyfully jumping when seeing an immediate change in my face. Most likely fear, but he didn't stop, continuing to use the bed as a trampoline. Hamar stood like a gun shooter, taking aim as she swiftly pulled off one of her hard wedged shoes. I tried alerting Shlomo, but my lips wouldn't release the words. In shock, I watched as Hamar flung her shoe, perfectly dismounting Shlomo from the bed, while in midair. She caught him cleanly in the back of the head, sending him rolling around on the floor, screaming in agony. Hamar was so stunned when hitting him, that she ran over to see if he was ok. Her face went from livid to "Oh my God". I didn't know if the shoe was really meant for me or not, but once she knew he was ok, the attack was on.

Hamar grabbed her weapon from the floor, turning into a wild banshee. She jumped on me, wildly hollering, "You stupid idiot. Jumping on my bed." As she screamed, the shoe kept banging down on my back and buttocks. "You wild bastard. Animal. You fucking animal. I can't take you animals anymore. Idiot. Bastard, I hate you." There were other Arabic and Hebrew obscenities added in when she finally got off me. That was the extent of Shlomo's beating and I don't think my father knew Hamar's kids were off limits to his fury.

Shlomo and I were avid football fans and during the playoffs that year, my dad and Hamar didn't want to watch with us. So Shlomo and I went with Mitch and Julie to another room to watch the game. It was an additional bedroom that came off the family room which they converted into a little TV area for us. While watching the game, Julie repeatedly kept coming in and out of the room. Each time rising to leave, she blocked the television set. As the game was coming to a climax, Shlomo had asked her several times to either stay out or sit down. Oblivious to his requests, Julie got up again and walked out, so Shlomo quickly jumped up and started to close the door. She didn't like the idea of being shut out, so they struggled with the door until Shlomo finally won the battle. But not before Julie removed her finger. There was a shrilling scream as my father instantly leaped up to see what was going on.

"What the hell happened," he yelled, looking at Julie. Shlomo was assisting her with opening the door while she was wailing and holding her finger. Her hand was trembling as she held the injured finger in her other hand. There was blood everywhere as Julie looked like she was going to pass out.

Shlomo became frightened, realizing he seriously hurt Julie. "Are you ok," he asked, staring at her bloody limp finger.

My father was extremely protective of Julie, with it being bad news if any of us hit her. It was a shame Hamar was excluded from that list, for Julie's sake. When my father got a good look at her finger, seeing the damage Shlomo did, he lost all control. "God damn it. Look what the fuck you did." He was holding Julie's bloody limp finger in his shaky hand, looking as though he was going to rip Shlomo's throat out. Shlomo turned white, in a matter of seconds, jetting up the stairs for his life.

Knowing my father's temper, Hamar started yelling, "Leave him alone, Sheldon. Sheldon, do you hear me?" She began chasing them, as my father was trying to catch Shlomo running for his bedroom. "Do you fucking hear me," Hamar screeched, doing her best to catch up with him. My father was deaf to her screams, only having one thing in mind, destroying Shlomo for hurting Julie.

Shlomo slid across the carpet on his knees, attempting to make it into his bed. My father fell down to his knees too, forcefully grabbing Shlomo by his shoulders. He pushed Shlomo's bulbous head against the side of the bed, getting directly in his face while trying to catch his breath and bellowed, "Where the hell do you think you're going? God damn it."

Just as he raised his hand to give Shlomo a powerful slap, Hamar jumped on his back, crying, "Get off him. Get the fuck off of my son, you bastard!" She was red in the face, looking ready to rumble with my father over the safety of her son. She spat while screaming, aimlessly grabbing for my father's cocked arm as he attempted to avoid her grasp. Shlomo sat on the floor, eyes shut with his head pinned between my dad's hand and the bed.

Then my father vigorously turned around, shoving her off of him. His face was stricken with anger as he looked betrayed. "Get off me," he responded, with a gruff shaky voice. Looking surprised and upset by Hamar's reaction, he didn't struggle with her, but stood up, shoving Shlomo with his foot. Then out of breath, he stammered, "Next time, keep your God damn hands to yourself."

Shlomo was wheezing in fear, as my father shot Hamar an evil eye, squawking, "*Your* son, huh? Make sure *your* son keeps his hands off my daughter." He emphasized *your* in his sentence.

Hamar caught on to his sarcasms, shrieking, "That's right, my son. Keep your fucking hands off, my son. You ever touch him again and I'll divorce you. Big shot. Idiot going to hit my son? Fuck you and your pig daughter. Your second wife."

Mitch and I followed everyone upstairs, but made sure to get down before our father noticed us. We didn't want to rouse him, possibly becoming his next victims. After all the chaos with Shlomo and Hamar, my father trotted back down the stairs, assisting Julie with her bloody finger. Hamar was too busy soothing her son, but when she eventually strutted down, her interest in helping Julie was nil. She played her usual martyr role since everything had to be about her. It didn't matter that Julie nearly had her finger severed. She insisted on being callous and curt towards my father for the rest of the evening. It was one of those squabbles which lasted for a few days. Hamar playing her silent treatment game, with my father refusing to give in. Eventually somewhere along the line, I'm sure he broke before she did, apologizing for his actions. That's how it worked in my house, whether or not she was wrong, Hamar would never bend to apologize. Mutual respect between the two of them was non-existent.

Shlomo and I were obsessed with anything to do with football; it was all we could think about. While messing around in the neighborhood, we came across an old discarded football, which we played with each and every day in our front yard. We constantly ran plays, with me at the quarterback position and Shlomo as the wide receiver. We became very good too, given as I had his timing down for running passing- routes. Playing so frequently, I could throw the football to him with my eyes closed. I don't remember if I used playing football as an escape to forget the yearning for my mother or if it was the one thing that made me feel alive.

Eventually, our interest evolved into collecting football cards, taking the place of our burnt Wacky Stickers. Shlomo and I were still embittered over losing them. Watching so many football games, we knew all the players, their teams and the numbers on their jerseys. We strived to acquire our favorite team's cards first, growing our collection into a huge hobby. While trading with a few kids in our neighborhood, we met other children from our school that collected and began wheeling and dealing with them. We didn't have any money, so we negotiated with whatever possessions we had.

One time we invited this kid over, pulling a fast one on him while playing a game. We suggested he toss up his cards to see how high he could get them and when falling to the ground, we assisted him by pocketing the cards. As the game progressed, he retrieved fewer and fewer cards, until there was only one left. At which point, he became very upset with us running home to tell his dad, but we never heard from his father or him again.

When first beginning our football card collection, it was so minuscule that we could fit all the cards in a shoebox. Then our collection grew so large, that we filled two trash bags. Each night we stayed up late reading and learning about the different players. Shlomo and I did our best to keep our voices to a whisper, but sometimes it got a little loud. When my father heard us, he yelled from the family room, "Go to bed. God damn it."

Shlomo always retorted, but only for our ears. "God damn we are." It made me laugh, even louder than before.

Then my father would give one last warning. "God damn it. You better be quiet. You don't want me coming up there." Shlomo was a sacred cow, so that left me to get my butt whooped. When I heard his last warning, I made sure Shlomo brought it down a notch, thinking how going to bed was a fine idea.

I made a few good friends at school, but really enjoyed this one guy, Danny, who was the class clown. He had this thing he did which made everybody laugh. Danny would lick his right hand, then while wiping his butt crack would say, "Tell ya what I do." I had no idea what it meant but found it awfully funny.

While walking home with Danny after school, he invited me over to help paint the fort he built in his backyard. Shlomo was walking along with us when my friend asked me, offering his help too. Once Shlomo and I checked in at home, we went over to paint. We were having a grand time, slapping yellow paint all over the walls and ceiling. It turned out looking great, with Danny thanking us when leaving. Walking home, Shlomo and I discussed possibly building our own fort one day, if we could gather enough wood. Then he came to a sudden halt, looking down at his pants. "We are dead," he exclaimed, with a dreadful look on his face.

"What are you talking about? Did something happen?"

"Your pants. My mom got us these new pants. There's yellow paint all over them."

Then it hit me and I knew we were dead. "Oh my God. You're right. She'll kill me. This is about all I have to wear. What else am I going to wear to school?"

On our way home, Shlomo was designing a plan. He suggested that when arriving at our house, we should run directly to our bathroom and try getting the paint out before his mother saw it. The only problem I could foresee, with his plan, was our red Toughskins looked more yellow than red. There was no way we were going to get all the paint out, but not having a plan of my own, I went along with his. As we walked home, I was biting my nails down to the bone, trying to rub out the paint. It only succeeded to making my jeans look worse, knowing we had no way out of this dilemma.

When reaching the front door, Shlomo cracked it open as we both rushed in. But not before we met Hamar coming down the stairs. Her venomous look was enough to kill us. Mortified by what she saw, Hamar staggered down the stairs as if in defeat and was so fueled with fury that she actually started crying. After a good look over, she sadistically screamed, "Get up to your rooms. NOW!" Shlomo and I hightailed it up, as he jumped onto his bed and I leaped on mine, shuffling a pillow for protection. Then she came running after us, climbing the stairs hollering, "You stupid idiots. You wait and see."

Stomping in our spooky bedroom with a look of death painted on her face, Hamar broke into a wild conniption. She grabbed the doors to our closet, repeatedly slamming them open and shut with all her might. While violently slamming the closet doors, she was screeching, "You fucked up your clothes. I don't have money for more clothes. You idiots." Then holding one of her shoes, just before reaching me, she whipped it across the room. It whisked right past my left ear, sticking in the wall like a dart missing a board. The hardwood wedge shoe stuck heel-first into the wall, with her demanding it back. Stupid me, turned around and yanked it out of the wall. Gasping for air, Hamar motioned for me to give it back. I knew it was a terrible mistake but tossed it back anyways. Then Hamar took another shot at me as if she were a gunslinger, ricocheting the shoe off my forearm. It hit me so hard that I heard something pop. While screaming and rolling around on my bed in pain, I gingerly held my arm.

"I think you broke it," I screamed. "Oh man, it kills."

Appearing nervous, Hamar realized she truly hurt me this time, most likely hearing the pop in my forearm as well. She never apologized or even asked if I was ok. With a queer look on her face, she quickly gathered up her shoes while yelling an array of obscenities in her language, then scrambled out from our bedroom.

The next morning my arm was in terrible agony, feeling like someone hit it with a steel baseball bat. I could hardly move my hand or jingle my fingers from the intense pain. When inspecting my injured forearm, it had an enormous bulbous lump on it, resembling a large plum in size and color. After getting dressed for school, I went downstairs to eat breakfast. Hamar was already in the kitchen preparing something when I greeted her with a "hello". She barely looked up, not saying a single word. A bowl was waiting for me, since we weren't allowed to take any plates or silverware ourselves. Hamar claimed to keep kosher, so she didn't want us to mix the milk with the meat utensils. I poured some cereal and sat down with Mitch and Julie. Mitch looked unhappy as usual, knowing it was invoked from rooming with Julie. They didn't talk much as he was getting more distant from me too. I could see he was having a difficult time adapting to Hamar's abusive ways. It seemed like he had a lot going on in his head, with little desire to share it with anyone. I found it sad, but was overwhelmed dealing with my own predicament. It was hard for all of us because we had hopes that our stay with Hamar and our father was only temporary. The fact was we were stuck here, needing to toughen up to endure it.

While I was in deep thought, Hamar blew out a horrid fart. It didn't even faze her but abruptly shook me back to reality. She simply continued to do whatever it was she was involved with and didn't even excuse herself like usual. Then I started feeling the pain in my right arm nagging at me again. Staring at Hamar, I inquired, "Mom, what should I do about my arm, it really hurts?" I was rubbing the plum size bump while speaking.

"I don't know," she curtly said, with disdain in her voice. Never even bothering to look up, she continued acting too busy to be concerned.

"Well, do you know when this lump will go away," I asked, lifting my forearm up to show her.

Without looking in my direction, she spitefully said, "When you get married, that's when it will go away."

I glared at Hamar in disbelief, thinking she was making a joke. I waited to see if she was going to crack a smile or say she was kidding, but neither reaction happened. Once knowing she was serious, I honestly didn't know what she meant. I was baffled by Hamar's reply and surprised by her aloof concern, since she caused my injury. At that instant, it occurred to me that she didn't have a motherly bone in her entire body. It was one of those defining moments, which solidified in my mind that emotionally I had to be hard. Motherly love and nurturing died when my father won custody of us.

****

Looking back, it was clear that Uncle Gus and Aunt Rubel were the closest relatives to us. They were constantly around with their two children, Sarah and Phil. We shared all sorts of occasions together like Friday night dinners, barbeques or just weekend outings. Mitch, Julie and I made sure to refer to them as uncle and aunt. It was getting easier as time passed, considering we didn't have any kind of contact with our real family. When summer arrived, we spent even more time with them because of their membership to the Red Hill Municipal Pool.

Getting into the pool was the biggest obstacle, messing with my nerves each time we went. My father and Hamar didn't buy a membership, so we had to improvise. Improvising meant, we would either sneak in or use Gus' membership cards. I hated the sneak approach, having been caught once before and it was humiliating as hell. When the pool attendant caught me, everybody was already inside and I had no idea what to do next. Not having a way to contact anyone, I simply waited outside the gate until they noticed I didn't make it in. Eventually, when they realized I was missing in action, Uncle Gus came out paying for my admission. My father gave him the money, but seeing that he held the membership card, Gus was one in charge of retrieving me. When coming in, Hamar and my father gave me the biggest guilt trip for getting caught and having them pay. It was as if I was a huge disappointment for not being smooth enough to slip by the pool attendant. Since unable to sneak in like Shlomo, they called me a chicken. Ever since my father busted me for the cigarettes and made me return them, I had a conscience about doing anything illegal.

The next approach was even better than sneaking in. My father and Hamar would pay for themselves while carrying Samara in, since she was free. That left the rest of us sitting in a car, waiting as the temperature reached as high as 110 degrees. Eventually, someone would run out with the membership cards so we could enter the pool. The first time this happened I was given Uncle Gus' card. The only trouble with that was it stated his date of birth and featured his picture. I was supposed to pass for a balding man in his late forties. Being ten at the time, I never thought it would work. While walking up to the entrance, a wrenching sensation upset my stomach and I was astonished when they allowed me in. The pool attendants were so careless that it worked every time after that.

The grocery store was another place where I always experienced awkward adventures. Hamar repeatedly exploited the produce section while switching the price tags on all the items she purchased. As soon as we walked in, she invited everyone to the fruit section, generously instructing us to eat as much as we wanted. Shlomo was in his glory, a natural, as he feasted like a famished animal without hesitation. His hands and mouth were all over the fruit, eating just about anything Hamar wouldn't buy for the house. Mitch and I were too reserved to do anything like that. Perhaps, we would sample a grape or two, but nothing to the extent of what Shlomo consumed. He had no reservations about eating entire plums or peaches and spitting the pits on the floor. I could never understand how a manager didn't approach, throwing us out from the store. Regardless, I couldn't stomach doing something as common as that.

After we were done with the fruit section, Hamar needed a lookout to watch while she changed the price tags on the groceries. I never accepted her dishonest requests, as she quietly cursed me under her breath, saying, "Stupid idiot. Chicken." Then she would summon old faithful Shlomo, directing him to be the lookout person. He honestly enjoyed the chore, never feeling ashamed for being dishonest. Hamar strategically positioned Samara in the grocery cart, blocking the view, as she hastily peeled off the appropriate price tags. Then she would replace them with cheaper ones, looking ridiculous as she worked through the task. It was like watching a squirrel quickly unraveling a nut, then eating it before anyone could take it away. Mitch and I kept our distance, quietly cackling as we watched her at work. It was one of the few times she didn't look overly confident, instead she appeared childlike. I couldn't imagine my father was doing so poorly that she had to be this thrifty and underhanded.

While switching price tags, Hamar would have Julie shoplifting to help out her cause. Julie was only too glad to assist, trying her best to be accepted and fit in with Hamar's natural children. By helping, she thought it was one more inch closer to getting a dribble of Hamar's love. It was a cold home with little affection, but we were all striving to assimilate. Julie was too young to remember our real mother, missing out on the love she shared with us. So having no memory of any kind of motherly love, she was constantly yearning for it. Her memory was being tarnished with horrible stories of sleazy sex and abandonment. All of us were plagued with such tall tales that it started to feel like it actually happened. My father and Hamar did an effective job of making sure we had no contact with our mother and grandparents that the stories slowly sank in. There was no advocate to defend our real family, so their existence began fading away. Our memories of them were like figments or shadows of our imagination. Mitch and I didn't necessarily believe the stories, but rather pondered them around in our heads. Julie was younger and much easier to manipulate, so she was most impacted by their malicious stories, taking them all to heart.

****

Hamar and my father still held going out on Saturday nights, as high as Shabbat dinners. Shlomo and I didn't mind, seeing how we had the run of the house when they were gone. He knew where they kept their secret stash of goodies and no matter how many times we moved, he found it. Our parents mostly went out with Hamar's wealthy sister, Muffy, and her husband, Douglass. They dressed up for the occasion too, since Douglass' friends were true socialites with plenty of money. They ate at the most exclusive establishments in Delaware; the kind of restaurants where jackets and ties were required. During the times we were still awake when our folks returned home, they raved over the incredible restaurant they ate at. My father would still be licking his chops, describing in detail how wonderful the food tasted. They normally had great leftovers like lobster, crab cakes or steaks, but we were never allowed to try any of it.

Douglass didn't care much for Hamar; a considerable reason why Hamar and her sister didn't spend more time together, except for Saturday nights. My father wasn't especially fond of Douglass either, perceiving him as a pompous ass and a showoff. Always accusing Douglass of belittling him and other family members when they were out with his friends. The demeaning comments were usually around the subject of success and money. A few times when they were out, Douglass made a few insulting remarks at Gus' expense in front of his friends. My father once told me how it infuriated him, because Gus was too nice of a gentleman to start an argument and defend himself in public. It was obvious my father didn't enjoy going out with Muffy and Douglass, but did it to avoid nasty confrontations with Hamar. She was incredibly enamored with money and socializing with people who had it. My father was not like that but she quickly changed him when they married.

One Sunday afternoon, Mitch and Julie pulled a disappearing act on us. Hamar had been looking around for a few hours but with little luck. She asked if Shlomo and I would go search for them, given that dinner was going to be ready shortly. We scouted most of the neighborhood, coming up empty handed. Finally, we started searching the small strip center by our house, hoping to find them wandering around in the stores. There weren't many places, but the grocery store had a broken gumball machine which many of us knew about. We figured they may have been there messing around trying to get free gumballs, but they didn't turn up at grocery store either. The last place we searched turned out to be where they were hiding.

We found Mitch and Julie sitting in the neighborhood park, alongside a little fire Mitch started. They were doing their best to be inconspicuous, while getting prepared to grill the steaks that Julie shoplifted. When we walked up, they were comfortably sitting Indian style around the piled wood as Julie smiled, appearing to be happy to see us. Mitch's expression was entirely different, looking like a man on a mission and wasn't as happy to see us as Julie.

"What in the world are you guys doing," I asked. "You could set the whole place on fire and what's with the steaks?"

Julie instantly jumped up, asking, "Do you guys want some? They're big."

"No," I said with a sarcastic tone. "You guys are in trouble. You better come back now. Mom has been looking for you all for a while and sent us to find you."

Mitch didn't look up, poking at the little fire with a bent twig. "I'm tired of living here. Julie and I want to run away and go live with our Mama Ida and mom."

I immediately thought to myself, "What a terrible thing to say in front of Shlomo." It was like committing suicide without knowing it. I tried convincing them to come along without any further explanations, seeing as Shlomo was present. Then Shlomo jumped in, saying, "Come on guys, my mom has been looking for you for a long time and she's going to be pissed if we're not back soon."

Julie leaped up at once, ready to head home but Mitch took some convincing. I don't think Julie understood why she was running away from home, even though she was catching most of the abuse from Hamar. Mitch was still determined to runaway, with no desire of hearing about going home. "I don't want to go back," he contended. "She hides all the food and we're not allowed to eat anything. She even took my Halloween candy. I'm tired of all the yelling too." That was the most Mitch had spoken in a long time.

I wanted to say I agreed but Shlomo was standing next to me. It felt uncomfortable speaking candidly in front of him. "I know," I said. "But we have to go. You don't want a beating from dad? Do you?" I hoped the threat of my father's hand on him would bring Mitch back to reality.

Reluctantly, he stood up still looking down at the ground, arguing, "I'll go, but I'm not talking to anybody." As Shlomo walked ahead of us with Julie, Mitch and I lagged behind while I listened to him complain. I thought it best Shlomo didn't hear more than he needed to about his mother.

As Mitch aired his thoughts for a while, we all walked back home. None of us told Hamar or my dad where they were or why they left. We didn't talk about it again, but I could see Mitch was adamant about getting out of this situation. I sucked up the bullshit, trying my best to get along with Julie doing the same. Even after all the abuse she endured, Julie stood strong wanting to fit in. Mitch continued with his current demeanor, which was acting very quiet and reclusive. I never really knew what he was thinking. Deep down inside I understood his hatred for living there, having the same sentiments but the reality was, we were stuck. It was like quicksand; the more we fought the nonsense, the more we sank into self-pity.

We never reached out for help from anyone either. We were too fearful of being punished, with nowhere to go since our real family had completely quit fighting for us. I understood the only hope was to slowly tolerate the suffering, eventually growing old enough to move out.

CHAPTER 22

A year had passed since living in the Red Hill house and our lease was up. My father and Hamar decided to downsize, moving us to an apartment that had three bedrooms and a den. We remained in Red Hill, which wasn't too far from where we lived before, and extremely close to my dad's lighting store. The apartment complex was off of Moss Lane, having some heavy traffic but we were permitted to go visit the stores in safe walking distance. One being the 7-Eleven, where we frequented when stumbling across some change from the coke bottles we cashed in. With our unit on the first floor, we had a feeling of having our own giant backyard. It was the size of two football fields and Shlomo and I spent most days practicing our passing plays. We were getting prepared for the season since my father promised to sign us up for tackle football that year. We were so enthusiastic that we practiced every spare moment. I hoped to be the starting quarterback as Shlomo had his heart set on being the starting wide receiver.

Everything was wonderful about the apartment except the interior. It was nice and spacious but infested with disgusting cockroaches. I considered myself a clean kid and the idea of cockroaches climbing around when I was asleep gave me the creeps. I continually imagined falling asleep with my mouth wide-opened, having one of them crawling in. It was an ongoing nightmare I had during my stay, with each night taking longer to fall asleep. I never realized how many of them there were, until going into the kitchen or bathroom at night and flipping-on the light switch. It was like they were having meet and greets, while we were sleeping. There were hundreds if not thousands of the nasty things, crawling all over the counters and cabinets. As soon as I turned on the lights, they scattered away in masses as if pulling a fire alarm. The roaches instigated my spine with a tingling sensation each time I encountered them.

When we first moved in, Hamar had Mitch, Julie and the baby sharing the same bedroom, but after a few weeks, Shlomo demanded his own room. He was tired of rooming with me, wanting his privacy, so Hamar converted the den into a bedroom for him. Mitch was ecstatic because for the first time, in a few years, he was able to room with another guy. It was nice for me too, since we didn't have much time to speak alone about our mother and grandparents. Even though I was working on erasing them from my memory to stay strong, deep down I didn't want to forget my real family. I had the fondest memories of my childhood with them, but those fine thoughts were beginning to feel like a dream. The effects of trying to forget my mother and grandparents, in addition to such extended absent contact really impacted me emotionally. It was a sad affair, but refreshing to discuss them freely with Mitch. It softened me up, reflecting on the last people who truly loved me. They didn't make us feel like we had to fight to be cared for or loved. It was unconditional and I felt like it ended too soon in my life.

Another problem we encountered, while living at the apartment, was Hamar and my dad lied to the rental agent. They stated only having three children on the rental agreement, knowing if they had been honest, he wouldn't have rented the unit to them. So that meant, we always had to enter the apartment at different times and never all together. On many occasions, two of us were let out from the car before reaching our unit, evasively walking around the back of the apartment building not to be caught. We even avoided going to the apartment's community pool since our parents were afraid of being busted, but we still had Uncle Gus' membership when we wanted to swim.

Rocking Horse Elementary was a magnificent fit for me, with none of the kids coming from rich families and dressing just like I did. They wore Toughskins jeans and Kmart sneakers. There may have been a few who wore Chuck Taylor sneakers, but for the most part we all wore the same attire. I was excelling in sports at the time, which helped me considerably to make friends. My two best buddies were Dominic and Fred. They knew each other for years and dominated the fourth grade, making me a popular guy for the first time. Still paranoid about being left back, I avoided mentioning my age at all cost. Dominic was a short Italian kid, who played like he was a tough guy, portraying to bigger than he actually was. He was a genuine smartass but funny as hell. Anytime someone would challenge him, he threatened to call his two older brothers who attended the junior high school, which conveniently was behind our school. It was funny to watch the other kids constantly back down to his threats. I didn't blame them since knowing his brothers; they weren't the kind of guys you wanted to mess around with if you wanted to live. Fred was a nice kid and unlike Dominic, never mouthed off to people. He was one of those kids who hit his growth spurt at an early age, looking older than he was, so no one picked on him.

My teacher was very helpful during the time I attended Rocking Horse. She was easy to learn from and cared about her students' education. My grades were practically perfect in her class, making school much more enjoyable for me. I liked going there so much, that I hoped Hamar and my father weren't thinking of moving anytime soon.

Shortly after we moved in, Papa Willie called my father. Sadly, he was dying of pancreatic cancer and wanted to see us before passing away. My father did not immediately agree, wanting to discuss it with Hamar first. I remember overhearing their conversation concerning my grandparents' visit. My father was totally against them coming over in the beginning, but then saw it as an opportunity to acquiring some money. Grasping how wealthy my grandfather was, he knew we would have a better chance of inheriting money if he allowed them to visit with us. After weighing out the options, Hamar and my father agreed to let them come for a visit. They were growing so excited about the prospect of acquiring quick cash, that they even discussed it in front of us. I recall my father talking about it in the family room and it wasn't focused around my grandfather's death as much as it was about his wealth.

My father sat on the couch next to Hamar, looking exceedingly intense when speaking. "Hey guys, mom and I agreed to let your grandparents come over for a visit. You probably don't know this, but we found out that your grandfather has cancer and he's pretty sick. I don't know how sick but he wanted to come by and see you kids. Thank your mother because I didn't want them to come over." Elated, he glanced over at Hamar smiling. None of us said a thing. He continuously played up to Hamar when it came to things like that. I think he did it so we would love her more or think she was wonderful for doing something kind. We never did, as Mitch and I caught on to this routine without putting any credence towards it at all.

After finishing his opening statement, Mitch and I were jumping for joy in our minds. We looked at each other with brows raised but never spoke a word out loud. We made sure not to look overly excited either, so not to upset my father or Hamar. Neither of us really comprehended that Papa Willie was dying, seeing how overwhelmed we were with the idea of visiting with them. It had been more than two years since the last time we had any kind of contact with our grandparents.

My father delved back into the discussion and this time, he and Hamar displayed big mischievous smiles on their faces. "Jim, your grandfather was buying you Israeli bonds before you were even born. You must have thousands of dollars by now." His smile enlarged like Dr. Seuss' storybook character, "The Grinch".

Seeing how happy he was, I smiled back, asking, "What's a bond? Is that good?"

"Are you kidding? That's great, kid. A bond can be cashed in for money and I was with him when he bought plenty of them for you."

Grinning, I replied, "Great! That sounds cool."

Then Hamar chimed in licking her chops, stating, "Of course it's good, stupid. It's money. We need money. Stupid, asking if it's good."

After her defining comment, it was quite obvious what was going on. They didn't care that my grandfather was dying. They were hoping I would be left money, so to get their greedy paws on it.

"How about me, dad? Did they buy any for me too," Mitch questioned, sitting on the floor next to me.

"They sure did, Mitch. I don't know if you have as much as Jim, but I know they bought all you kids Israeli bonds."

Even Shlomo was becoming excited, slapping us on the back, shouting, "Good job guys. Wow, that's great. Make sure to be real nice to them. We can sure use the money."

Then Julie, jumping up and down, asked, "Me too? Me too?"

Looking like the bearer of great news from Mount Sinai, my father exclaimed, "Yes honey, you too. He got them for all you kids."

Hamar and my father sat on the couch with great anticipation in their expressions, while we remained on the floor listening. By their large gracious smiles, it looked as if it were their inheritance we were discussing, as they continued on with the conversation. I found it strange that they were chatting about such issues in front of us. Mitch, Julie and I didn't care about the bonds or even if we could convert them to cash. We were just so happy to see our true family again, making me feel like a missing part of my life was returning. It was all Mitch and I could talk about until the day they arrived. Apparently, our mother was not allowed to come. Building up the confidence to ask my father why she wasn't permitted to see us, he explained how she was too dangerous to be around. I couldn't understand the logic in his explanation or see what kind of danger he was referring to, that would justify such a threat to us. I understood they only permitted my grandparents over to get their money. Also realizing, if my mother had any wealth like her parents, they would have certainly allowed her to come as well.

At last, when the day came for my grandparents to visit, Hamar metamorphosed into someone I had never met before. She made sure, when our grandparents walked in, that she looked the part of a loving mother. She had Julie sitting on her lap with Mitch and me sitting on either side of her on the couch. What struck me strange or rather gave me the chills, were the loving rubs and touches Hamar gave us on our heads. It just didn't feel natural. My grandparents arrived, carrying armfuls of presents for all of us, even gifts for Shlomo and Samara. I never could figure out how they knew about them, but it was awfully nice that they were included. When saying hello to my grandparents, Hamar looked as though she plucked a smile from a caricature that an artist had drawn and superimposed it on her face. I laughed to myself, thinking how it must have hurt considering I never saw her smile that big before. It looked so phony that I knew anyone with some kind sense could read right through it.

Mitch, Julie and I stood up immediately to say hello. While hugging each of them, I hoped they could read my mind because it said, "Help. Please try to get us back again. Don't give up." Regrettably, I recognized it was false hope.

Papa Willie appeared very thin and weak. He was always a thin man, but looked sickly this time. His arms were like pixie sticks, swimming in the sleeves of his shirt, with his belt looking as if it was wrapped around his waist twice. Mama Ida looked to be the healthier of the two, still full figured with a glowing smile. While conversing with us, her happiness was illuminating and I could see a soft sparkle in her blue eyes, which I missed very much. It was a comforting look that I hadn't received from anyone, in quite some time. I wanted to ask about my mom to see how she was doing, but I knew better. All of us knew better than to ask that question or look overly elated to see them. I had a sense of needing to put up an imaginary line, so not to get too close to my grandparents.

My father paced the family room during our visit, smoking one cigarette after another. The room was filling up quickly with so much smoke that Hamar asked if he could go outside. She even asked in an unusually nice manner, shocking the hell out of me. Mama Ida made small talk with Hamar to be polite, but Papa Willie directed his full attention on us. He was vivacious while playing with us, showing little signs of being deathly ill. It was refreshing to be the center of attention for once, since Shlomo and his sister received all the attention in our house. I normally felt like a third wheel or even a stranger when Hamar's family came around. So it was nice to finally have my own family show us some love, reassuring me that someone still thought we were special.

As the clock was ticking down, despair was coating my mind with the reality that this was probably the last time I would see Papa Willie. The death of my dad's father taught me there was no coming back once you died. I remember being truly focused on him, trying to appreciate the short time we had together. Eventually, the visit came to an end and it was time to say goodbye. I hugged my ailing grandfather snuggly, hoping he knew how much I loved him. I didn't cry but the pain knotted strongly in my stomach as I watched them leave. Still owning a guilt complex about following my father's instructions in court, I prayed Papa Willie either forgave me or didn't know what we were coerced into saying. I didn't want him dying, thinking I betrayed him.

It didn't take long, from the time my grandparents left, for Hamar to switch back to her old self. As soon as the door shut behind them, she jumped on my father with all of us still around. "Well, what did he say to you, Sheldon?"

My father, looking surprised by the question, said, "What do you mean? What did he say to me? Nothing. You saw the old man. He was with the kids the whole time?"

"Schmuck. That's because you're smoking. Smoke, smoke! That's all you know. Stupid idiot. Big shot. I had to tell you to go outside. The whole house was filled with your smoke." Then she glanced at Shlomo. "Right, Shlomo? Wasn't he smoking the whole time like an idiot?"

This was the first of many times, when she dragged him into their arguments, which amazed me. Shlomo looked as disappointed as his mother, sadly grumbling, "Yeah dad, you were."

My father lit another cigarette, resembling a cornered tiger ready to pounce on his victim. His eyelids turned red as he squinted, coldly shouting, "Shut your mouth, Shlomo. Ok?"

"You shut your mouth, potato," Hamar hollered, with a ferocious demeanor. "Big shot, telling my son to shut up. Why didn't you use your big mouth with their grandfather," she screamed, then turning to face me. I took a slight step backwards. This was beginning to turn into a war zone and I wanted no part of it. "And you," Hamar called out to me, with a yucky look on her face.

"Hugging your mama and papa like a baby. What? You don't like it here? Stupid idiot. I'm not a good enough maid for you? Shit head!"

My father's complexion was white from anger, as he began shaking. I'm sure the nicotine didn't help, but I think it was more his nerves from Hamar's vicious attack. "Watch your mouth. Ok? What is it with you and your dirty filthy mouth?"

"Fuck you! You're going to take your son's side over me? Huh? Is that what you're doing?" I wanted to crawl under a rock and hide, possessing no desire for this argument to be about me.

My father completely lost his temper, screaming, "All you kids get the hell out of here."

Jumping in fear, we all darted for our bedrooms to take cover. Then through the walls, I could hear my father roaring at her with a wicked vengeance. "You listen to me. That old man is a cheap motherfucker. Ok? I didn't want those fucking people in my house and I told you I didn't want them in my fucking house. But no, you had to have them here. I hate the fuckers. Do you understand me? I hate the fuckers. I wish they both would fucking die. I hate that cunt more than the old man."

Remarkably, Hamar was quiet during his outburst. I was dumbfounded, presuming this would be it for Hamar and her two kids. My father would definitely divorce her after this battle. "No way," I thought to myself, was he going to put up with her and Shlomo on his back. I still couldn't fathom the fact that she asked Shlomo's opinion and he actually gave it, without any hesitation.

Hamar didn't yield long, firing back, "Just shut your mouth."

"You didn't want them here," she screamed to herself.

"You wanted them here. You're the one that told me about all their fucking money. What, did I make it up? Stupid. Just shut up already. I'm tired of your big mouth," Hamar hollered with malice.

It sounded as if the argument came to a halt after that barrage, until I heard Hamar belly-aching to herself. "Stupid idiot. Like I know they have money. Stupid. Like I need these bastards in my house. Potato, opening a big mouth on me." Then thrusting out one last insult to my father, she yelled, "Next time open your big mouth on somebody else, potato. You do that to me again and I'm leaving."

I could not comprehend how a woman, who was beaten the way she describes, could be so defiant. My father was a scary guy when becoming enraged, but she didn't waver, pushing him to the far limits. There were times when I honestly thought he was going to punch her through a wall. I could never figure out why he put up with so much of her bullshit.

The selfish thing about my father's hatred, towards my grandparents, was he never told us when Papa Willie died. He absolutely had no empathy for our feelings, robbing us of the opportunity to attend his funeral. The first time I found out he died was when he allowed Mama Ida over for a visit a few years later. He kept beating on the fact that my grandfather was a wealthy man and couldn't understand how he didn't leave us anything. "He had so many bonds for you, Jim. I can't believe he didn't leave you kids a penny. At least for college, he could have left you something. Jesus Christ, the money those people have. And that bitch won't give you a dime. You wait and see. Ida and Paula always said, in front of the old man, how they couldn't wait for him to die because he was so tight with his money." From the tone in his voice, it sounded like he was the one jilted out of the money. It was difficult for me to listen to his nasty comments about my grandparents, considering they were very loving and giving to me. More so than he ever was.

While school was in session, Shlomo and I joined the Montgomery County Football League. We had a tough coach named Mr. Norton who worked us real hard, but was always nice to me. He was a hefty fellow with average looks, except for his right index finger. He had a noticeable fingernail growing out from the end of it, similar to a claw, which I found a little creepy when shaking his hand. Mr. Norton rarely gave me a rough time since I was the smallest and youngest player on the team. My weight class was unable to form a team due to a lack of players that year. I wanted to play football so badly that I moved up a division just to be able to be on the field. My goal of being a starting quarterback was stunted that year, but at least I was out there getting experience. Since I was so small, Mr. Norton had me playing second string offensive guard and defensive guard. He sort of made me feel like the team mascot, but I was able to play each game.

Our home life at the new apartment remained the same. Hamar continued beating on Julie, inflicting awful comparisons to my mother's fabricated behavior. It severely changed the way we thought of Julie, imposing an animosity which grew amongst us. Relentlessly, we heard Hamar calling her a pig or a whore like our mother. It went on for so long that we were beginning to believe the manufactured slurs. All of us were trying to win Hamar's acceptance, which meant following her contemptuous lead and agreeing with whatever she said.

Julie was in trouble with Hamar on a regular basis and it wasn't for talking back. It was for stealing food or candy as she defined it. Whenever Hamar would find a candy wrapper or a peach pit in the trash, she went crazy because whomever ate it did not ask first. Mitch and I were becoming hostile towards Julie since Hamar was cross examining all three of us, trying to determine who the thief was. Invariably, Julie was found to be the criminal. Hamar knew exactly how much food or candy was missing, simply by eyeballing the pantry. When finding Julie guilty of taking food, Hamar went insane and it was a scary sight to witness. She portrayed a mad woman, hitting Julie with whatever was in her hands at the time. I witnessed Hamar throwing forks, knives, scissors and several other sharp objects which made me hold my breath, hoping it didn't seriously injure Julie. During those monstrous attacks, I could swear Julie had an invisible angel protecting her. When it looked like a dangerous kitchen utensil was going to strike Julie, somehow it was magically diverted. Hamar grew even more enraged when missing, with Julie feeling the wrath far worse once Hamar grabbed a hold of her.

The situation was escalating out of control with Hamar accusing Julie of stealing candy and food. It was evolving into a daily witch hunt, with serious consequences. One night, Hamar had all of us sitting in a circle as though we were going to play duck duck goose. Everyone was present except my father and Samara. He was watching television in the next room as Samara was asleep in her crib. Shlomo was running this little pow-wow, trying to convince Julie to admit that she stole a candy bar. Apparently, Hamar noticed a chocolate bar missing from the Halloween candy we collected from the year before. She didn't have a wrapper or any evidence, but was convinced Julie stole the candy. Shlomo and Hamar were playing good cop/bad cop, attempting to get a confession out of Julie.

Shlomo was acting like the good cop, coaxing her on by saying, "Come on Julie, just tell us you did it and no one will hurt you. I promise."

Julie sat staring into his eyes and wouldn't give in. "I didn't steal the candy. I swear. It must have been somebody else. I swear to God." This time she looked like she was telling the truth, but Shlomo wasn't giving up.

"Julie, we know you took the candy bar. Come on, mom won't hurt you. I promise." Hamar was sitting quietly next to Shlomo. She didn't say a word, but I could see her patience was running thin through the glare of her dark eyes. "Come on Julie, what do you say?"

Julie stuck to her guns and the odd thing was how relaxed she appeared. It was like she actually thought by not admitting the crime, Hamar wasn't going to hit her. But I knew Hamar was going to punish her with or without a confession and the beating would be horrendous. Julie continued sitting there, calmly rocking back and forth on her rear-end.

Losing patience, Shlomo decided to change his strategy. "Listen Julie, if you admit it, you won't get hit. But if you don't, mom is going to beat you. Just say you did it and you won't get hit. Ok?"

Mitch and I chimed in, saying, "Come on Julie, just admit it." It was getting late, with us wanting to watch TV before going to bed.

At last, Julie gave in. She smiled, glancing at Hamar who looked stone cold, casually stating, "Ok. I did it."

I was listening to Julie when my attention was distracted by Hamar. She transformed from a motionless mummy to a ferocious mountain lion, jumping from a sitting position, landing on top of Julie. It started snowing blond hair as Hamar was pulling the hair from Julie's head and scratching her face. She was yelling at the top of her lungs, "You fucking bitch whore. Liar thief pig. I've had it with you. You stupid pig. I hate you."

Suddenly, my father dashed over with a cigarette hanging from his bottom lip, bellowing, "Hey. Hey. What the hell is going on here?" Gently, he was pulling his wife off of poor Julie, but his attempts were going nowhere, so he yelled, "Hamar! Come on. Stop it already. What are you doing?"

Hamar gave Julie's head two last slams into the carpet for good measure, then faltered up with two handfuls of hair. "Your fucking daughter is a liar thief pig." Breathing heavily, it sounded difficult for Hamar to squeeze the words out from her lungs.

"Come *on*. Watch the language," my father pleaded.

"Come on? You come on. You fucking moron. Idiot." Hamar's chest was furiously pumping in and out, with a serious gasping for oxygen. She was directly in front of my father, barking inches from his face, probably close enough for him to smell what she ate for dinner, which I think was liver and onions.

"What the hell is going on here? What happened," he asked sounding confused, peering at Julie on the floor. She was out for the count, looking as though she were rolled by a few hoodlums. Julie's hair was so disheveled and strung out that she displayed an image of suffering from bad static cling.

"Your pig daughter is stealing food. That's what's going on. I am tired of this shit. Do you understand me? I am tired of being your kids fucking maid."

"Maid? What do ya mean," my father asked, with a befuddled expression.

"Just shut up you idiot. You don't know anything that goes on. Go ahead, keep smoking your cigarettes and drinking your vodka. I've had it."

Then my father looked at Shlomo for answers. "I don't know dad. I guess Julie took some candy and mom wanted her to admit it. That's all."

Julie was standing up by now, uncontrollably crying. She was trembling terribly from Hamar's malevolent attack, as her knees knocked together, crying out, "They told me to say it. I didn't take the candy." Her mouth was agape now, with saliva webbed between her lips, while having a difficult time squeezing the words out in between her whimpering.

Hamar harshly jumped in, cutting Julie off. "Just shut up. You pig. Fucking liar. You should drop dead."

As she was reaching for Julie again, my father grabbed her hand, shouting, "Ok, enough. Enough already. Julie get out of here. Go to your room."

While staggering off in obvious pain, Hamar removed her shoe, flinging it at Julie with full force. "Ooh," Julie bawled, as the shoe ricocheted off her back. Then reaching behind, Julie held the aching spot, moaning in pain.

"Don't wake the baby when you go in, pig liar," Hamar demanded, without showing an ounce of empathy.

My father watched, then shouted, "Ok, all you kids get to bed." As Mitch and I ran off to our room, my father sternly said, "What the hell is wrong with you?"

"Just shut your mouth. Stupid. You don't know anything. Are you defending your wifey? Is that what you're doing?" Mitch and I closed our bedroom door, so the rest of the argument was muffled. This was the beginning of Hamar accusing our father of siding with Julie over her. These fights were the most horrible ones, perpetuating to so many potential divorces. It caused harsh animosity between Hamar and Julie, encouraging Hamar to refer to Julie as my father's second wife or wifey. The more my father defended her, the more abuse Hamar inflicted. Julie desperately needed someone to be her advocate and it was a shame my father fell short to ward off Hamar's vile scorn. It proved to be a devastating blow to Julie's sanity.

The roach population was growing out of control and the longer we lived there the larger they seemed to get. One night after switching on the light, a huge black and tan one wasn't fast enough and I crushed him by accident. It scared the hell out of me because I thought I heard it scream. These roaches were becoming entirely too cocky, as they started showing up in my breakfast cereal in the mornings. Hamar refused to call the maintenance man in fear he would see all the beds. She thought he would figure out that we were too many living in the apartment, with a chance of being evicted. I was sick of the living conditions but without an exterminator, I had no choice.

Shlomo and I were sitting in our parents' bed, watching the *"Dirty Dozen"* during one of our parents' Saturday night excursions. We were looking forward to seeing the movie all week, since Jim Brown was starring in the film. While sitting in their bed eating candy, which Shlomo took from Hamar's private stash, a big roach came crawling over Hamar's nightstand. Without any hesitation, I reached out snagging it with my bare hand. Normally, I would have never done that, but it was getting intolerable being pushed around by these pests. Shlomo stared at me like I was crazy, expelling an unstrung cackle. "Jim, what are doing with that cockroach?"

I felt it crawling around in the palm of my hand, giving me a tickling sensation. Then searching around the room, I noticed Hamar's sewing kit. "You know what? I want a pet. How about you?" Standing up, with the roach still cupped in my hand, I reached into the sewing box, pulling out a needle and a piece of thread.

Shlomo's eyes were inquisitively fixed on me, as he nervously asked, "What are you going to do with that?"

"I'm going to make a leash for our new pet," I replied, starting to thread the cockroach through its belly. Initially, it was tough getting the needle to penetrate. But once through, I tied a knot on the other end of the thread and it worked like a charm. It's like the feeling you get from baiting your fishing hook for the first time with a worm. At first you get the willy's, but then you work-up enough confidence to actually stomach doing the dirty deed.

"*Ohhhh* my God," Shlomo half-laughed, shouting at the same time. "I can't believe you did that. Oh my God. You're gross." He continued to nervously laugh and I could sense, by the anxious expression on his face, that he was sickened by the whole thing.

The roach didn't appear hurt, as I began taking him for a stroll along my parents' bed. "Look man. I'm walking the cockroach. Isn't that cool," I said, as the roach appeared to be obedient.

"Dude, you are gross. I can't believe you," Shlomo gasped through a grin. He was backing away, as I slowly strolled the cockroach closer to him. "Get that thing away from me," he cried out, while laughing.

Then suddenly I came up with a brilliant idea. I decided to get even with Hamar for having us live with all these pests, by scaring her with the roach. Taking the thread with the cockroach still attached, I put it underneath the telephone that was on her nightstand. I assumed the weight from the phone would keep the roach from scurrying away. Shlomo was laughing at my prank and couldn't wait to see if it was going to scare his mother. After everything was in place, we continued watching the movie, periodically checking to make sure that our little friend remained on the nightstand. When Hamar and my father returned home, we were still in their bed watching television. We nervously cackled under our breath, listening to my father describe their night out. As he went on with his trite story, Shlomo and I kept peeking over at the roach that was trying everything in its power to get loose. Neither of them ever noticed our prank while we were in the room, eventually sending us to bed. After lying in bed for a while and almost falling asleep, I heard a shrilling scream echoing from their bedroom, as Hamar was cursing in Arabic or Hebrew. It was hilarious and I felt somewhat vindicated. Smiling and giggling myself to sleep.

The next morning, while poking through my cereal looking for cockroaches, my father staggered into the kitchen. "Ok. Who was the wise guy that put the cockroach on your mother's nightstand?"

Shlomo and I immediately began laughing out loud. Then Shlomo said, "Jim. He is gross. He actually made a leash for that thing too. Did you see that?"

Lighting a cigarette and taking a deep drag, my father shot me a queer look, simply shaking his head in disbelief. He smirked as if he wanted to laugh at the prank but something stopped him.

Things were beginning to look up for my father, as his lighting store was taking off, making a fair amount of money. I remember him coming home one evening, surprising Hamar. Slipping in while she was busy in the kitchen, he elusively hid cash throughout the entire apartment. When finished, my father prompted her to go find the money. He made the first few dollars easy to find, enticing Hamar to go search for the rest of the stash. The money was buried in the beds, the lights, the couch and a few other sneaky places. As Hamar impatiently found the money, she tightly caressed the bills in her palms, smiling like a child opening birthday gifts. It looked like so much fun that we wanted to join in and help, but Hamar wouldn't have it. She almost bit our heads off for offering. "No. No. Everyone get away! I want to find it."

All of us stood back watching, as she pecked and cooed for the money like a pigeon looking for bread crumbs. She reminded me of a spoiled child who didn't want to share with others. When all the money was eventually found, she sat down in the family room counting it. I don't know how much she collected but her enamored reaction showed instant gratification. It was one of the fewest times, I actually ever saw her content.

Later that night, I decided to hit my dad up for an allowance since he was in such a generous mood. Shlomo and I knew their anniversary was coming up and wanted to get them a gift. After Hamar's scavenger hunt, my father went to his room to change, so I followed him in, gracefully saying, "Hey dad, I was wondering. Do you think it would be possible for me to get an allowance from you, please?" I stood with great anticipation, waiting for him to say "yes".

Without as much as a moment's consideration, he responded, "No."

While sitting on the bed, with his back to me, removing his socks, I asked, "How come?"

"Because I don't have enough money to give you an allowance, that's why."

I wasn't giving up so easy. "Well, Shlomo and I want to buy you and mom an anniversary present and we need some money. How about a dollar a week? I already shine your shoes and maybe there's something else we could do."

"No," my father shouted, without any hesitation again. He didn't bother looking in my direction, busy neatly hanging up his slacks. With the slacks under his chin, he gently slid them on a hanger.

"What about fifty cents? Do you think you could spare fifty cents," I asked, starting to feel like a pauper.

Then going to his dresser, my father picked up his pack of cigarettes, then began lighting one. "Jim, I'm not giving you any money. That's the end of the story." It was evident that he was perturbed with my pestering.

I thought to myself, "If he was able to buy all those packs of cigarettes, how was it he couldn't throw some change our way?" I threw out my last offer as a joke, but he didn't laugh. I wanted to see what he would say. "Ten cents. Could you spare ten cents?"

He merely looked at me, as if I was a joke, walking out from the room. After that night, I told Shlomo we better think of something else, because my father wasn't letting go of his change.

We started our babysitting careers after my failed negations with my father. Shlomo babysat for Aunt Muffy's two children, as I was hired to watch over Aunt Rubel's kids. It was an easy job and they paid us about five bucks, each Saturday night, for watching their children. Eventually saving up a few dollars, we combined our earnings to buy our parents an anniversary gift. Hamar was impossible to buy for and anytime we presented her with a gift, she was brutally honest about hating it. She repeatedly returned all our gifts, then keeping our money we spent on her. Cash was hard to come by, so when telling us how much she disliked our gifts, it felt like a piece inside of me was chipped away. But instead of cursing under my breath and vowing never to buy her another gift, strangely it inspired me to get something that she might keep. It was bizarre thinking, but pleasing Hamar was the constant theme in our house. Starting with my father, then trickling its way down to us. This onerous to appease Hamar, even haunted us through our adulthood.

When Valentines Day came around, my father took everyone shopping to get Hamar presents. He bought a heart shaped candle for Julie and Samara to give Hamar. Then purchased a stuffed animal and a little heart shaped box, filled with chocolates, for the guys to give Hamar. During the drive home, we were so excited to give her our gifts that it was all we could talk about. Shlomo, Mitch and I even devised a plan of how we were going to present our gifts. We decided that each of us would have our hand on the gifts when presenting them to her. When arriving home, everyone darted straight for Hamar, struggling and fighting to make their gift the first she would receive. All of us were so wrapped up with giving her a present that we forgot our plan, which we worked so hard on. While Hamar was picking the presents out from the bag, I stood smiling in great expectation of her loving ours'. The first item she lifted out was the stuffed animal. Managing a smug smile, Hamar said, "Ah, that's nice," handing it over to the baby.

"Hey mom, why did you give that to Samara? It's for you," I proudly said, smiling.

Still looking through the bag, she sarcastically shouted, "It's for babies. Let Samara have it." Then pulling out the heart shaped candle, which Julie and Samara got her, she glared at it with disdain in her eyes. "Sheldon," she said with an obnoxious smirk. "What is this? Is this what you wasted our money on? Stupid. Like I need this shit."

Julie looked very hurt, as I presumed all of us were, since Hamar completely sucked the air out of all the fun and excitement. My father squinted at her, while grinding his teeth saying, "Come on Hamar. The kids did a nice thing." Grinding his teeth was a habit of his when upset. "Just say thank you. That's all you have to say." He acted aggravated while speaking his peace.

Hamar roughly slammed the bag down, holding the last gift blurting, "Just shut up, Sheldon. You didn't give me a chance. Thanks," she muttered through clenched teeth and pursed lips. It looked utterly painful for her to have to say.

Then Shlomo asked, "Mom, are you going to open the chocolate?" I was thinking the same thing since I was sure we all wanted a piece.

"No. I'm going to save it for later," she said, grabbing the boxes and shoving them high in a cabinet out from our reach. I never saw the chocolate or the candle again, given that she later returned everything and kept the money.

After my father's lighting company proved to make a little profit, our Sundays were spent driving in the family car. My parents were determined to build their own home and it was pure torture for five children to be jammed in a car, searching for lots all day. Every Sunday morning my father read through the real estate section, then out we went, hunting for potential lots to build their dream home on. Muffy and Douglass had recently purchased a brand new home in Parkview, where Hamar desperately wanted to move to be by her sister. We searched for what seemed like months but everything was completely out of their price range. Hamar and my father had a few nasty arguments over the price range, but in the end, they finally found a parcel they both could agree on. It wasn't in Parkview, but instead they settled for the city of Red Hill again. Hamar refused to admit the property was located there, since she considered Red Hill beneath her. Bass was the next best thing to Parkview, so she told everyone we lived in Bass.

My father took on the job of being the general contractor and after all the plans and specs were completed, they broke ground. While working his lighting store with my uncle, he also oversaw all the tradesmen he hired to construct the home. Every weekend was devoted to building the new house, as it turned into a family project. My father cut many corners by doing things himself, using us to help with partially finishing the home. The one job I remember doing, which I thought was far out of our expertise, was laying the drainage hose around the foundation. This procedure was to prevent potential flooding in the basement. He had all of us running around the first floor, which at the time was covered in pressed wood, laying this contraption into a deep hole that was trenched out around the basement. He screamed and pointed in frustration until we got it right. Hamar was so used to running the show at home that she didn't like taking his tongue lashing. Frequently, she got into big arguments with him which were the only times he refused to back down. Being so focused and serious on building the house, he habitually cursed, never finding a reason to say please or thank you. I think that's what drove Hamar batty. The unfortunate outcome was how badly we botched up the job. Anytime we had a strong rainfall, our basement turned into a swimming pool. It was an ongoing problem which we could never correct. I feel bad for the poor sap who bought their house.

The home was on target to be built by the time our next school year started and it was looking very promising. Before finishing out my school year at Rocking Horse, Mama Ida surprised me. An announcement came over the loud speaker while I was sitting in class. "Will James Wilde please report to the school office before going home today. Thank you." Everyone ooh'd and ah'd after the announcement, assuming I was in some kind of trouble and in fact, so did I. Vigorously biting my fingernails, I tried imagining what I could've possibly done. Even my buddies were looking puzzled, as they stared at me. When class was over, I quickly gathered my things and hurried to the front office. I was responsible for walking Mitch and Julie home, so I knew I had to hurry not to miss them. When approaching the front desk I peeked over, introducing myself to the lady who was in charge. "Hi, my name is Jim Wilde. You wanted to see me?"

"Oh yes, Jim," she replied with a friendly smile. "Your Mama Ida dropped this off for you. She wanted me to make sure you got it." While speaking, the lady picked up the box from behind the elongated desk and passed it over to me. "Here you go," she said half-laughing, commenting how heavy the box was.

I quickly snatched it, thanking her as I ran off to meet up with Mitch and Julie. It felt good to get something from Mama Ida and it was nice that she was still thinking of us, even though we weren't permitted to speak with her. The box was quite a load but I didn't care. The only thing on my mind was rushing home to find out what was inside. Julie and Mitch were overwhelmed with excitement when I told them we got gifts from Mama Ida. Even as I ran, we couldn't get home fast enough to open the large brown box. On the entire way, all I could smell was the scent of cardboard under my nose and couldn't wait to tear the thing open.

Passing through the sliding glass door in the back, it occurred to me that it would be prudent to show Hamar the gift before opening it. I knew how she had to have total control over every situation and it wouldn't be worth getting into a scrap over. Walking into the kitchen, we found her busy preparing something for dinner. I was the first to kiss her and say hello, which was a must in our house. We always kissed both sides of her cheeks when leaving or entering. It was a major crime not to do it immediately either; you were in the doghouse if you happened to mess that up.

Proudly, I held up the brown box saying, "Look what the other grandmother dropped off for us." I was careful to call Mama Ida the "other grandmother". I had to preface anyone from my former family as the "other", otherwise it was grounds for sizable trouble. There was only supposed to be my father's mother and her parents as our acting real grandparents, so I used this term to avoid controversy.

Hamar instantly grabbed the box from my weary arms claiming ownership. "How did you get this," she inquired, making sure we didn't have contact with Mama Ida.

"From the school. They called me up from class to pick it up."

Hamar blasted a nasty look my way. "Was she there?"

"No," I adamantly said. "She must've left it at the front desk. I never saw her."

Hamar was preoccupied with unwrapping the box, while Mitch, Julie and I conversed amongst ourselves. She was attempting to rip the packing tape off with her nails, but was unsuccessful, so she resorted to using her teeth. She resembled a rat trying to gnaw its way through a piece of cheese, when Shlomo promptly showed up to see what great treasures were locked inside the box. All four of us stood anxiously awaiting, as Hamar struggled with the packing tape. At last, when the box was opened, she hastily pulled out a card that Mama Ida had addressed to Mitch, Julie and me. Hamar quickly skimmed through it, then tossed it over to us. After reading the kind sentiments inside, I noticed it was signed by Mama Ida, Papa Willie and mother Mindy. I thought it was very thoughtful and was pleased to see my mom signed the card too. Watching Hamar burrowing through the box, I almost forgot the gifts were for us. She harshly yanked out clothing while taking quick glances, then abruptly tossing them to the side. I didn't know what she was looking for, but it didn't seem as though she liked anything Mama Ida had bought for us. At the bottom of the box was a watch for me and a few toys for

Mitch and Julie. Hamar opened a jewelry box as she curled her lips in disgust. Plucking the watch from the box, she commented, "Ugh, this is like an old man's watch. What an ugly watch."

Wanting a better look, I asked, "Can I see it please?"

She held it between her index finger and thumb while saying, "Here. But I wouldn't wear it. It's ugly and it looks like an old man's watch."

Retrieving it from her greedy fingers, I looked it over, replying, "I like it. I think it looks cool." Then smiling, I tried it on my right wrist.

"You would. You have terrible taste," Hamar said, with a sly snicker. Shlomo agreed with her, as they laughed together out loud.

I couldn't comprehend what she didn't like about the watch. It had a beautiful silver band with a blue face and little dots in front of the numbers. The dots resembled diamonds, adorning the watch with a dressy appearance. I decided not to care what she or Shlomo thought. I found it sad that she couldn't be happy for us, figuring she was upset because Mama Ida didn't send anything for her children. She and Shlomo looked like a pair of jealous immature children, mocking us for the gifts they didn't receive. Unfortunately, we never did get to wear the clothing since the closest we ever came was watching Hamar fondle them, with her ravenous hands. She brought everything back to the department stores, pocketing all the cash for herself. Most likely, she would have returned the watch as well, but luckily Mama Ida tore off the tags.

Shortly after Hamar returned our gifts, a fire ignited in my belly which couldn't be extinguished, evoking me to rebel with a wise-ass mouth. I didn't have the same patience for her usual evil ways, itching for an opportunity to blurt out something obnoxious at her. I understood it would lead to a beating, but was far beyond falling to my knees due to physical violence.

School was out, with Hamar having no choice but to drag us along while she shopped for the new house. It was nearing completion, as she was trying to get it decorated before moving in. During one of our shopping sprees, Hamar and I got into a screaming match, standing in the middle of Montgomery Mall going at each other. She kept coming at me with intolerable insults, until I finally lost my temper, calling her a miss know-it-all. It shocked the hell out of me how those words escaped my mouth and I guessed it stunned everyone else too. Shlomo, Mitch and Julie all stared at me dumbfounded with their eyes bulging out.

Hamar was stumbling with several bags, appearing to be holding her breath not to embarrass herself by screaming at me in public. "Ooooooh. You wait til we get home," she mumbled under her breath, with torrid fire in her voice. "I'm going to call your father when we get home and make sure he comes from work and kills you. You just wait. You bastard. Piece of shit, you just wait."

Knowing I was dead, my face took on a white complexion as all the blood rushed to my stomach. Walking back to the car, Hamar was livid and began talking to herself. "Stupid idiot. Calling me miss know-it-all. Wait, just wait, til I tell your father. You piece of shit. You can go to hell. You bastard." She carried on the entire drive home but in extra high volume. With each threat, I could vividly see my father viscously attacking me and as we inched our way home, my stomach was churning from nerves.

When we got back, Hamar hollered for me to get into my room, immediately calling my father. I could hear her on the telephone, screaming about what a piece of shit I was and he better get his ass home to beat me now or else. With the combination of her insane yelling and my father having to leave work, there was no doubt I was in severe trouble. I sat on my bed like a pig waiting to get slaughtered. The only difference between me and a pig was I knew what I was waiting for. I wished I had to the gumption to run away, but it would only prolong the inevitable.

It didn't take long for my father to get home, considering he only worked five minutes away. When he arrived, the door sounded like it was kicked opened and I recognized his heavy footsteps right away. Then I heard him ask, "Where the fuck is he?"

"He's in the bedroom," Hamar instantly replied in a spiteful tone.

I sat on the bed with my legs dangling over, as my body violently trembled, slowly going numb. It was a feeling like being in the doctor's office, waiting for the biggest needle you ever felt. My fingers dug deep into my bedspread as I heard him getting closer. The door slammed opened, hitting the door stopper with a heavy loud thud. My father walked in with malicious drooling eyes and fists clenched. Squeezing my eyes tightly shut, I waited in slow anticipation for a brutal beating. Without a sound out of my father's mouth, he whacked me right across the face. I saw bright circling stars, then felt my brain rattle in my head. Every muscle in my body tightened up, waiting on another blow but there was none. Opening my eyes after a few dull moments, I saw him walking away.

Hamar was leaning against the doorframe to my bedroom, yelling, "That's it? That's all you're going to do? I told you to kill him! You stupid idiot."

I thought to myself, "Please shut up lady. No more hitting for God sakes." I was still trembling, thinking she was going to convince him to beat me some more.

"What the fuck, do you want me to do? Huh? Do you want me to kill him? Is that what you want?" My father was screaming so loud that the room felt like it was vibrating. Hamar stood with a wicked look in her eye as my father reiterated, "Do you want me to kill him? Is that what you want?"

I was praying he was just bluffing.

"Fuck you. Just go to work. You stupid piece of shit too. I've had it with you and your pig kids already," she shouted back in a cruel manner.

Then glaring at me, Hamar spitefully hollered, "You stay in your fucking room. You big mouth bastard. Piece of shit. I'm through with you. You can feed yourself and clean your own clothes. I don't give a shit about you anymore. Piece of shit. Calling me a know-it-all. You should drop dead." Slamming my door shut, she repeatedly screeched obscenities in English, Arabic and Hebrew out loud.

I heard my father screaming at her when leaving. "I don't have time for this shit. I'm working, trying to earn money and you're calling me home for this shit." The front door ferociously slammed for a second time, then he was gone.

After the commotion settled down, Mitch came back into the

room to see if I was ok. Hamar didn't appreciate that. She and my father were experts on engineering gimmicks to pin one sibling against the other. It was barbaric but we all fell for it, whether we honestly believed it or not. It was like a sick psychological study that we all participated in. If one of us were in trouble with Hamar, then the other siblings would ride on her bandwagon. Whether she was right or wrong, none of us ever stuck up for the other. We were deathly afraid of getting beaten ourselves, so we wanted her to like us for taking her side. It manifested into a contest, with everyone striving to win her love and acceptance.

CHAPTER 23

The new dream house was finished in the nick of time for us to start school. I was entering the fifth grade, with Shlomo being the first child in our family to reach junior high school. Our elementary school was so small that they mixed a few fourth graders in my classroom. I found it odd that all of us were learning the same curriculum, but as time passed I became accustomed to it. Initially, I was afraid of not being smart enough to be in a classroom with just fifth graders. But it turned out, that was a standard practice since the school wasn't large enough to accommodate all the children attending. Still harboring my dark secret of failing second grade, I was paranoid of anything happening out of the ordinary.

Shlomo had a complete personality makeover after reaching the seventh grade and we didn't do as many activities together as before. Our interests changed as he became more focused on his friends than our relationship. We stopped our combined hobbies and every day football workouts. He was more concerned with hanging out with his school buddies than messing around with me. There seemed to be such a big difference between elementary school and junior high from his descriptions. It sounded so exciting that I couldn't wait to go.

It was cumbersome starting new schools year after year and making new friends. I missed my old buddies, finding it difficult to fit in to certain circles sometimes. The only attribute saving me was being a good athlete. The majority of the kids attending this school all came from very wealthy or well-to-do families. My family was financially struggling, as I was sent to school wearing Kmart plastic tennis shoes and Toughskins jeans. The other kids were wearing leather Nike's and Levi jeans. Fortunately, I made friends with a very popular guy named Dave. Not only was he a great athlete, who all the kids looked up to, but was quite the stud with the girls. He immediately took me under his wing as we began hanging out in school together. Dave gave me a hand in making other friends, helping me avoid ridicule about my cheap attire. At that time, I only had two different shirts and two different jeans to wear to school. I was getting weary of trying to mix and match my clothing each morning. There were only so many combinations I could put together and I was struggling with my self-confidence about it. I did everything in my power, day after day, not to think about what I was wearing. The only person whoever teased me about my atrocious wardrobe was Dave, but it was always in private. He was more inquiring why I was dressed the way I was, rather than ridiculing me. He actually offered his Nike shoes to me when he got a new pair, but I was too proud to accept them. He was my best friend and I truly looked up to him.

I don't think I slept or took ownership of my new bedroom for at least a year. Each of us were slotted to have our own bedroom in Hamar's new dream house, but the only problem with that was Hamar's parents moved right in when we did. Mitch and I were tossed out of our beds like Bedouins and given army cots. Somehow, Hamar came by these cots which Mitch and I were forced to sleep on. I was made to share my room with papa and Mitch with mama. The bedrooms were average size at best and when adding an army cot, there literally was no room to walk around.

Hamar and her parents loved eating Moroccan dishes, which consisted of a multitude of beans and fried foods. Needless to say, they walked around billowed with horrid smelling gas. Papa had a habit of getting up in the middle of the night and farting, as he maneuvered around looking for the bathroom. Unfortunately for me, he expelled gas in my direction each night before making it to the toilet, giving off a revolting odor. The smell was indescribable, making it almost impossible to fall asleep after one of his episodes. Mitch and I were disappointed by the intolerable arrangement but wouldn't dare say a word if we wanted to walk again.

Football season started and this time I was enrolled in the appropriate weight class. Most of the kids who played were from different elementary schools, since not many who attended my school were interested in playing tackle football. They were primarily focused on playing soccer, with my best friend Dave being one of them. I was a rarity, loving football far more than soccer. Mitch joined as well, playing second string center on my team. Upon winning the starting quarterback position, I remember how proud I was to come home and give my father the big news. When breaking the news to him, he couldn't have been happier. After slapping each other's hand in victory, I asked if he was planning on coming to my games. He explained that he would try, but never showed up to a single one. When we played, most of the kids usually had one or both of their parents on the sidelines, but mine never showed. It was difficult to get a ride to the games on Saturdays as well, since my dad and Hamar weren't interested in watching us play. Being close with my coach, he was kind enough to pick Mitch and me up for each game.

As the season progressed, we won so many games that we made it all the way to the championship. I was overwhelmed with pride, feeling as though we were going to the Super Bowl. When finding out, I knew my father had to make time to come to this game; it was too important for him to miss. That night I told him all about the championship game, but he explained how he and Hamar already had plans to go away on vacation. With disappointment clogging my windpipe, I asked, "When did this happen? We didn't know about it."

He had a surprised expression on his face, taking a sip of vodka, saying, "I didn't think I had to clear my vacation with you."

"I know that, but we didn't know. Mitch and I have this big game and I thought you'd want to come," I said, feeling slighted.

"I would, Jim but we already have this planned. Your mother and I need to get away together. Next time I'll see your game."

"Just forget it. Who knows if there will be a next time for a game like this. Plus, you never came to one of our games anyway." He was such a disappointment that I gave up on our conversation, sauntering up to my bedroom. Hamar happened to pass me, as I stomped off shedding my enthusiasm.

As I walked away, I heard my father lighting a cigarette in frustration, then telling Hamar what just transpired between us. "Do you believe this shit? He's mad at me about this vacation?"

"Who cares? Stupid, like I'm going to miss my vacation for his stupid football. That's all I need, is to miss my vacation for his football. Stupid, like I'm going to miss my vacation," Hamar remarked so eloquently.

I was terribly upset by my father's lack of interest, choosing never to discuss my football games with him again. I figured he would be proud that I was a quarterback, using football as topics for us to speak about. But instead, my participation in football was only a good conversation piece when he was listening to other proud parents boasting about their children. Then he would use it to position a counter attack. His disinterest never swayed me from playing football, seeing as it was the only thing in my life which made me feel good about myself. I liked achieving great grades in school, but there was something vastly special about being on a football field.

Our weekends were busy and except for playing football, my time was devoted to helping Hamar finish her dream home. At first, it started with the lawn. They purchased three quarters of an acre, without a single blade of grass growing anywhere. Our job was to prepare the property for the lawn people, so they could spray the grass seeds before winter. To our chagrin, the entire lot was overwhelmed with rocks. Hamar and my father had us on our hands and knees, picking a plethora of them up, one by one, and disposing of them. We spent days performing this task until one afternoon, we noticed a neighbor from across the street with an old Ford tractor. My father and Hamar sent Shlomo and me over to ask the guy if he could help us out. Thank God for his kindness, because at the pace we were moving, it would have been months before we finished. It also saved my aching back from permanently being hunched over.

Now that the lawn was out of the way, Hamar had other projects we needed to work on. The time spent doing her chores were extremely tiresome and mentally brutal, leaving no time to play with my friends.

I felt like a slave, as if my life was not my own. I didn't mind helping out, but her projects were consuming all my weekends. This wasn't a short-term endeavor either, as it continued to go on for two years. My friends couldn't understand what was going on at my house that exhausted so much of my time. Whenever having a sleepover at my friend Dave's house, Hamar, without fail, would call his home by 8am to make sure I was on my way home. Dave couldn't believe it and I recall him saying, "Jim, I don't know what you're going to do when you grow up, but you work so hard I bet you'll be richer than all of us." It was terribly embarrassing, but with no choice, I ran my butt home to help.

The next project we worked on was the basement. It was left unfinished, with Hamar wanting it to resemble a New York Disco Tech. I found it hard to get myself overly excited for this project, after anticipating all the hard work. My father always excused Shlomo from helping out. Whatever the job, his excuse was Shlomo was more of a hindrance than a help. I could never understand that one, so Mitch and I were stuck helping with the construction. This happened on every project we worked on. Shlomo somehow wasn't needed for building the deck, the bar, laying cement or any other large jobs which were demanded of us. It became the unspoken rule and such the norm, that Mitch and I never gave it a second thought.

By the time we were finished with the basement, it did look like a Disco Tech. After installing all the drywall, we painted everything purple. That was Hamar's idea of what an upbeat Disco Tech should look like. The bar was huge, being about ten feet in length with a neat bending design for the facade. It was a beauty, exemplifying a bar you would find in a fancy nightclub. During the grueling project, Hamar and my father constantly argued about an array of different things, like where to put them or how big to make something. She truly slowed us up, using a filthy mouth towards everyone if we tried defending our work. My father repeatedly told Hamar to watch the language, but he only enticed her to become even nastier. Never backing down, she made an assertive point of showing us who the boss was in the house. Usually the scraps lasted about ten minutes, then we resumed working.

Hamar was insistent on having a dance area, so we laid down a linoleum floor, while adding string lights to cover the back wall. The only thing we didn't do was lay the carpeting. We even hung the drop ceiling, which involved installing the ceiling tiles in place too. When done, the basement looked incredible. I wasn't crazy about the color Hamar picked, but overall it resembled a little dance club. As much as I hated not spending time with my friends, I was proud of the jobs we completed. The only issue that bothered Mitch and me was how we never received a thank you. We weren't given an allowance and never dared ask for one either, so all we wanted was acknowledgement that we helped out. It was beneath them to show appreciation, which eroded my mind and stomach walls. There were times I wanted to jump out of my shoes, questioning why it was so difficult to show a little appreciation. But I knew it would only backfire, so I remained stifled in my shoes.

A few weeks later I heard a terrible cry seeping from the basement. It was Hamar yelling for help. "Someone get down here fast. There's water everywhere. Yala, I need a bucket and some rags."

Her loud voice carried for miles and if you didn't move the instant she called, it was trouble. Scrambling to see what all the chaos was, we found Hamar wading in two feet of dirty brown water. She was standing by the dance floor, as the water was creeping in through the back wall where the string lights hung. It was difficult to pinpoint the exact location where the water was coming in, but it was inching through the bottom of the entire back wall.

Staring at us with evil eyes, Hamar noticed no one brought down a bucket or any rags. "Idiots! Where's the bucket and rags? Stupid, fast go up. Idiots." She didn't speak to anyone in particular, so dumbfounded, we stood looking at each other. That enraged Hamar even further, as her face contorted with anger, shrieking, "Now! Go now, idiots. What are you waiting for? A special invitation?"

Mitch, Julie and I jumped at once, scampering to go find the supplies she needed. My father quickly arrived looking at the back wall, trying to find the origin of the problem. Shlomo didn't care to run, casually sauntering where my father was doing his search and following him around. Feverishly digging around the laundry room for rags, we weren't having much luck. Hamar used anything that was too old for us to wear as a rag, which left very little with any substance to use. Eventually, we came running down the stairs, carrying old yellow stained underwear and Swiss cheese torn t-shirts. As we worked on the dirty water, it just continued pouring in. No matter how fast everyone labored, we couldn't keep up with the flooding, so my father decided to run out to buy a shop vacuum.

While he was out Hamar was in a state of insanity, shouting over and over again that we weren't moving fast enough. We were all thankful when our father returned, since the vacuum swiftly did the job to her satisfaction. Nothing was too badly ruined but the room emanated an odor of sewer water. The carpet was slightly stained a light brown, however, everything else seemed shipshape. This problem never went away, becoming an ongoing nightmare, seeing as anytime it rained, Hamar sent us downstairs to check on the basement's condition. My father opted to buy a sump pump for the window well, hoping it would cure the problem. It did work, until it rained hard and steady, making the job impossible for the sump pump to keep up. My parents didn't want to spend the money to have a professional out, so we took our chance every time it rained. It felt like all our work was melting away with each storm.

Soon after our football season came to a close, Hamar and my father had a birthday party for Mitch in the new house. He had the first non-traditional birthday party there. By saying non-traditional, I mean he was allowed to invite friends outside the family, which was a no-no in Hamar's rulebook. She didn't like wasting money or food on people who didn't bring the proper gift and the only acceptable gift was cash. Hamar invited the usual aunts and uncles with their children. My cousins, Jeff and Dan, were there too, which was great because we didn't see much of them since my father married Hamar. If I didn't occasionally bump into them at the lighting store, it would take until the next Jewish holiday before seeing them again. I wasn't sure if it was that last fight at Uncle Stewart's home or something else, but we didn't see them as often as we had when my father was married to our real mother.

There was no entertainment like a puppet show or a clown doing silly stunts at Mitch's party. We simply played around, talked amongst ourselves and ate lunch. The house was Hamar's palace, so she was on the warpath that day, policing everyone around. Being this was her new dream home, she refused to stand for any rambunctious children making a mess of it. After the cake and ice cream were eaten, Hamar was all business. Announcing it was time for the presents to be opened, she assembled everyone in the family room. She sat directly in the thick of things, putting someone in charge of jotting down what each aunt, grandparent and friend gave as a gift. Hamar used this method in order to appropriately reciprocate. Usually, she invited one of Muffy's wealthy friends to the party, anticipating a very handsome gift. But if it wasn't satisfactory, she would bitch about it for days.

Mitch's handful of friends brought gift-wrapped presents, which didn't surprise Hamar. She made obnoxious comments under her breath while cackling, as if the gifts were as good as junk. It was loud enough for everyone to hear, but she didn't care. When it came to the family's gifts, which consisted of envelopes filled with money, Hamar smiled patiently waiting for Mitch to read the cards out loud. Once he finished reading, she hastily snatched the cash, squeezing it tightly in her greedy fists. She always told us that she wanted to hold the money so we wouldn't lose it. The problem with that idea was it magically disappeared and you wouldn't dare ask for it back either. She undoubtedly pocketed the money, never saving it as promised.

I was stereotyped as cheap by Hamar, since I caught on to what she was doing. She didn't appreciate my intelligence, which ignited quite a few battles between us. After one of my birthday parties, Hamar insisted on holding my money, but I thought it in my best interest to hold it myself. Infuriated that I would suggest such a thing, she turned the situation into a gigantic ordeal. "What do you mean, you want to hold it? What do you think, I'm going to steal it? Is that what you think? Stupid idiot, like I'm going to steal his present," she screamed, trying to bully me.

All the guests had gone home by now, as this was happening in front of my father and siblings. "I didn't say that. I don't think you would steal it. I just want to hold it myself, so I don't have to ask you for it later," I gently said.

She was furious that her authority was in question, as I refused to roll over like everyone else did. Glancing over at my father, she sarcastically snickered, saying, "Do you believe this, Sheldon? This idiot thinks I'm going to steal his money. Right, you think I'm going to steal your money? Cheap. Cheap, like I'm going to steal your money. Piece of shit. Everything I do for you and this is the shit I get. Keep your fucking money. You should drop dead."

Everyone was looking at me like the bad guy but I knew at least Mitch knew where I was coming from. Shlomo didn't care because whether he gave his money to her or not, his mother always made sure to take care of him. Mitch, Julie and I had to pray for her to throw us a crumb.

I realized I was going to lose the fight, considering how she was doing everything in her power to make me look like a shit. "I'm not cheap. I just want to buy some things with my birthday money. That's all," I answered, feeling a queasy sensation in my stomach.

She was beyond angry and of course, working to manipulate everyone to join in with her abusive tactics. Shlomo came to her defense pleading, "Come on buddy. You sound really cheap. All she wants to do is hold it for you so you don't lose it. We all give it to her to hold. You'll get it back. She's your mother," he exclaimed. "Do you really think your mother would steal from you?"

"Hell yes," I thought to myself. I knew he was feeding me a bunch of bullshit and in the end she would steal my money. Naturally my father never came to my aid, so I had no choice but to give in. Otherwise, I would look like a piece of shit, condemned to the dog house until giving her my money. So, I thought it wise to hand it over, taking my losses now, rather than later.

Even after handing over the money, Hamar walked away counting it while calling me all sorts of colorful names. She gave me the silent treatment for the longest time as well, until my father finally coerced me into apologizing. It still didn't end after my apology as she went on with her chastising, calling me cheap and other demeaning names.

Mitch was immersed in his glory, while in possession of all the new presents. We never received toys unless someone brought them over for a special occasion. Our typical present was a pair of socks and pajamas or slippers and a robe. Eventually, our parents became very creative, presenting me with handwritten IOU's in my birthday cards. Mitch opened a few of his gifts, with one in particular being the most popular one amongst all the kids. It was a little football player who kicked a small plastic football through a field goal when smashing down on his head. Everyone took turns smacking down on the little guy, seeing who could kick the longest field goal. As the party died down, Hamar hurriedly began collecting the presents. She even repacked some which had been already opened. Breathing heavily, she coldly broke the news to Mitch, saying, "Mitch, pick two presents and the rest go away." She was ruthless, showing no emotions as she broke his heart.

Mitch was left appearing devastated and I felt horrible for him, as his rare smile transformed into an awful frown. We were sitting by the unused virgin fireplace when I looked in my father's direction. I was hoping he would say something in Mitch's defense but instead smoked his cigarettes, pretending not to hear a thing. I wanted to jump to his defense, asking why Hamar found it necessary to return his gifts. But I knew better. I already traveled down that road before, which only leads to tragedy. Mitch languidly made his decision, choosing the football guy and the magic set. Without hesitation, Hamar swooped away the rest of the gifts, storing them high on a shelf in the hallway closet. Her eyes were full of greed and impervious to emotion as she completed the task. I knew exactly what she was going to do with them and so did Mitch.

Mitch wasn't the same after that day, becoming more withdrawn and depressed as time crept on. I remember him coming downstairs in the mornings, quietly eating breakfast while facing the wall. The kitchen had a built in counter, where we ate the majority of our meals, with Mitch's stool being the closet to the wall. When eating a meal, he wouldn't acknowledge anyone, especially Julie. If she happened to be sitting beside him at breakfast, Mitch would turn the box of cereal not to have to look at her. He used Julie as an emotional punching bag, verbally abusing her with the same names he heard Hamar using. Once in a while there was hitting involved, but that was on rare occasions since our father wouldn't stand for that kind of behavior from any of us. If he found out we were slapping Julie around, he was sure to kick our asses. Only Hamar got away with that crime.

We all picked on Julie at times. She started assuming our mother's persona, influenced by Hamar constantly pounded in our heads how much Julie was like her. The malicious name calling and beatings made it seem ok for us to act out in the same manner. I think Mitch and I were resentful towards our mother for leaving us with this dysfunctional family, taking our hostility out on Julie. It wasn't something I analyzed at the time, but looking back, it all makes sense.

My father and Hamar made it a tradition to have my grandma over every Friday night for Shabbat dinner. She was my father's mother, who practically raised us, so Mitch, Julie and I loved spending time with her. We genuinely enjoyed her company because she was our real grandmother, making us feel like we were important to her. Feeling any kind of worth in our house was a rarity, since our lives were primarily filled with Hamar's side of the family. We were viewed as outsiders to them, so I developed this unexplainable warmth in my heart when it came to real family. Mitch and I had a special bond with our grandmother, stemming from our Rolling days together. She was like a mother to us, something we never forgot. After our birth mother was taken away, she was the closest person we ever had to one.

When coming over for dinner, Hamar was kind enough to fix my grandma's hair. It was a nice gesture, but my grandmother paid it back many nights by biting her tongue. She was one to always know her place, which had to make her a daughter-in-law's dream. She sat through many Friday night dinners while having to stomach Hamar's cruel remarks. Hamar hated fat people and if my grandmother wasn't my father's mother, she would have been more wicked than she already was. Subliminally, she poked fun at my grandma during her visits, which nauseated the hell out of me.

I remember one instance when the peas were being passed around, while eating dinner. We had a long rectangular table where my father sat at one end and Shlomo at the other. My grandmother's seat was on my father's right with Hamar on his left. When the peas made it over to my grandmother, she spooned a few onto her plate to eat, as Hamar snickered, commenting, "Come on, mom. That's all the peas you're going to take?" All of us stopped what we were doing to take a look at her plate.

My grandmother also looked down at her plate, sweetly answering, "Yes dear. I have plenty of food here. I can't eat much more."

Hamar peered at her with a disgusted expression on her face, as I sensed something unpleasant was going to crawl out of her mouth. "Please, ok mom, nobody gets fat from the air. You can take some more peas."

I nearly fell under the table with embarrassment, not wanting to look at my poor grandma. I couldn't believe my ears as Shlomo joined Hamar with a smug little cackle. Then acting like a smartass, he added, "Come on grandma, have some more. Don't be shy."

Blown away, I looked over at my father waiting for him to put Hamar in her place, but he merely looked like it went over his head. So after dinner, I approached him while he was getting another vodka. "Hey dad, I can't believe mom said that to grandma. It was rude as hell. How come you let her talk to her that way?"

Innocently looking at me, he said, "Oh, she's only kidding. She doesn't speak right sometimes so it comes out wrong."

"Well, I think it was nasty and she knew exactly what she was saying. And what's with her and Shlomo laughing at grandma? I can't believe you didn't say anything." I wasn't giving up, thinking to myself, "This was bullshit already and she needed someone to put her in her place." I had him alone in the family room, which was unusual, so I wanted to be heard.

My father didn't get angry with me but instead argued in Hamar's defense. "Oh please, your mother loves grandma. She wouldn't have her over every Friday night for dinner and do her hair if she didn't." His eyes were red and slightly lazy when he finished his speech. Acting as though I couldn't top what he said, he stood aplomb with a confident demeanor

I knew this was a no win argument, given he and Hamar had no respect for children or what they had to say. It was well noted, so I stuck to my guns arguing, "Well, you can think what you want. But she was rude and I'm sure she hurt grandma's feelings. If she was my wife, I would've never allowed her to talk to my mother that way. I bet if you said that stuff to her mother you'd be dead."

My dad stood there about to say something when Hamar broke his concentration. "Sheldon! What are you and Jim doing in there? Are you getting another drink? You idiot. Alcoholic drunk."

"No," my father shouted back, giving me an awkward look. "Let's go back to the kitchen. I'm sure grandma is fine."

I was angry with my father, knowing very well that my grandmother's feelings were hurt. Anybody's feelings would have been hurt after hearing a rude and malicious comment like that. My father's problem was he never put his foot down when Hamar was out of line. He thought turning a blind eye was the answer, which was why Hamar behaved the way she did. My grandmother was a saint, never putting her nose in my parent's business. There were times I wish she had or anyone else for that matter, but she was an extraordinary woman with tact. I don't think many mother-in-laws would have held their tongues after a lashing like my grandmother received.

Halfway through the school year, Hamar and Shlomo surprised me. One afternoon, I noticed Shlomo sporting new converse sneakers and Levi jeans. I found it hard to swallow, since the only new clothes I got were Jeff and Dan's hand-me-downs and I was still wearing my old Kmart plastic tennis shoes. Deciding to confront Shlomo, I questioned him in his room. "Hey man, where did you get those new shoes?"

"Mom. Since I'm the oldest, I get the clothes first then you get 'em," he proudly stated.

Having no response, I walked out of his bedroom feeling miffed. Each day I was trekking off to school ashamed of what I was wearing and here he was privy to new clothing. We were only five months apart, so it didn't seem fair to me. I was wearing plaid pants and turtleneck shirts with fake sewn on vests. Granted, it was the seventies but I looked like Bozo the golfer. It was a wonder I wasn't tortured at school. Thanks to my new best friend, Dave, I was able to walk the school hallways without being verbally assassinated.

Finally digging deep enough, I found the courage to ask Hamar about this situation, which she wasn't happy about. Later on that day, before my father returned home, I found Hamar in the kitchen. "Hey mom, can I ask you a question?"

She didn't appear happy, half listening when I strutted in. Her mother was in a chair kneading dough, reflecting her best genuine smile at me. "Huh? What is it," she curtly asked.

Biting my fingernails, I said, "I was wondering how Shlomo got new Converse sneakers?"

She picked her head up from the mixing bowl, scowling at me. "What do you mean? Why does Shlomo have new sneakers?" I could see she was ill-prepared for this question, as her first reaction was to get upset.

"I saw he had new shoes and I was wondering how come I didn't get any." My voice was a bit high from being nervous.

With a grimacing look, she snarled, "What business is it of yours? Who are you to come and ask me?" I knew mama didn't understand English, but she shot a look of concern while quietly kneading.

"I was just wondering because mine are falling apart. I'd like to have the Converse sneakers too. Nobody wears the ones I have." I didn't want to say that no kid in this neighborhood would ever dream of wearing Kmart tennis shoes.

Her eye-lids parted wide like the Red Sea, as if to swallow me with her thunderous rage. "None of your business. Ok? None of your business. Big shot, like you're going to come in here and ask me where he got his shoes." She could see I wasn't leaving, shouting, "He paid for half of them. Ok? With his own money. Now what? Give me half the money and I'll get yours."

Knowing full well Shlomo had no money, I asked, "What money did he have for the sneakers or the new clothes?" I sensed she was going to bite my head off but I was already in the eye of the tornado.

"His own money. That's what money. Stupid," She screamed, shaking in rage. "Like I need to answer to you. Who the hell are you? You bastard. It's none of your business, like I said." Then taking a deep breath, she noticed I wasn't budging. "Go. Get out of here. Like I have to explain myself to you. Piece of shit. Yala! Get out of here."

I knew she was screaming like a maniac because she wasn't being honest about Shlomo contributing money. She felt challenged and irritated that I painted her into a corner. As I walked up the stairs, Hamar refueled her batteries, yelling, "Your brother goes to junior high school now and he needs to dress better. You stupid idiot. Big mouth asshole." Her voice echoed up the stairs, as I faintly heard her carrying on with her mother while resting on my bed.

After my confrontation with Hamar, things were actually starting to look financially good for our family. My father surprised us one day, rolling up in his new Datsun 280Z. It was an unbelievable looking automobile, painted metallic blue with a sporty elongated hood. I thought it resembled a bullet. He purchased the 2+2 series which added a backseat to the car. When arriving home, he blasted the horn and Hamar must have known he was coming with it, because she didn't act surprised. Everyone ran out of the house excited and in awe when seeing the car. Hamar's mother came bumbling out behind us with a cup full of milk, chanting some prayer as she began pouring it on my father's tires. Never seeing that ritual before, I asked, "Hey mom, what's mama doing? She's getting dad's new car dirty with all that milk she's spilling."

"It's for good luck," she said, trying to get inside the driver's seat.

My father had been driving a little Capri for a few years and I could see how proud he was of his new automobile. He already treated Hamar to a brand new station wagon, so now it looked like it was his turn for a little fun. I was happy for him, knowing how hard he worked to acquire it. My only hope was that it would still be around when I got my drivers license. After drooling over the car, my father sped us around the block, giving everyone a taste of what the 280Z could do. He tried convincing mama into taking a ride, but she was too afraid and wobbled back into the house. After my father finished giving rides, that left us, the three boys, to go joy riding with him. We spent time together seeing what this baby could do on the beltway.

CHAPTER 24

When you have a pool, it's fascinating how many people start flocking to your house. Soon after my father bought his car, our new swimming pool was installed just in time for summer. It seemed like my parents had hit the jackpot. Hamar's family and friends started popping by quite frequently, especially Aunt Rubel and Uncle Gus, with their two children. Every weekend we were throwing pool parties in the backyard, spending little time as a family since Hamar was constantly entertaining. When guests came by, they stayed around until after dinner. I remember my father grilling out every Sunday night with our guests finally leaving after it became dark. On Saturday's my father worked, then he and Hamar always went out, so Hamar's family and friends were gone by 4pm. It was like a revolving door at our house.

Complaining about how much food she was going through during the summer, Hamar blamed Mitch, Julie and me. But it was very apparent that the shortage was from all her entertaining. The security on the refrigerator and pantry were increased, as she reminded us that we were not permitted to take anything unless she gave it to us.

Hamar was opposed to us inviting our friends over, due to the food shortage. The only one excluded from the rule was Shlomo. He somehow managed to have a friend or two over, but it didn't make a difference to me, since most of my buddies were gone for the summer. Dave and a few other guys, who I was friendly with, were all sent off to camp, making summers a little lonely for me. They didn't go for a few weeks either, these kids went for the entire summer. Some of them even staying at two different camps, but between the manual labor and the pool, I kept fairly busy.

The summer months were filled working on Hamar's projects, which kept my mind off my friends. Shlomo was sent off with his buddies, due to his lack of labor skills, leaving only Mitch and me to help our father. Our initial project was building a mammoth deck for one of Hamar's elaborate parties. When we finished, it was an awesome ten by forty foot structure, with two enormous trees sprouting out from beneath.

Hamar didn't stop with the deck though. Guessing we did such a terrific job, not because she said so or even thanked us, she insisted we complete a few other assignments. We built a brick bar, which was assembled with left over bricks from the front of the house. She needed the concrete pool patio enlarged, so we put on our masonry hats and did a fine job laying concrete. When we were done with the patio, she converted us into landscapers, instructing us to plant pine trees and little shrubs around the circular driveway. The house was taking so much energy and time from me, that I began to hate it. The house was a never-ending project, completely exhausting Mitch and me. We began reminiscing about times with our mother and grandparents, knowing they would have never treated us like manual laborers. Out of all the projects during that summer, helping my father install the fence was the most grueling. We had to dig these three foot deep holes and install a wooden fence around the entire back of the house. It was brutal work, as the hot summer sun sucked us dry. When school finally started, so did my vacation.

I welcomed the new school year with open arms, overjoyed to get away from Hamar and her slave-driving. It was the first time, starting a new year at the same school where I attended the year before. I didn't count Rolling's debacle as a complete school year because of the inconsistency of attending school. It was also great to get back to see all my friends again.

The sixth grade was my favorite year yet, since having a male teacher who made school more enjoyable than any other teacher I ever had. Being that Mr. Univack was a sports enthusiast, we hit it off right away. He was more like a friend than a teacher to me. Through

Mr. Univack I became friendly with our principle, Mr. Snead, who was an ex-baseball player for the Pittsburgh Pirates. I enjoyed visiting with him so much that I frequently stopped by his office just to talk. There were rumors going around that we spent more time at recess than learning in class, which wasn't the case. Mr. Univack loved sports but made sure we were well prepared when graduating the sixth grade. My grades flourished, finally receiving straight A's for the first time.

While school was in session, I noticed Julie was becoming a fixture in the hallway. The first few times it was nice seeing her on my way to the cafeteria, but then it became embarrassing. I found out she was getting punished by her teacher for being unruly in the classroom. Hamar brought that to my attention by beating the crap out of Julie on a regular basis. She was receiving phone calls from Julie's teacher about her clowning around in class and deplorable schoolwork. Julie was failing miserably with her reading and writing. Her teacher was suggesting my parents consider sending her to another school that better suited her needs. It was a wonder Julie could think at all, after all the beatings she took to the head from Hamar. My father was terribly aggravated by Julie's activities at school, doing his share of disciplining as well.

The finishing blow was when Julie and a friend reached into their teacher's desk, taking out some money. Hamar was called to the school and had to sit through all the details of how Julie stole from her teacher. Ultimately she was expelled, prompting my parents to find another school for her to attend. When getting home that day, I found Hamar chasing Julie around our pool table like a wild banshee.

We had a pool room located between the kitchen and family room and when walking in, I instantly heard an array of chaotic screaming. "Stop running you pig. When I catch you, you're dead pig. Come here you pig whore," Hamar was shrieking.

I didn't know what had happened at the time, but by the look on Hamar's face, I realized it was serious business. She was infuriated while running out of breath from being unable to catch Julie. Then picking up a pool ball, Hamar heaved it at Julie with all her might.

Holding my breath, I prayed it would miss as the ball loudly crashed against the paneled wall without striking Julie. Hamar was furious for missing and barely able to get out the words shouted, "You bitch. You better stop. When I catch you pig, you're dead. Get over here you pig bastard."

As they were running around the pool table, Julie was yelling out crazy sounds, reminding me of Curly from "The Three Stooges". "Woo, woo woo, woo. Woo, woo woo, woo." They looked like a couple of characters straight out of an old black and white comedy from the 1920's. I was laughing inside as Hamar was having no luck catching Julie.

Unable to stay silent any longer, I barked, "What's going on? What did she do?"

Weary and still trying to catch her breath from hunting Julie, Hamar bellowed, "Stop her. Stop that pig."

"I can't do that," I said, stepping back.

"You piece of shit," she cried out, rounding the table.

Then picking up another pool ball, Hamar whipped it at Julie's head. Luckily, the hefty ball missed again, slamming against the paneled wall with a deafening thud, as Julie looked behind still screaming, "Woo,woo woo, woo. Woo, woo woo, woo."

Running thin on patience and breath, Hamar stopped where the pool cues were hanging and grabbed one. Taking careful aim not to miss this time, she stood like an African warrior ready to strike his prey, then flung the stick. This time she connected, striking Julie directly in the back. Stunned by the blow, Julie fell to the ground like a wounded gazelle. I watched her rolling on the ground and crying in pain as Hamar leaped on her back. Grabbing two fists full of Julie's hair, she began relentlessly slamming her head on the steps, leading down to the family room. Hamar resembled a determined lunatic, trying to milk water from a well. Standing motionless, I did not know what to do or say to help Julie. Hamar was in a fit of rage and I wasn't about to grab her and throw her off, so I hoped it would end quickly.

While slamming Julie's head into the carpeted step, Hamar was howling, "Why did you steal that money? You fucking whore pig. I hate you. I hate you. You should drop dead." Hamar had absolutely lost her marbles.

Julie's head was bobbing up and down as she cried out, "I wa wa was hun hun hungry. I wa wa wanted." Before she could finish, Hamar maliciously grabbed her mouth squeezing it shut. She looked as if she was trying to smother Julie to death.

As Hamar was beating Julie, she hollered a word with every smack and punch. "You fucking piece of shit. Wait til your father gets home. You're dead. Dead, you pig whore." After the fierce beating, Hamar languidly stumbled to her feet walking off with a triumphant swagger. I was sickened by the whole chaotic episode. It was unbelievable what I just saw, wishing she would be dragged off to jail like the common criminal she was. When turning around, Mitch and Shlomo were standing behind me. I was so drawn in by what was happening, that I didn't notice when they came in.

Julie was lying in a puddle of her own tears, while her body trembled uncontrollably. I went over to see if she was ok, but she shooed me off. Then slowly pushing herself up and hunched over, Julie shuffled up to her bedroom as her bottom lip drooled with saliva. Her crying and moaning from the bedroom was horribly loud, as Hamar screeched from the kitchen, "Shut up, you pig bitch or I'll come up there and give you more. Do you hear me, pig? WHORE!"

Mitch and I were upstairs talking when we heard Hamar call us down for dinner. Julie didn't make it down. She was still up in her room while the rest of us quietly sat at the dinner table. Hamar was slopping some soup in our bowls when noticing Julie wasn't at the table. Glaring in our direction, she hollered, "Where's the pig? Where is that fat ass? Someone go call her, right now." Hamar was getting all worked up again, so I swiftly went to call Julie down.

When reaching the bottom of the stairs, I called up, "Julie, come on down. Mom wants you down here for dinner."

She faintly moaned, "I'm not hungry."

Hamar yelled again from the kitchen, "Where's that pig? She better get down here now. And I mean now. Fat ass, where are you?" Her voice was sounding vile and I knew it was in Julie's best interest to get downstairs.

After climbing up the stairs, I found Julie laying face down on her bed. "Hey, you better come down. It's not going to be worth another beating. Believe me."

She looked at me with tears dribbling from her eyes, quietly whimpering, "Ok, I'll try." She got up, but literally had to hobble down the stairs. It was a dreadful sight and I felt awful for her.

Hamar showed no pity towards Julie at dinner, standing behind the kitchen counter repeatedly chastising her. "You just wait 'til your father gets home, pig. You'll really get it then, fat ass. You stupid, just like your mother, Mindy. You can't even write your own name on a piece of paper." It sounded like she was trying to make a point, boldly speaking out loud as if to justify the savage beating she gave her. Julie was still trembling at the table and it was difficult to look at her after seeing the kind of turmoil she went through. Hamar was dishing out so much abuse that Julie appeared to find it difficult to swallow her soup. Then we all brought our bowls over to Hamar, as she rinsed them out, tossing our dinner right back in.

As we were finishing dinner, the front door opened then quickly slammed shut. My heart dropped to my stomach, when hearing my father's familiar footsteps approaching. I was scared to death for Julie, knowing Hamar was going to lay into him pretty hard about her stealing. Like an assembly line, each of us walked up placing our bowls in the sink, then kissed our father hello. He only required one kiss on the cheek, so it wasn't very time consuming. Still standing behind the counter looking evil, Hamar began provoking my father right off the bat. "Well, there's your daughter. The pig stealer."

My father shot Hamar a disturbing glance, as she hollered, "Don't look at me with your chicken eyes. Big shot. Like you're going to look at me with those chicken eyes. You better take care of this. I am tired of taking care of your fat ass whore daughter."

"Come on already. I told you about that shit," my father said, edging towards anger. Julie was standing against the wall that separated the pool room from the kitchen. Acknowledging something horrendous was going to happen, I went upstairs to spare myself from the nasty situation.

For the first few minutes it sounded civilized downstairs, hearing voices but no yelling or screaming. I figured maybe everything would work itself out, but it didn't last long. I nearly hit the ceiling when my father roared one of his belligerent yells. It raised the hair on my back as I thought the roof was going to blow off. Julie was crying and howling at the same time. I couldn't make out what was being said through my father's hollering, but he was completely out of his mind. Not being able to take it anymore, I went downstairs to see if I could calm him down.

By the time I came down, Julie and my father made their way into the pool room. His eyelids were tainted red, as he was shaking while pinning Julie against the dark paneled wall. He had one hand holding her by the neck as the other was doing all the slapping. He was screaming directly in her face as she was pleading with him. "Please, dad. Ok. I understand. I understand. It won't happen again. I swear. Oh God, please." Her words were choppy, as she begged him to stop hitting her. Gasping rigorously for air, Julie couldn't close her mouth looking as if she was on the verge of fainting.

"I don't know if I can believe you, Julie. You're a liar. Do you hear me? A… liar…," he was shouting in her face while slapping her legs. He even punched her in the gut, which surprised the hell out of me. It appeared to surprise Julie too since she went cross-eyed when feeling the blow.

Finally, I interrupted saying, "Come on, dad. I think she's learned her lesson. You're breathing hard and she's crying. I think she gets it." My father was as white as snow and was so out of breath that all he could do was wave me away.

Hamar had a front row seat for the entire show. Standing in the doorway that separated the kitchen from the pool room, she spitefully added, "Yeah Sheldon, you can't even breathe. She's not worth it. Stop before you give yourself a heart attack." She was very nonchalant when speaking, like the show was taking a nosedive.

My father didn't let Julie go after our requests. He still had her in his grasps, barely capable of completing a full sentence. Then drawing her closer to his face again, he gruffly said, "I better not… hear about… you getting in trouble… again. Do you hear me? Because the next time… there won't…. be a next time. Now get the fuck…

out of my face!" Suddenly Julie found this extra ounce of strength, and hightailed it upstairs.

No one said a single word when Julie disappeared. And as my father hastened to the kitchen, we all backed stepped clearing a path for him. Weary and disheveled, he staggered to get a glass with ice. Even Hamar was silent when he faltered to the family room to pour himself a drink.

About a week later, school broke for Christmas break. We were just about done gathering our things for the Florida trip when there was a knock at the front door. My father answered it, as a well dressed man and woman were standing on our front stoop. Looking confused, my father said, "Hello, can I help you?"

The well dressed man spoke first, introducing the lady and himself, explaining that they were with family services. My father's face dropped, as he looked perplexed with redness draping his facade. Then the man spoke again, "Are you Mister Wilde, sir?"

My father sounded as if he had cotton balls in his mouth, eking out, "Yes. What can I do for you?"

"We received a call from Luxmanor Elementary School about your daughter, Julie. Can we come in please, Mister Wilde?"

Every one of us gathered in the foyer, wondering what was going on. My father immediately took notice, sending us upstairs. Then he invited them into the family room where they spoke for a while. Being nosey, we stood at the open area on the second floor above the foyer, trying to listen in on their conversation. We couldn't catch a single word, but it was obvious they came because of Julie's beating. I remember seeing the bruises on her body, they were hideous. She had actual black and blue handprints pasted on her back from my father's horrific beating, in addition to other bruises covering various parts of her body. Julie was a walking billboard for child abuse if you happened to look under her shirt. I was surprised someone finally noticed, but her wrists were a dead give away. It was a wonder the police weren't there to arrest the both of them, instead of these two social workers.

After what seemed like hours, Hamar and my father walked the social workers back to the front door. I could tell Hamar was playing the mother of the year part, as she and my father bid them farewell. They were all smiles like they just became the best of friends. Once the social workers left, all at once we asked our folks what happened. My father said, "Nothing happened. They were checking on what happened to Julie, that's all. They asked about her bruises."

Then Hamar cut my father off, looking victorious exclaiming, "And he told them that he spanked her for stealing money from her teacher. That's all. They even said they would do the same thing." Then she peered at Julie with squinted eyes, meanly squawking, "All because you had to steal from your teacher, fat ass. Pig stealer."

"Hey, watch your mouth. I told you not to call her pig," my father blurted out, sounding disturbed.

"Oh, just shut up. What? Are you going to protect your second wife? Shmuck. Stupid. Now, because of your second wife we're running late," Hamar sarcastically shouted, as everyone went along with her giving Julie a once over look.

Shlomo wasn't pleased either, snickering, "Nice job, Julie. Now we're really going to be late."

After the excitement came to an end, Hamar herded everyone into the family station wagon and off to Miami, Florida we went. The ride was horrendous, even with the extra space the car was jammed packed with luggage. Five kids in the back of a station wagon for twenty hours was an ingredient for disaster. On the way down, we found an array of different activities to keep ourselves occupied. Mostly, the fun was teasing and picking on each other, with Julie getting the grunt of it. My father and Hamar quickly grew tired of our silly games, relentlessly screaming and slapping us from the front seat. Digging deeper into the road trip, we were getting tired and Julie started laying her head on our shoulders. While she was trying to sleep, we found it amusing to knock her head off our shoulder with a quick shrug. Each time her head flung from one shoulder to the next, with her yelling for us to stop, but we continued to do it until our father lost his temper. He created such a scene in the car, that we had no choice but to allow Julie to fall asleep on us. He threatened a beating if we carried on with our bullshit, which certainly didn't sit well with Mitch or me.

The highlight of the trip was our pit stop at a small motel. Hamar became irritable, complaining of being tired and wanting to stop. My father wouldn't hear of it, struggling to drive further through the night. Hamar didn't help with the driving, so my father's eyes were growing weary with every mile he drove. Loosing her patience, Hamar put her foot down moaning, "Sheldon, let's stop. Your chicken eyes are so small you can barely keep them open. I want to stop, right now."

Being so exhausted, my father didn't argue this time, pulling into a small motel off the highway. They rented a single room, with the entire family managing to somehow sleep in it. The next morning, my father was the first one up, bellowing for everyone to get ready. He wanted to make good time, insisting each of us use the bathroom before getting back on the road. As Hamar was packing the overnight bag, I observed her stuffing the motel towels in there too. Staring at her, I said, "Hey mom, why do we need the towels? Isn't that stealing?"

Hamar broke a nervous smirk, as I noticed lipstick stains on her two front teeth. "Just shut up and move out of the way, stupid," she demanded, cackling and sliding past me to the bathroom. Once in there, she snatched the unused soap, shampoos, ice bucket and glasses. Hamar even swiped the ashtray my father was still using.

"Hey, hey," he shouted. "What are you doing? I'm using that."

"Shut up and get dressed already. We need another ashtray for you, potato," she shouted, getting annoyed.

From the time Shlomo started junior high school, he was getting very cocky, doing stupid things in an attempt to be funny. He was definitely his mother's son, as he started stealing items from the motel room. Shlomo went through the drawers first, swiping the pens, the paper and all the postcards. He would have stolen the bible as well, if we weren't Jewish. Then looking at me with a devious smile, he said, "Come on buddy, get with it. We need stuff. Start getting some things, man."

I looked at Mitch as if these people were nuts, then we stood observing while they stole everything that wasn't mounted down. Shlomo was enjoying the activity so much, that he actually tried stealing the color TV from the room. He asked for my help, but I refused. Then he asked Mitch for his assistance and he echoed my same sentiments. Shlomo struggled for some time trying to pry the TV loose, but with no success. When my father finished dressing, he happened to catch Shlomo wrestling with the TV set. Immediately becoming upset, he shouted, "Shlomo! What the hell are you doing?"

Shlomo was still working when he answered, "Hey, don't worry dad. I thought we could use a new TV, but I can't get it loose."

Slightly laughing, my father said, "Ok, let's go. Everyone in the car."

Hamar was having such a terrible time trying to zip up her billowed bag that she called Shlomo for his help. She had him firmly sitting on it, as she vigorously zipped the bag shut. After a few minutes, we were all in the station wagon except Shlomo. My father stepped out of the car, calling out, "Shlomo. Come on. What the hell are you doing?" Peering out my window, I watched as he scurried down the stairs carrying a trash can in his arms.

"What the hell is that," my father questioned.

Shlomo stuffed the trash can on the roof of the car, along with the other luggage, then jumped in smiling. "Don't worry, buddy. I need a trash can for my room. One less thing you have to buy."

"Just come on, Sheldon. What do you care? You're wasting time. Let's go," Hamar impatiently barked, as my father hunched back into the car.

He shot Hamar a disgusted look. "Real good. You're setting a real good example for your kids."

"Oh, shut up, you potato," she screeched, with a guilty cackle. By the look on my father's face, I could see he wasn't amused. Then, just as he started accelerating out of the parking lot, I happened to glance up noticing a cleaning woman hollering at us. She was shaking a fist in anger, while running down the stairs to catch us.

As she was making progress, I quickly shouted out, "Dad, you better hurry. I think a lady is trying to catch us because of Shlomo's trash can."

He looked out his side view mirror, simultaneously slamming

his foot on the accelerator and off we went. After a couple minutes, he looked out the rearview mirror to make sure the coast was clear, then sarcastically said, "I hope the two of you are God damn happy. You, with your God damn towels and you, with your damn trash can. Next time keep me the hell away from your games." Hamar snickered under her breath, as she gazed out the passenger window.

A few months later my actual age surfaced at school. I turned thirteen years old and was having a Bar Mitzvah a month later. So naturally, I had to send out my invitations with the expectation of my cover being blown. I confessed to my friend Dave, and our new best friend Stanley, what I had experienced in my past. I explained the divorce issue, all the different schools I attended and the hiding my father dragged us through. They completely understood my predicament, promising to keep my little dark secret between us. Hamar only permitted me to invite six friends anyway, so very few people from school figured out my tarnished past.

Since Shlomo and I were only five months apart, Hamar and my dad decided to combine our Bar Mitzvahs to save money. Hamar stuck to her philosophy, allowing us to only invite a few friends. The majority of the party was reserved for her friends and family members. This would guarantee a better return on her investment. Through all the planning, there was no mistake that this was Hamar's party, as she acted accordingly. We never had any input, seeing as it was more for an adult party than a kid's Bar Mitzvah. The only thing we requested was a football theme, which Hamar agreed on doing. I had Shlomo pitch the idea, knowing she would listen to anything he had to say. The theme was only going to be displayed on the sweet table and when the guests first arrived to the party. Hamar's idea was to have a large photo of Shomo and me dressed in our football uniforms for the guests to sign when entering the party room.

Prior to the Bar Mitzvah, she had a good friend who offered her husband's services to take the photo for the guests to sign. He came over one snowy day, taking several shots of Shlomo and me standing in the snow in a three point football stance. He was a little slow snapping the photos, as our fingers froze from being buried in the snow. When he finally finished taking the pictures, we couldn't have been happier. Then handing the roll of film over to Hamar, he instructed her to have the pictures developed right away. She assured him she would, while setting the canister on the kitchen counter. The film was stored in a little black canister and for some reason Hamar believed it would be ruined if opened.

Later that day, Mitch and I were in the kitchen talking about the photos when he picked up the little black canister, taking a peek inside. Hamar happened to be walking in at the same moment and went berserk. Her eyes ran wild with anger, as she darted towards Mitch with sparks flying from her hard wedge slippers. She briskly grabbed the canister from his little hands, snapping the top shut. Her expression contorted into a crazed maniac when snatching him by his hair and swinging him in the kitchen.

"You fucking stupid. Idiot. You ruined the pictures. Shithead," she screamed in a violent rage, heaving him through the dining room door. Mitch went flying with a yelp, hitting the floor with a thunderous bang. I ran around to the other side, watching from the foyer as Hamar beat the hell out of him. She ferociously started stomping on Mitch with her infamous hard wedge slippers, screaming a variety of curse words in Arabic and Hebrew. I still had no idea what they meant. Then grabbing two fists of his hair, she pulled until his follicles finally gave way. It looked like she was holding two dead chipmunks in her fists when done. Mitch was rolling around on the carpet in tears, appearing disoriented. Hamar stomped on him one last time for good measure, hollering, "You'll never touch my things again, you piece of shit. Now I have to ask my friend's husband to take more pictures, you stupid. Idiot. Drop dead, you shithead." When Hamar was done yelling, she tossed Mitch's hair in the air like party confetti and stormed away.

He was crying, looking up as his supple hair gently floated in midair. I watched him catch his fluffy remnants, lamenting over them in his open palms. With ownership of his hair again, Mitch remained sitting on the floor and gingerly tried replacing them back into his head. He tenderly attempted pushing the hair back into his scalp over and over again, but unfortunately, with no success. I was still in the foyer biting my nails, as I watched Mitch struggle with his detached hair. Frustrated and torn apart, he languidly stood up, walking up the stairs with his hair neatly resting in the palms of his hands. He went bald in his early twenties, claiming it was induced by Hamar's evil attack.

The Bar Mitzvah party was sensational, but leading up to the big event Hamar annoyed the hell out of me. She constantly reminded everyone, on several occasions, how much this shin-dig was costing her and my father. What bothered me most was this affair primarily consisted of Hamar's friends and family members. My friends were buried in the crowd and I actually didn't see much of them unless I was sitting at the table. We had a live band playing a variety of the big hits as everyone drank themselves silly, dancing all night long. The enlarged photo of Shlomo and I turned out extremely nice, with most of the people signing it in a tactful manner. There were a few smart asses who wrote and drew some colorful things, but it turned out to be a fun keepsake. When the back door opened for the sweet table, it was a great presentation. Not a thing was missing as the football theme was placed around the desserts. They had inflatable football players and footballs, which people snatched up to take home with them. In the middle of the table was a realistic football field with two little football players standing in each end zone. At the end of the party we thanked everyone for coming, eventually arriving home well after midnight.

Bright and early the next morning, Hamar was already down in the kitchen counting the checks, cash and the US Bonds. My father had a cup of coffee in his hand with a cigarette in the other. His hair had a bad case of bed head and his eyes looked like a bloody wreck. Julie and Samara were already eating breakfast, as Mitch was just finishing up. I walked over to Hamar smiling and asked, "So, how much do you think we got?"

Glaring up at me with her crowfeet lines, which accentuated her dark lifeless eyes, Hamar snarled, "I'm trying to count and you just messed me up. Shut up. Just be quiet."

"Sorry," I facetiously said.

"So, how was your party, Jim? Was it everything we said it would be," my father inquired, with an arrogant look on his face as if he already knew the answer.

"Thanks. I loved it. It was great, but I'm sad it ended so quickly."

Then winking at me, my father motioned in Hamar's direction. I looked at him confused, so he whispered, "Say thank you to your mother."

I nodded my head and said, "Thanks mom. That was a real cool party last night."

Without looking up, Hamar harshly said, "You're welcome. It only took your father to tell you before you could say it. Shmuck." Then holding up a dictionary, she spitefully shouted, "Here's that shit present your friend got you. That's why I didn't want all your friends invited. See what I mean? You were complaining about the number of friends you were allowed to invite. I paid a hundred dollars for her dinner and all I got back was a shitty book. That's why."

I took the red dictionary from her swollen fingers, angrily refuting, "I like it. I don't have one."

That dictionary was the only gift I received from my Bar Mitzvah. If not for the dictionary, I wouldn't have received a single gift. After Hamar counted the money that morning, she promised to open savings accounts for Shlomo and me for our college fund. When it was time for college, a few years later, Shlomo had two years paid for and a Fiat Spider convertible sports car purchased for him. When it was time for me to attend college, my father drove me directly to a bank, instructing me to apply for a school loan.

There was no allowance like Shlomo's $25 per week spiff for college or a sports car. In fact, I was only able to buy my first car by getting into a car accident, using the money from the lawsuit to purchase my first automobile. Hamar also had us liquidate the bonds when they matured. Driving us to a Metropolitan Bank, she had us endorse the backs of the bonds to cash them in. Once finishing our bank transaction, she pocketed the money. There was no smooth talking of a savings account or even a checking account to candy coat the crime. By this time, she apparently thought it was owed to her. It certainly made it difficult for me to get my college financed.

CHAPTER 25

My folks had a lawsuit pending from the time we lived in the Red Hill apartment. Hamar was involved in a bad car accident with another woman, who recklessly drove her car up on Hamar's trunk. Due to the accident Hamar wore a neck brace daily, then had surgery performed for the constant pain. Her case was built on the premises that she was incapable of moving her neck or picking anything up, leaving her permanently injured for life. They hired Uncle Douglass to represent her when the case finally made it to court. Hamar and my father were so sure they were going to be victorious, that they were spending the money before the case ever made it to court. They were suing for an absorbanent amount of money, counting on hitting the mother-load. To be sure everything went smoothly in court, Hamar and my father coached us on what to say in case we were called up to testify. They instructed everyone to tell the court what a great mother Hamar was before the accident and how much she loved playing with us. My father wanted us to testify how she loved wrestling on the floor and spending time playing fun games with her children, prior to being injured from the car accident.

As luck would have it, we never made it to the witness stand since the defending attorney hired a private detective, who shot some interesting film of Hamar. The stunned courtroom watched, as she was filmed lifting large tree branches, rocks, heavy boxes and all sorts of other objects, which testifying earlier she couldn't do. The judge was appalled by what he witnessed, throwing the entire case out. Hamar was infuriated, bitching about losing for years, while

Uncle Douglass was anything but pleased by the outcome. He was a prolific attorney in the area, with Hamar's silly antics not helping his untarnished reputation. I'm sure the court proceedings didn't help her relationship with her sister, Muffy, either.

I was a big fan of the Jewish holidays because we spent half of them with my father's side. He never put up a big fuss with Hamar about other holidays, so most functions were done with her side of the family. If it wasn't for the Jewish holidays, we would never see my dad's side for some reason. Uncle Stewart and Aunt Carly were the only family my father had, except of course his mother. The holidays were usually at their house when getting together. It was obvious Hamar despised going, making it quite evident by her pretentious actions and remarks. She wanted everything to be done with her family, so it was aggravating when she gave my father such a difficult time. Hamar made it a point to blurt out terrible insulting comments, imposing sly remarks under her breath with every visit. Performing like a child because she didn't get her way, Hamar put forth an aura that she was better than anyone else. She played this infantile game, believing she was rich and beautiful while everyone else was beneath her. It was extremely embarrassing and I wanted no part of it, always making sure to keep my distance from her.

The moment we came walking through the front door, Hamar would begin, strutting in the house with her chic designer clothing, Gucci purse and a snotty attitude to match. She ignited the evening by giving everyone a once over look, which meant looking them up and down to see if they were dressed to her satisfaction. If not, the inevitable would happen. This was a practice her family performed on us whenever we came for a visit. It made me exceedingly uncomfortable, since I was always self-conscious of what I wore anyways. Hamar's favorite target was Aunt Carly's brother's family. Her brother and sister-in-law were super nice people, who had two cute little girls. They were on the short side like their mother, Trudy and whenever Hamar spotted them, she began her nasty remarks. Usually, Shlomo, Samara and even Julie would be beside her when she made these despicable comments, reminding me of high school bullies. Hamar referred to Trudy and her two girls as, "the little people", while maliciously snickering and staring at them. Then pretending as though no one heard, Hamar and company gave phony warm salutations. I never understood why Julie gave in to Hamar's vulgar antics, but I suppose she was doing her best to fit in. It was very unusual that she wasn't the scapegoat, so Julie stood a better chance of winning Hamar's acceptance, at least for that night, if nothing else.

However it didn't end with Aunt Carly's brother, the ridiculing perpetuated from Aunt Carly's food to other members of her family. As the night progressed, I could sense the tension thickening but fortunately no one lost their cool. Jeff and I normally had a conversation about my home life, with him questioning how I was getting along with Hamar and her two children. I wasn't too forthcoming at the time, being still apprehensive about divulging full disclosure after the hamburger incident. But Jeff grasped how crappy I had it under these circumstances, sympathizing with my discouraging situation. It was very transparent to him or anyone else, who came into contact with my insane family.

My father and Uncle Stewart expanded the lighting store to an additional location in Virginia. The business was going so strong, that Hamar wanted my dad to hire her sister's husband to run the new showroom. Agreeing with her, they brought Hamar's sister, Edith and her husband, Yuli, from Rhode Island. Yuli worked in a furniture showroom as a salesperson, but with the business plummeting the way it was, he was looking for a change in career. In addition to Yuli's struggle with his current employer, Edith wasn't happy living so far away from her family, which made the move to Delaware such a success for them. Uncle Stewart and my father did a kind thing by hiring Yuli. When the time came for Yuli's family to relocate, my uncle and father helped with the purchase of their house, by lending them the down payment and co-signing for the home loan.

Around this time is when our parents began occasionally taking us out for Sunday night dinners, as a family. We were all excited with great anticipation, having never been out for dinner with our folks before. Going out to eat was reserved for their Saturday night excursions. There was one place in particular where they liked to go, which we frequently went with Uncle Gus and Aunt Rubel's family. It was an "all-you-can-eat" seafood restaurant, which was Gus' pick. Being the true miser with money, he knew better than anyone where the best value was. Gus was cutting coupons before it was even fashionable and if he happened to be at our house on a Sunday, he started clipping ours. This inspired a couple of good scraps between him and Hamar over those coupons.

Since Hamar considered herself kosher, I found it strange that she would eat in a place like that or bring home the seafood. Each time, before heading out to the restaurant, she lined her purse with a plastic produce bag to sneak the food out. They had deals like, kids under six ate for free or buy any item on the menu and eat as much as you want of any other item that was the same price or less. Samara was legitimate for the "eat for free deal", but Julie pretending to be six was hilarious. She was nine years old when we started going and was very tall for her age. She's almost six feet as an adult, so back then Julie looked sixteen years old. Every time we went, Hamar and my father forced her to declare that she was six years of age, which worked for a few years. For some reason, the restaurant's servers never questioned Julie.

Hamar was the most demanding and insensitive person I had ever eaten with at a restaurant. She's one of these individuals who were so rude to the servers that I made sure to order anything but what she wanted to eat. I would dare to guess, that Hamar was the restaurant patron who you heard about, where the people in the kitchen took turns spitting, farting or pissing on her food. Undoubtedly, she ate her share of booger laced meals. The pompous behavior would commence as soon as we were seated, with Hamar ordering the servers around like they were dirt under her feet. "Where are the hush puppies? How come the hush puppies aren't here yet? Do you believe this, Sheldon? There's no hush puppies." Then she would call the server a schmuck under her breath, as if they wouldn't hear it. Not only did they hear it, but everyone had common knowledge of what a schmuck was, since it wasn't just a Jewish expression anymore. I wish my father would have conveyed that to her.

The servers were very polite, responding, "No problem. I'll get those for you right away, ma'am."

I wanted to slide under the table, hiding until dinner was through. My father would look at her with an uncomfortable expression, quietly saying, "Hamar, we just sat down. Give them a minute."

"Just shut up, potato," she would defensively answer, while turning her head.

Chesapeake Bay Seafood House was known for their fabulous hush puppies, being the first thing the servers carried out to the table. They were little deep fried cornballs, which became addicting after merely eating one. Hamar and Shlomo invariably started the dinner off by warning everyone not to eat too many hush puppies, since they were so filling.

The ordering was comical, as the server went around the table, starting with Shlomo, Mitch and me ordering the spiced shrimp. Then Hamar and my father, without fail, ordering the Alaskan snow crab legs. The plan was, once we ate our first serving, my dad and Hamar would continue ordering the crab legs, throwing them around the table for all of us to eat. As the server went around writing down what everyone wanted, we all giggled in anticipation of Julie's order. She only had a choice of three things, which were fried chicken, fried flounder or fried gulf shrimp. Julie constantly went for the fried gulf shrimp which were about the size of sea monkeys. Countless times, I sat in my seat waiting for Julie to get busted, but she never did.

When it was Hamar's turn to order, she didn't look at the server. Her face was turned with a sourpuss expression, as she callously demanded, "I want the crab legs and don't give me a little bit either or I'll keep calling you to get me more. The last time I was here, they only gave me five legs every time they refilled my bowl. I want a bunch."

The server normally smiled, assuring her they would be sure to bring plenty. When all the orders were placed, my father would throw an incentive to the server. "Listen, bring the food fast and I'll give you a real good tip." He always kept his word, leaving the server a very generous tip.

Then Uncle Gus would chime in before the server left, saying,

"Wait a while wa wa would ya, me too. I'll give you a good one." My father told me how Gus was a lousy tipper, so I couldn't imagine what he left as a tip.

The waiters instinctively brought the drinks to the table before the meal, disturbing Hamar to no end. The sodas weren't part of the "all-you-can-eat" deal, so she never wanted us to get them before dinner. When the server delivered the drinks, Hamar was verbally abusive to them, sending everything back.

The food usually came quickly, with the server nearly losing a finger when placing the bowl in front of Shlomo. It was brutal watching Hamar and Shlomo eat, as they made it look like a pie eating contest at a state fair. They shoveled food in their mouths so rapidly, that sometimes the shell was still on the seafood. Shlomo was a complete animal when eating. In fact, my Uncle Stewart nicknamed him "the animal" and for good reason. When he ate, everything was all over his face, hands and clothes. If you happened to be sitting next to him, you weren't going home clean. Shlomo didn't believe in flatware or napkins, managing to get every part of his body in the bowl, except his feet. Before their plates were clean, Hamar and Shlomo were the first to demand more food and God forbid if the server didn't make sure it was a robust portion.

When everyone was done eating, Hamar ordered more spiced shrimp and hush puppies. The servers would look at her as if she were insane but always brought more. When they returned with the last order, Hamar would open her purse shoveling all the food in it. Her purse was like a bottomless pit, as she continued ordering until it was bursting at the seams. Being so humiliated, I would slide my chair back pretending like I didn't know her. Everyone at the table laughed hysterically, but I couldn't believe no one stopped her. There was no way that restaurant ever made a profit off our family. Coming back at a later date, I recall noticing a sign which read, *"Please do not share your food."*

One morning changed the way I ate food for the rest of my life. I came downstairs finding Mitch and Julie waiting to eat, while Hamar was bringing out the cereal. Samara was already eating her Pop Tart as Julie, like usual, was gobbling up the leftover crust that

Samara refused to eat. It was the epitome of how Julie was treated in comparison to Samara. Here was Julie munching on scraps at the table like a stray dog, as Hamar's daughter was gorging on the best part. Julie was grateful just to be able to eat the crust since, besides Shlomo and Samara, we were not permitted to touch the Pop Tarts. It was another fanatical rule put in place by Hamar, with her reasoning being Samara didn't like cereal. Hamar looked miserable pouring the cereal into the bowls, as she took out two one gallon containers of milk from the refrigerator. There wasn't much left in one of the plastic containers, but Hamar refused to be wasteful. I happened to be watching when she was pouring the milk into Julie's bowl and couldn't believe what I was seeing. The milk that Hamar was pouring out, plopped onto Julie's cereal in a cottage cheese consistency. She didn't seem to care, continuing to shake the milk container until every last drop was out, then served it. I thought for sure Julie was going to send it back, but instead ate it. I waited for some kind of sign like a yuck face or something after her first bite, but she didn't have a negative reaction at all.

Startled, I said, "Mom, that was gross what you gave Julie."

"What was gross? Stupid, it's milk. How can milk be gross? Just shut up, ok," Hamar lashed out at me, with a nasty tone.

"Yeah, I know what milk looks like and you gave her old spoiled milk that looked like cottage cheese."

Then Hamar's mood changed, shouting in a rabid fit, "Just shut your mouth. Like I don't know what milk looks like. Stupid. What? Am I going to poison her? The milk is fresh. I just got it two day ago. Stupid. Like I'm going to poison her. Stupid. Just mind your own business. Idiot, like I don't know what milk looks like."

Losing my appetite, I hastened from the house as Hamar repeatedly screamed in hysterics. I could still hear her voice shuttering through the house when closing the front door behind me. Thinking how inhumane Hamar was to feed Julie stale milk, I informed my father. He insisted I was over exaggerating, doing his finest to make it sound as far-fetched of a story as possible. So trying to add some validity to the mix, I shared a past experience. Describing how I watched Hamar take a block of blue molded cream cheese and serve it after skimming it off. Not just an end piece either, but most of the block of cream cheese. Even after the story he refused to believe me, insisting she was an excellent cook.

After that day, I made a habit of smelling everything Hamar served me. I didn't know if my nose was sensitive enough to detect whether something was spoiled or not, but I wasn't taking any chances. Whenever catching me sniffing her food, Hamar became infuriated. I remember one instance when she became violent, screaming, "What? Do you think I served you poison? Is that what you think? Piece of shit. Like I would serve poison. You can go to hell!" I found it better to do my sniffing when she wasn't paying attention.

CHAPTER 26

During the time I was attending the seventh grade, Mama Ida came back into our lives again. Hamar and my father sat us down in the family room, explaining that they were allowing her over for a visit. Surprised, but excited at the same time, I asked, "Hey dad, how come you're letting the other grandmother come over?"

He looked at Hamar, signaling for her to take over the question. Gladly taking control, she said, "Well, she called and you have a new baby brother that she wants you to meet. She thought it would be nice if he met his brothers and sister."

I wasn't buying that explanation. There had to be a carrot dangling in the wind somewhere for my father to permit Mama Ida over for a visit. He absolutely loathed her, telling me some very explicit things which made me uncomfortable. He made it perfectly clear how much she disgusted him and what he would like to do to her. During one of my father's animated outbreaks, he said, "I hate that woman. I would like to take a knife and slice her from her cunt to her mouth." This was a conversation we had after my father found out that Papa Willie didn't leave any money for us. After hearing him divulge that scenario to me, I was sickened, wishing he kept things like that to himself. It didn't sound like something a grandson needed to hear about his grandmother.

After Hamar's reasoning for permitting Mama Ida over, I picked at her brain. "Oh, so that's why she's coming over? She just wants us to meet our new brother?"

Hamar pushed up her lips with great effort, projecting a phony smile. "I wanted to wait until your grandmother came, but I'll tell you anyway. She has some things for you guys from your grandfather's death. I told her it was ok to come. I didn't ask your father because he hates her. He would never want her here." Then glaring at him for support, she shouted, "Right? Right, Sheldon? You'd never let her over?"

"That's right. If I had my way, that bitch wouldn't step foot in my house. You have your mother to thank, because my answer was no."

I wasn't thanking her and neither were Mitch or Julie. I was old enough by now to realize the game they were playing. He was placing Hamar on a high pedestal, treating her as the divine one who was allowing our grandmother, from exile, to re-enter our kingdom. This ploy never enticed me to alter my opinion of Hamar, knowing her evil ways better than he did. She was cold and incapable of kindness, making this visit about them and how they could take advantage of three children. My father and Hamar were under the illusion that Mama Ida was going to walk through our front door, showering us with Israeli Bonds that Papa Willie left for us.

The day Mama Ida arrived at our house, she wasn't carrying any bonds. She came with my mother's two year old son and a few gifts. This was a simple social call like she mentioned to them on the telephone, not Ed McMahon walking in with a giant check.

It was wonderful seeing her again, but unfortunately it was without Papa Willie this time. He died a few years earlier, which we were never made aware of and it was sad to think we never attended his funeral. When Mama Ida arrived, her eyes still held a wonderful blue warmth to them, but she looked as though she aged slightly. Ordinarily, my grandmother was on the chunky side, however this time, looking thin as her face revealed more wrinkles induced by her weight loss. Mitch, Julie and I semi-warmly hugged and kissed Mama Ida hello, being very cautious not to upset Hamar. She looked so elated seeing us again, then introduced our new half-brother. He was a cute little kid with blond hair and blue eyes. He looked very much like Julie, which Mama Ida commented on when we met him. Quickly gravitated to the pool table, he started pitching the heavy pool balls at us. Mama Ida did her best to stifle him, but it took Julie to divert his attention on something else.

Since it was Saturday afternoon my father was at work, which was exactly the way he wanted it. That left Hamar alone with us to entertain Mama Ida, as she put on a splendid performance. She did her best to show our grandmother how much she adored her grandchildren, while smiling and gingerly speaking when addressing us. It was scary the way Hamar could portray herself as another human being, giving me the impulse to want to throw up. I kept waiting for her slip and revert back to normality, but she was good.

Apparently, our mother was terribly sick. Mama Ida explained how she was incapable of walking on her own and confined to a wheelchair. Later on, my father told me how the doctors warned her not have anymore children, since she had symptoms of MS. Sadly, my mom didn't listen, marrying a fellow for a short period of time and getting pregnant. Once giving birth, the MS was triggered which debilitated her in the most aggressive way.

Sensing the gloom brought on by our mother's condition, Mama Ida changed the mood reaching into the bags, cheerfully saying, "Here are a few gifts I brought for you children." Bending over, she pulled out an array of different presents while passing them out to us. Hamar was captivated with salivating eyes, waiting for something with value to emerge. Then Mama Ida reached into her purse, taking out a small jewelry box. "Jim, Papa wanted you to have this," she said, handing me the box. "I don't know if you remember or not, but papa always wore this ring. He was a mason. Do you know what that is?"

As my grandmother was explaining what a mason was, I gently opened the velvet black box, looking inside. It was a magnificent diamond ring, set on a white and yellow gold band. The diamond looked exceptionally large, sparkling as the light swam through its facets. Never holding anything so elaborate before, I carefully removed the ring from the box slipping it on my finger. "Wow, this is beautiful. Thank you so much," I said, stunned by such a luxurious gift. I wanted to call her mama, but I knew that wasn't acceptable in front of Hamar or my father. So I opted not to call her anything, feeling safer by being silent.

Mama Ida's eyes brightened when seeing the ring on my finger. "That is beautiful. I wish your Papa Willie could have seen it on you. It looks big though. Be careful not to lose it, Jim." I nodded my head agreeing, feeling so proud that Papa Willie chose me to have his ring.

Then standing up, mama suddenly remembered something. "Oh Jim, I almost forgot. I brought Papa Willie's golf clubs for you. They're in my trunk. The clubs were too heavy for me to carry, so I had Lisa put them in the car for me." Then she paused, saying, "By the way, Lisa said to say hello to you kids."

I loved her and shouted, "Tell Lisa I say hello too. She used to make me the best BLT sandwiches and give me rides on the vacuum cleaner. Tell her hi." Catching myself, I quickly glanced over at Hamar, waiting on a nasty look but she still had that phony smile glued to her face. After that, I was cognizant of each and every word I breathed.

Handing over the car keys, Mama Ida said, "Go out to my car and bring in papa's golf clubs. Lisa put them in the truck."

Smiling, I hurriedly dashed out from the family room to go collect the golf clubs. When opening the front door, I spotted mama's Cadillac, finding it funny that she was still driving the same type of automobile after all these years. Mama was one not to break tradition and it looked brand new too. Going around to the back of her car, I popped open the trunk. A large green canvas golf bag was lying back there with the name, Moss, written across it. It appeared as if someone wrote his name with a thick black marker. Seeing his name on the golf bag, gave me a guilty complex for taking ownership of his bag. It didn't settle in my mind yet, that my grandfather had died as I began feeling like a scavenger. First it was the ring and now it was his golf clubs. Setting my thoughts aside, I staggered while lifting the clubs out, surprised by how heavy they were.

When I stumbled into the kitchen with the golf clubs, my grandmother chuckled. "Well, I guess you'll have to learn how to play golf, huh, Jim?" As she chuckled, it sounded like a great idea to me.

Grinning with appreciation for the gift, I couldn't create a complete smile since being saddened by the circumstances. It felt as though my grandfather was a ghost in the past, with so much of my youth spent without him. When it was time for Mama Ida to leave, I knew it would be the last time she would be allowed over. She brought no money or bonds and that was the premise of her visit. I watched as she grabbed her new grandson's hand, reminding me of myself years before, as they walked out to her car. It was a disparaging time and I never knew when I would see her or my mother again.

As soon as my grandmother left, Hamar's face and demeanor made a complete switch back to her normal persona. When I came back to the kitchen, she was looking in the direction of my golf clubs. "Ok, take that shit out of my kitchen." Picking them up, I started towards the basement until she yelled, "Where are you going with that?"

"Downstairs. I thought I would put them in the basement."

"No, no. In the garage. That's all I need is that shit in my basement. No, no. Put it in the garage. Putting it in the basement. That's all I need is more shit in my basement," Hamar sarcastically shouted in anger.

After returning, Hamar looked aggravated. "Where's the ring your grandmother gave you?" She had this snarling expression which revealed her teeth and for some reason a joke my father told me came to mind. Hamar's teeth and feet were so dreadful, that my father warned me before I marry a woman to make sure to check her teeth and feet, like the Arabs do when buying a camel. It was an ongoing joke he told me, after each time he needed to pay for one of Hamar's surgeries. It didn't make her laugh, but I got a chuckle out of it.

When we were living in the Red Hill apartment, my father was kind enough to bring home a few McDonald's fruit pies. Hamar split them in half for us to eat, seeing as there were not enough to go around. Excited about the cherry pie, I was sitting at the kitchen table when I quickly snatched a bite. While chewing, I felt something hard in my mouth, but before I could swish out whatever it was, I bit down almost breaking a tooth. Fishing around in my mouth, I finally picked out something small and hard. As I studied the hard object between my fingers, Hamar burst out laughing so hard that her mascara began running down her face.

I didn't recognize what I pulled out. The hard object looked like a little rock, so feeling ill, I asked, "What? What so funny?"

Hamar could hardly get out the words, as everyone else at the table began laughing along with her. "It's.....my.....tooth," she erupted through her laughter.

I started gagging and screamed, "Oh my God, how did that get in there?" I thought I was going to vomit and uncontrollably dry heaved. Shaking from all the hysterics, Hamar scurried over snatching the rotted tooth from in between my fingers. Then still cackling, she opened her mouth pushing the tooth back into place. I never looked at pie the same way again.

Hamar was still waiting on an answer about the ring and I knew why. "It's in my pocket," I said with my hand protecting it.

"Give it to me and I'll put it with my jewelry. I'll lock it away so you don't lose it."

"Why can't I hold on to it? I won't lose it," I argued, knowing it would vanish in her possession.

"Just give it to me. What? Do you think I'm going to steal it? Stupid! Like I would steal it," Hamar screeched, sounding hostile.

Hearing the chaos, Mitch, Julie and Samara filed into the kitchen. "I'm not saying you're going to steal it, but I want to hold on to it. What's the difference?"

"What's the difference? It doesn't fit you and I'll give it to you when it does. Idiot. That's what's the difference." Then Hamar didn't want to continue arguing, so she exploded. "Ok, give me the ring. That's it." Then glancing at her audience, she cried out, "Do you believe this? This piece of shit thinks I'm going to steal his ring. Cheap. That's what you are, cheap."

No one made a comment when I finally gave in. "Here, take it," I cried in frustration. Angrily, I yanked the box from my front pocket, tossing it on the kitchen counter. "Here you go. Happy?"

That ignited Hamar's fuse, incensing her to call me a nasty word in her language. Then while walking out of the kitchen, she screamed, "Shithead. You piece of shit. Fuck you. This is the last time I help you. This is the thanks I get for letting your piece of shit grandmother over. Now you're a big shot again, huh? Don't you talk to me. You piece of shit. Wait until your father gets home. Piece of shit, thinking I'm going to steal his shitty ring."

When making it to my bedroom, I heard her calling up, "You should drop dead. You piece of shit. Drop dead. You're the thief, not me." I closed my door, shutting out her vile scratchy voice. Standing in my room, feeling paralyzed by grief, I violently punched a hole through my wall. I could not hold my temper any longer from her driving me crazy with her bullshit antics.

Hamar was already in the process of getting spruced up for their big Saturday night splurge, when my father returned from work. I was still in my room simmering down and listening, as she jumped all over him about our confrontation regarding the ring. She was yelling and swearing about what a piece of shit I was and how I thought she was a stealer. When hearing enough, I strutted into their bedroom to defend myself.

As soon as I entered, Hamar hollered, "Get out. Get out. You piece of shit. You should drop dead."

"Hey! Hey," my father bellowed. "What kind of talk is that?"

"Just shut your fucking mouth," Hamar yelled, with her head bobbing up and down with every syllable. "Stupid. Now you're going to defend your cheap fucking son. You can drop dead too. Asshole!"

"What the hell happened," my father asked, looking like the rage was building inside of him. Hamar always knew which buttons to push.

"She wanted my ring and I wanted to hold it myself," I gently replied.

Hamar was fuming. "She. Who the hell is she. Do you believe this shit, Sheldon? She. Like I'm a piece of shit."

Sternly staring at me, my father corrected me. "Mom. She's your mother. You call her mom."

Then he focused on Hamar. "Well, do you have the ring?"

"Yes. He gave me the ring. I told you that already. Stupid. Asking me if I have the ring. Stupid idiot."

Wisely, my father changed the subject, squawking, "That's it, a ring? All the money that old man had and she brought you a ring?" He was growing emotionally annoyed over my gift.

"She also brought me over his golf clubs too," I proudly stated, feeling honored to have them.

"Jesus Christ," he yelled out, lighting a cigarette. "With all that money and that cheap old bitch comes over with a piece of shit ring and clubs. She should be the one to drop dead and the old man should go to hell. With all their money, I figured he'd leave something for you kids. At least for college."

Then peering over at Hamar, he exclaimed, "The next time you want that old bitch over, don't. Didn't I tell you? I know these people. They are the cheapest garbage of the earth."

Hamar cooled down a notch or two, declaring, "Believe me. After the way this piece of shit talked to me. There will never be a next time."

CHAPTER 27

Mitch was beginning to show signs of an unusual debilitating disease. It initiated with the swelling of his left middle finger, leaving it bent at the middle knuckle. It looked like he broke the finger at one time, never properly resetting it. Then shortly after that happened, Mitch's left hip bothered him so horribly that he started limping like an old man with arthritis. He favored his right leg, using it to support himself as he hobbled around. Hamar and my father waited to see if it would heal on its own, but it went on for weeks. Progressively, Mitch was getting worse, as my father decided to take him to our family pediatrician. After the evaluation, the doctor determined that Mitch was going through growing pains and with time it would pass. But the symptoms never disappeared, with Mitch's growing pains by no means evolving in to any kind of a growth spurt. Being twelve at the time, Mitch stood well under five feet tall, so my father continued searching for someone with answers.

Mitch was having a difficult time doing the simplest chores, like getting out of bed or putting himself together in the mornings. Distressed with Mitch's diminishing condition, my father took him to see his orthopedist who couldn't find anything wrong with him either. The only idea he had was inserting a needle in Mitch's finger, so to draw fluid in hopes of relieving the pain, but that didn't help. Mitch was still agonizing over his hip and now, newly injured finger. The orthopedist didn't have a prognosis, managing to injure Mitch's finger worse than it was before he came in to the office.

After a few months went by, my father was growing desperate.

He was losing time from work, without a single doctor forming an opinion of what was wrong with Mitch. Hamar was absolutely no help, since being unwilling to call any doctors, grumbling that no one understood her accent over the phone. By this time, Mitch had advanced to spending the better parts of his days chained to the commode. He was wiping his undercarriage so incessantly, that only blood stained the soiled toilet paper. He complained how just the smell of food was enough to stimulate his bowels. My father expressed extreme concern when Mitch appeared to have lost a significant amount of weight. He was so weak that attending school was becoming a serious challenge. Finally giving up the conventional doctors, my father rushed Mitch to Seneca Hospital in hopes of finding a solution.

The doctors at Seneca were as stumped as the prior physicians. After they had Mitch endure more probing and needles, the doctors opted to draw fluid from his left hip. They were hoping to find something in the fluid that would shed some light on his illness. When all the tests were completed, they regrettably found nothing and suggested Mitch be taken to John Hopkins. The doctors felt that Hopkins was better equipped for someone in his condition.

Mitch left the hospital on crutches, which were more of a nuisance than anything else. His left hip still terribly ached, as his mobility was so deplorable that he found it impossible to get on the school bus with the crutches. The only upside to his handicap was being excused from any of Hamar's house projects. Mitch had a good sense of humor during those occasions. When I was recruited for new jobs, he would laugh, mocking me with silly expressions. He appeared so depleted and hindered with terrible pain, that I would have rather done the projects than traded places with Mitch.

Nearly a year after my father shuttled Mitch around to all the different medical experts, they diagnosed him with Crohne's disease. The doctors were so stumped that a psychiatrist at Children's Hospital actually suggested that Mitch was faking it. In her opinion, he was pretending to be sick for attention. Mitch was sent home that day with a plastic bucket to prove his innocence. The psychiatrist wanted him to collect the entire stool he passed in a day and bring it back.

That was the only appointment Hamar attended and Mitch said she was against it. She made him do his business in the basement bathroom, then store it under the vanity when done. Apparently, when my father and Mitch returned with the bucket of crap, the doctors were flabbergasted by the plethora of poop. They decided to refer him to a specialist in Florida who specialized in Crohne's.

Thanks to Mitch, the whole family was treated to another Florida vacation. He and Hamar flew down together, while the rest of us made the trip in our trusty paneled station wagon. They departed earlier to make Mitch's doctor's appointment, but the specialist turned out to be an allergist. He wasn't the Crohne's guru that Mitch was hoping he would be. Dissatisfied with the results, Mitch considered the doctor a quack, suffering through a series of skin pricking and scratching tests to uncover what was ailing him. When the allergist was finished, he merely suggested Mitch stay away from all wheat and dairy products. Mitch was furious with the prognosis, feeling like it was a waste of time. He received no explanation of why he wasn't growing or any kind of real treatment for the pain and excessive bowel movements. It seemed to him to be a family vacation rather than a cure for his horrific disease.

When returning home from our trip, Mitch was put on a strict diet avoiding all foods containing wheat or dairy products. He religiously adhered to this alternative medicine for months, but there was no improvement in his condition. He reminded me of the Tiny Tim character from the movie, *"A Christmas Carol"*. At thirteen years old, he was still less than five feet tall and a mere bag of bones. The crutches, meant for assisting Mitch, didn't give the support needed, leaving him in constant pain. While watching him get around, I noticed how his limp was very defined, like he was stepping up on a curb every time he utilized his left foot. Mitch's hopes were deteriorating with every passing day, as he was becoming very depressed.

Hamar and my father were convinced that the allergist knew what he was doing. They tried comforting Mitch by telling him the doctor was world renowned for his expertise in curing people, but it didn't alter his attitude. He transformed into a true loner, avoiding any type of interaction with us and coming across as very angry and hostile towards everyone. One morning at breakfast Shlomo joked around with Mitch, nicknaming him, side-face, since he ate staring at the wall. Mitch hated being called side-face, exploding in fury anytime Shlomo antagonized him with that name. It was the only way we could get a reaction out of him, so I started referring to him as side-face too. Sadly for Mitch, Hamar liked it so much she resolved to calling him side-face. Eventually, side-face became a household name for Mitch.

CHAPTER 28

My father and Uncle Stewart had built the lighting store up to three locations by this time. The third location was opened in Bistle, Pennsylvania, but breathing a short lived life seeing as Jimmy Carter was in office and the economy took a downward spiral. Painfully, one by one the locations were shut down until they were left with only the Red Hill store. It blind-sided me, impacting the entire family out of the clear blue sky. Hamar and my father's lifestyle illuminated a well-to-do appearance, showing no signs of erosion. In fact, he traded in his 280Z for a Cadillac Coupe de Ville as she upgraded her station wagon for a Cadillac Sedan. They were still dressing up and running out to fancy restaurants every Saturday night, so it took us by surprise.

One evening my father came home after an exhausting day at work. He and my uncle were in the process of liquidating the inventory, hoping to recoup as much cash as possible before going belly-up. Looking ghastly, my father worked long hours, as the pressure was physically eating him away. His eyes were badly sunken in and the black circles underneath didn't help to hide them, resembling an old weary raccoon. We were all in the family room while he was complaining to Hamar about his day. All of us kids were nosey, sitting around eavesdropping and waiting for the unpleasant details. Something detrimental was happening, but I didn't know how much worse it could get for Mitch, Julie and me. While Hamar's kids benefited from my father's short success, we still resembled hobos.

During their conversation, my father made a suggestion which drove Hamar to insanity. "Listen Hamar, I was thinking that we need to sell the house. If we sell it then we could take the money and start our life over again," my father explained, as he rocked back and forth looking fatigued.

Hamar glared at him as if he were out of his mind, shouting, "What did you say?"

Without hesitation, my father repeated himself. "I think it's for the best if we sell the house because...." Before completing his sentence, Hamar was draped over him like a grizzly bear ripping apart a deer.

"My house? You're not selling my house. You piece of shit, shithead. This is my house," she shrieked, yanking ferociously on his hair. Mitch, Julie and I stood astounded, watching Hamar attack our father with brutal force. This was the first time we witnessed someone else receiving a beating from her, besides us. It was vindication as far as I was concerned. Now he was experiencing our agony, feeling her wrath when she went into insanity mode.

My father stood patiently without moving, while Hamar beat the crap out of him. "You're not selling my house. Do you understand me? You can get the fuck out, but you're not selling my house." She was violently clawing at his face and eyes with her painted fingernails like a fierce cat. My father continued standing there like a dolt, taking her abuse as though he had it coming.

No one attempted to stop Hamar, as she was now slapping his face and pounding on his chest with tears flowing from her eyes. "This is my house. You lost everything, you stupid idiot. All the money from my house you took. You bastard asshole."

My father was speechless, looking as if his eyes were going to roll back in his skull. Hamar was brutally coming at him with full force, but I could see she was winding down, as her breathing and crying soon transformed into hyper-ventilating and raspy yelping. Finally, Shlomo stood proudly next to his mother, putting an arm over her shoulder. "Yeah, dad. We're not giving up this house and moving into an apartment or something. I'm with mom."

My father's appearance looked as if he just rumbled with a

mountain lion. His face and chest were completely red, scratched from top to bottom. "Listen, I don't want to sell the house any....."

Hamar suddenly cut him off, as she belligerently started jumping and screaming in place. She looked like a child at Toys R Us having a temper tantrum over a toy. "Just shut your mouth. You shithead. Piece of shit trying to ruin my life. You'll never get my house. Do you understand me? Never!"

Passively looking at Shlomo, my father gruffly said, "Would you please calm her down."

As Shlomo moved to comfort her, Hamar yelled, "You calm down. You piece of shit. Idiot. I need to calm down? You need to calm down. Idiot. Like I need to calm down. Drop dead. Go to hell, you bastard asshole."

"Come on mom, calm down and let's hear what dad has to say," Shlomo squawked, struggling to keep her off my father. Hamar acquired a second wind and was off to the races again.

"Stop it already. Ok," my father refuted, finally showing some assertiveness. "I'll try to say it again for the hundredth time. I don't want to sell the house, but I don't have another idea. If we sell it, we can at least have some money after we lose the business."

"And I told you, I'm not selling my house," Hamar forcefully said, spewing out her words in a deliberate manner.

"Yeah dad, I'm not willing to sell it either. Mom's right," Shlomo shouted back, acting like his mother's advocate. Hamar was still under his arm breathing heavily.

"You know something Shlomo, this is something for me and your mother to talk about." My father sounded perturbed, having his fill of Shlomo's interference. Then walking over to the bar, he lit a cigarette with very shaky hands. "Ok, you kids go out. Get upstairs or something. I need to talk to your mother alone."

While we were upstairs, I could overhear them loudly arguing in the family room. It wasn't clear, but it didn't have to be for us to know what was going on. After some time, Hamar stomped out of the family room grabbing her car keys. I heard my father pleading, "Come on. Don't be silly." Then the front door slammed as Hamar sped out in her car.

My father was left standing alone in the foyer holding a drink. I leaned over the banister, whispering, "Hey dad, is everything ok?"

Jerking his head up, my father threw me a sullen look. "You kids just go to bed. Just go to bed," he demanded, sounding upset.

Hamar eventually came back and I lost my childhood forever. Instead of selling the house and downsizing like my father suggested, I tasted the workforce at the age of fifteen. Hamar and my father decided to send Shlomo and me out to find jobs. Shlomo accepted a job working at a department store, in the deli section, while I found a job at Woolworth's pushing a broom. I didn't think Woolworth's would hire me since I was under age. But after spending an entire day submitting applications around Montgomery Mall, they were the only ones interested. I was working four days a week, which left no time for playing sports anymore, so I had to quit my junior high school basketball team. The most devastating sport to give up was football. I was one year away from playing high school football and it didn't look like it was going to happen for me.

Quitting basketball was extremely difficult to deal with, but football was my life. I had played since the fourth grade, with my ultimate goal being to play starting quarterback for my high school team. Being told I couldn't play football was like cutting out my soul with a jagged knife.

My father elected to go back on the road as an outside salesman. It wasn't in the lighting field anymore but instead, women's clothing. He was selling for a few different companies, trying to get the high-end boutiques to carry his merchandise. Reluctantly shedding the Cadillac, he purchased a Datsun 310, traveling on the road most of the week. There were many nights when he didn't come home at all, since traveling to many different states. Still bitter over the loss of his lighting business, my father frequently complained about his new found profession. I sympathized with him, seeing how it was thriving for a few years. As time went by, I often wondered what became of Uncle Stewart and his family, since it was obvious Hamar and my dad cut all ties with them.

The last occasion we spent with them was for dessert at our house during Rosh Hashanah. Hamar received a phone call from Aunt

Carly, explaining how they were going to a new temple where their kids wanted to join. She mentioned that there was a good chance the services would end later than expected. Hamar was curt with her and didn't appreciate the warning. Her side of the family was coming on time, so she found no reason why Aunt Carly's family couldn't do the same. My aunt's response was that she would do her best to be on time. Hamar was inflexible and rude, telling her dinner was going to be served at the original time and if they wanted, they could show up for dessert.

Hamar was enraged, knocking my father over when spilling the dilemma on his shoulders. "Would you believe this shit? Carly called to tell me that they would be late for dinner tonight," Hamar cried out to my father, with smoke fuming from her ears. She was standing in the kitchen, while mama was busy preparing for dinner.

My father acted dumbfounded, asking, "Why? What happened?"

"What happened? I'll tell you what happened." Hamar was hot now, shouting with toxic venom in her voice. "All of a sudden your brother, Stewart, is a big Jew. Jeff and Dan picked a new synagogue they want to join, so your shmuck brother and Carly are going with them instead of being here on time."

"What? What temple are they going to? I thought they went to mom's old temple," he said, sounding bewildered.

Hamar's face had a distorted livid expression, as she screamed, "Stupid. I just told you. They're going to the temple that Jeff wants to go to. Idiot. Stupid. Open your fucking ears."

"Hey, don't start, ok," my father shouted back in anger.

"You don't start. You idiot. My family who's orthodox is going to be here and your schmuck brother who's reformed is going to be late. I'll tell you this, Sheldon, if their not here on time for dinner, it's the last holiday I spend with your family. Ok? I'm not putting up with this shit. All of sudden your brother is this big shot Jew. Idiots. All of them. Like Jeff and Dan know a temple. Idiots. Especially your brother. All of a sudden they're religious. What a joke."

Mama was busy cooking away, never flinching as Hamar hollered her nasty loud remarks. I suppose not understanding English had its advantages sometimes, but the screaming was enough to get your heart racing. My father didn't give Hamar an answer and left to indulge himself with a cocktail.

The worst scenario happened when Uncle Stewart and his family showed up for dessert, missing dinner. I never found out where they ate, but they showed up in good spirits, which rubbed the fury deeper in Hamar's face. She didn't directly say anything to my uncle or aunt, but was brutally laconic and tactless when greeting them. She chose to be snotty, making no small talk while ignoring them the entire night. I overheard Hamar telling her sisters, "Do you believe this shit?" Then she switched over to Hebrew or Arabic, so no one could understand the rest of her insulting conversation. It was quite obvious what she was orchestrating, but my father stayed away instead of correcting the situation. I didn't think it was a crime to be a little late because they wanted to be with their children for the holidays. Hamar and my father never understood that the holidays were about spending time with your immediate family. Not dressing up with the intention of putting on a fashion show for the extended family. That was an ingredient always absent from my childhood.

After that night, the holidays were never split up again. Hamar got what she wanted, so that every holiday, from that point on, was spent with her side of the family. Mitch and I were distraught over the situation, blaming our father for agreeing with his wife. It was another step towards dismembering his family. We couldn't understand how he could let this happen, but later I noticed how his mentality was cohesive with Hamar's.

I'll never forget picking up my first paycheck. My father was driving me to Montgomery Mall, smiling proudly saying, "It must feel good to pick up your first paycheck, huh?"

I glanced over at him trying to crack a smile, but it was impossible. "Yeah, I feel real good about it."

"Listen, when you get it, give it to your mother. I'm sure she'll be real happy," my father said, still smiling.

When he dropped me off at Woolworth's, I snatched up my check and ran it over to Sears to cash it. I think it was around forty-five dollars, minus the little service fee which they charged me, but

I didn't have a bank account. While driving home, I felt a proud sensation shower over me, holding the cash I earned in my hand. I wasn't happy about the arrangement but at the same time, I was helping my family. If nothing else, I considered that an honorable deed.

When we arrived home, my dad strutted behind me, saying, "Don't forget what I said, ok?"

Nodding, I searched in the kitchen for Hamar feeling full of pride. When first finding mama busy making mini loaves of bread, I stopped to say hello and kiss her. Then my father and I found Hamar in the master bedroom. I smiled, puffing my chest out, saying, "Hi mom." Then gave her the routine double kiss, handing her the cash. After her normal cold hello, she snatched the money from my grip slowly counting it. Once the task was completed, she walked over shoving the cash into her nightstand without as much as a thank you. I felt my chest deflate and languidly sauntered out of the room.

A few minutes later I heard Hamar screaming at my father, purposely loud enough for my ears. "Thank him? Fuck him. He should be kissing my feet that he still has a house to live in. You go thank him. If it was up to you, we'd be living in a apartment. Schmuck. Like I should go thank him. He can drop dead before I thank him. You too. You can go drop dead with him."

"Hey, hey, what's wrong with you? Watch the way you talk," my father said like he was pleading with her. Everyone always had to walk on eggshells around her.

"Just shut your mouth! What's wrong with me? What's wrong with you? Go. Go. Go with your son. Piece of shit, telling me to thank him. That's all I need to do is thank him." Then I heard my father stomping down the stairs, while Hamar continued her wretched rambling. "Stupid. Like I need to thank him. He should thank me. Idiot. You and him are idiots," she screamed with fire in her lungs.

Turning on my receiver, I listened to the radio hoping it would cheer me up, but I was too torn apart for it to help. My mind was plummeting deep into a dark pit, with anger compelling my fist through the wall again. I acknowledged that from this point on, it was a lost cause with Hamar. There was no way of breaking through her icy cold exterior and I was beyond requiring her love or acceptance anymore. That thought process is what guided me through her contemptuous behavior, since this was the ongoing treatment after giving her my paycheck each time. There was never a simple thank you or even a smile, just Hamar snatching the money from my hand as if I owed it to her. My father was no better, quickly assimilating to her mindset. People from the outside world of normality and reason never saw this side of Hamar or my father. The infamous cliché, when I told my friends about what I was doing, was, "At least you're helping out your family." I always had to chuckle to myself, feeling as though I didn't have a family. This house was filled with poison and cold heartless bitterness. I could almost see my own breath when exhaling in this cold abode. Hamar thought this house was the world, which it was to her and her two children. I think that's why I hated it so much. Besides the house stealing my soul and leaving me barren, I felt being loved and cared for was more important than a damn house.

My father picked me up from work late one Saturday afternoon, looking concerned. "Have you heard or seen Mitch today?"

I shook my head, replying, "No. Why? Was he supposed to be at the mall or something?"

"Your mother and I are worried. We haven't seen him or heard from him since this morning. I even called his friend, Carl but his mother said they weren't together today." He sounded irritated as his knuckles were white from squeezing the steering wheel so tightly.

"Well, has he come home yet," my father asked Hamar, as I followed him into the kitchen.

"No. Do you believe this idiot? No phone call or anything," Hamar rumbled, hastily rummaging through her kitchen drawer for something.

Just as I sat next to my father at the kitchen counter, Mitch came strolling in from the laundry room. The front door was normally locked so we always came in through the garage door. His expression and demeanor showed no indication that he had any idea Hamar and my father were looking for him. Hamar stood leaning against the counter, with a cold abrasive look on her face when Mitch double kissed her hello. But that was typical Hamar, he would have never picked up a signal of being in trouble from her behavior. My father's demeanor, on the other hand, was a dead give away that he was upset. His face was white since the blood migrated to his eyes and eyelids. Mitch, still looking clueless to the situation, scooted over to my father giving him a kiss and saying hello. Nonchalantly my father offered him a cheek, without returning the kiss. "Where were you today, Mitch?"

Mitch stood directly in front of my dad, casually answering, "Oh, I was at Carl's house today."

Deciding to let Mitch bury himself, my dad said, "Really? What did you guys do?"

Mitch looked like he was slowly leaking confidence, stammering, "We, ah, we played in his front yard."

Before my father stood up, he backhanded Mitch across the face, screaming, "You're fucking lying. I called Carl's mother and she hadn't seen you all fucking day. Now, I'll ask you again. Where the fuck were you today?" My father was shaking with rage, appearing ready to throw another slap as he waited on Mitch's answer.

Mitch slammed into the pantry closet with a loud thump, when backhanded by my father and was now rubbing his cheek which instantly reddened. Tears were trickling from his eyes as he shouted something that rocked my world. "I was with the other mother and grandmother," he blurted out, with his hands defensively covering his face in anticipation of a flurry.

Everything suddenly stopped around me, with a sense of being mentally paralyzed. I couldn't believe those words lingered over his lips without a struggle. It was astonishing that he didn't try another bullshit story, but instead blurted out the truth. I knew as well as he did that he was committing instant suicide.

Mitch's confession catapulted my father on top of him. "You motherfucker," he screamed in a crazed rage of violence, physically throwing Mitch against the oven. Then grabbing him by the throat, my father lifted Mitch up to his height hollering in his face, "This is what you do to your mother and me? You fucking piece of shit! After everything we've done for you."

Mitch tried squealing something out but there was no chance. His face was turned to the side as he was gradually turning red. Hamar was standing behind my father with her arms crossed resting on her chest, chiming in, "You piece of shit. Huh, you went to see your mother and grandmother? You should drop DEAD," she spit out with a disgusted tone in her voice.

Hamar's comment was a sure death sentence for Mitch. My father was already fighting for her honor, so her remark only added fuel to his fit of rage. Taking Mitch by the throat, my father tossed him about eight feet against the standing freezer we had in the laundry room. Mitch's head and back hit it with such a ferocious crash, that the freezer almost toppled over. Then my father attacked him as if he were a heavy bag in a gym, belting Mitch with a flurry of vicious punches to the mid-section.

Keeping a safe distance, I scampered over trying to reason with my father. "Come on dad, enough already. The kid's sick."

Looking livid, Hamar unfolded her arms answering for him. "Sick? He wasn't too sick to go see his whore mother and shit grandmother. Right, you piece of shit," she berated, as my father was still working on Mitch. "After I took you to all those doctors and flew you to Florida, this is how you pay me back. You should drop dead. You bastard." She was nauseating to watch as it seemed like she was living vicariously through my father's attack on Mitch.

Mitch was shrieking in agony with every blow and slap my father landed. I pleaded again, fearing for his life. "Come on dad, I think he's had enough."

Consumed with Mitch while trying to gather his breath, he yelled, "Just shut your fucking mouth. Get the fuck out of here."

Mitch was crying out in pain as my father firmly pushed him against the freezer. Then while huffing and puffing, he yelled at Mitch. "Is that what you want, to go live with your fucking mother? The whore that fucks men in front of you. Huh, is that it? You and your fucking mother and your cunt grandmother? You all can live together happily. After all the shit you put us through and this is the thanks. You fucking shit."

Then ruggedly dragging Mitch by his neck, my father pulled

him into the finished part of the garage. "Now you can go fucking live with your piece of shit cunt grandmother and that pig whore of a mother," he gruffly hollered.

Hysterically crying, Mitch was frantically swinging his arms in an attempt to get loose. Following closely behind them, I watched as my father maliciously hurled him into a wall. Mitch hit it so hard that it sounded like an explosion, with the impact embedding his entire body into the drywall. The collision actually formed a silhouette of Mitch after he finally oozed out. Once able to escape, he made it to a shopping center where he called Mama Ida to send a cab for him.

My father couldn't stop trembling when sitting back down on his bar stool. The confrontation with Mitch caused his breathing to become noticeably short and heavy. Hamar scowled at him, saying, "Sheldon, you have to calm down. You're going to give yourself a damn heart attack over that piece of shit." She hurried over to the sink filling a glass of water, then sliding it over to him. "Here, drink this."

Temporarily, Hamar looked pleased that my father defended her honor, but it didn't last long. "Sheldon, I'll tell you this. That shithead is never allowed back into my house again. Do you understand me? He's fucking dead. Dead, do you hear me? I mean it."

My father's head hung low, as if he were looking at something on the kitchen floor and didn't answer. While struggling to catch his breath, I saw that his complexion was a sickly light shade of green. "Sheldon, do you hear me? That piece of shit is dead. After all I did for him. Taking him to all the doctors to find out why he was a midget. I made him all that special shit the doctor told me to make. He's finished," Hamar yelled, without barely taking a breath.

"I heard you. Ok?"

My father was perturbed, as I watched him finally pick up his head seeming weary. "I can't believe it. He just stands there and tells me that he's seeing his fucking mother and that cunt grandmother of his." Then my father turned, glaring at me. "Did you know about this shit he was doing?"

I was surprised and biting my nails replied, "No. I didn't know anything. He doesn't really talk that much."

"I can't believe this shit. All I've done for you kids and this is the thanks I get. He was treated the best, out of everyone. He was sick, so we didn't have him help with anything around the house or even cut the lawn. Nothing," my father said while staring at Hamar.

"That's right, nothing. I didn't ask that shithead to help even to pick up a dish. Piece of shit. My own children I didn't treat as good as him. He should drop dead."

"Ok already, with the dropping dead," my father squawked, looking annoyed.

"Just shout your mouth. I'll say it as many times as I want. You stupid idiot. He should fucking DROP DEAD," Hamar screamed, clearly challenging him. "Remember what I said, that shithead isn't allowed in my house."

The next day Mama Ida called, asking my father to pick up Mitch. She thought it better that he should grow up with a father in his life, feeling too old to handle him herself. She explained how her hands were already full with a grandson and a daughter, who was suffering from MS. Against Hamar's wishes, my father went and brought Mitch back home. During the drive back, he made it clear to Mitch that he was to beg and plead for his mother's forgiveness. My father knew it was the only possible way Hamar would accept him back. Without Mitch's cooperation, he would have to make a very difficult choice between being married to her or ostracizing his son. Mitch never spoke in the car, so my father was bushwhacked when he never apologized to Hamar. In fact, he never acknowledged her at all, simply going about his day and giving her his famous side-face. It drove Hamar insane, convincing me that she would surely divorce my father over the whole ordeal.

Each night after Mitch returned, we could hear them furiously fighting over him. Hamar was the louder of the two, constantly on my father's ass to get rid of him or she was leaving. The tension between the two grew so bitter, that they didn't speak unless it was about throwing Mitch out of the house. Hamar was shameless, as she taunted my father with a number of insulting remarks, trying her best to push every one of his buttons. I overheard her discussing Mitch with Shlomo and Samara. Those two even tried convincing my father to dump Mitch for Hamar. She was using any tool at her disposal.

During all that chaos, Mitch and I would sit in his bedroom discussing how his visits were with our mother and grandmother. I was grilling him with all sorts of questions. We sat on his floor while he spoke more than I ever heard him speak since joining this new family. Revealing a rare smile, he confided in me how he had been visiting them for over a year. I could hardly believe he was able to keep a secret that long without getting caught. "How did you get there all those times?"

"It was easy," he told me. "I called Mama Ida Saturday mornings and she would send a cab for me. It was great being there. I could eat whatever I wanted without being screamed at and my stomach never hurt. It was nice and peaceful over there. No screaming or being made to pick rocks out of the ground on my hands and knees."

He looked extremely happy sharing the stories, as if he found utopia being at Mama Ida's home. "How is everyone," I asked.

"Our mother is real bad and she's in a motor scooter now. You know those things you see crippled people in? Mama has a nurse to take care of her. She can't walk so she needs help going to the bathroom and washing up. She's real skinny too. You wouldn't recognize her if you saw her," he added, looking concerned.

Curiously, I asked, "How about Aunt Paula and Uncle Charles? Did you see them? And how about Lisa? Have you seen her too," I persistently asked before letting Mitch answer. I was overwhelmed with excitement to finally hear about my real family.

"Yeah, I see everyone. They all look the same. Aunt Paula stills puts up that great Christmas tree too. Uncle Charles got fat though. He has a big belly now like, ah, Santa Claus."

Staring at him in amazement, I said, "I can't believe you've been doing this for so long. Why didn't you tell me?"

"I didn't want to get in trouble. You might've slipped or something and I didn't want to take a chance. But I'm glad they know now. I just want them to send me back. I hate living here and I hate all the shit they make us do." He smirked, appearing determined to move on with his life. I could tell his plan was to infuriate Hamar enough to get bounced out of this hell hole.

About a week later Mitch's wish came true, with nobody happier than him. Hamar and my father were having one of their big pow-wow's, arguing more intensely than usual because she wanted him gone that night. No questions asked, she wanted him gone. I was upstairs with Mitch that evening when hearing Hamar cursing at my father in three different languages. The argument or should I say, the war was out of control as she was at the very end of her patience.

"I want that shithead son of yours out of my house. I'm sick and tired of telling you this every night. I want him gone tonight. Do you understand me? Tonight! I won't be his fucking maid or yours. I'm not going to clean his shitty stained underwear or cook his fucking food anymore." Hamar's voice stirred the house as her volume elevated from a frightening scream to an all out conniption. I felt nervous for Mitch, praying he wouldn't get another beating like the last one.

My father was muffled at times, but he did his share of screaming as well. "What do you want to do? Send him back to that fucking whore mother of his and that bitch grandmother. Is that what you want?"

Hamar's voice became more deliberate, exclaiming, "Yes! That's what I want. I want him fucking gone. He walks around this house and gives me his fucking side-face. That bastard who I took to all those doctors and to Florida. He should drop dead." Then she screamed at Mitch from the family room. "Do you hear me shithead? I want you gone. Dead. Drop dead. You idiot piece of shit. Go. Go back to your whore mother who doesn't give a shit about you. That bitch who was fucking all those men."

Then she sounded like she was stuck in between hyper-ventilating and crying. "Shel..don, if he's not out by to..night, I'm pack..ing and me and my kids are leav..ing to..night."

Suddenly, I heard Samara from the top of the stairs call down, "Dad! Just get rid of him. He's not worth it. Get rid of him." Mitch and I looked at each snickering.

My father's voice weakened, sounding profoundly defeated. "You know something? Fuck it. He's gone. That's what you want? He's gone. I can't do this shit every night. You know something, I'm not stupid. I can see he doesn't want to be here anymore. I'll drop him off at my mother's tonight and take him to his wonderful new family tomorrow."

That night Mitch was dishonorably discharged from the family. As my father whisked him out into the crisp dark night, he was shunned by everyone except me. I could tell, during this whole charade, that Hamar was upset with me. She acted cold and distant because I was speaking with Mitch throughout her battles with my father. She wanted me to ignore Mitch like the rest of the family, taking her side. That was the unspoken rule in our family and since I was conversing with him, I was the enemy too.

The next morning I joined my father when he drove off to pick up Mitch. My grandma looked very concerned and agitated as we walked into her apartment. She didn't say much more than hello and her demeanor was curiously rigid. I couldn't make out if she was upset that Mitch was leaving because Hamar forced my father or because he was sneaking around and got caught. My grandmother never interfered, but I always wondered what she was thinking at that moment. Her and my dad went to talk quietly in the kitchen while Mitch and I stood around waiting. He was electrified with excitement, talking my ear off about moving out. But when my father returned, he became very reclusive, not speaking another word. Mitch carried an awkward smirk on his face when leaving, looking like he was ready for his destiny as my grandmother gave him a tight squeeze good-bye.

We stopped back home for Mitch to collect whatever he needed, which really wasn't much but a few pairs of Tough Skins and one or two shirts. I distinctly remember him smiling and blissfully humming while gathering his things. It was almost a joke as we looked at each other laughing, since it was so out of character for him to hum or sing. Mitch kept repeating the same little melody, "Dee, dee dee dee, dee, dee dee dee." If my father every saw or heard what was going on, I think there would have been a murder that morning.

The drive in the car was like being in a morgue. It was snuffed out by complete silence, with the only sound being the sizzling tobacco from my father's cigarette when he inhaled. Mitch sat in the backseat of my father's Datsun 310, focusing out the window the entire ride. I was in the passenger seat biting my nails, finding it crazy that all three of us were actually driving to Mama Ida's house. I never fathomed that this day would come. My father seemed like he was waiting on Mitch to apologize or say something, but he did neither. When reaching the house, Mitch simply popped open the back hatch of the car, throwing his little duffle bag over his shoulder. I gave him a hug good-bye as he smiled, but never once did he acknowledge my father. I contemplated walking him up to the door, but I firmly stood my ground. Unlike Mitch, I wasn't ready to end my relationship with my dad quite yet. I realized at that moment, as much as I resented him for leaving us in Hamar's care, I still loved him.

On the ride home, my father furiously vented. "God damn it. I told your mother not to have that bitch over the house. Now look what happened. She bribed him with all kinds of fucking toys and candy. Stupid, stupid guy. He's going to find out what kind of miserable people these are." Then going temporarily insane, he shouted, "I hate that cunt. I'd like to take a fucking knife and cut her from her cunt to her mouth." After the outburst, he lit another cigarette, chain smoking the rest of the ride home.

I looked out the window, laughing to myself after hearing his outrageous remarks. He didn't understand and never would. It wasn't bribery that drove Mitch to Mama Ida's, but love and warmth. Something his children weren't getting and he could never honestly address that issue. He failed to unselfishly look in the mirror, admitting to himself that his own kids were being emotionally and physically mistreated.

CHAPTER 29

Being a late bloomer, I finally had my first girlfriend when I was in the ninth grade. I met her at a celebration party that my best friend Dave took me to, while playing a kissing game. His basketball team had just finished their last game of the season, so the cheerleaders threw them a farewell party. After a few dates, I wanted to double with Dave and his girlfriend, but I was broke since Hamar was taking my entire paychecks. Dave's girlfriend and mine were close friends, so I knew they spoke. He was taking his girl out to a movie or dinner on the weekends, while I was taking mine nowhere. Feeling embarrassed about never taking my girlfriend out, I was determined to join Dave and his girl.

One Friday after cashing in my paycheck, I decided to ask Hamar if I could keep some money this time, knowing very well she had been giving Shlomo money from his pay. It was becoming obvious seeing as he was lining his closet with Polo clothing and going out with his buddies drinking beer every weekend. At that time, I was bringing home around fifty dollars a week, never seeing a single cent. When coming home that day, I rushed upstairs with my pay to Hamar's bedroom. I greeted her while handing over the money and without saying a word, she snatched it from my trembling hand. As she was counting the cash, I felt nervous to ask but pulled myself together, saying, "Hey mom, I was wondering if I could have some money this week?"

She immediately gave me look as if I insulted her. "What for," she asked, glaring in my direction.

Biting my nails, I uneasily answered, "Well, I want to take my girlfriend to a movie or dinner with Dave and his girlfriend."

She pulled out a five dollar bill from the money I gave her, saying, "Here." Then she rolled the rest up jamming it in her drawer.

I was disappointed looking at the five dollar bill in my palm. "This isn't enough," I said, feeling a frown appearing on my face.

"What do you mean that's not enough? What, I should give you more," Hamar shouted, getting defensive.

Standing my ground, I couldn't believe she thought five bucks would be enough for dinner or a movie. "Well, I can't do anything with five dollars. That's not even enough for a movie and popcorn," I firmly said. I was feeling slighted, knowing how Shlomo was getting money for months and there was no way it was only five dollars.

Hamar erupted in a raging fit, reaching in her nightstand, then furiously throwing the money in my face. "Here. Here you piece of shit. Take it all. You disgusting pig. Cheap. That's what you are, cheap. Take it and get the fuck out of here. Stupid idiot. I'm tired of you already. Money for a girlfriend, like you're a big shot already with a girlfriend. Get out!"

I tried explaining that I didn't want the whole thing, but she wouldn't listen. So I left the money on the floor, nervously trotting out of the room holding the five dollar bill in my fist. Then she chased after me, yelling, "Here! Take it. You bastard. Shithead." She was screeching like a crazed maniac, throwing the money in my face again. "Drop dead," she added, clumping back to her bedroom.

After scooping up the money, I sadly sauntered back to my bedroom. I was on the verge of seriously running away. It burned me that I simply asked for a few bucks and Hamar turns into an all out war. There was no doubt in my mind that when my father came home, she was going to blow the whole story out of proportion, with me paying dearly. Not too long after my confrontation with Hamar, the front door opened. I heard my father's powerful footsteps in the foyer while nervously awaiting another blowout. Profusely sweating, I was imagining what my fate was going to be for this infraction. I could hear Hamar shouting from her bedroom but couldn't clearly understand what she was saying. Whatever it was, I most definitely knew it pertained to me.

I was slumped over sitting on my bed, when my father reached my room looking overly tired, which I thought could work in my favor. "What the hell went on," he bellowed, slamming his clenched fist onto my desk. "I can't take this shit as soon as I walk in the door. What the hell is going on," he demanded again.

"All I did was ask for some money to take out my girlfriend and she started throwing money at my face and telling me to drop dead. She only gave me five dollars and you know I can't do anything with five bucks." I was careful as I spoke, not to provoke him.

"She said she gave you five dollars and that wasn't good enough for you. You know the problems I'm having. You're a real piece of shit. Where's the money," he asked, searching around my room.

I pointed to my dresser, feeling defeated. "Over there."

He grabbed the cash, tightly squeezing it in his fist. "Take this fucking money and give it back to your mother and then apologize. I mean now. You're a real piece of shit to make your mother beg you for money," he screamed, making sure it was loud enough for his wife to hear. "Now take this God damn money and get out of my sight."

Shoving the cash at me, he glared with a look of disgust. I grudgingly took the crumpled money, wallowing down to the kitchen to find Hamar. She was at the sink when I found her, wearing a look which resembled a spoiled brat who didn't get their way. Unwillingly, I held out the money and with the most sincere voice I could contrive, said, "Sorry about our argument, please take the money."

She continued playing in the sink, refusing to acknowledge me. Then my father interjected, "Hamar, he said he's sorry. Take the money," he gently said.

"Fuck him. I don't want it." Then looking at me with hatred, she shouted, "Go. Go take out your girlfriend, you cheap piece of shit. Idiot."

I glanced over at my father feeling perplexed, but he seemed to be out of ideas too, motioning for me to leave the money on the counter. Neither of them spoke, as I placed the money down while the tension felt overwhelming. Shoving my hands in my Tough Skin pockets, I walked back up to my bedroom as my father scampered to get a glass of ice.

My brain was rattling from all the turmoil and I was disappointed that my father failed to come to my aid once again. It was constantly disappointing how he never monitored a level playing field between his kids and hers. I knew he realized Shlomo was getting money from Hamar, but chose to be blind, so for years to come that was his defense. After that night, my regular stipend from Hamar was five dollars per pay.

A few weeks after Mitch moved in with Mama Ida, my father received a telephone call. My grandmother had the same discussion with him, explaining how she thought it was in Mitch's best interest to grow up with his father. She felt too old to raise him, our half-brother and my mother who was slowly dying. My father got smart with her, blurting out, "Well, you should have thought of that before you bribed him with toys and all that other shit to get 'em to come over."

Overlooking his comment, Mama Ida also explained how Mitch was playing jokes on her and she was too old for things like that. Apparently, she thought he was putting little pebbles of poop all around the house as a gag to scare her. But instead, discovered a chipmunk had found its way into the house and was trapped inside. At the end of the conversation, my father informed her that he would check with his wife and let her know.

Hamar and my dad were struggling terribly, desperately needing money for their lavish lifestyle. My father went as far as attempting to collect money from Hamar's sister's husband. I remember him calling Yuli from the family room one night, asking for the thirteen or fifteen thousand dollars back, which he lent him for the purchase of his home. Yuli refused to give it back to him, saying how he was stuck in Delaware with no job thanks to my father. Losing his mind in anger, my father hollered, "You fucking kike. I'm coming over right now to collect my fucking money." Instantly slamming down the phone, he rushed to get to his car, but Hamar wouldn't allow it. She convinced him to let it be since it was her sister's husband. My father almost killed him another time when Yuli had taken home an expensive crystal chandelier and a few mirrors from his lighting store without paying. Needless to say, Hamar saved Yuli once again from my father's fury.

Around that time, my father had been seriously considering opening a cab company, explaining to Hamar that if he had $250,000 he could swing it. The idea presented itself after he met up with a friend of Uncle Douglass', who owned one and was a multi-millionaire from the business. After hanging up with Mama Ida, a light bulb went off in his head, which precipitated a big discussion with Hamar about the Mitch acquisition.

My father called back Mama Ida, offering to take Mitch off her hands if she gave him $250,000 to open a cab company. Being so repulsed by his vulgar suggestion, she slammed the phone down on him. Mama told the story to Mitch, apologizing for almost sending him back to such an appalling so-called father. That was the last time the subject ever came up, officially taking Mitch off the market.

Shortly after that, I started getting in touch with Mitch to find out how he was doing. During our conversations, he would hand the phone over to Mama Ida and my mother to talk. It was amazing to hear all their voices again, bringing back so many incredible memories. I especially was overcome with joy to hear my mother's voice. It had been six or seven years since the last time we had spoken. Her voice sounded very different though. It wasn't that once strong deliberate tone I remembered, but weak, shaky and frail now. After speaking with Mama Ida a few times, she offered to send a cab for me, which I instantly accepted. I understood the consequences, but missing them so much gave me the strength to take the chance. In my mind, I determined that a malicious beating was worth seeing my family again. At the very worst, I would be banished back to Mama Ida's house, which wouldn't have been such a bad thing.

While waiting for the cab on that Saturday morning, I couldn't stop shaking and biting my nails from all the excitement. I was so overjoyed to finally reunite with my family again. The feeling was so immense that it didn't even cross my mind to be caught. I stood down at the end of the street, preparing myself to wave as the cab drove up. When the cabby finally arrived, reality blew me over with the feeling that it was really going to happen. After all these years, I was going to break protocol and see my family again. During the drive to Mama Ida's, I tried imagining how everyone was going to look, hoping my mother would recognize me after all this time. I threw away all the bad things that I had been brainwashed with and smiled, waiting to see their faces again.

Mitch and my half-brother opened the door when I arrived. We were elated to see each other again, cackling because we knew it was a criminal offense for me to show up for a visit. Hamar and our father would have had a fit, if they had an inkling I was there visiting. Mama Ida was standing in the kitchen smiling when I came walking in, with a million memories going through my mind. As we embraced, I could feel the sincerity in her hug, an experience I had not felt in years. She still looked great despite her age. Her hair was a nice golden tint of blond and she was wearing a wonderfully put together attire. My mother was sadly the complete opposite of a vision, being utterly demoralized when seeing her. She was sitting in her yellow motor scooter, with her arms agape, waiting for a hug from me and was hardly recognizable. The MS had eroded my mother so dreadfully that she was just loose skin and bones. Her face was horribly gaunt and protruding outwards taking on a skeletal appearance. Apprehensively I staggered over, trying my best not to look shocked. She appeared so frail that I was concerned of hurting her with a tight hug. But we exchanged loving hugs and kisses, as it felt great to be in her arms again.

My mother was all smiles when we broke from our embrace, extending me an endearing stare. I was feeling awfully teary inside, finding it difficult to believe she was the same woman who gave birth to me. Empathy was bursting from my bodily seams, seeing how withered away she was from the disease. Her hair looked to be the strongest and healthiest attribute about her, as it was pure white and managed in a big healthy bouffant. She resembled a drawing that a child would have created, with unusually large characteristics, greatly out of proportion. Her hands and feet didn't seem to belong to her, looking oversized for her body since they were the only two features not plagued by the MS. My eyes could barely meet hers as I asked, "How are you feeling, mom?"

Trembling terribly, she comically slurred, "Well, what do you think? I can't walk or go to the bathroom myself. I piss my pants plenty though," she jokingly said, with faint laughter. "I'm sorry you have to see me this way, Jim, but I'd rather see you this way than not see you at all." She was still smiling ear to ear and I literally mean, it was ear to ear. Then examining me up and down, she shouted, "Boy! You're looking handsome. Isn't he, mother?"

Grinning proudly, mama remarked, "Yes, I think Jim looks a lot like you and Mitch looks just like his father. Sometimes I have to tell Mitch to turn his head because at times he looks just like Sheldon. Right Mitch?" He just laughed at her.

My mother pulled out a long girly cigarette from a leather pouch and while shaking, lit it. She was barely able to put the butt in between her lips, as the smoke even appeared to quiver as she exhaled. "So Jim, the girls must be chasing you around, huh?"

Nervously giggling, I answered back, "No. But I had a girlfriend for a little while, but that was it." I was still finding it difficult to make eye contact with her.

"What do you think of your new brother," my mother asked, peering at Albert.

"He's cute," I said. "He looks a lot like Julie with that blond hair."

"You should have seen him last week," she chuckled. "He ate a jar of cherries and then drank all the juice. After a few minutes his lips blew up like these big mamma jamma lips and every time he talked his lips smacked together. He was a real sight to see. Right mother?"

She began laughing uncontrollably with everyone joining in. Albert didn't find it as funny, screaming, "Shut up!" And then he stomped away.

"So, Mitch tells us you work at the five and dime store now, Jim," Mama said, nervously twitching her nose from side to side. "Do you like working there?"

Before I could answer, my mother sarcastically asked, "Why

does Sheldon, Feldon, Weldon have to make you work and take your money? Can't he find a job that pays or is he still lazy?"

I was beginning to get accustom to my mother's appearance, somehow overlooking her boney façade and recognizing the mother I once knew. Her familiarity returned through her eyes and sense of humor. Then returning to reality, I said, "I'm not crazy about working there, but I don't have a choice. My dad and his wife say they need the money."

With a concerned expression, my mother firmly slurred, "Mitch and mama tell me they live in that big house and drive Cadillac's. They don't need your money. I'm sick over them taking your paychecks and so is mama." I quickly took a peek at mama, noticing she was nodding her head in agreement while twitching her nose.

"I heard that stepmother of yours is a real treat. Mitch and mama tell me how you guys can't eat anything over there. What the hell is that? I never heard of keeping food away from children." Mitch had a hand over his mouth as he snickered.

"I know. I think it's crazy too, but my dad doesn't do anything about it. God forbid you open something that was never opened before, you'd get killed for it."

Mama jumped in, critically shouting, "Mitch told me how she pulled out his hair. He said she yanked gobs of it out and threw it at him. I also heard how she beat and pulled out your father's hair too. Let me know the next time she pulls out his because I want to see it. He deserves it after all the bad things he's done to you kids. That man disgusts me and they both make my stomach sick. How can they be such showoffs and then can't afford to feed their children? My God, it makes me sick. Thank goodness papa isn't alive to hear this."

My mother, looking distressed, slyly remarked, "The Pop Tart story is ridiculous. Mitch tells me how that wild Arab gives her kids the Pop Tarts and Julie eats the crust like a dog. What's wrong with your father? He doesn't say anything? Mitch eats anything he wants here. Even Pop Tarts." Her face jetted out at me as she spoke and her obvious disbelief confirmed my own feelings over the years. At home, everyone automatically backed Hamar's decisions, making me second guess my sanity.

"Yeah Jim, I can eat anything I want," Mitch chimed in while laughing. "Are you hungry because mama has all the stuff you like? She even has those pickled watermelon rinds you love." Getting up from his chair, Mitch hastened towards the kitchen.

"Jim, go get something to eat. You look like skin and bones," mama commented, looking upset over the contents of our conversation.

After Mitch and I feasted on a variety of foods and goodies, mama, Mitch and me strolled around the house reminiscing. Mama pointed out all the pictures she had of us, complaining how much she missed seeing me. Everything still looked the same as it did when I last saw it. I felt at home again as we walked around the house, but saddened that I wasn't able to grow up knowing them. Mitch was right about the house being peaceful. I felt it too, noticing how my nail biting and aggravated stomach pains were absent. There was no yelling or screaming and I wasn't looking over my shoulder, concerned I did something wrong. The one big difference I felt was the warmth, there was actual heat blowing in the house. Hamar kept our thermostat around sixty degrees in the wintertime, freezing my ass off night and day. She did buy everyone these cheap heating blankets which were supposed to solve the heating problem. Unfortunately, my blanket never worked, so I spent my nights rolling around trying to stay warm. When finally falling asleep, that was about the same time I needed to get up to prepare for school. It took a couple hours to fully awake each morning, since I was suffering from sleep deprivation.

Eventually, the time came for me to leave, kissing and hugging everyone goodbye when the cab pulled up to the house. Mama walked me to the door, along with Mitch, saying, "I don't like the way they're dressing you and that coat you're wearing is not warm enough. The next time you come over I'll buy you a new winter jacket and some decent clothes. It'll be around your birthday, so that'll be your birthday present. Ok?" She nervously twitched her nose from side to side smiling, then gave me hug.

The consequences of being caught managed to start tearing at my stomach walls. I sat in the cab, slouched over so no one would see me in the backseat. When the cabby was close enough to my house, I asked him to go a little further away, so not to take any chances of being spotted. Once paying the fare, I crept home finding everything just as usual. My blood pressure dropped back to a normal rate and no one was the wiser.

The house felt especially cold when I returned that day, with the stress and bitter chill grabbing ahold of me. It invoked a sense of bleak existence, erasing the warm glow I had at Mama Ida's house. Already having an emotional attachment to my real family, I couldn't wait to see them again. It was gratifying to feel loved and important to somebody, which sounds peculiar but when you live without it for so long, you forget how it feels. I conditioned myself to be strong, emotionally blocking out the urge for love and warmth at a young age. The mindset made it easier to deal with the coldness that hovered over Hamar's house.

The next morning I heard Hamar banging around in Mitch's bedroom. Her gold bracelets clinking were what really woke me, in addition to rolling around all night trying to produce adequate body heat. I jumped out of bed, finding Hamar moving around furniture as Julie was ripping down Mitch's posters. "What are you doing," I asked, shivering in the hallway.

Julie stopped what she was doing for a moment and turned around smiling. "Mom is making Mitch's old room into a guestroom. It's going to look great when we're done, right Mom?"

Looking as miserable as usual Hamar ignored Julie's question, trying to push Mitch's desk away from the wall. Hamar wasn't even dressed yet, still wearing her nightgown with her face and hair looking like they suffered from a bad case of bed markings. Then peering at me while struggling with the desk, she shouted with a nasty tone, "Are you going to just stand there or are you going to help? Stupid, just standing there looking at me like I'm the maid. Yala, come on already."

"Ok, all you had to do was ask," I grumbled, feeling attacked.

"Stupid, like I have to ask him. You see me trying to move the desk, don't you? All I have to do is ask," she said, mocking me. "Just get over here and help."

I stomped in feeling like I was able to pick the whole damn thing up myself, boiling from her offensive attitude. "Alright, look out," I said to her, sounding irritated. Bending down on all fours, I shoved the desk as hard as humanly possible. It wasn't as heavy as Hamar made it appear, so it easily slid away from the wall with one good shove. When the desk was moved out, all of our eyes were feasting on what Mitch had been hiding behind it for years. There was a plethora of various candy wrappers, peach pits, plum pits and several other discarded remnants, which Mitch disposed of behind his desk. It struck us like an epiphany. The expression on Hamar's face was like the look on the warden's face from the movie *"Shawshank Redemption"*, when he realized how the prisoner, Andy, escaped from his prison cell.

Julie was the first to speak, victoriously shouting, "Look mom! See, I told you I wasn't stealing the candy. You didn't believe me. See, I told you." Julie was so wound up with happiness that she was actually jumping in place.

"Oh my God, that fucking liar. Piece of shit," Hamar said slowly over her lips. "All this time that shithead side-face let Julie get all those beatings for him stealing the candy." Then she eagerly hollered to my father. "Sheldon. Sheldon, you have to see this."

I heard my dad's rushing footsteps, as he popped in with his cup of coffee and cigarette to see what was happening. "What? What's all the screaming about?"

Hamar forcefully grabbed my father's arm, dragging him over to the pile of evidence. "Look at this shit. Look what your shithead son has been doing since we lived here," Hamar loudly squawked, while pointing at the evidence.

My father smirked, shaking his head in disappointment. "Oh my God, he was the one eating all that shit and blaming it on Julie. That's terrible. Letting Julie get hit and he was the one stealing the candy." Then my father shot Julie an apologetic look through his red eyes. "Sorry kid. We didn't know he was the one stealing the candy. We thought you were lying."

Julie grinned and still looking energized shouted, "See, I told you I was telling the truth. Do you remember in the apartment when I had to admit stealing candy and Shlomo made me lie and admit that

I did? Mom beat me up and I still told you I didn't steal the candy. See, he was the one the whole time. I'm not a liar."

"Do you believe this piece of shit son of yours, Sheldon? Acting like he's this sick kid who can't eat anything and then letting his sister get beaten up for him being a stealer. Disgusting. He's disgusting. Piece of shit. I'm glad he's gone. That fucking stealer. He should drop dead."

Hamar used this episode to justify ostracizing Mitch from our home. She knew Julie had a very special place in my father's heart, almost divorcing him a number of times over it. She manipulated the situation by pinning Mitch to be the culprit for getting Julie in trouble for years. My father bought into it, which I think justified in his mind that he made the correct decision by letting Mitch leave.

Julie was in the limelight that entire Sunday, as she and Hamar were buddies for a day. Julie strutted around the house like a hero, acting the proudest I had ever seen her. Hamar explained the Mitch story in great detail to everyone, ending it each time by saying, "Can you believe this shit. This whole time that piece of shit was letting Julie get the beating for him stealing."

Julie's hour of heroism didn't last long though. Days later she came home past her curfew, throwing Hamar into a violent frenzy. Julie was attending another elementary school for her learning disability, but still had a close friend in the neighborhood. That day she was over her friend's house playing when she lost track of the time. Hamar was merciless towards Julie, beating the crap out of her for being late. As she was finishing administering the punishment, my father happened to arrive home catching Hamar in action. She had Julie in the family room, pounding her excessively with brutal force.

Looking surprised, my father rigidly yelled, "Hey, hey. What the hell is going on?"

He surprised the hell out of Hamar, who was sitting on Julie's back. She quickly turned in his direction, irritably screeching, "What's going on? You want to know what's going on?" She was huffing and puffing miserably, gasping for air as she shouted. "Your pig fucking daughter here, came home late again. I….warned her. I warned her before, not to be late." She still had a handful of Julie's hair in her shaky grips, shrieking, "Right pig? Didn't I warn *you*?"

Julie was yelping in pain when my father sternly shouted, "Ok, Hamar, I think she's had enough."

"You just shut your mouth. You should be screaming at this piece of shit. Don't tell me what's enough, you potato. Stupid idiot."

Insulted by the potato remark, my father shouted, "I told you, I don't like you using that word *pig* in this house anymore."

Hamar stomped off of Julie, giving her one last hit as she stood up perspiring. "You're going to come home and tell me what to do. You take care of it then. You stay home with this whore pig. She's just like your ex-wife. I'm sick and tired of you sticking up for your second wife."

"Who's sticking up? You punished her and that's that. I told you that I don't like you calling her pig," my father answered, sounding less rigid.

Julie was leaning against the couch quivering as they quarreled. Her bottom lip drooped so low that it almost looked as if it touched the carpet, with saliva cascaded from her mouth. Hamar was panting and snarled, "I told you once before. If you take that pig's side, I was leaving you. Now I'm leaving. I've had enough of your shit and being your kids fucking maid. You can go to hell. You piece of shit. Do you hear me? Go to hell!"

Then my father pleaded, "What are you talking about? Please, stop talking stupid, ok?"

He struck a nerve with that comment, instigating Hamar's fury. "Stupid. Who are you calling stupid? You're the stupid one. Shmuck, calling me stupid. You are the stupid one. Bastard. Asshole. I'm leaving, that's it. You should go to hell. Drop dead."

By this time, Shlomo found his way to the family along with the rest of us. "Yeah dad, why are you sticking up for Julie? You're not here to see what goes on," Shlomo said, challenging my father while standing next to his mother.

"Do you believe this, idiot? He's sticking up for his second wife like always. I'm sick of this. I'm leaving. I can't take this idiot anymore," she angrily blurted, addressing Shlomo.

As Hamar quickly marched out of the family room, Shlomo stammered, "She's leaving dad. You better stop her."

"Shlomo, just shut up. Ok," my father scowled, reaching out for Hamar's arm.

"He should shut up? You shut up. Why don't you say for your second pig wife to shut up? Schmuck, telling Shlomo to shut up. You shut up. You fool asshole."

"Come on, don't be silly," my father called out, chasing her down the hallway.

"You'll see silly," Hamar retorted, as she grabbed her car keys slamming the front door behind her.

After Hamar left, my father sent everyone upstairs and within an hour she returned as usual. I heard the front door open, but there wasn't any speaking or yelling that I could hear. Then she immediately shot up to her bedroom. My father was punished by having to endure a few days of the silent treatment, which I considered a gift. No screaming was a faint commodity that wasn't regularly offered in our house.

My father finally caught me after a few visits with my mom and Mama Ida. Around the time of my sixteenth birthday, my grandmother had a cab pick me up and bring me to Montgomery Mall. When meeting up with everyone, I was a little nervous to be out in public. The mall was a popular social venue, making it almost inevitable that I was going to run into somebody I knew. We must have been spectacles, with my mother motoring around in her yellow scooter. Those scooters were not prevalent at the time, compelling a majority of the people walking by to stare at us. I did my best to keep somewhat out of her range, having a strange notion that someone was going to see me that day. We looked too conspicuous for it not to happen, but I still took my chances.

Mama kept her promise as she dragged me through her favorite department store, searching for my birthday gifts. I forgot what it was like to shop for clothes since the last time I did was with her. She had me trying on all sorts of things and it was nice to have someone concerned about the way I looked for a change. After a while of trying on an assortment of clothing, mama purchased a new winter jacket and a few other things for me. I felt like a new man when shedding off my old attire and couldn't thank her enough for all the gifts. My only concern was how to get everything home without Hamar and my father getting suspicious. It troubled me throughout the afternoon, as the anxiety circled around in my mind.

When we were done shopping, mama treated us to lunch at her favorite restaurant in the mall, Three Kings. It was owned by two very nice Greek gentlemen, who served the best food. I was especially fond of their burgers and steak fries. At that time, they were the only restaurant which had seating out in the mall, adding to my jitters from anxiety. I spent more time people-watching than eating my meal or concentrating on the conversations transpiring at the table. We knew the owners for years given as mama had been bringing Mitch and me there as far back as when we were infants.

After lunch, we all went back to mama's house where they had gifts and a birthday cake for me. Aunt Paula showed up too, which was nice considering I hadn't seen her in a long while. Mitch and I were at her house once, which was an unique log cabin converted into a single home. When all the fun stuff was over, I wanted to get back home. I was nervous of being caught like Mitch, in addition to having to sneak all the new clothing in as well.

Gnawing my nails and cuticles on the taxi ride home, I was anticipating the worst. My stomach was grumbling from being anxious as I prayed, hoping no one would be home. Luckily for me, the house was a ghost town when arriving, making it easy to smuggle up my birthday gifts. Soon after strategically hiding my things, the front door opened as I instantly recognized my father's heavy footsteps. With my heart racing abnormally, I quickly finished squirreling my presents away and stammered down the stairs to say hello.

When entering the kitchen, I found my father hastily chomping on roasted peanuts from the jar. Hamar didn't permit him to eat peanuts but once a day, which was only when he was having a vodka on the rocks. He always took advantage of jumping on the opportunity to sneak snacks when she wasn't around. He looked

edgy while approaching him to say hello. "Hey dad, how's it going," I cheerfully said.

"Let me ask you a question," he said, trying to swallow a mouthful of peanuts. "Where were you today?" His tone was gradually changing.

When he prefaced a question that way, I knew he was on to something. Feeling warm blood slowly blanketing my face, I began blushing. "I was at the mall with my friend, Dave," I managed to force out, without hesitation.

"Really? What if I tell you that I saw you with that white haired piece of shit whore mother," he shouted, loudly slamming his fist on the kitchen counter. The volume of his voice increased with each colorful adjective he added about my mother.

I started biting my nails while shaking. "I don't know," was all I could drum-up.

"Did you like walking around the mall with her and that white hair?" He paused for a moment, waiting on a response from me. "Well, did you," he bellowed as I jumped back.

"No. I don't know," I stuttered, waiting to get my ass kicked.

"You fucking disgust me. You're an ungrateful piece of shit, just like Mitch. I don't know how you met up with them, but I better not see that shit again. Do you understand?"

Trembling, I waited on him to throw a blow, but he was still screaming. I nodded my head while agreeing with him, hoping he was letting me off with a verbal warning.

His eyes and lids were a deep shade of red as he gave me a loathing stare. "I don't believe you, Jim. Mitch, I can see, but you. Do me a favor. Don't come to me for anything anymore. I don't want anything to do with you. This was the worst possible thing you could've done to me. I'm not even going to tell your mother about it. She'd have a heart attack if she knew. You're just lucky she didn't see you."

"She would have sent my ass packing to mama's house, like Mitch, if she knew," I thought to myself. "And you would've probably lost the rest of your hair from her pulling it out."

"I'm not going to say a thing to your mother about this shit. But I'm telling you, Jim, I hear about you seeing those fucking people again, no one's going to hold me back. You got me," he threatened, throwing a handful of peanuts in his mouth.

I nodded my head, saying, "Yes. I understand."

"Good, now get the fuck out of my sight. You disgust me," he said with a nasty expression on his face.

Quickly, I shuffled out with my head still attached, which was good enough for me. I felt fortunate, in comparison to Mitch, to get out without absorbing the same brutal punishment. After that afternoon, I stopped seeing mama, my mom, Mitch and everyone else for a while. I decided to cut it off since I didn't want any more trouble.

CHAPTER 30

Time had gone by, with all the excitement over Mitch coming to an end. It was like he never lived with us, as his name was rarely mentioned in any conversation. That was until my father received a phone call approximately five months later, informing him that Mitch was going to need an operation. Mama Ida had been taking Mitch to see the same doctor our mother was seeing for her MS. After a number of visits, the doctor determined that Mitch needed part of his intestines removed, in order to put the disease in remission. My father was called in because the doctor needed him to sign-off on the operation. He still had custody of Mitch, so nothing could be done without his approval. Apparently, when meeting with the doctor, a big argument erupted concerning the operation. The doctor threatened to take my father to court if he didn't sign-off on the papers, giving him permission to operate on Mitch.

The doctor was appalled by how malnourished Mitch was from the crazy diet the specialist from Florida put him on. He argued that if Mitch continued with this diet, he would surely die from malnutrition. Mitch had not yet hit his growth spurt and most of his days were spent in the bathroom. The doctor was confident by performing the operation, Mitch would grow to his normal potential height, with his symptoms greatly diminishing. After everyone had their say, my father signed-off and Mitch went through with his operation.

A few weeks later, the bills started flying in and Mama Ida paid for the operation by putting Mitch on her health insurance plan.

Mitch wasn't sure how he got on to her policy, but remembers going to court so she could obtain custody of him. But like all insurance companies, there was a deductible to be dealt with and mama was convinced that Mitch's father should assume that responsibility. She called my father, asking him to pay for the deductible, but he kept putting her off. One day, she caught him while Hamar was around and when hanging up the phone, she asked, "Sheldon, who was that?"

He looked perplexed, as if he didn't know how to answer the question. "It was God damn Ida again. She's looking for money for Mitch's operation."

"Sheldon, I'm going to tell you right now. I'm not paying for that shithead's operation," she squawked, putting her foot down. "I told you this before, so don't you come asking me to pay for this shit. She wanted him, now she has the shit," Hamar declared, while raising her voice.

"I already told her, we weren't paying for it," my father stammered, not looking very convincing.

"Why is she still calling if you told her that? I'm telling you, Sheldon, you pay for that shithead's operation and I'm leaving you. I am not paying. That's it. The both of them can go to hell before I pay for that shithead's bill. Let her break her head over the bill."

"Do me a favor, ok? Don't start fucking threatening me. I'm not in the mood right now." A rage was building up in my father, becoming very apparent in his voice. It sounded like frustration from being coerced into doing the wrong thing, instead of paying my grandmother for the deductible.

Hamar wasn't intimidated by his anger and retaliated. "Do you a favor? Do me a favor, stupid. Like I'm in the mood. I can see you're thinking about paying that bitch for your shithead son's operation and I'm telling you. I am not paying. Stupid shmuck, telling me you're not in the mood. Fuck your mood. I'm not in the mood. Big shot. All I have is problems ever since I met you and your kids."

Then Hamar began mimicking him with a nasty tone. "I'm not in the mood. He says. Big shot's not in the mood. Don't you think about paying her. That's all I can say, potato."

My father's face had an expression as though he was holding his breath, trying to time how long he could hold it without breathing. I thought he was going to explode, until he reached for a cigarette and lit it. After one long puff, he filled a glass with ice tramping angrily to the family room, while Hamar was left in the kitchen, still talking to herself. Mama Ida never did get paid since they ignored her phone calls. Hamar and my father justified stiffing her with the deductible, by saying she was rich enough to pay for it herself. They manipulated the story, referring to her as cheap for even asking for the money in the first place.

That same summer, Hamar and my father came home all excited, proceeding to elaborate how they found a new career move for me. While purchasing shoes for Hamar, they met the manager of the store who was looking for a new salesman. I wasn't as enthusiastic since I was working in the music section for Woolworth's and was very comfortable there. "I don't know," I said, feeling intimidated to move to another job.

Surprised by my answer, my father said, "I thought you would be excited. You can make great money selling women's shoes. They pay commission and spiffs on shoes and purses. Don't you want to make more money?"

"Yeah," I thought. "For who? You?"

Hamar jumped in, attempting to sell me on the idea. "At my work the guys make like $50 or $60,000 a year. Your cousin Jeff is begging me to get him a job where I work."

Hamar was hired by an expensive department store, selling women's dresses. The store was located in another mall in Red Hill, which was considerably newer than Montgomery Mall. It was considered nicer and a step up because they had several chic little specialty shops.

I thought a moment about the change, asking, "Well, how much do they pay?"

"You have to meet the guy, Jim. I told him you'll call to make an appointment for an interview," my dad said, grinning as if he gave me the key to a bank safe.

I didn't have any suits or slacks to work at a place like that, so

Hamar grabbed a few suits from Uncle Douglass. They were more intent on me getting the job than I was. When trying on the suits, I looked absolutely absurd. I was sixteen at the time and wasn't finished growing, so the two suits literally looked like they belonged to my uncle. The jackets were too long as my fingers barely peeked out of the sleeves. The slacks were so large that my belt needed to be pulled extra tight just to keep them from falling to the floor. Hamar and my father suggested I keep the jacket on, so no one would notice the extra material bunched under the belt. The finishing touch was definitely my father's 1970's wide clown ties. He didn't want to part with his new thin ones, sticking me with his old, bold colored and offensive ties, which made me look like a fool when peeking in the mirror. I was appalled strolling in public looking the way I did, but of course, they tried convincing me how great I looked, with me knowing better.

On the way to the interview I was preoccupied, thinking how I would never get the opportunity to play high school football. It burned me inside, with a sense of my childhood being ripped away from me. Playing football was all that mattered to me while growing up, being the one thing that instilled a sense of worth. I felt like I belonged somewhere when playing the game I loved most and doing something with kids my own age. When the tenth grade began, the JV football coach grabbed me in the hallway, asking, "Where were you for football tryouts? Everyone's telling me you're the quarterback and you never showed up. You better be there today after school if you want to play this year."

Excitement was gushing through my veins, when hearing the opportunity of my dream position waiting for me. But sadly, I knew what my answer had to be. "Sorry coach, but my parents need me to work."

"Work," he shouted. "Why are you working? You should be playing football. Your parents really need you to work," he said sarcastically. "I don't get it. Well, if you change your mind, let me know because we could use you on the field."

He strutted away shaking his head, as I felt tormented knowing I could walk on the field assuming the starting quarterback position.

Frustrated, I decided on confronting my father when he came home, hoping to appeal to his masculine side, but unfortunately it didn't work out that way. He was agitated that I even asked, telling me how they couldn't manage without my paycheck. The only suggestion he had was for me to wait and maybe things would be better the following year. Well, next year came around and the year after that and I never played.

When I arrived at the interview, the first thing grabbing my attention was that it was an all women's shoe store. My initial thought was I would feel a little uncomfortable working there if hired. I didn't know anything about women's shoes nor did I have any experience wearing them. During my interview, I was surprised the manager was a man since I figured a woman would be more fitting for the position. But he was extremely enthusiastic about his work and I liked him from the get-go. Mel was definitely straight when we spoke, with a very deliberate baritone voice. I didn't know if it was his real voice or if he was just acting for the interview to sound important. Mel was in his mid-twenties, sporting a dark heavy beard and what I remember most about him was his accent. Since relocating to Delaware from Boston, he picked up this strange accent sounding like a Bostonian Elmer Fudd. I loved it but had to pinch myself not laugh out loud.

I was never in a sales position before, but Mel made it fun and challenging at the same time. He suggested I could make great money by knowing how to sell, which he offered to teach me if I wanted the job. Stunned by the offer, I almost fell off my chair seeing how I was dressed like a rag doll and my only work experience was at Woolworth's. I jumped at the opportunity, accepting the position to work with him, which seemed like a step up since the money would be better.

On my first day, Mel and another salesman named, Bart, decided to have some fun at my expense. Mel asked if I could go ask another shoe store, if we could borrow their wall stretcher. Quickly, I marched around the mall going from one shoe store to the next asking to borrower a wall stretcher. Each time I asked, I received the strangest stares from the salespeople I approached. After four or five places, a sales guy pulled me aside explaining how my manager was pulling a fast one on me. He told me to think about what I was looking for, so I repeated it to myself a couple of times. After doing that for a few seconds, it finally came to me. Then I explained to the man that I thought I was looking for a shoe stretcher and we both laughed.

When I returned, Mel and Bart hysterically laughed while pointing at me. Mel shouted from the back of the counter, "Well, did you find the wall stretcher, Jim?" Then he slapped Bart on the back, who was in hysterics. I knew from that moment this was a great place to work, feeling like I definitely fit in. After a few months, Mel had taught me so well that I was his top salesperson. I was making anywhere from $150 to $200 a week selling shoes and totally enjoying my job. He had me working every Saturday and Sunday plus two weekdays so I could make great commission. Hamar gradually became a bit more generous, allowing me to keep $20 of my pay each week.

My whole life started revolving around the shoe store, with my closest friends becoming my co-workers. High school wasn't going as well as I thought it would. All my friends were playing sports as their closest buddies became their teammates, but unfortunately, I didn't fit in those circles. If there was a football or basketball party, I wasn't invited, which made sense considering I wasn't participating. My best friend Dave and I had a falling-out over a girl and simply stopped speaking to one another. Stanley became like the rest of my friends, tagging along with his sports buddies. The one friend I still had left was Jed, but he fell into the same category as everyone else when it came to the weekends.

By the time I entered the eleventh grade, my only buddies were from work and the people I knew from around the mall. I was a ghost at high school thereafter, which poisoned my grades as they suffered terribly. My grade point average went from practically a 4.0, down to a 2.7 by the time I graduated. I wasn't involved with the proper crowd for my age, paling around with people who were much older than me. Most of them were three to ten years older and since football was out of the question, I started picking up bad habits. Smoking cigarettes was the biggest sin, something I promised myself I would never do, but everyone I socialized with smoked. My weekends didn't involve high school parties like a normal high school kid, but instead I was spending my free time bar hopping with work buddies and getting loaded on cocktails and beers. It was exciting and couldn't be compared to going to high school parties, watching kids getting drunk and falling down stairs. I was out dancing and meeting girls from all over the area. I found a whole new world out there, never feeling the urge to attend another high school function again.

Mama Ida and Aunt Paula occasionally dropped by the shoe store to visit. My mother was so bad off she didn't even leave the house anymore. I stopped by mama's house a few times to visit her, but it was pure torture to see the suffering. The MS had eaten her up so rapidly, that she couldn't have weighed more than seventy pounds and her uncontrollable muscle spasms were heart-wrenching to watch. I remember being there once, as my mom's left eye involuntarily twitched for what seemed like thirty minutes. She somehow kept a good sense of humor about it, half joking slurring to my grandmother, "Look mother, my eye." She stuck out her skeletal neck like a crane to give mama a closer look. "It won't stop blinking," she said while laughing. Almost like she had given up on life, accepting her dreadful fate. Then she started winking the right eye as a joke, slurring, "Now they match."

Mitch never dropped by my work like the others and I lost touch with him for a couple of years. Mama Ida told me he dropped out of high school to work at a hardware store full-time. She explained how she was against it, but he insisted that he hated school. Eventually Mitch made a surprise visit, dropping by our house a few years later. He parked down at the end of the driveway in his 1970's Charger, waiting for us to come out. I was lying at the pool when he showed up, shocked he had the moxie to face everyone after leaving on such bad terms.

It was a Saturday when he came by and I practically didn't recognize him. He shot up like a weed, standing taller than me with a thin built. It was like a miracle how much he grew. When I last spent time with Mitch, he couldn't have been more than five feet tall. We smiled when seeing each other, exchanging kisses on the cheek.

"I can't believe the operation worked as well as it did," I said to him, staring in amazement.

"Yeah, I know, Jim. I'm taller than you now," he bellowed with a crazy smirk drawn across his face. I noticed his voice had become deeper since the last time I saw him.

As we conversed, family members slowly started coming out to see him. Hamar refused but my father curiously made his way over. He managed a slight smile, being overwhelmed by how much Mitch had grown. My father and I asked him several questions as we stood by his car, checking it out. I got a sense that Mitch came by solely to show everyone how he had grown and that he was doing ok for himself now. I found it quite humorous, given that my father and Hamar said he would be a complete screwball, having grown up in Mama Ida's house. But he stood looking healthy and driving his own automobile. I didn't even have my own car yet. He didn't stay long and when he left it was another few years until I met up with him again.

Hamar was infuriated with my father for going out to see Mitch. "Stupid. You went too? To see that piece of shit. After everything we did for him and he fucked us over to live with those shit people and you run out to see him. Idiot fool," she cruelly spewed when we came back to the pool area.

My father ignored her insults, exclaiming, "You should see how tall he is now, Hamar. He's as tall as me. You wouldn't believe it."

"We saved his life, stupid. If it wasn't for me, he'd still be a midget. I was the one calling all the doctors, trying to find somebody who could help him. I even took him to all the doctors when I couldn't speak English. I didn't even know where I was driving when I took him for the appointments. And this is the thanks I get from your shithead son. Stupid. Go back out and talk some more, you idiot."

Then she started mimicking my father, saying, "You wouldn't believe it. Of course I believe it. I took him to the best specialist in the world down in Florida. I flew him myself with nobody's help. This piece of shit. He should drop dead," Hamar vilely shouted as she laid back in the sun.

My cousin Jeff and I started spending a lot of time together that summer. We ironically grew up sharing many of the same interest, even though we hadn't spent much of our childhood together. Occasionally, he dropped by with his bathing suit to swim and tan and to catch up on our lives. My bedroom window looked over the pool, so I would lean my speaker out to play a variety of albums we both enjoyed. Jeff and I shared the same taste in music, ferociously collecting albums and dubbing cassette tapes. But he didn't share in my passion for The Doors, so I stuck with what we both liked, Little Feat and The Allman Brothers. Once figuring out the music selections, we spent our days lying in the sun and drinking cocktails from my father's bar.

Jeff was a hearty eater, with the ability to put away huge amounts of food, but you wouldn't know it by looking at him. One afternoon when Hamar was at work, Jeff gorged himself with her flank steak, which was out defrosting for our Shabbat dinner. I didn't know he went in the house to feast and almost lost it when I found him shoving his face with her precious meat. It was the biggest crime you could commit in her house. She made it a point to warn everyone not to touch the flank steak, so I was in pure shock when noticing Jeff demolishing over half of it. I already had vivid sounds and visions of Hamar in my mind when she discovered the meat massacre.

Nervously laughing, I stammered, "Jeff, my mom is going to freak when she sees that you ate all that flank steak."

He had an extremely loud voice which was profoundly deliberate when he spoke. I forever compared the volume of his voice to Fred Flintstone's, free flowing and loud. "What are you talking about, man? It's food, here on the counter. I'm having a little snack. She can't be pissed over that."

"You don't know her, man. She loses her mind when we eat her food. She even told me that meat was for dinner tonight and specifically told us not to touch it."

"Man…, if she has a problem with me eating the meat, tell her to call me," Jeff shouted while burping out loud.

When Hamar came home that night, I thought I felt the house rumble from her robust yelling and hollering. She verbally attacked me, calling me every name known in the English, Hebrew and

Arabic book of curse words. If Jeff was listening, I'm sure he could have heard every nasty name she called him from his house, which was about ten miles away. Until this day, she stills gets angry and red in face from the loss of her precious flank steak.

During this same year, Hamar and my father sent Shlomo to an out of state college in Pennsylvania. He was in a downward spiral, as his grades and disposition were less than appealing. He was getting himself involved in all sorts of mischievous activities, so they thought it best to get him away from his current friends. Before he left, we weren't on speaking terms and that was by my choice.

Shlomo and his friends had been spending a majority of their time with a group of girls they met out one night in a bar. Coincidentally, they lived in our old neighborhood where we rented after the townhouse burnt down. One afternoon, Shlomo insisted I take out one of the girls from the group. I hated being fixed up on blind dates, but he did a hell of sales job persuading me. Seeing as I wasn't dating anyone at the time, I finally caved in and went along with his plans for the night. Shlomo instructed me to pick up the girl, take her out for something to eat, and then meet him at Rootie Kazootie's. That was a new bar that opened in Bass which was the big hot spot back then. They were also infamous for not being overly strict about checking ID's. It was interesting because I never walked in the place without seeing several familiar faces, dancing and drinking that were as young as me.

On the way to pick up my date, the neighborhood evoked some old memories I had while driving through it. I started rubbing my right forearm, remembering the terrible beating I absorbed from Hamar's shoe and the knot it left. When arriving at the girl's front door, I was surprised to see that she was fairly cute. After the introductions, we went out to eat where the drab conversations during dinner were primarily around Shlomo. I began wondering if this date was for me or him. Connie seemed nice enough but was incredibly jumpy throughout dinner, speaking without a single pause. When I found out she had a kid with some old boyfriend of hers, I wanted to murder Shlomo. The last thing I needed was to be fixed up with a teenage girl who had a baby.

After dinner, she quickly wanted to leave to meet up with Shlomo and his buddies at Rootie Kazootie's. As we walked in the bar, Shlomo immediately requested my dad's car keys. I didn't think much of it, passing them over without asking any questions. Instantly, Connie glued herself to Shlomo and his buddies while I scooted off to grab a couple of cocktails. When I returned with the drinks, Shlomo and Connie had disappeared. I thought, perhaps, they were out on the dance floor, so I stood around mingling with a few people waiting for them. Finally, a mutual friend of Shlomo's and mine confided in me. "Hey man, I can't stand to see your brother make you look like a fool anymore," Jack said, looking distressed.

"What are you talking about," I shouted over the music.

"Dude, Shlomo is in your car with Connie, doing blow and having sex."

This is approximately the time when Shlomo started really getting involved with cocaine and becoming a habitual user. I was furious by what he was suggesting, yelling over the music, "What the fuck are you talking about? He set me up with that girl."

Jack's expression looked sincere, as he calmly said, "Sorry dude, but I went outside with a few other guys and we saw them in the car screwing, so we walked back into the club. You're like the only one that doesn't know."

Feeling like a total jackass, I instantly gulped my drink down along with hers. It didn't take long for the both of them to return and I asked Shlomo for the car keys back. Snatching them roughly from his hands, I darted out of the bar in anger. While storming off, Connie asked where her drink was as I heard Shlomo shouting, "Where are you going man?"

Overcome with fury, I hastily jumped into my father's car peeling out of the parking lot. I didn't even consider how much I drank, realizing now I could have drawn attention to myself by driving like an idiot in front of a cop. By the time I got home, my gut was killing me from nerves and hostility. I was so overwhelmed with rage that I was compelled to punch another hole through my bedroom wall. Luckily, I didn't hit a two-by-four, otherwise I would have broken my hand for sure. Slamming my door shut, I played what I always did on my turntable, The Doors. I was hooked on their music, being the only band who played through my speakers. For some reason, I was deeply drawn to their music and lyrics. It helped get me through some really tough times in my life, giving me peace of mind. I actually started writing poetry which was invoked by the emotions I experienced while listening to their music.

After a few hours, Shlomo had the audacity to walk into my room, asking me to drive this bitch home. I literally lost my mind, screaming, "Are you out of your fucking mind? Do you think for a moment that I'm going to drive home some whore that you just screwed?"

He stood there looking as innocent as a new born baby. "Come on man. Do you actually think I screwed a girl that I hooked you up with? This isn't nice, the girl's waiting in the car for you."

"You brought her back here, thinking I was going to bring her home after you had sex with her? You better get out of my room, now," I violently screamed, with The Doors loudly playing in the background.

"Dude, she's your date. You have to bring her home."

"My date," I echoed. "She's my date? That's why you screwed *my date* in the car after I spent my time and money taking her to dinner." Suddenly, I ran to my closet in complete madness, grabbing my BB rifle and chasing him into his bedroom with it. But before I could crack it against his head, he slammed the bedroom door in my face. I was so furious that I slammed the barrel of the rifle through his door, hoping to hit him on the other side. Hastily yanking out the rifle, I hollered, "Fuck you, man. Don't you ever call me your brother again. You fuck, now you drive that bitch home!"

I stumbled back to my room, feeling dizzy from the inflicting hostility rumbling through my head. Then slamming my door shut, I rested on the bed as The Doors were playing through my mind. While lying there, I tried to get control of my emotions, but it was a terrible feeling being duped by someone who was supposed to be family. I had serious reservations about trusting anyone again after the crap Shlomo pulled that night.

CHAPTER 31

My senior year of high school flew by like colors on a spinning top. Everything was an absolute blur, seeming to mend together in one vast day. I was in the work release program, which meant I attended school for half a day and the other half, I went to work. I was picking up as many hours as possible to stay away from home. Hamar worked most days but when around, she was grumpier than ever. She constantly hollered for Julie to get her different things or to pick something up, maliciously referring to her as fat ass in place of pig. It vigorously reverberated off the walls, ruffling my nerves to the point of not wanting to be around the house any longer. Hamar was using anyone in sight as a punching bag for taking the edge off her daily stress, which was usually Julie, who absorbed the grunt of it.

Work was my second home and I was the happiest when at the shoe store. I had a sense of pride being there because of my friendships and work accomplishments. My manager and I became close friends over time, as he entrusted me with the key to the shop. There were days when he allowed me to open and close the shoe store without a manager around. I appreciated Mel's confidence in me, taking the responsibility to heart. Although, I did break the rules a couple of times by having a few get togethers in the stockroom, but it was always civilized. Typically, it was a few of us after work, hanging around chatting while indulging in a few beers. Work also became more fruitful, seeing how my father and Hamar cut me loose, allowing me to keep my entire earnings. I finally felt what it was like to receive a paycheck. Hamar was constantly on my back about holding the cash for me, but I opted to hide the money in my bedroom instead. She chastised me to no end, calling me cheap and other obnoxious names. But at the end of the day, I still had my earnings.

I wasn't taking school very seriously any longer, using it more for a place to hang my hat for a few hours. Being so withdrawn from all the other students and past friends, I didn't even consider going to prom. A girl I was friends with from junior high happened to ask if I would like to go with her. I didn't really see the sense in it, since all my friends weren't going. But she expressed a sincere interest in attending, so I decided to change my mind and go. I was glad to have gone because it was one of those things in life you would like to say you did. She was a fun date as well with her quirky sense of humor and we had a blast dancing and laughing the entire night. It turned out to be my last high school function, before graduating.

I decided on attending the University of Delaware after graduating high school. It was my only choice seeing how affordable it was and I already knew many people who were attending. My immediate downfall was entering without being serious about my education, majoring in business management. I don't think at the time that was what I really wanted to major in, but the majority of the people I knew were going in that direction. Sadly, I was more preoccupied with escaping from my home life and college seemed like the best way to accomplish that. Doing more clowning around than anything else, I found myself on academic warning after my first semester. I didn't actually focus on my strengths or interests to graduate, sticking with business out of pure laziness. I was more consumed with finding the *"Animal House"* experience than my studies, so in my second semester I joined a fraternity.

Through a frat house, I counted on finding more opportunities to party and meet women, which was the case. I was drinking like a buffoon, running around so much that I couldn't find time to go to my classes. Bedtime was at four in the morning every day, so I was getting up at one or two in the afternoon. To make matters worse, I moved into the frat house halfway through my second year of college and maybe attended a class or two a week. My overzealous desire for escaping burned my chances for graduating. The world offered so much in college, and I wanted to gulp it in faster than I should have. Moderation was never in my personal card catalog and I realized that too late.

Before leaving school, I received a dreadful phone call from Hamar. I was still in bed when answering the telephone, which was out of the norm for me. Ordinarily, I would have let my roommate's answering machine pick it up. "Hi Jim, it's mom," she said, sounding as if she were forced to phone. This was the first time Hamar ever called, so I was curious what the special occasion was. "I thought you should know your other mother died yesterday and if you want, I could take you to the funeral," she nonchalantly offered, as if she fulfilled her duty.

Hung-over and disoriented, I was completely taken back by the horrible news. Regrettably, I was so self-absorbed with my own social life that I hadn't visited her in quite some time. Mama Ida and I spoke often when I first started college, meeting up for lunch once, but that slowly dwindled away.

I was speechless by Hamar's news and without thinking answered, "No thanks," slamming the phone down. I found it revolting how my father put her up to this phony bullshit charade. Outraged by the call, I thought neither of them had the right to insult me with their fake support. Especially after the malicious and wicked comments they imposed on me over the years about my mother's character. Out of all the people to awaken me with the news of her death, Hamar would have to be the worst choice. How my father thought that was the appropriate way to inform me of my mother's passing is beyond me.

Lying in bed, I was more upset how I found out about my mom's death, than her actual demise. I didn't cry nor did I feel like I lost anyone in my life. The feeling was more cold and impassionate, like I conditioned myself to be when it came to the subject of mothers. I did a fine job conditioning myself over the years, becoming impervious to any such feelings. My mother was only 41 when dying, leaving me with a sense of being shortchanged, since Hamar and my father set too many ironclad obstacles in my way to hurdle. I lamented more over her death later in life than earlier, in response to a dramatic change I made in my own life.

My father began managing an electrical supply house when I was a senior in high school and hired me to work for him part-time. I spent the summers working in the warehouse, occasionally selling in the lighting showroom too. When expelled from college, I worked fulltime while attending night school to be reinstated at the University of Delaware. Since being employed full-time, I decided on moving out to Galley from my frat house, sharing an apartment with a fraternity buddy of mine. I was so consumed with being a failure, that I made focusing on my work a priority and as luck would have it, caught a break. The acting purchasing agent got fed up with his job, quitting without giving any notice. Immediately, I attempted to convince my father that I could take over his job. So temporarily he gave me the opportunity, while searching for someone else to fill the position. After a few months, I proved my worth by showing him several areas where I was saving the company money. Being so impressed with my work, he had me generate a progress report of all my savings. My father brought that with him on his next meeting with his superiors and I was officially hired as the new purchasing agent. I also received a generous raise, which boosted my confidence making me feel like I was on the right path.

Friday nights were a must-show at my parent's house for Shabbat dinner. I reluctantly went while all my buddies were out meeting girls at happy hour. At the time, Oscar's was the in spot for all young professionals to meet and drink. In fact, it was so popular that even a few Washington Redskins players showed up once in a while.

As much as I didn't like dedicating every Friday to Shabbat dinners, they were never boring, with interesting things happening quite frequently. Julie was in the limelight often, seeming to be dating a new guy every other month. For some reason, she had to bring these boyfriends to our dinners, constantly looking for Hamar's approval and acceptance. It was a disease with her, as Julie waited after dinner to hear whether Hamar approved or disapproved of her date. I noticed how most of the guys she was bringing home were of Moroccan decent. For the life of me, I couldn't understand the intensity of her motivation for Hamar's acceptance. Why she wanted to be reminded of Hamar by some other Moroccan's accent was puzzling. Julie was so severely beaten and verbally ridiculed, I figured she'd run away instead of trying to appeal to Hamar's better side.

Julie was around nineteen during this time and truly a modern day Cinderella. She complained innumerable times how Hamar purchased her own daughter, Samara, new clothing, leaving her wearing all the hand-me-downs. I assumed Julie grew a backbone, asking why she wasn't privy to new attire because Hamar's explanation was Julie ruined all her clothing. She described her as a wild animal that didn't brush her own teeth or even want to bathe. I found it incomprehensible that my father never put his foot down, demanding Julie be entitled to new clothing as well, since she was the eldest.

Julie was always compared to Samara by Hamar in every way, shape and form. She made Julie the ugly duckling while building up Samara as the beauty queen, outwardly doing this in front of my father. He covered his ears and eyes, never coming to her rescue. He still contends there was never any favoritism. Hamar thought nothing of commenting how beautiful Samara was in front of company, then elaborating how Julie wasn't as pretty. I wondered how she never lost her temper, tearing Hamar to a thousands pieces. By this time, Julie was nearly six feet tall, certainly capable of fending for herself. It still seems hard to swallow how cruel Hamar was, but it happened and the abuse continues on, even today. Julie's mental stability was irrevocably damaged by Hamar's verbal torture and long stretch of physical abuse.

Mitch surprised me one afternoon when stopping by my place of work for a visit. The last time I saw him was when he came to visit me at my fraternity house with Julie. My fraternity brothers and I encouraged him to drink while he miserably lost playing our drinking games that night. He was so inebriated that he barely found his way back home. Later I found out that a forty-five minute trip home took him nearly three hours.

When Mitch showed up at my work, I couldn't stop staring at him. He was attempting to grow this grotesque beard which didn't totally fill in, leaving him looking like Abraham Lincoln. I had to tease him about it and it felt like old times. He was much better at taking a joke now, not trying to swat me with one of his shoes. Mitch was doing well for himself, bragging how he was managing an automotive store, attempting to work his way up to the purchasing department. As our conversation progressed, we started comparing our home lives. He was very content how everything turned out for himself and before finishing, my father happened to walk by my office. Surprised to see Mitch, he briefly stopped in to say hello. He looked a little more comfortable speaking with him this time, given that Hamar wasn't around to jump all over his ass. Mitch and my father made small talk, which didn't consist of much substance since they both had hard feelings towards one another. After catching up, Mitch left to go back to work and I didn't see or hear from him again for another year. I don't know why we didn't keep in better touch, but back then that was the way we were.

When Mitch left, my father laughed, inquiring, "Did you mention anything to him about that awful beard he's trying to grow?"

I cackled as well, saying, "Yeah, I was kidding around with him and said he looked like Abraham Lincoln. He was cool with it."

"Yeah, but is he going to shave it?"

"I don't know," I answered, feeling as if there were bigger issues for him to be concerned about. "I was just kidding around with him. If he likes it, he should keep it."

My father walked out of my office, shaking his head with a smirk on his face. "He looks terrible. You should've told him to shave it."

Not long after Mitch's visit, the owners of our company sold the business to another supply house. It was truly a sad affair since the business had been around for decades and the owners milked it dry. I was devastated, not knowing what I was going to do for a new job. To make matters worse, I had just purchased a new Mustang convertible, having no idea how I was going to make the payments. Hamar still insisted on holding my paychecks, so I had no idea what money I had in the bank. For all I knew, I was broke. She even mailed in my car payments which I agreed to, just to keep in good graces with the family. I knew if I didn't allow her to do my banking, I would be called cheap while ruffling her blasted feathers in the process.

My father decided on opening his own electrical supply house, bringing me on as an employee. I was responsible for managing and purchasing supplies for the store, while his job was canvassing and bringing in new clients. He hired a gentleman named, Sam, who previously worked for my Papa Willie for several years. Sam had a great customer base, with years of knowledge for the business. Our hope was all his customers would follow him, giving our new store a good jumpstart. The timing was perfect for him too, since he was looking for a job. After my grandfather passed away, he left his supply house to my Uncle Charles, who ultimately ran it in the ground. Unfortunately for Mama Ida, Charles had been milking the business for years, until there was nothing left. Sam told me that in the end the sheriff came in, throwing everyone out of my grandfather's store and chained up all the doors. Apparently, Charles took out a million dollar line of credit without my grandmother's knowledge and never paid it back. Needless to say, that was the end of his marriage to my Aunt Paula.

During our fist year, everything went smoothly and I even got married. When I was completely moving out of Hamar's house, I asked her for my grandfather's mason ring. The look on her face alone was enough to tell me that she never imagined I would ask for it back. "I don't have the ring anymore," she said, looking upset that I had the moxie to even request it.

"Where is it," I asked, knowing very well she pawned it.

Appearing annoyed by my question, Hamar shouted in defense, "I gave it to Aunt Rubel when we went to Israel. I asked her for it and she told me that she couldn't find it. I think she lost it."

I was enraged. "She lost it? What was she doing with it? She went to Israel too. What makes her house any safer than ours?"

Hamar was sitting on her bed while my father was undressing. Infuriated that I wasn't accepting her first explanation, she violently screamed, "Who the hell are you to ask me? It's gone that's all. What, you think I stole it? Piece of shit," she screeched at me, along with a number of other curse words in Hebrew and Arabic. "Like I need your fucking grandfather's shitty ring. Get out, just get out of my room. You cheap. You should drop dead."

Then she looked over at my father. "And you. You potato. You're going to sit there and let him talk to me like that. You big nose potato. Stupid idiot."

I stood holding my ground, refusing to leave. I really wanted her to admit that she pawned the damn thing. It would have been worth the loss of my grandfather's ring just to hear her admit it. I couldn't stand her lies any longer and her poised confidence when she did. No one in the family ever challenged her, so she constantly got away with bullshit like this. Staring at my father, I stated, "I just don't understand how Rubel could have lost the ring or why she would have it in the first place."

He was speechless as Hamar grew completely belligerent. "Get out of my room, you piece of shit. You should die. Do you hear me? You should die. Like I took the ring? Fuck you and that ring. Drop dead, you fucking cheap piece of shit. Idiot," she viciously yelled as I stomped back to my bedroom.

"Here we go again with this nonsense," I thought, resting on my bed. When we went to Israel, I had to pay my own way and give her $600 to hold for me. She of course insisted on it, so not to make trouble, I gave in without a fight. When we arrived at the hotel, I asked for the money back. As Hamar proceeded to hand me $350, I was left flabbergasted. Doing my best to hold my temper, I asked where the rest of the money was and she gave me the same reaction I received from the missing ring. Then she made a point of ignoring me throughout the entire trip, treating me as though I was the criminal. My father eventually convinced me to apologize to her. Hamar gave him such heartache, because I wouldn't cave in to her demands, that he had no choice but to twist my arm. It felt demoralizing afterwards, knowing very well she stole the money, but that was the insane protocol in my family. Mama Ida was absolutely sickened when I told her the story.

We were growing the business at a fast rate, but after our second year, I was finding it hard to replenish the inventory. Around this time, my father hired Shlomo to work with us. His responsibility was bringing in a flock of new customers since my father felt he was an extraordinary salesperson. I was perturbed because we didn't have enough money to buy new merchandise, so it didn't make any sense to bring on a new salesman. I confronted my dad about it, but he was just elated with the idea of bringing him on. "Oh, are you kidding me? Shlomo is the best salesman. He's got a great mouth. Believe me, with him and me on the road it'll be great."

I didn't want to make waves, so I bit my tongue, sitting back and watching. I didn't understand what we were gaining by hiring Shlomo, since he had no electrical background experience. All of his jobs were bartending, until he fell into a commercial Real Estate position. He held the job for a short period of time, then had a falling out with his boss and either got fired or quit. Like Julie being compared to Samara, the same thing happened with me being compared to Shlomo. Hamar would sit at the dinner table, slobbering about what a great salesperson Shlomo was and how he had the best mouth, as she put it. Then going on to say how he was the best looking and the coolest with women. She was totally in awe over him joining us, believing his presence would make the difference in our success. This crap repeatedly went on in front of my father, with the artistic way she positioned it meaning to belittle me. Hamar infused these contemptuous comments to insinuate that I didn't measure up. It was uncanny how I was capable of reading through the lines, but my father couldn't. I only wish that was the case. He chose to plead ignorance, going along with her and never feeling she was out of line.

A few months later, the existence of our supply house was miserably snuffed out. Sam tragically died of a heart attack, which forced my father to basically hand the business over to another electrical supply house. My wife and I were speechless at the time, seeing as my father never conferred with me that the business was in dire straits. He and Hamar were even trying to convince us to purchase a condo, while all this was going on. Fortunately, we decided to hold off.

CHAPTER 32

After the demise of our company, I was seriously thinking of doing my own thing. I didn't know what it was going to be, but I was getting nervous not having any control over my destiny. While on unemployment, my father rented a warehouse and started a new company selling only light bulbs and fixtures. He based the business around his past cliental and Sam's customer list. Shlomo and I stayed on, but I promised myself to give it one last try with my father, then I was gone.

From the beginning, the model was looking like a slip shot business plan and I didn't foresee any real substantial financial future. I was in charge of purchasing and some selling, while my father and Shlomo were pure sales. Things were not progressing as fast as we would have liked, which caused a cloud of tension to hover over the office. To get things going, my father opted to start having meetings a couple times a week at his house after work. The meetings were borderline ridiculous, as we sat around the family room drinking cocktails and brainstorming. Primarily, my father and Shlomo ran the discussions. I tried my best to interject good ideas, but they always fell on deaf ears. My father was enamored with whatever Shlomo and he had to say, making those the only topics for discussion. I was quickly losing my patience and faith in the whole summit idea, eventually clamming up. With all the vodka and bullshit between the two of them, anything they uprooted was thought as an uplifting idea.

One unique idea, Shlomo and my father contrived, was approaching churches and convincing them to sell light bulbs to their members.

Then they went even further, suggesting church children fill their wagons with light bulbs to sell door to door in their neighborhoods. The discussion and idea became so absurd that they volunteered me to fill a little red wagon to go knocking door to door selling light bulbs too. Becoming inflamed with their futile idea, I argued my case, but they both accused me of being negative, suggesting that the idea would work. I was so enraged by their mockery that I stormed out of the house and went back to my apartment. Things evolved into a rocky relationship after that.

After we were opened for a while, my father hired Julie to answer phones and do odd jobs around the office. She did work for us back at the first electrical supply house and did a decent job. She needed the money too, given that Hamar threw her out of the house for dating a guy whom she and my father loathed. At first, Hamar loved him because he was Moroccan and of course, they had many things in common. But after speaking with a few of her friends, she found out he was married before and physically abused his wife. Once that was common knowledge, Julie was given an ultimatum, either she stopped dating the guy or they would throw her out. She decided to keep her Moroccan boyfriend and moved in with him. Hamar happily cutoff all ties with Julie, leaving my father to continue his relationship with her by himself.

Since Julie was working in the same office, we started to become close. My wife, Jen, and I invited her and her boyfriend, Mel, over to our apartment for dinners. In return, we went to their place for a few dinners as well. Most times, we sat around drinking while talking about our crazy colorful childhood. Jen and Mel were entertained as Julie and I discussed our old war stories, starring Hamar and my father. We half-laughed over tales such as the Halloween candy story, comparing whose beatings were worse. It felt different to be around Julie as an adult and seeing her with a guy. I always pictured her as this little girl, squirming around telling lies, while being beaten for things she didn't always do. Her beatings were so embedded in my head that I equated her face with tears and suffering, rather than smiles and joy. Even though we all laughed over the stories, I could see the sorrow buried deep in her eyes. Not being dramatic, but it was easy to confuse her laughter with happiness than a shroud for sorrow. Some people have a knack for that kind of behavior and with Julie, I could see right through it like glass.

She wasn't mentally all together at work, portraying to be slightly quirky. Julie was on the telephone most of the time with either her boyfriend, Mel or friends. But what I found to be quirky was how she had this habit of being hooked on a word and constantly repeating it all day long. On one particular day, no matter if she was sitting at her desk or walking around, I kept hearing her repeat, "Shmear. Shmear. Shmear." I contemplated saying something to her but let it go for a while.

My father closed the office door to have a meeting with the light bulb rep when Julie started again. He excused himself, then walking over to my desk, whispered, "Do me a favor. Go tell that idiot to stop making those fucking noises already. I'm embarrassed sitting here listening to that *Shmear* shit, with this guy in my office."

Stepping out from the office, I found Julie at her desk. "Julie, you have to stop saying *Shmear* already. Dad's getting pissed off. Where the hell did you learn that word from anyways," I asked since it sounded like something Mitch would say. He had the same kind of personality as Julie, with a passion for repeating silly words. I remembered that he especially liked that word.

"Mitch. He loves saying, *Shmearrrr*," Julie replied, accentuating the word while laughing.

"Well, just be cool because dad's getting embarrassed."

Crazy little things like that kept Mitch and Julie tightly knit through the years. They had this closeness, which I didn't have with either of them, because of these little quirks. Even through their rocky relationships, it inevitably glued them back together from broken times.

One night, Julie asked Jen and me to meet her out for a few drinks. When we arrived, it was one of those nice rustic bars with the loud music and smoky atmosphere. They had a minuscule menu, as the real focus was drinking and smoking. When we met up with Julie, Mel hadn't arrived yet and she was unusually serious. We ordered a couple of beers while leaning against one of the tall tables.

Then Julie began uncontrollably trembling, acting as though she was going to cry at any given moment. "Are you ok," I asked, feeling concerned.

Upon hearing my question, her face reverted back to the same expression I remembered from when she was getting a beating. "I have to tell you something," she mumbled, with her bottom lip quivering.

"Ok," I said, taking a sip of my beer. "Go ahead. What is it?"

"It's really bad," she shouted over the music. "Really bad, Jim." She was looking exceedingly ill, as her whole body caught up with her bottom lip and violently shook.

"Julie, what is it? It can't be that bad," I shouted, feeling edgy how long it was taking her to spit out whatever it was she needed to say.

Then cupping a hand over her mouth, she forcefully swallowed. "What's wrong? Are you ok," I asked.

"I'll be right back. I think I have to the throw up," Julie shouted in a panic and rushing to the bathroom.

While she was gone, I said to Jen, "I've never seen Julie act this freaky before. I can't imagine what she has to get off her chest that's making her so crazy."

Just as I finished, Julie came sauntering back and frustrated from the suspense, I barked, "Ok Julie, just tell us what the hell you want to say. This is taking too damn long."

"Ok, I'll tell you, but you have to promise not to get mad at me." Then staring at me for my confirmation, I nodded my head, agreeing. She stuck out her right hand, waving it up and down as if to calm herself, but not before having a shiver attack. Her entire body quaked, looking like she got the chills from seeing a snake or rat. "Shlomo and papa raped me," she exhaled, stomping in place like she was trying to put out a fire.

"What did you say? Did you say that you were raped by Shlomo and papa," I questioned, not trusting my own ears.

"Yes," she shouted, beginning to cry.

Seeing how sensitive the conversation was getting, I gently stammered, "How? How did it happen?"

"Shlomo used to take me down to the basement when mom and dad weren't around and do things to me."

I was totally perplexed and started stammering my words. "What? What things are you talking about?"

Julie began crying and shivering. "Do you hate me? Do you think I'm a bad person?"

"No! No," I shouted, feeling concerned. "No. I don't think any of those things. It's not your fault. How long has this been going on for? Where was I when this stuff was going on? Was I home?"

Wiping her flowing tears, Julie's cried through a weeping voice, "For a long time. I think since I was around twelve or eleven years old. Somewhere around there, I guess." Then she peered at me. "You weren't around, but Samara came down to the basement one time and she saw. She saw what he was doing to me and she ran back upstairs."

"Why didn't you tell anybody or at least tell me? I can't believe this has been going on for so long."

"You know why," she said sobbing. "I'm the liar in the house. No one would believe me. Do you believe me?"

"Yes. Of course. I don't think you would lie about something like this, Julie. Lying about eating candy or food isn't the same as lying about something like this," I said, trying to console her. "Have you talked to Samara about this?"

"Yes, and she remembers coming down and seeing something. But that's it."

Trying to put all the pieces together, I continued with the questions. "What's this with papa? What the hell did he do?"

Julie began quivering again, looking as if she were overloading her mind. Appearing to almost go into a trance, she shouted over the music, "He used to come into my room. I still remember what his breath smelled like. Do you remember how he used to drink that stuff that smelled like licorice? I can't remember what you call it."

"Yeah, I can't remember the name of it, but it was some kind of a liqueur."

"Right and his breath smelled like it. He would come in my room and lay on top of me. He also tried to kiss me, but I always turned my head and then there would be all this wet sticky stuff on me. Then he would take a tissue and wipe it off."

I was truly mortified by her story and felt like vomiting myself. I knew she wasn't making this crap up and curiously asked, "Julie, your room was across from mom and dad's. How didn't they see this going on? Wasn't papa nervous that someone was going to catch him?"

She almost looked upset, as if I was questioning her integrity. "They were downstairs. He would sneak up." Then swallowing a large gulp of beer, she said, "Don't you remember that I put a lock on my door like you did, and mom beat the hell out of me for it?"

"No. But I believe you," I responded, wondering where this was going.

"Well, she did. I put it there to keep him out. He was disgusting and I wanted to keep him out. Remember how he always gave me candy and everyone said he loved me the best?" I nodded as she continued. "Yeah, he gave me candy to keep me quiet. But I would've told if I knew someone would've believed me. I feel like garbage that I took the candy. Like I'm cheap. I feel like it's my fault."

I was feeling extremely bad for her, wanting to make a point of letting her know that it wasn't her fault. "You were just a kid, Julie. That fucking garbage, Shlomo and that old man knew exactly what they were doing. You can't blame yourself," I rigidly stated, doing my best to sound convincing. It disgusted me how the old man strutted around like he was holy and meanwhile, was having his way with a child.

Julie seemed like she was ready to keel over from exhaustion. Her shoulders were slumped downwards, as if she just laid down an armful of bricks. Then wavering back and forth, I held her as she quickly gulped down some more beer. My mind was swirling around with an abundance of questions. I felt overwhelmed with remorse since I wasn't able to be there for her, not understanding how all this happened for so many years without anyone finding out.

Still in shock over her disturbing accounts, I asked, "Are you ok? Can I get you another beer?"

She appeared stronger now, as if dropping that armful of bricks gave her strength. Her eyes went from reflecting sorrow to projecting hatred and anger. "I can't believe mom used to send me to the grocery store with Shlomo. She knew he was raping me. Anytime she sent him to the grocery store, she yelled for me to go with him. Why would she do that? I know she had to know. There was no way she didn't."

"I don't know," I said, shrugging my shoulders. "Do you really think she knew? That's kind of strange."

"She knew," Julie blurted out with confidence. "Do you remember the parking lot across from Magruders," she shouted over the music, failing to wait for my response. "He used to drive me over there and have sex with me in the car. That's where he did it when we went to the store. I prayed someone would see us but no one ever did."

"Does anybody else know about this," I asked, feeling bewildered.

"Yeah, dad and mom know now. I took dad with me to the psychiatrist," she said while gulping down another beer.

"I didn't know you were seeing one. What did the doctor say?"

"The psychiatrist told dad that I was telling the truth and she believed me about being raped by Shlomo and papa. Dad believed that Shlomo was experimenting with me, but just doing stuff like fondling and touching. He didn't believe he was having sex with me. He told the doctor there was no way he believed that papa would ever touch me because he was so religious."

Julie looked weakened after a couple beers, but appeared more comfortable talking. "I would think the same thing about papa, but how does dad think you're making up something so disgusting like this. Even the psychiatrist confirmed what you're saying is truthful. And fucking Shlomo, he doesn't think he did anything? That guy's been in more trouble than anyone I know."

Staring down at the dim wood table, Julie quietly said, "They want me to face Shlomo at their house and say what he did right in front of him." She started sobbing and shaking again. "I can't do that. He has this power over me. I don't know why, but he does. Shlomo and all of them will just say I'm lying anyways and I can't go through that."

I couldn't comprehend not wanting to face her attacker, so I fiercely said, "Julie, what are you talking about? Here's your chance. You know it's the truth, so just face him and bust him right in front of everyone."

"I can't do it," she sobbed. "Mom and dad don't believe me and they'll never take my word over Shlomo's. Mom said she believed papa did it because he used to cheat on mama back in Morocco, but not Shlomo."

Half-laughing in disbelief, I said, "That old guy? What did he do?"

"Mom said something like, these boats would bring over these young girls to work when he owned his bar and he would sleep with them. But she doesn't believe Shlomo did anything to me." Julie's voice dropped in despair.

"Mom also told me that she never wanted us," Julie snapped. "She said that dad tricked her into having us live with her. She made it out like it was my fault for living with them that Shlomo and papa did this stuff to me. All this time and she tells me that she never wanted us?"

"She's been saying that shit forever. I can't believe this is the first time you've heard it," I said, feeling disgusted that Hamar used that as a defense.

Then I got back to her confronting Shlomo. "Listen, it's up to you, Julie but I would personally confront Shlomo if I were you. I'll say one more thing, if you don't show up, they will definitely say you're lying."

Julie looked so exasperated that I didn't want to challenge her anymore. I presumed she was going to do whatever made the most sense and left it at that. As it worked out, she never showed up and stopped talking to Hamar all together. Shlomo got off because of her absence, giving everyone the impression that Julie was full of shit. Even my father, who admitted he believed that Shlomo was doing something sexual to her, never came to Julie's rescue. Along with all the other crap that happened to Julie, he allowed this crime to go unpunished under his own roof. It was the epitome of our lives with this family and also the demise of Julie's mental stability.

Going to work was difficult, considering I sat adjacent to Shlomo in the office. The old man was dead, but Shlomo was still around and it disgusted me to look at him. The topper was when Julie told me he was still having sex with her in the warehouse when my father and I were out on calls. I couldn't understand it, but she said he had some kind of power over her. I wasn't a psychiatrist, but the situation completely baffled me, as my stomach churned just by the sight of him. Julie didn't want me to confront Shlomo, so I never let on that I knew what he had done or what he was currently doing.

Jen and I spoke afterwards, determining that we wanted to get the hell away from this family. I knew if my father allowed this monstrosity to happen to Julie, than nothing good would ever come by being connected to this so-called family. Repeatedly, I tried appealing to Hamar, hoping to be accepted as a true son but I knew years back it was impossible. My own father showed more love and kindness to Hamar's children than his own, which I never understood. I lamented the years spent with them, finally wanting to restart my life. Jen was from New Jersey, so if I was really set on leaving Delaware, she wanted to move back by her folks. She left that decision up to my discretion, even though Hamar and my father accused her of pushing me to move.

I found myself fed up with all the fighting and animosity created by Hamar and my father, between friends and other family members. The favoritism and the unfavorable comparisons made between us and Hamar's children were cruel and intolerable. I knew if I didn't leave Delaware I would end up like Julie. I wasn't interested in spending the rest of my life sitting with therapists, bitching about what changes I could have made to avoid being unhappy. I felt it was time to reach out and find happiness wherever that may be. It was the hardest decision I ever had to make, but it was most gratifying in the end.

A few days after Julie's confession, Shlomo and I got into a heated argument. He felt I wasn't working hard enough and I thought otherwise. After all, who was he to make that accusation. Before long, we were at each other's throats squaring off ready to go at it when Julie came in screaming for us to stop. I quickly left, scampering to my car to get a crowbar. Then Julie came running out, shouting, "What are you doing?"

Shaking with adrenaline, I hollered, "I'm going to take this crowbar and bash the fuck out of his head. I'm tired of this fuck screwing you and getting away with it. And I'm tired of listening to his shit."

"You can't do that. You'll go to jail. Please just go home and cool down. I promise you'll feel better tomorrow."

There was no tomorrow for me. My mind was made up the moment I drove away from that warehouse. Returning home that afternoon, I explained to Jen about my confrontation with Shlomo and called my cousin Jeff. Ironically, he lived in New Jersey for two years selling tennis shoes for a major manufacturer. I met one of Jeff's friends at his wedding and had a great conversation about what he did for a living. Richard was in banking, managing a group of guys who originated mortgage loans. I enjoyed our conversation, seriously thinking it would be a great opportunity for me.

I confided in Jeff before we opened the new business, expressing my concerns about working with my father and Shlomo again. He was immediately against the idea, profoundly saying, "Man..., you've got to get away from that situation. Go and do something on your own. I'll help you, just let me know when you're ready."

I took Jeff up on his offer and he was happy that I finally came around. We were fairly close for being cousins and throughout the years he expressed concern for my wellbeing. After talking with Jeff and getting his input, I contacted Richard in New Jersey for an interview. I felt confident our conversation went well at the wedding, so I scheduled an interview that Friday. Jen and I dropped everything we had planned to secretly drive up. Before leaving, my father called several times but I never answered the telephone. He left a number of messages, attempting to get me to come back to work but my mind was stuck on moving.

When we got back to Delaware, I came home with a new job and a place to live in Shaker Heights, New Jersey. This was the first time I truly felt proud of myself. It lifted my confidence, which had been badly deflated by Hamar's ruthless abuse. The first thing I did upon returning was stopping over at Hamar's house to confront them about my decision. They were in the kitchen speaking when Jen and I arrived. As I broke the powerful news to them, Hamar had a hokey smile on her face, looking as though she knew something I didn't. I imagined she was happier than hell that I was going, since it only left one of my father's kids in her care. My father's expression was entirely different, as he seemed to take the news to heart. He looked like I just hit him below the belt, but even though I felt guilty for hurting him, I knew this was the prudent thing to do.

He was too hurt to speak, but Hamar managed to spew out an obnoxious remark. She smirked while displaying a sarcastic laugh, saying, "We knew, Jim. What, you think we're stupid? We knew the two of you went to New Jersey." Then glancing at my father, she barked, "Right, Sheldon? Didn't we," she shouted, waiting for a response.

My father simply nodded at her, then sardonically said, "Well Jim, good luck to you and your wife and your new family up there. That's all I can say."

As elated as I was, I had a knot in my stomach thinking about leaving Julie with all these awful issues to deal with by herself. I felt she should have been the one inspired to move and get the heck out of Delaware. I recognized Julie had a knack for survival but as soon as she acted on it, she always went running right back to them. She could never separate herself from those people, using anything possible to get Hamar's approval. My father held Hamar so high on this imaginary pedestal that Julie feverishly bought into it. She would actually make up bullshit about me, Mitch or anyone to get in Hamar's good graces. It was like a sickness, something she admitted to, but for some reason couldn't stop. Hamar loved nothing more than hearing what someone else said about her or anything to do with her. It was cause for an all out feud and when Julie joined her side, she had her acceptance.

CHAPTER 33

When we moved to New Jersey, I found out Julie left Mel and moved into an apartment with a friend. Mel was slapping her around so roughly, that it got to the point where Julie was telling people she had fallen down the stairs. Surprisingly, Mitch started visiting her on a regular basis and they became rather close. It was odd for me to envision those two as friends, since they fought like cats and dogs as kids, but I thought it was great they had each other now. While living in New Jersey, I wasn't speaking much to my father, given he was extremely upset I had left. We conversed about once a month, without any substance to our conversations. Every so often, he would put Hamar on the telephone, pretending I requested to speak with her. It was his way of upholding the peace, attempting to keep her off his ass. Hamar was getting annoyed because I wasn't calling for her, which was disrespectful in her mind. It was always about respect but why she thought she was entitled, was beyond my comprehension.

New Jersey was my great escape, evolving into a colossal eye opener over time. I hurdled some defining fences, piecing together parts of my shattered soul. I struggled for the first few years but as time went by my career progressively improved. While there I made great friends, feeling an air of confidence which was refreshing and stimulating. After working for a few banks and a mortgage company, I found a small community bank that was a perfect fit for originating mortgage loans. Shortly before joining the bank, Jen and I had a baby girl and named her Ricky. She was a beautiful little blond with big blue eyes. My father and Hamar were not at the hospital for the birth but wanted me to call them once the baby was born.

At the time, they were enamored with Florida and were looking to migrate down there. It was a must for Hamar to be by her sister, Muffy, who had recently moved to Miami. Not to break protocol, Hamar and my father were hunting for a place to live while their house was on the market. Interestingly enough, my father wasn't arguing about the move. He loved the warm climate and Hamar promised to allow him to buy a boat when they got down there. Knowing when Ricky was to be born, they planned another excursion to drive down to Florida.

They were the first ones I called when the baby was born. I was thirty-one and Ricky's birth felt like the biggest accomplishment I had made in my life. Trembling while dialing my father and Hamar's number, I congratulated them for being grandparents for the first time. They sounded very excited and left early the next morning. When they came in, we all hugged and drooled over the baby. After about an hour of holding Ricky and taking pictures, my father and Hamar took me out for lunch. Jen was weak and still bedridden, so I offered to bring her something back. During lunch, we briefly spoke about the baby since the majority of the conversation revolved around their desire to move to Florida. On the way back to the hospital, they congratulated me again and swiftly dropped me off. My father and Hamar explained how they were running late, needing to drive to Florida that same day. The car was packed to the gills and they never had any intention of staying longer than they already had. I understood Ricky meant nothing to Hamar, but my father broke my heart. It was terribly difficult for me to accept he would take a mere glance at his first grandchild, who was named after his mother, then choose to run to Florida rather than visit for a few days.

Like a good soldier, I never mentioned a word about it, even though I felt like I was spit on. I learned by now it was a no win battle and best not to ruffle any feathers. I became a guru at swallowing bullshit from them over the years, but what troubled me most about their visit was the excuse they used for not staying longer. Years later, it was brought to my attention how they were telling people that they didn't stay because Jen wouldn't allow them to stay at our house. We had a three bedroom home and the rooms were all taken, so she requested they stay at a hotel. Apparently, they were insulted by Jen's suggestion and hurriedly sped to Florida. The interesting part about their story was the conversation never took place. They simply made up the story to cover their ass because they knew their friends and family would inquire why they didn't stay longer. A story like that was more palatable than admitting that going to Florida was more important.

A few years after Ricky was born, I did some soul searching and Jen and I were divorced. I discovered that my accomplishments at work seemed to make me the happiest and it became my major focus. My father and I started speaking more frequently after my divorce, which brought us closer than we ever had been. The combination of years spent away from them and he and Hamar living in Florida full-time, slowly melted my treacherous childhood memories away. I shelved the disparaging memories in a holding cell, keeping them locked deeply in my mind.

My life richly improved and five years later, I met the girl I always pictured would be on my arm. This time I made that portrait come to life, as my new found confidence catapulted me into a wonderful marriage. Michelle's beauty illuminated from within, which electrified my heart. Her sister fixed us up and she was a jewel of perfection from the first time I saw her. Her long blond curly hair and deep brown eyes swallowed me emotionally and we married soon after.

I felt like I was getting a second shot at life. Being forty, I wanted peace and a comfortable relationship with my father and Hamar. I truly wanted family to be a priority in my life, making an effort to expunge my poisonous childhood from my veins. Mitch and I were always close, but I avoided Julie from the time I moved to New Jersey. She was confused with her relationships, using her survival tactics a couple of times on me to reach her goal of acceptance from Hamar. It was nothing dramatically devastating, but I wanted to be as far away from family feuds as possible.

During my first year of marriage, the bank I was working for got sold. The new owners' interest in making loans died out and I was left with very few options. I saved a good amount of money over the years, knowing one day it would come in handy and decided to go into business for myself. I wasn't sure what I wanted to tackle but had several ideas going through my mind.

One of Hamar's nieces was getting married, so Michelle and I went to Florida for the wedding. On one of the free evenings, before the event, my father and I had an extensive conversation about my future. We had discussions over the past few weeks how I wanted to open my own business. He was looking for an opportunity as well since his business with Mitch was sold.

While Mitch lived in Florida, he reunited with Hamar and our father, and this time stuck around longer than usual. Mitch and my dad were looking to do something different and decided to jointly open a carwash. Unfortunately, the location was a large problem, forcing my father to ultimately sell the business. Mitch was married at the time and prior to the carwash being sold, he and his wife constantly bickered with Hamar and my father. They were putting a strain on Mitch's marriage, nosing around in their personal business. Eventually, word traveled back to Mitch how Hamar and my father were telling friends and family members that he ruined the business. They went as far as blaming him for its demise. Reaching his boiling point, Mitch decided to write a heartfelt letter to my father, explaining his disappointment towards him. In his letter, Mitch was excessively candid, writing how our father destroyed our childhood and lives by marrying that crazy-ass Arab. It closed the door to their relationship forever, with my father vowing Mitch was dead to him. Mitch felt the same way and when diagnosed with MS, my father stuck to his promise. He never wavered to see if his son would live or die from the terrible disease. In fact, Hamar made light of his illness, saying MS wasn't that bad of a sickness and Mitch would only need shots to live.

Not learning from Mitch's experience, I went forward and opened a flea market with my father in New Jersey. We equally invested in the business, which I was in charge of running the day to day operations while he remained in Florida. My father really wanted to retire and I figured it made good sense to share the risk with somebody and who better than someone I thought I could trust. During our venture, our relationship became rocky. Hamar was wickedly working on my wife the same way she had with Mitch's. It started when Michelle questioned me whether or not I really wanted to marry her.

"Why in the world would you ask me something like that? You know I love you."

Her eyes looked solemn, as she apprehensively responded, "Well, I was on the phone with your mom and she told me how you called her upset about making a mistake by marrying me. She said you were crying like a little boy and told her you were sorry you ever married me. She said you haven't cried like that since you were a little boy crying to her."

Michelle knocked me over like a whirlwind when hearing Hamar's lie, so infuriated I shouted, "Are you kidding me? She told you that?" Michelle nodded her head, implying yes. "I never told her that and definitely don't feel that way. Who the hell gets married and a few months later says something as ridiculous as that?"

I was shaking with fury while grinding my teeth. I couldn't believe my ears nor wrap my arms around what she was saying. "What kind of person would suggest such an evil lie," I thought to myself. "Especially, someone who wants the respect of a real mother and then makes a wicked statement like that, jeopardizing my marriage."

I looked at Michelle, convincingly saying, "I love you. I never had a conversation with her about that. In fact, she complains to my dad that I never call to speak with her. And if I were at odds with our marriage, do you think out of all the people in the world that I would choose her to confide in? For your information, I never cried to her as a child either. She was as comforting as a stone. The only time I cried as a child was when my father was beating the crap out of me."

The next time my father came into town I exploded in anger, telling him the bullshit lies Hamar conveyed to Michelle. He was staggered by what I had to say and could only shake his head in disgust. Whether he went back to her with my news or not was very doubtful. They constantly fought and she publicly humiliated him about his weight and his big red nose, so he avoided confrontations at all costs with her. I found it consistent with my childhood, how he would rather avoid a fight than confront her about trying to destroy his son's marriage.

CHAPTER 34

My early forties was the conclusion of my relationship with Hamar and my father. After years of trying to hold together a relationship with them by a thread, I could no longer sacrifice my marriage or soul. My father had been gradually showing signs of becoming more vindictive towards Michelle and me. He was coming in once a month to collect money from our business and I could feel the tension during his stay. I had an idea what was bothering him, so one evening I confronted him about it in my house. My father angrily expressed that he was upset with me for still having a relationship with Mitch. He was also furious that I allowed him and his wife to come to New Jersey for a visit. My father expected me to ostracize Mitch from my life because of the letter he wrote. This was an activity that went on when we were children and I couldn't believe he expected me to end my relationship with my brother.

I was livid by his expectation and angrily barked, "You expect *me* not to speak to Mitch and his wife because of the letter he wrote *you*?"

We were having cocktails at the time and my father's eyes looked spitefully redder than normal. "That's right. I do expect you not talk to him again. He's dead to me. Do you understand me? Him and his fucking piece of shit wife. After your mother took him to all those doctors when he was sick and she didn't even speak English. If it wasn't for her he'd be dead today. So to me, he's DEAD. And by you having them here condones his letter to me. Don't you see that?"

Not backing down, I shot back, "So you want me to banish Mitch from my life because you did? I'm not doing that. I didn't just start speaking with him yesterday. I've had a relationship with him for years. And I have to tell you, if I hear the story of her taking Mitch to the doctor again, I'm going to be sick. What parent doesn't take their child to the doctor when they're sick?" My father shot me a venomous look, as he sipped on his vodka. "If I was his father, instead of throwing him out of my life, I would've asked him where a letter like that originated from," I exclaimed with my own daughter in mind.

"I don't give a shit where it came from. He's dead. You don't understand me. When I say he's dead, I mean he's dead."

Actually hearing him use those words struck me as cold, struggling to swallow after hearing them. "I don't understand how you could throw your own son out of your life for a letter. How about Shlomo? You didn't throw him out of your life after he spoke disrespectfully to you and cussed you out to your face."

"I don't care what Shlomo does. He's on drugs, ok? So he acts like that because he's on drugs. This other one is my son and he's a piece of shit. I'm the first to admit it. He's a piece of shit and has always been a piece of shit. He's dead to me and that's it," my father shouted, waving his arms in the air like he was flagging down a helicopter.

Befuddled by his answer, I questioned, "So because Shlomo's on drugs, that makes it ok for the way he's spoken to you over the years. And milking you for thousands of dollars and not working. That's ok?"

"What thousands of dollars," he asked, sounding whiney.

I was getting annoyed with this game, so aggravated I shouted, "You told me that he used up your business line which had $250,000 left on it. You also told me how he charged up all your credit cards eating at the Palm Restaurant. On top of that, you told me that you let him borrow $150,000 to help him and his wife out since her father wouldn't lend them the money."

"Oh please, I never said that. All I said was I didn't know what happened to the money for the business line of credit. He never used my charges."

My father had complained to me on several occasions about his issues with Shlomo and I was enraged that now in the heat of an argument, he was denying it. "Well, you're the one who told me those things. No one else did and I'm not making it up."

Our talk was going nowhere without accomplishing anything, so I asked, "What else are you upset about? I can see something else is bothering you."

His eyes went from red slits to opening exceptionally wide, as he righteously shouted, "You want to know what's really bothering me, do ya?"

I was sitting on the couch, sipping on my cocktail while my father went for another drink and nonchalantly said, "Sure. What else is bothering you?"

"When I went in for my surgery last month you never came. How about that," he justly yelled.

I was surprised he brought that up and grew very defensive. "Your wife told us not to come," I angrily shouted. "Michelle was going to buy the tickets but when I called she told me not to come."

"Yeah, because you called the day before," he said, looking insulted.

I knew Hamar was up to something and was ready for it. She used anything to cause a conflict between my father and me. She despised the fact that we became closer and her son was drifting away with his excessive drug abuse.

"The day before," I asked, feeling my heart rate increasing. "She told you that?"

My father nodded his head, saying, "Yeah, she told me that. She told everyone that, even Samara."

Enraged I stood up screaming, "Well, that's a fucking lie. I have the time and date on my cell phone as proof. I called her and it was ten days before your surgery. Michelle was going to buy the tickets and I made her hold on while I called your wife on another line." I couldn't stop calling her "his wife" seeing how I was fed up with Hamar trying to muddle up my life. "She told me that Uncle Stewart and Aunt Carly were staying over, along with your friends the Finkels and there was no room for us. Then she told me not to come, that there was no room. 'Don't come,' were her exact words." I was furious, letting it all go now.

My father pensively scratched his balding head, then looking stumped, said, "She told me you called the day before. She even told Samara that too."

"Well, it's a God damn lie. I have it in my phone if you want to see. I was in total shock when she told me not to come. Michelle couldn't believe it either. I thought you knew since she was at the airport with you picking up Samara and her husband on their way into town from London."

I wasn't sure if he was truly perplexed or playing a game to backup Hamar's lie. I started thinking that he had to know, since they were together when I called. Peering at me, my father squawked, "Well, that's all I can tell you. That's what she said."

Feeling as if I needed the hatchet pulled out from my spine, I asked, "Do me favor? When you get home, I would appreciate it if you asked her why the hell she made up that lie. I'm pissed off now about it. All this time and she fucking lied to you. This is unreal."

Since having his attention, I decided to elaborate and shouted, "It's like Julie. Her whole life is destroyed because of your wife. She beat the living shit out of her and called her nasty names for years. Julie is fucked up in the head from all her abuse. All she did was make her out to be ugly and fat. She always told her how she wasn't as pretty as Samara and other malicious comparisons. She even told my wife how much prettier Samara was than Julie. It was embarrassing for me. Michelle met Julie for the first time and told mom how beautiful she was. Do you know what your wife said?"

My father sat in silence, smirking like he knew the answer.

"She said, 'You should see my daughter Samara if you want to see a beauty.' Michelle was blown away by her comment. Parents don't talk about their kids like that."

We both were standing by now, as my father's face reflected a greenish tint. He took another sip of his drink, giving me a serious stare. "You don't talk to Julie. Why don't you talk to her and why didn't you try to help her, if you care so much," he questioned, attempting to turn the tables on me.

"I don't speak to Julie because your wife has fucked her up so badly. Julie uses any kind of ammo to get her acceptance and I don't need that kind of trouble. And you asked me why I don't help her. Are you kidding me? I'm not her parent. That's your responsibility," I shouted, feeling insulted that he would think it was my responsibility to stop his wife from physically and mentally abusing Julie. "What are you saying? That I should've stopped your wife from beating her all those years? That I should have stopped you? You even beat the shit out of me," I screamed.

"Oh, come on Jim. I may have slapped you once or twice, but I never beat you," he causally squawked.

I felt the steam profusely shooting out from my ears. "Are you kidding me? You beat the hell out of me and it was more than just once," I profoundly said, snickering.

The conversation was a lost cause, as my father confirmed everything I believed all the years we lived with Hamar. He justified her revolting actions by pretending not to know what was going on under his own roof. Deep down inside, my father realized he threw us in a snake pit with a stepmother who despised us. Because of his denial, we were bitten by her venomous fangs each day we spent with her. That night just about closed the book on our relationship, but there was one more episode to top this one.

CHAPTER 35

While my father was in for his last visit, I didn't mention the fact that he and his wife planned a two week vacation exactly when Michelle was due. We were expecting our first baby together and Michelle was so overjoyed about being pregnant, that she informed everyone when the due date was. When you hear about women glowing, that was my wife and she wanted to make sure Hamar was a part of our child's birth. She constantly nagged at Hamar, expecting her to come to New Jersey as soon as the baby was born. Michelle wanted her to feel as wanted and needed as her own mother. When we found out they were leaving on a trip a few months after our announcement, Michelle was mortified. I didn't have the same reaction, remembering back where I was on their priority list at the time Ricky was born. I kept reminding Michelle not to get her hopes up because ultimately, Hamar doesn't give a shit. It's not her real grandchild and she hates traveling to New Jersey, but my wife was convinced otherwise.

Samara married a wealthy guy and they were treating Hamar and my father to an expensive trip out of the country. Michelle discovered the news one evening during a discussion with Hamar. They made it a habit of speaking once a week while Michelle was pregnant. When Hamar told her the date of their trip, Michelle was terribly hurt and asked, "Do you know that's my due date?"

Hamar casually sounded surprised. "Oh, it is? When are you due again?"

Michelle was internally on fire with anger, given as Hamar asked that same question during each phone call. "April fourth," she snarled out of the side of her mouth, feeling repulsed.

"April fourth? I forgot. I better check with Samara," she said, playing stupid.

Michelle slammed down the phone in dismay and for the first time, told me I was right. I knew Hamar and my father didn't forget when the due date was. I believed they were getting even with us for not coming to the hospital when he had his surgery. It wasn't important to me anymore if they came or didn't come for the birth of our child. I found their plot nauseating, especially when my father knew the truth about Hamar lying about the time of my call. Putting my foot down, I demanded that Michelle never ask them to come to our home again. After over thirty years of kissing Hamar's ass and being abused to keep a relationship with my father, I didn't think I deserved this. I couldn't find it in my heart to continue a one-sided relationship and sure as hell wasn't going to allow my wife to experience what I ran away from.

Hamar never called Michelle back regarding the conflicting dates, as their future conversations went with the absence of that subject. Weeks before Michelle was due, my father finally mentioned how they were taking an elaborate trip with Samara and her husband. He repeatedly boasted how amazing the trip was going to be, while showing no regard for my baby's birth. I didn't engage him or utter a word concerning my sickened outrage over his decision. I came to grips with it and honestly ran empty on caring anymore.

As the delivery time was creeping upon us, my father was insisting that Michelle go in early for a C-section. The tables were being turned, as he was attempting to make me out to be the bad guy for not forcing the doctor to take Michelle in sooner. He started taking an interest in the delivery time, riding me hard after Michelle's last few appointments.

"So, did you ask the doctor if she could have an early C-section?"

Michelle would invariably be sitting next to me during his requests, which got me hot under the collar. "No dad, I didn't ask him about that. I'm not having my baby born early, risking any kind of health issues. Whatever the doctors says, is what we'll do," I roared in anger.

"Listen, I talked to a doctor friend of mine here in Florida and he said it's fine for the baby to come out a couple of weeks early. Your sister, Samara, had an early scheduled C- section both times and the kids were fine," my dad combated back.

"That's great. I'm not doing it. We decided to listen to the doctor. I'm not jeopardizing my kid's health."

Then his tone would swell in anger. "I don't understand why you won't ask. What? Are you afraid of asking? He's your doctor, you can tell him what you want."

"I'm not doing it. If he wants us to do it, then we will," I hollered back, feeling miffed.

A week before Michelle was due, the doctor decided to take her in for an early C-section after all. He was concerned that the baby was going to be enormous, predicting it to be over nine pounds. Once our child was born, my father was the first person I rang. When getting him on the telephone, I proudly exclaimed that we had a boy, which he was completely indifferent about. I went as far as saying, "I thought you would be more excited than this?"

"I am," he said, still unmoved. "I just didn't know today was the day."

I embraced an urge to holler, as if someone was sticking pins in my eyes, but since I was in the hospital, I kept my cool. "Why wouldn't you think it was today? I told you Monday that it was this Thursday we were having the baby and Michelle told mom as well," I firmly barked back.

"I don't know," he managed to say, sounding preoccupied.

Then suddenly a nurse scurried over, ordering me off the phone since I was directly outside the delivery room. "I have to go," I said, feeling as though I emotionally had no breath left to speak.

My mother-in-law was on her mobile phone, breaking the exciting news to Hamar when the nurse abruptly instructed her to hang up. Soon after, Hamar called on my cell phone while I was still in the recovery room, bawling me out for not calling. I hurriedly told her that I couldn't speak and hung up the phone. I was angered by her audacity to think my mother-in-law's call wasn't good enough. After she and my father intentionally scheduled a trip during the time of my child's birth, they were lucky I still had the respect to call at all.

Later in the day, when I was out of Michelle's hospital room, Hamar phoned to congratulate her. The next day Hamar's call to Michelle instigated a desperate phone call from Shlomo. He was talking a mile a minute, like he drank ten cups of super leaded coffee or snorted a few lines. "Hey buddy, you have to tell Michelle to call mom."

Puzzled by his request, I asked why as he frantically stammered, "Mom said she was going to come in after their trip and Michelle made it out like she had to make an appointment. Tell her to call quick because they're sitting on the runway waiting to take off," Shlomo spewed out, without taking a single breath.

I was roaring mad at his suggestion, with the temper of a tiger that hadn't eaten in several days. "Are you fucking kidding me," I asked. "There's no fucking way that I'm having my wife call them. No one is going to call them. I'm done with all this showing respect shit after what they've done to me," I distinctly professed.

I knew all the words that escaped from my mouth would make it back to them in care of Shlomo. I was certain my father put him up to it since Shlomo could care less if I was on good terms with them or not. I made sure, through him, they would know my exact sentiments.

"Oh come on, buddy," he said with a counterfeit tingle in his voice. "They could die in the plane. For all you know the airplane could crash and you'd never have the chance to say you're sorry."

Snickering from anger, I sternly shouted, "I don't give a shit. Michelle is not apologizing for shit. That's it. Now you can go tell them that."

Hamar needed that bullshit lie about Michelle in order to explain going away to her friends and family members. In fact, that was one of the reasons she said she didn't want to come in. Michelle was stunned to hear the story, explaining how she was grateful for the call and thanked her. At the end of the discussion, Hamar mentioned that when they got back from their trip, she would stop up for a visit. Michelle said great and told Hamar just to let her know when.

A couple of weeks later, Michelle received a stern unfriendly phone call from my father, informing her that they were coming in to see the baby. She asked what time they were getting in so I could pick them up from the airport. My parents refused to stay in a hotel when they visited and would never consider renting a car. So when my father harshly said for us not to bother picking them up because he had rented a car and a hotel room, we knew the wrong people were upset. I could smell a horrific battle brewing in the air.

The Friday they came over was the last time we ever spoke or saw them again. I made sure my daughter, Ricky, was over that night for dinner. She rarely heard from them and I thought it would be nice for her to see her grandparents. The last time Hamar and my father spent time with Ricky brought back terrible memories of Julie's childhood. Hamar mentioned how big and pretty Ricky was getting, but jousted in a nasty comment by remarking how fat her ass was getting. Ricky came to me in tears, complaining about the degrading comment. I had to smooth it over with a lie, so she wouldn't hold a grudge. The crazy thing about Hamar's remark was that Ricky was never heavy and the comment was meant to be purely mean to hurt her feelings.

Around dinnertime I heard a knock at the front door and anticipating an ugly evening, I went to answer it. As I opened the door, both Hamar and my father came bustling in with all intentions of not saying hello. I quickly blurted out, "Hello," to Hamar, as she stared forward allowing me to peck her on one cheek instead of the usual two, due to her swift entrance. Then I took the same approach with my father, as he abruptly darted by. Neither of them even slowed down to say congratulations and when they passed me, I took a stunning notice at Hamar's profile. Anytime I saw her, there was ordinarily some kind of new plastic surgery done to a different part of her body or face. This time I did a double take when seeing the length of her eyelashes. I didn't know whether they were implants or glued on, but only Minnie Mouse had longer lashes in my estimation.

After locking the front door, I followed them into the family room where Kari, Michelle's sister, was gently handing over the baby to Hamar. My wife was sitting on the couch recovering from her surgery and neither of them made a single attempt to acknowledge her. I silently watched, biting my nails in anger as Michelle struggled up from the couch to say hello. Hamar and my father were staring at the baby, trying to avoid eye contact with Michelle at all cost. They looked like two patrons at a museum reading the brief description on an exhibit.

"Hello, mom," Michelle proudly said, while eyeing the baby. Hamar still avoided eye contact, curtly saying, "Hello," allowing my wife to peck her on each cheek.

I was finding it hard to keep my lip zipped, watching as Michelle said, "Hi, dad." Again she followed her salutation with a kiss on each of his cheeks.

Neither of them, to this point, had extended a congratulations to either of us. Being that I was very familiar with this type of situation and dealing with internal rage, I simply tried to make the best of it. When everyone sat down on the couch, I excused myself to retrieve the appetizers from the fridge and get glasses. As I re-entered the room, Hamar and my father were still focused on the baby while speaking to Kari. I don't think it was possible for them to situate themselves any further from Michelle than where they were sitting. After I put down the platter, my father grabbed a cracker and slapped a piece of cheese on it. "Here, Hamar," he said, offering her the cracker and cheese.

She snubbed her nose at it and still not looking up, snickered, "No. I don't want it and you don't need it either, fatso."

Regardless of Hamar's remark, my father still found the courage to eat the cracker and cheese. I stared in Hamar's direction, still consumed by her flamboyant eyelashes and casually asked, "Hey mom, can I get you a glass of wine?" I was still attempting to make this evening cheerful, even though the mood was very somber. Babying Hamar was what we all did. It usually put her in a good mood but she wasn't budging this time.

With her head still remaining in a downward position, she snapped, "No. I don't want anything."

"Jim, I'll take a glass full of ice and vodka," my father modestly requested.

After quickly getting the drinks together, I joined everyone back in the family room where my father was boasting about his trip. Hamar remained in her assumed position when I requested my father's assistance with grilling the steaks. I felt bad leaving Michelle with Hamar, but she had Ricky and Kari as buffers. I needed my father's help since Hamar would never be happy with my grilling. So I utilized him as my fall guy in case the steak wasn't to her liking.

While everyone was seated and eating, Hamar instantly proceeded to tear up her T-bone, complaining out loud and making nasty comments. "This steak is shit. I can't eat this shit. I only eat New York strip. I don't eat this shit. This is garbage"

Kari looked mortified and immediately said, "Hamar, why don't you take my steak if you want? I don't mind the way yours is cooked." Kari was hastily holding her plate in Hamar's direction.

Still looking down while pulverizing her steak, Hamar yelled, "It's not the way it's cooked. I don't like T-bone. It's cheap shit. I don't eat anything but New York strip."

Seeing how my father found it appropriate for her to insult my wife and me, we all just ate and ignored her. I found out a few weeks later that a T-bone is half strip and the other half is filet, which was information I wish I had that night. After dinner, I asked my father to come outside for a talk in my Florida room. I didn't want to ask but I knew if I didn't confront him my mind would eventually burst.

While the girls were cleaning up, I said, "Dad, I have to ask you a question that's bothering me." My heart was furiously pumping as my insides felt cramped from holding in the anger for so long. "Why did you go on vacation when you knew my kid was being born?"

Peering at me through his red slits, he nonchalantly replied, "You know something, I told you to tell the doctor to do the C-section earlier, so we could be here. But you argued with me and never asked him."

I cringed with irritation and bellowed, "So you went on your vacation because the doctor wouldn't take the baby out early? Do you really think that I'm going to knowingly risk my baby's life for your trip? You all knew the date months before you made your plans."

"Well, we didn't know it was going to be a boy."

"What does being a boy have anything to do with you coming in? So, if it were a girl it would be ok for you not to come in. It's funny because you guys made sure to go to London to help Samara when she had her two girls. What do you think Samara would do if her mother didn't show up when she had her kids? She'd never speak to you guys again. Your wife would never miss her own daughter giving birth, but it's ok to miss my kid being born. Her son had a girl and she was there for both of his kids too. This is your grandson and obviously it didn't mean anything to her, but I can't believe you'd miss the birth and the bris."

Staring into my father's red eyes, I waited for his answer as he stood there thinking. "Ok. You want to know what it really is? Do you? Your wife. How about that?"

Stepping backwards in shock, I demanded, "What about my wife?"

"Your wife makes me and your mother feel uncomfortable every time we come here, ok? That's why," he firmly shouted back, looking confident with his answer.

I was flabbergasted and angrily yelled, "My wife makes you feel uncomfortable? You have to be kidding me. She puts little gifts on your beds from the Crabtree store and she asks your wife what you guys like to eat. She even goes to the store and buys all kinds of stuff that you all like. That's my crappy wife," I sarcastically screamed.

"Oh please, ok? Your wife makes us feel like shit. She's just like your first wife. She makes it very apparent that she doesn't want us here."

Mentioning my first wife in the same sentence with Michelle made me blow up like a flare. I knew how much they hated my first wife, so his comment was meant to be very belittling. It was an all out battle and I was livid. "What kind of shit is that to say, that Michelle is like my first wife? She's nothing like her and you fucking know it."

The screaming was getting louder, which provoked Kari to charge out sounding annoyed. "Guys, don't fight. Ricky's inside and she's getting scared. You're father and son for God sakes. What's going on?"

My father gave her a dirty look, grumbling, "Nothing. Just go back inside. Everything's alright."

Then he looked at me fuming. "You want to know really why I didn't come?"

"Sure," I said, trying to count which "Really why I didn't come" this one was. "Why didn't you come?"

"Because you didn't come to my surgery. How about that? When I had my surgery, you were the only one not there."

"What," I shouted, knowing that we covered this before. "We talked about this the last time you came in. Didn't you talk to your wife about it," I roared. I had no use for Hamar anymore and used the "wife" comment to show the disconnect. My father finally succeeded in pushing me to my limit with all his bullshit, leaving me with no desire to continue our relationship. I was so enraged that I was seeing only darkness.

"My wife, as you put it, is none of your fucking business. You weren't there, ok? You weren't there," he repeated, taunting me.

What I said next, never left my lips in over thirty years, but like I said, all I could see was darkness. "Well, your BITCH wife lied and I want to fucking know why." I hollered so loud that I'm positive the neighbors heard and probably thought I was insane.

Before I could turn to go into the house, my father snatched my wrists in his grasps and almost shoved me through a glass plated door. My wife and Kari instantly barged out the other door as all hell broke loose. "Get your hands off my husband," Michelle yelled, stomping her feet. I mean it, get off of him."

I could see Ricky in the background crying, as Kari shouted, "What is wrong with you? This is your son. I can hear everything through the door. He's only asking why you didn't show up for your grandson's birth. Get off of him."

My father and I were struggling during their outburst and I said, "Don't worry guys. Just go back in the house. I'm not going to fight my father. Don't worry about it."

He was still speechless as Michelle demanded, "Get off of my husband. I mean it or I'm calling the police."

After breaking our grips, my father irritably barked, "Just go back in the house. This is about me and my son."

"I don't care what it's about. You just keep off of him," Michelle warned, as she ran back inside dragging Ricky upstairs with her.

Kari was still outside shrieking at my father, but she eventually went back in to keep Hamar company. While Michelle was upstairs with Ricky, Hamar had the nerve to backstab and insult her the entire time to Kari. This woman had no shame. Kari kept reminding her that Michelle was her sister and didn't appreciate the remarks. But Hamar refused to yield, continuing her wicked attack on Michelle's character anyway.

My father and I were still outside going at it. I was in a blind state of fury, as he was trying to talk to me but my rage was far too intense to hear his reasoning. I finally said, "That's it man. You blew it. You blew everything," I bawled. Meaning, we were done. Whether he knew it or not, there was no going back anymore. All that was said and all that was done was irrevocable damage. Nothing could salvage our tattered relationship now. I even named my son after his father, so I couldn't imagine there was anything left to do to show him respect. At that moment, I finally came to grips with understanding that all the respect and all the efforts I made over the years, without any sacrifices on his part, was pointless.

I went into a fit of rage, screeching, "I want to know why your wife lied about me. I want to know why she lied and told you that I called the day before, when it was actually ten fucking days before."

I started pushing my way through the Florida room doors, as he jumped in front of me. "I want to know where you were during my surgery. Where were you?"

I kept pushing my way in through my father, until I saw Hamar scrambling out of the family room and hightailing it out the front door. "Why did you lie? Why did you have to make a fucking fight between my father and me," I screamed, as he stayed in front of me so I couldn't confront her.

"Fuck you," I heard Hamar echoing, as she ran down the front stoop. "Fuck you! You idiot. Piece of shit."

With Hamar outside, my father kept repeating while waving his arms, "Where were you? Where were you?"

"Where were you? I was in the hospital a few times you knew about. Where were you?" I imitated him.

Then he jumped out the front door, as Hamar was standing at the car still screaming, "Fuck you! Drop dead, you piece of shit. Fuck you!"

Taking a deep breath and filling my lungs, I finally yelled the words that I wanted to holler at her for years. "FUCK YOU! You should drop dead. You drop dead. You're the piece of shit. FUCK YOU," I shouted out like a mad man, as my father started the car and they drove away.

CHAPTER 36

Nearly two years later, I received a call from Julie. She eventually migrated to Florida like everyone else and did some soul searching herself. She quickly met up with Mitch, who also moved down a few years earlier. They lived together for a short period of time, until she tripped into a few potholes. One being, Julie eloped with a man who she wasn't completely in love with and broke all ties with the family. She had a habit of doing that over the years, but soon divorced him and came running back to Hamar and my father. Since moving to New Jersey, Julie and I lost contact and the last time we saw each other was at her engagement party, four years prior. She remarried a doctor, which of course, made Hamar and my father very happy.

Julie began leaving messages for me to call her, but I vowed not to speak with anyone who associated with Hamar and my father. After that infamous blowout, I had no intentions of ever speaking with them again. My personal life was never more blissful. Mentally, I had a sense of freedom from their tyranny, and memories of my horrific childhood. After five or six messages, I finally picked up the telephone, feeling guilty since the messages sounded like an outreach for help.

"Hey Julie, what's up," I casually asked.

"You're fucking ignoring me. You're not picking the phone up on purpose because it's me," she hysterically shrieked.

I didn't expect an approach like that from Julie. She never spoke to me in that manner before, so I was taken by surprise since we hadn't spoken in years.

"I've been calling you for weeks and leaving messages. You're not picking up the phone or calling me back," Julie screamed, while bawling in excitement.

Defensively, I shot back, "Well, you know, Julie, the last time we spoke was when Michelle was pregnant with my son. You became buddies with her and spoke all the time. Then you just disappeared. We never heard from you again. I don't know if it was from the fight I had with dad and his wife, but you didn't even call to say congratulations."

"It wasn't because of them," she cried. Then there was a pause. "It wasn't because of them."

Confused and not knowing where she was going with this, I said, "Ok. What was the reason? Why did you disappear?"

"Because I'm fucked up. I'm fucked up in the head, that's why," Julie sobbed, sounding like she wasn't all there. "I'm seeing a psychiatrist again and they have me on this medicine. I haven't slept in weeks because I haven't talked to you. I have to tell you what happened. I need you in my life. I need family. I need my real family not that fake step shit anymore. I need real family in my life. I hate her and dad. They are out of my life. I swear on my kids, Jim."

She was very convincing, as I could see something tragic must have happened between her and my father. One of her phone messages specified how she got a restraining order against him. So sensing she was looking for my support, I gently asked, "Ok, calm down. I'm sorry, stop crying. What happened?"

She proceeded to explain how Hamar and my father were giving her a hard time about her children. Hamar had gone as far as telling Julie she couldn't bring her daughter for Friday night dinners anymore, because she constantly vomited in her presence. Julie explained that anytime she brought her daughter and son over to their condominium, her daughter would refuse to go to Hamar and threw up at the sight of her.

"She's calling my daughter retarded. She says she looks retarded and acts retarded. Do you believe that shit and she says it right in front of dad," Julie screamed but this time in a more deliberate voice, as her whimpering subsided.

"I can't believe what you're telling me. Who the hell says that stuff? You're telling me dad just sits there while she's insulting your daughter?"

"Yeah, he agrees with her. They say it's weird that my daughter clings onto my husband and doesn't want to say hello to them." Then Julie continued with her deliberation, yelling, "I'm a mother now. I'm not this little girl that they can say that shit to anymore. My family comes first. I have children now and I can't allow them to be called nasty names by this animal. I'm a mother and my kids come first."

"Julie, what happened with this restraining order you were telling me about?"

"Oh yeah, dad came over to my house after I told them I never wanted to see them again, because they said that shit about my daughter. I cussed them out and ran out of their apartment. I hate them. I can't take them anymore," Julie cried out, failing to finish the story.

"So, what happened," I asked, trying to move her along.

"Oh, dad came running into our house, threatening to beat up my husband, Cory. Cory started yelling for dad to get out of the house and dad wanted to fight him. Cory told him that he wasn't losing his doctor's license over him and I called the police. Then the police came and threw dad out of the house."

"Jesus, that's unbelievable. So now you guys have a restraining order to keep him away, huh?"

"Yeah, he's not allowed to come anywhere near us or my children. I'm never going to speak to them again or see them. My psychiatrist told me that I need to speak to my real family. I know we haven't talked for a long time but I want us to have a relationship again. I want me, you and Mitch to be a family again. I don't want any more of those people in my life," she convincingly swore.

Julie sounded different and sincere, but she always managed to run back to Hamar and my father. I was reluctant to invite her into my life because of that threat. "Julie, I'll be honest. I love you and you're my sister, but I don't trust that you won't go back to them."

"I swear on my kids, Jim. I know I've fucked up in the past but this is it. I swear. Did you hear me? I swore on my kids," she shouted in a state of panic.

"Ok, I hear you but everyone is afraid to believe you because you always find your way back to them. I'll tell you something because I'm your brother and I care. You must and I mean must, never talk with them again to get well. You sound really bad and I'm sure the doctor told you the same thing. These people have done nothing but destroy the person that you are and that you could've been."

"I know, Jim. Believe me, my psychiatrist told me never to talk to them again and stick by you and Mitch. She wanted me to get a hold of you because she thought you could help me."

I was feeling like a big brother to Julie at the time, as my heart trembled for her sorrow. I was overwhelmed that she came to me for help and at that moment, I felt a need to have my sister back in my life. From the sincerity in her voice, I couldn't in good conscience turn my back on her. "Julie, I'll tell you this. You're my sister and I'll try to have a relationship with you, but you have to promise to take your medicine and continue to see the psychiatrist. If I hear you didn't and that you went back to dad and his crazy wife, that's it. I can't help you anymore."

"I swear, Jim. I promise. All I want is you and Mitch in my life. I just want my real family. That's all I want. I'm almost forty and wasted my time trying to get love from them and I give up."

After a mouthful of other complaints, Julie decided to tell me something about myself. "Jim, you wouldn't believe the things they're saying about you. They're terrible things."

I wasn't shocked and inquired, "Yeah, what are they saying about me?"

"Oh my God, they told everyone down here that the night you got into that big fight with them, you were so drunk that you jumped on mom." Then Julie swiftly corrected herself, saying, "I mean the animal. And then you started choking her to death on the couch. Then dad had to pull you off and run out of the house before you killed her."

I started scratching my head while laughing hysterically. I found it hilarious but not shocked over their ridiculous lie, as it went hand in hand with all their fabricated nonsense during my entire life with them. Laughing with sarcasm, I said, "You've got to be kidding me? They told you that?"

After explaining the true story to Julie, she had some more shocking news which really irritated me. "They also said that dad opened up the business for you with $250,000 and that you and Michelle stole all the money and now he's broke."

"Are you serious? They're telling everyone that?" I thought I was going to punch a hole in my own drywall. "That is total bullshit. In the beginning, we both put the same amount of money in and in fact, I even put in more because he was in Florida. Needless to say, the $100,000 loan we took out, I had to repay it myself when I sold my house. The bank put a lien on my home and took the money out before I could close on the deal. The rest I had to pay in cash. He's a God damn liar," I shouted, finding myself sweating in fury. "How about that?"

"Oh my God, Jim, if you hear them, you would believe they're telling the truth. They are such good liars. They're telling everyone that story. Can you believe it?"

"Well, I'll tell you this. He got back every cent he put in and more. He never worked there nor paid back a nickel for the loan. I don't care what he's telling people. As long as my true family knows the truth, that's all I care about. I don't think anyone really believes that I took his money and Michelle and I pushed him out of the business. Anyone who knows him wouldn't believe that bullshit."

After my eye opening conversation with Julie, I was reminded of the reason why I chose not to socialize with anyone associated with them. I felt the stress and helplessness feeling coming back. Not being able to defend myself against their outlandish lies killed me inside, but I learned how to ignore it. Over the past couple of years, I conditioned myself not to emotionally get bothered by their garbage. My mental freedom was more important than stewing over their pathetic lies.

Lying in bed that night, I felt energized by the candid discussion I had with Julie. It gave me a triumphant and gratifying sensation to know that all of us finally had reunited. We unified after all these years, with the strength in that notion being unparalleled. We managed to rupture the insidious efforts of Hamar and my father, which they successfully pulled off for decades. I knew we were stronger together and eventually, most of our shattered pieces would be reconciled. However, some would elude us since time has a precarious way of swallowing tarnished memories.

After my initial conversation with Julie, she kept to her promise with Michelle and I hearing from her once or twice a day. I normally spoke to Mitch a couple of times a week, so it was refreshing to add Julie into the mix. She projected a vigorous tone in her voice, which seemed to inflate as time passed. I was overjoyed by her massive progress, as she repeatedly reminded me how happy she was for eliminating my father and Hamar out of her life. One late night, Julie surprised me with a completely different tone in her voice.

"Hi, Jim, it's Julie," she meagerly dragged out.

"Hey Julie, what's up," I asked, knowing there was something behind her altered voice.

Almost sobbing, she said, "Did you hate me for all the years you lived in New Jersey?"

"No, I never hated you. Who told you that?"

"Oh my God," she bellowed as if she could breathe again. "All this time I thought you hated me. Mom and dad told me that you moved to New Jersey because I told you about the things Shlomo and papa did to me. Oh my god, I'm so happy to hear that."

"Julie, I left because of those things you told me, but not because you did anything wrong. What happened to you wasn't your fault and you have to remember that. I left because it was torturous for me to be around all that shit. I wanted to leave for a long time. You just gave me the push I needed. After years of our father allowing us to be abused was bad enough, but then he does nothing about what Shlomo did to you. I couldn't stick around anymore. I thank you for coming out and saying what you did. What this Shlomo did to you was an atrocity and dad should have never allowed it to go unpunished." I found myself getting loud, with the habitual anger building up from the subject of Hamar and my father.

"They gave me shit for years about you moving. Over and over

371

again. They blamed me and I think I started to resent you because of the way they treated me. I'm so glad you didn't hate me," Julie said, with a sense of relief.

We talked a little more as our voices toned down to a whisper. "Jim, can I tell you something that I never told you before?"

"Sure," I softly said, while rubbing my weary eyes.

"Do you remember when you were about sixteen and you were in Shlomo's room getting ready to go to work and I walked in and told him my vagina was bleeding?"

Uncomfortably, I said, "Yeah, I remember that." I knew where she was going with this.

"You teased me and called me names."

"Yes. I remember. Sorry about that."

"You remember that," she questioned, sounding surprised. "Well, the reason I went to him was…" Then Julie took a deep breath as I heard her taking a sip of something. "Was because of what he did to me down in the basement." Her voice sounded like she fell off a cliff when finishing.

"I remember that. It didn't strike me back then what could have happened to you. I just thought you got your period or something. I was surprised that you had him checking out your vagina from all the people to choose from."

"Oh my God, so you do remember. So you believe me? You believe I'm not a liar," she said, with hope in her voice.

"I believe you. I always believed you. When I moved to New Jersey, I started thinking of clues that I may have missed and that story did come to mind."

"So, you do believe me? They tried brainwashing me so much and calling me a liar that I began to think it was a dream. That maybe it never happened. Thank you. Thank you so much for believing me."

Julie sounded as if an enormous boulder had been lifted off her back, something that had been crushing her insides for years. Then sounding emotionally exhausted, Julie said, "Jim, I love you."

Looking at the time, I whispered, "I love you too, Julie. Goodnight."

"Goodnight, sweetie."

"Thank you to my wife for all her love and support during my long journey."

Manufactured By: RR Donnelley
                     Breinigsville, PA USA
                     October, 2010